John

I pray this is
a blessing to you and that you
will find Treasures in the Psalms.

God Bless,
Charles

# Finding Treasures
## in the PSALMS

My dear John,

I hope you find many "Treasures" as you read this Devotional. You are one of God's Treasures to me!

Love you,
Gran
Christmas 2022

# CHARLES HALL

# Finding Treasures in the PSALMS

DAILY DEVOTIONAL

XULON PRESS

Xulon Press
2301 Lucien Way #415
Maitland, FL 32751
407.339.4217
www.xulonpress.com

© 2021 by Charles Hall

All rights reserved solely by the author. The author guarantees all contents are original and do not infringe upon the legal rights of any other person or work. No part of this book may be reproduced in any form without the permission of the author. The views expressed in this book are not necessarily those of the publisher.

Unless otherwise indicated, Scripture quotations taken from the Holy Bible, New International Version (NIV). Copyright © 1973, 1978, 1984, 2011 by Biblica, Inc.™. Used by permission. All rights reserved.

Scripture quotations taken from the King James Version (KJV)–*public domain.*

Printed in the United States of America

Paperback ISBN-13: 978-1-6628-0766-4

To my wife Vivian,
my daughter, Emily, and son, Bren and his wife, Austin,
and my grandchildren; Brynlee, Walker, Tatum, Reese, and Luke.
As David writes in Psalm 91, I pray that God will cover you with
His feathers, and that you will take refuge Under His wings.
Let His faithfulness always be a protective shield.

# Acknowledgments

First and foremost, I want to thank God for entrusting me with the responsibility of writing a devotional book on the Psalms. Without the guidance of the Holy Spirit and His daily provision of ideas, this may have become a lifelong project, instead of a finished book.

Second, I would like to thank my wife, Vivian, for her prayers, encouragement, support, and allowing me to have hours of uninterrupted time to write. Also, I appreciate her permission to turn our kitchen table into an office.

Lastly, I would like to thank Amy Baumgartner for the many hours she spent editing the manuscript. She is a wife, mother of three teenagers, works full time, yet undertook the task of reviewing each devotion. I also appreciate the support given by her family allowing her time to spend editing the book.

# INTRODUCTION

When our family goes to the beach, my favorite past-time is searching for shark's teeth. I have literally found thousands of shark's teeth, most of which are pretty small. However, on rare occasions, I will find a larger one laying in the sand. When I find a larger one like the one on the cover, it motivates me to search even more. My passion for searching for shark's teeth led to the inspiration for the title and cover of this book. Even though the Psalms were written thousands of years ago, they speak to our pain, joy, sorrow, and need for God in our lives on a daily basis. They describe a Sovereign God who loves us and leads us to salvation through Jesus Christ. I pray that your journey through this book will draw you closer to God, His purpose and plan for your life and that your search will lead you to find treasures of forgiveness, redemption, salvation, joy, hope, and confidence in the God who loves you. As you begin to find those treasures, hopefully they will motivate you to search deeper into God's Word.

Each devotion explores a verse or a combination of verses from the Psalms and includes Bible and personal stories to help us better understand the character of God. They close with the following thoughts to help reinforce God's Word in your life:

**Acknowledge:** How is God's love, power, and presence acknowledged in today's reading?

**Confession:** Is there something in my life that I need to confess to God?

**Thanksgiving:** What can I give God praise for today?

**Prayer:** Lord, what can I learn and apply from today's verse?

May God richly bless you as you spend time in His Word.

# Day 1

Psalm 1:1 Blessed is the man who does not walk in the counsel of the wicked or stand in the way of sinners or sit in the seat of mockers.

I think it is very appropriate that the Psalms begin with Godly wisdom about the paths we choose and the friends we keep. Our friends have a huge influence on our lives. The question is what kind of friends do you have? Are they like the people mentioned in today's verse? Are your friends influencing you to do things that are harmful to yourself or others? If so, you need different friends. Hopefully, you have found friends who are supportive, always there for you and care for your well-being. Being a friend takes effort and selflessness on our part. I was very fortunate to have a nucleus of good friends who love God. Our friendship has continued for many years. Over the years we have stayed in touch and have been there for each other. Think about your friends. What type of influence are they having on you? Can you thank God for the people He has put into your life? Notice the status of the person who avoids bad company; they are called blessed. What does blessed mean? According to www.oxford-learnersdictionay.com blessed is defined as: 'Made holy, consecrated, endowed with divine favor and protection.' So, to be blessed is not simply good fortune and prosperity. It is being made holy through the saving grace of Jesus. Our greatest blessing is that our sins have been forgiven and we have eternal life with the Father. Do your friends help point you closer to knowing and obeying God? Or do they sit around mocking you for your relationship with God? If that is the case, you need a change of friends. Psalm 1 is a good Psalm to commit to memory and guide you throughout your life.

**Acknowledge** – Lord, You put the right people in our lives to be our friends.

**Confess** – Lord, forgive me for allowing people who are a bad influence into my life.

**Thanksgiving** – Lord, thank You for friends who are closer than a brother.

**Prayer** – Lord, I thank You for the gift of friends. Help me to be a good friend to someone, let us share in Your blessings.

# Day 2

Psalm 1:3 That person is like a tree planted by streams of water, which yields its fruit in season and whose leaf does not wither, whatever they do prospers.

Yesterday we learned that blessings come to those who choose their friends wisely and avoid the ungodly. In verse two David tells us, a blessed person is one who seeks God's guidance instead of following the crowd. Today, we see the blessings God provides when we follow Him. The Psalmist uses an analogy of a tree planted by the water. Do you have a mental picture of a huge tree, full of leaves, and standing firmly on the bank of a large river? This tree withstands the buffeting winds and seasons of drought. It provides shade, fruit and nourishment to those who come around it. This tree will face hard times, but is anchored by the river and does not wither when those times come along. Jeremiah 17:7-8 gives the same promise of a person who trusts the Lord. 'But blessed is the man who trusts in the Lord, whose confidence is in Him. He will be like a tree planted by the water that sends out its roots by the stream. It does not fear when heat comes; its leaves are always green. It has no worries in a year of drought and never fails to bear fruit.' I hope your roots are firmly planted in God's love. If so, then you will have no problem praising Him for seeing you through the storms of life. However, maybe your roots are not so deep and you are being buffeted by the winds of confusion, loneliness, worry, a failed relationship, or financial problems. If that is the case, you can claim God's promise of strength and blessing today. Put your trust in God, allow Him to strengthen you, encourage you, and shower you with His peace.

**Acknowledge** – Lord, You are a river of blessing.

**Confess** – Lord, forgive me for allowing doubt and fear to take over my life.

**Thanksgiving** – Lord, thank You for planting me beside the river of life. Let me bear fruit for all to enjoy.

**Prayer** – Lord, I put my faith and trust in You. Plant me beside the river of living water so that I may bear much fruit (love, joy, peace, patience, kindness, goodness, faithfulness, gentleness, and self-control).

# Day 3

Psalm 1:6 For the Lord watches over the way of the righteous, but the way of the wicked will perish.

Today we learn that the Lord watches over the way of the righteous but the way of the wicked will perish. Verse four tells us the wicked are like chaff which gets blown away by the wind. What direction is the wind taking you? Are you gone with the wind or is your life firmly planted in God's promises? Is the Lord watching over you or are you wandering around making bad decision after bad decision? Ultimately, you will decide your destiny. Do I want a destiny where the Lord is watching over me and directing my steps, or do I want a destiny where I wind up being blown away like the chaff? There are very few people who would consider themselves a wicked person, but without Christ in our lives, we are wicked in His sight. It is through the blood of Jesus Christ that we are made right with Him. Yet even before we came to know Him, He loved us and had a plan for us. If you trust Him, He will not leave you to perish like the wicked. Proverbs 3:5-6 tells us how the Lord directs our way. 'Trust in the Lord with all your heart and lean not on your own understanding; in all your ways acknowledge Him, and He will make your paths straight.' Do you trust the Lord with all your heart? Or, are you trying to make it on your own? Have you plotted your own path of life? How is that working out for you? Whose understanding would you rather trust, yours or God's? If you trust God's understanding then seek Him each day and ask Him to guide your steps. He will if you ask Him and allow Him to. Psalm 37:23 tells us, 'The steps of the godly are directed by the Lord. He delights in every detail of their lives.' The path of life is filled with many options, obstacles, detours, and turns. Stay on the straight path, the one that God has prepared for you. You will not regret it.

**Acknowledge** – Lord, You have a plan for our lives.

**Confess** – Lord, forgive me for taking the wrong paths in life.

**Thanksgiving** – Lord, thank You for watching over me and ordering my steps.

**Prayer** – Lord, each day is a gift from You. Help me to trust You and lean on Your understanding.

# Day 4

### Psalm 2:1 Why do the nations conspire and the peoples act in vain?

HISTORY TELLS US THERE IS NOTHING NEW ABOUT THE BEHAVIOR of people. Today there is political and social unrest in many areas of the world. Within the United States, there is division and conflict. Riots are breaking out across the country due to the murder of a black man while in custody of the police. His tragic death sparked peaceful demonstrations which quickly turned into riots. The riots escalated to mayhem, looting, burning, destruction of property, and the death of several police officers. It seems that our nation is split in two, divided upon political lines. Our country is not alone with its struggles. In Europe, Britain is trying to withdraw from the European Union. Refugees are pouring into many countries there because of war. Unfriendly nations are working to develop nuclear weapons for war. Foreign citizens are being held hostage. We see the unrest, wars, persecution and wonder where God is. If all you watch are news channels, the barrage of bad news would make you want to stay at home and never leave. Fear and anxiety can easily paralyze you. Take heart, there is good news! Jesus said in John 14:27, 'Peace is what I leave with you; it is My own peace that I give you. I do not give it as the world does. Do not be worried and upset; do not be afraid.' God still reigns, and we can take refuge in Him. The Psalmist says their actions are in vain. We can be intimidated by all the chaos and persecution or we can put our faith and trust in God. Isaiah 54:17 tells us, 'No weapon forged against you will prevail, and you will refute every tongue that accuses you. This is the heritage of the servants of the Lord, and this is their vindication from Me.' God is in control. Continue reading Psalms 2, the rest of the story is revealed. Are you worried about the future? Trust the God who triumphs in the end.

**Acknowledge** – Lord, You are in control.

**Confess** – Lord, forgive me when I worry and lose faith in You.

**Thanksgiving** – Lord, thank You for preparing a King, Jesus, to rule the world.

**Prayer** – Lord, although the world seems to be in chaos and turmoil, I trust in You. Help me to be ready to face those who are against You and Your people. You know the end of our story.

#  Day 5

**Psalm 2:5-6** He rebukes them in His anger and terrifies them in His wrath saying, I have installed My king on Zion, My Holy mountain.

TODAY'S VERSE IS VERY CHALLENGING BECAUSE WE SEE GOD rebuking people in His anger. We would rather think of God as a loving and caring God who is 'gracious, and full of compassion; slow to anger, and of great mercy.' (Psalm 145:8) However, God can get angry and will not hesitate to take His wrath out on anyone according to His plan. It is God's holiness that makes sin offensive to Him. However, His anger towards sin is always under control and righteous. God can be angry and not sin. The good news is that God is also a God of mercy and forgiveness. God is willing to forgive us and not hold us accountable when we repent of our sins. The Psalmist begins by saying God rebukes them in His anger. Verses 1-2 tell us that God is rebuking the people who stand against His 'Anointed One.' God's rebuke can be very powerful and terrifying according to the Psalmist. He is also not hesitant to confront the wicked. John 3:36 tells us, 'Whoever believes in the Son has eternal life; whoever does not obey the Son shall not see life, but the wrath of God remains on Him.' Those who do not trust Him as Lord and Savior will one day face God's wrath. Until Jesus returns, we will face persecution, problems, strife and disappointment because of the sinful world around us. So, how do you plan to live until He returns? Will you live in fear and dread each day? Will you withdraw and hide? I hope not. This is a time when we should be sharing the good news of Jesus and His salvation to everyone. This is a time when we should be on the offensive lines helping the poor, the homeless, and the needy in Jesus' name.

**Acknowledge** – Lord, You are our King. You will make the nations prove, the glories of Your righteousness, and wonders of Your love.

**Confess** – Lord, forgive me when I fail to submit to Your lordship in my life. My selfishness and pride get in the way.

**Thanksgiving** – Lord, thank You for Your love for us that You would send Your Son to die for me, that I might have eternal life.

**Prayer** – Lord, there is strife, difficulty, envy, murder, and terrorism all about the world today. Let me take refuge in You.

Psalm 3:1 O Lord, how many are my foes! How many rise up against me!

HAVE THERE BEEN TIMES IN YOUR LIFE WHEN YOU FEEL LIKE EVERYONE is against you? This is how David felt when he wrote this Psalm. His son, Absalom, had just led a successful revolt against him and established himself as King. David and his supporters fled Jerusalem and barely escaped capture. On his way into the wilderness, a family member of Saul, whom David replaced as King, cursed David and threw rocks at him. It had to be a very low time in his life. Even though David wrote this Psalm about his circumstances, it also foreshadows the death Christ faced on the cross. Jesus stood before Pilate with an angry mob shouting, 'crucify Him!, crucify Him!' He was alone when a legion of Roman soldiers beat and taunted Him. He was nailed to a cross carrying the weight of our sins. The onlookers mocked Him. A thief hanging beside Him joined in with the mockers. The physical pain overwhelmed Him. The Father turned away while He hung there. Satan and his demons rejoiced as His blood was pouring out. Jesus suffered that much for you and me. When I think about His sacrifice for my sins, my troubles seem small. Yet, I still have problems. People haven't changed. They still gang up against each other. Jesus' crucifixion and David's escape from his son, Absalom, highlights the dark side of the nature of people. They will take advantage of the situation and pile on while you are down. In verse two of this Psalm, David goes on to say, 'Many are saying of me, God will not deliver him.' That had to be a low point of David's life. Are you at an all-time low in your life? Do you feel like there is no hope? Take heart, there is a God who loves you and cares about you. He has a plan for you. David had a good ending to his situation. Jesus rose from the grave. Your story is only half-written.

**Acknowledge** – God, You are in control of our lives, even when we don't see how things will work out.

**Confess** – Lord, forgive me when I doubt Your hand of mercy in my life.

**Thanksgiving** – Lord, thank You for the story of David and his trials.

**Prayer** – Lord, I know You are working in my life, even when it feels like everyone is against me. Thank You for loving me

# Day 7

Psalm 3:3 But You, Lord, are a shield around me, my glory, the One who lifts my head high.

AT THIS LOW POINT IN HIS LIFE, DAVID FINDS HOPE IN GOD. He compares God to a shield that has protected him in war. Paul, writing in Ephesians 6:10-18, tells us to put on the armor of God. Verse 16 says, 'In addition to all this, take up the shield of faith, with which you can extinguish all the flaming arrows of the evil one.' With God as his shield, David knew he would be okay. His faith kept him going. As he continued to trust God, his confidence and hope grew. When he left Jerusalem; his head was low, filled with worry and fear. Now he takes his mind off his troubles and shifts his attention to God. His circumstances do not change, but his outlook on life changes dramatically. The Lord lifts his head. Instead of walking away completely defeated, David realizes that no matter the outcome, God will restore him and lift him up. What is God saying to you today? Are you at a low point in your life? Are you so low that when you look up, the only thing you can see are the soles of someone's shoes? Where is your shield of faith? Did you leave it behind after the last crisis in your life? Do you need to pick it up and dust the cobwebs off? Satan loves nothing more than to pile on more trouble while you are down. It is his way of keeping you full of worry and fear and separated from God. Call out to God today! Ask Him to be your shield and the one who lifts your head. Then, use your shield of faith each day to protect you from the arrows of the evil one. Ask God to restore your confidence and hope despite your current circumstances. The good news is that He will answer you.

**Acknowledge** – Lord, help me not to fear the future, for I can rest on Your word from where deliverance comes.

**Confess** – Lord, forgive me when I try to do things on my own power and skill. I need to put my full faith and trust in You.

**Thanksgiving** – Lord, thank You for deliverance. You are a shield around me.

**Prayer** – Lord, sometimes we don't even know who our foes are, where they come from, or why they are against us. Help me to trust in You.

# Day 8

Psalm 4:1 Answer me when I call to You, O my righteous God. Give me relief from my distress; be merciful to me and hear my prayer.

How often have you prayed this same prayer? I confess that I have prayed it many times, often over things which I put myself in to begin with. The Book of Job gives us an example of a person who experienced a lot of trouble in their life. The Bible tells us that Job was blameless and upright. He feared God and avoided evil. He was very rich and had a large family. However, in the span of one day, Job lost his children, his livestock, and his servants. To make matters worse, Job's health was attacked. He was covered with painful boils. They were so bad, that Job sat among some ashes and scraped himself with a broken piece of pottery. If that is not enough, his wife's advice to Job was to curse God and die. But through all this, Job remained faithful to God. Even when his friends came to see him and tell him that he had done something to deserve all that happened to him, Job remained faithful. Yes, he tried to argue and reason with them that their arguments were off base. Yes, he called out to God for relief and answers to his distress. At the end of Job, God answers him and eventually restores all that was taken. Our situation may not be as dire as Job's, but to us it is just as important. Do we wonder if God is listening to us, or if He will answer our cry for help? The answer is yes, God is listening, and He hears our prayers. He heard Job's prayers and He hears ours too. However, there are three possible answers to our prayers: yes, no, or not now. We must wait on God's timing for answers to our prayers. Like Job, the wait can seem like an eternity. But, His answers are always on time. Cry out to Him today! Let Him know what you need. Ask Him to be merciful to you. He loves you and will answer your prayer.

**Acknowledge** – Lord, You are in control and hear our prayers.

**Confess** – Lord, help me to truly repent when I seek Your help out of situations of my own doing.

**Thanksgiving** – Lord, thank You for Your mercy and deliverance.

**Prayer** – Lord, help me to know the joy and peace that comes with Your presence in our lives.

# Day 9

Psalm 4:8 In peace I will lie down and sleep, for You alone, Lord, make me dwell in safety.

BEING ABLE TO SLEEP THROUGH THE NIGHT IS PRICELESS. PEOPLE spend millions of dollars each year on sleep aids. Although Jesus was the Son of God, He needed sleep too. The Book of Mark tells the story of Jesus asleep in the back of a boat. He had a long day teaching and healing and was exhausted. A terrible storm suddenly blew up causing waves to break over the boat. The boat was filling with water and the disciples were scared for their lives. Jesus was so tired that He had no trouble sleeping through the storm. The disciples woke Him saying, 'Teacher, don't you care if we drown?' After calming the storm, by simply speaking to it, Jesus' response to the disciples is His response to us as well, 'Why are you so afraid? Do you still have no faith?' Why are we so afraid when life's storms rage around us? Why do we stay awake at night worrying about tomorrow? Even though we are exhausted at bedtime, our minds start to race as soon as our head hits the pillow. As our minds race, so does the clock. After several hours you might drift off to sleep. If I had to make a list of the things that have kept me up nights, it would start with issues at work and disagreements with others. Your list may include health problems, broken relationships, family problems, or financial problems. The good news is that after I learned to give my problems to God, my sleepless nights have been few and far between. The problems didn't go away or become any less daunting. It is just that I began to trust God more to handle them. Let's get back to David. He had many challenges in his life, but he said, 'in peace I will lie down...' Do you want the same peace David had? Turn your cares over to God. Give them to Him! He will carry them for you. Don't lie awake at night wondering if God cares about the problems you face.

**Acknowledge** – Lord, You help us dwell in safety even when life around us is in turmoil.

**Confess** – Lord, forgive me of worry I take upon myself.

**Thanksgiving** – Lord, thank You for the peace we can have in the middle of the storm.

**Prayer** – Lord, help me to be able to lie down and sleep peacefully.

# Day 10

Psalm 5:3 In the morning, Lord, You hear my voice; in the morning I lay my requests before You and wait expectantly.

IN TODAY'S VERSE, DAVID REMINDS GOD THAT IT IS IN THE MORNING when God hears from him. Charles Spurgeon, a great Preacher and writer in the 1800's, wrote about prayer, 'An hour in the morning is worth two in the evening.'[1] He also wrote, 'prayer should be the key of the day and the lock of the night.' Are you a morning person? Do you like to rise earlier than necessary to get ready for your day? Or do you sleep to the last minute, hitting the snooze button several times before getting out of bed? In either case, I hope that you allow some time in your morning to reach out to God before you head off to work, to school, or your normal routine for the day. God wants to hear from you. The Creator of the universe wants to have a relationship with you. Get your day started off right by spending time with Him. Vivian and I have a saying, 'sometimes it is good you do not know what your day holds. If you did, you may not get out of bed.' That is why it is so important to start your day with Him. Having that time with God, seeking His presence in your life gives you the strength and faith to live each day. I make an effort to read the Bible each morning and pray before heading out. I have to admit, there are days when I don't allow enough time to do both, but I try to set aside time to pray. It takes discipline and resolve to have a daily routine of reading God's word and time communicating with Him. Identify and set aside the world's distractions you think are so important, that drain your time and prevent you from having a close relationship with God. David did. Can you, like David, say, 'Early in the morning I lay my requests before You...'?

**Acknowledge** – Lord, You want to have a relationship with me.

**Confess** – Lord, forgive me when I put other things ahead of the time I could spend with You.

**Thanksgiving** – Lord, thank You that You hear and recognize my voice when I call to You.

**Prayer** – Lord, help me to have a daily time set aside to get into Your word to commune with You.

# Day 11

Psalm 5:11 But let all who take refuge in You be glad; let them ever sing for joy. Spread Your protection over them, that those who love Your name may rejoice in You.

Several verses earlier, David describes the character of his enemies. As a king, he was in constant danger from those who would want to take over his kingdom. That is why most kings had cupbearers who would sample their food and drink to ensure it wasn't poisoned. They also had armed bodyguards to protect them. However, in today's verse, David changes direction to describe the righteous. He said they take refuge in God and love His name. Let's look at why the righteous should love God's name. Loving God should be easy because God loves us and cares for us. 1 John 4:19 tells us, 'We love because He first loved us.' God even sent His Son to pay the price for our sin. That should be reason enough for us to love Him, and to rejoice and sing praises of joy. The righteous should also take refuge in God. Taking refuge represents trust in God. No one would seek refuge in something they didn't trust. For example, I wouldn't seek shelter in a mobile home that was in the direct path of a tornado. I would be looking for shelter that could withstand the strong winds. In the same manner, we should be seeking refuge from the God we can trust when the storms of life begin to rage. Unfortunately, we live in a time where the potential for harm is very real. There is hardly a day when the news doesn't contain a story of a mass shooting, drive-by shooting, attack on Christians at church, or a terrorist attack somewhere in the world. Not only is physical danger real, but there are many forces in the world that can ruin us economically, emotionally, and spiritually. We need God's protection. We need to do like David and take refuge in God. Seek His hand of protection in your life and the life of your family.

**Acknowledge** – Lord, thank You that You love and care for us.

**Confess** – Lord, help me to remember my own sin, so that I can come near to You.

**Thanksgiving** – Lord, thank You for Your protection from our enemies.

**Prayer** – Lord, help me to hate sin, but love the sinner. Help me to be able to separate the two. Thank You for Your protection over my family.

# Day 12

**Psalm 5:12** For surely, O Lord, You bless the righteous; You surround them with Your favor as with a shield.

David closes this Psalm with a promise of God's blessing and favor on the righteous. He uses the picture of a large shield surrounding God's people. We have already learned about the shield of faith, several days earlier in Psalm 3. A shield is not only referred to throughout the Psalms and in Ephesians, but in other places as well. In Genesis 15:1, the Lord speaking to Abram said, 'Do not be afraid, Abram. I am your shield, your very great reward.' In the following verses of Genesis 15, God made a covenant with Abram, promising his offspring will be as numerous as the stars in the heavens. He also promised the land of Canaan for him to take possession. God's grace and His favor go hand in hand. It is by God's grace that we can have eternal life with Him. It is also God's grace or His favor that gives us the ability to live for Him no matter our circumstances. Abram's life didn't end up on 'Easy Street' after God appeared to him and changed his name to Abraham. In fact, there were several times when Abraham felt his life was in danger. Also, it wasn't until he and his wife, Sarai, were 100 years old before their promised son, Isaac, was born. Abraham's faith was even tested by God when God asked Abraham to sacrifice his only son. God's favor on us may not be as broad as the covenant He made with Abram, but He surrounds us with His favor. His favor and blessings come in all different forms, shapes, sizes and quantities. There are times in our lives when we face difficult circumstances and struggle to find Him. We wonder if He is even paying attention to what is happening. However, weeks, months, or even years later we can look back and see how God's hand of favor was on us. Seek God, put your faith and trust in Him. Let Him surround you with His favor as a shield. Thank Him for the protection.

**Acknowledge** – Lord, You are our shield and protection.

**Confess** – Lord, forgive me when I doubt that You care for me.

**Thanksgiving** – Lord, thank You for Your favor and protection.

**Prayer** – For thou, O Lord, are a shield to me, the glory and the lifter of my head. Thank You for Your love and protection.

# Day 13

Psalm 6:1 Lord, do not rebuke me in Your anger or discipline me in Your wrath.

IN DAVID'S DAY, CALAMITY AND ILLNESS WERE VIEWED AS A PUNISHment from God for sin, so David was asking that God not punish him while He was angry. However, in John 9:1-7, we find Jesus dismissing that theory. As Jesus and His disciples were walking down the road, they saw a man who had been blind from birth. The disciples asked Jesus, 'Rabbi, who sinned, this man or his parents?' Jesus replied, 'Neither this man nor his parents sinned, but this happened so that the work of God might be displayed in his life.' Have you felt like David? Have you felt that God was punishing you for something you had done? Have you been so sick, your bones ached? Have you walked with pain and sickness more than you thought you could bear? This is how David describes his sickness. Notice how David starts his prayer to God. Instead of asking for healing or relief from pain, he asks God not to take out His anger upon him. David knew he had sinned and felt God was chastising him. So David is asking for mercy from God and that He would not impose the full measure of the penalty for his sin. What is the penalty for our sin? Paul writes in Romans 6:23, 'The wages of sin is death, but the gift of God is eternal life.' Because of our sin, we deserve the death penalty, not a sickness or disease. Remember Job? The Bible said he was blameless, upright and feared God. He wasn't deserving of the problems he faced. Satan attacked him because of his faithfulness to God. However, as sinners, we deserve the punishment of death and hell for our sins. God can use calamity and illness to get our attention and bring us to Him. Thank God, He sent His Son to pay the penalty for our sin. Because of Jesus, we can seek His mercy and forgiveness and not receive the punishment we deserve.

**Acknowledge** – Lord, we deserve the penalty of our sin. However, through Your Son, Jesus Christ, we can have eternal life.

**Confess** – Lord, forgive me when I think You don't care that I am sick.

**Thanksgiving** – Lord, thank You that you don't discipline us as we deserve.

**Prayer** – O Lord, please do not rebuke me in Your anger.

# Day 14

**Psalm 6:6** I am worn out from groaning; all night long I flood my bed with weeping and drench my couch with tears.

On the evening before Jesus was crucified, He and the disciples shared the Passover meal together. Afterwards, Jesus and the disciples went to the Mount of Olives, where He withdrew from them to pray. Luke 22:44 tells us, 'And being in anguish, He prayed more earnestly, and His sweat was like drops of blood falling to the ground.' Jesus knew what was about to take place and prayed for God to 'take this cup from Me, yet not My will, but Yours be done.' He was in such anguish, that He was sweating droplets of blood. Have you ever cried until you could cry no more? Have you been completely worn out from crying? During those long hours, have you wondered if God was listening to you? Rest assured that God heard your prayers and has seen your tears. Just as God heard Jesus praying that night, He hears your prayers. A few verses later David tells us that God has heard him. Verse 9, 'The Lord has heard my cry for mercy, the Lord accepts my prayer.' Isn't it comforting to know that God hears us even when we feel like He is a million miles away? At our lowest point, God hears our prayers. Just the assurance that God loves and hears us can change our attitude about our current situation. Jesus prayed for God to change what was about to happen, but wanted God's will above His. Like Jesus, God may not change our circumstances but He will change our perspective on them. Because of Him, our hope is renewed. Our energy is restored. We are able to resume the fight, to continue our battle with the circumstances we face. Lord, thank You for Your love and concern for Your children. We know that it is okay with You for us to cry and fall on our face before You to change our circumstances. But even better is Your presence in our lives that allows us to run the race You have placed before us.

**Acknowledge** – Lord, You hear us when we pray.

**Confess** – Lord, forgive me when I doubt that You hear my cries for help.

**Thanksgiving** – Lord, thank You for Your encouragement or hope.

**Prayer** – Lord, although I flood my bed with weeping and drench my couch with tears, I trust in You to answer my prayers.

# Day 15

Psalm 7:1 Lord, my God, I take refuge in You; save and deliver me from all who pursue me.

Psalm 7 was written by David regarding Cush the Benjamite, an apparent supporter of Saul, who was part of a group persecuting him. David begins the Psalm asking God to deliver him from all who pursue him. In 1 Samuel, we read that David spent much of his early adulthood running from Saul who was jealous of him and wanted to kill him. Even after Saul was killed in battle and David was made King, he still faced difficult situations throughout his entire lifetime. His own son, Absalom, tried to depose David as king, going to war against David and his men. Also, during David's lifetime, he fought many battles against the Philistines. It seems as if he had a lot of enemies who were out to get him. With all this turmoil going on in his life, notice how he starts this Psalm, 'Lord, my God.' These names express supreme reverence, yet absolute confidence in the One he is speaking to. He continues to say, 'I take refuge in You.' Notice he didn't say 'I will take refuge.' There is a big difference. He has already taken refuge in God. He is already safe. No matter the immediate outcome, God is his refuge. God will deliver him from all who are after him. Our enemies may not be out to kill us, but may be out to slander and ruin our reputation. Our so called 'friends' may be out to get that promotion ahead of us by telling the boss untruths about us. They may say hurtful and mean things about us. However, no matter our situation, if we trust in God's wisdom and His will then we, like David, will have peace regardless of the immediate outcome. Take refuge in God; allow Him to deliver you from all who pursue you.

**Acknowledge** – Lord, You are our refuge and strength.

**Confess** – Lord, forgive me when I try to take control and do things my way.

**Thanksgiving** – Lord, thank You for the peace that passes all understanding, even in the midst of trials.

**Prayer** – Lord, as David prayed, I take refuge in You, save and deliver me from all who pursue me.

# Day 16

Psalm 7:10 My shield is God most high, who saves the upright in heart.

Yesterday we read that David sought refuge in God from all those who were pursuing him. In the verses leading up to today's verse, David is pleading his case before God. David insists he is innocent of any wrongdoing against his foes and has given no cause for attack from his enemies. He wants God to rise up and take action against the wicked. In today's verse, David expresses confidence that his prayer will be heard, because his 'shield is God most high who saves the upright in heart.' This is the third reference we have read about God being David's shield. By now we should have a good picture of the purpose and value of a shield. David also said that God saves the 'upright in heart.' A person who is 'upright in heart' is one that has high moral standards in all areas of their life. They are honest and want to do what is right. There are very few people who measure up to this high standard. Even David had his faults and failures. However, we have a Savior, Jesus Christ, who has made us right with God. His blood has washed our sins away and cleansed our hearts. Like David, have you been accused of things which you have not done? Have your actions and words been misunderstood, misinterpreted, and misconstrued which has led to conflict with others? Have you tried to take matters into your own hands to rectify the situation? How has that gone for you? Have you made matters worse? Instead of trying to solve things on your own, why not follow David's actions? Take your burdens and cares to the God Most High. Recognize that He is your Shield, your Deliver, and your Savior. Ask Him to go before you to work things out instead of you trying to fix things and making them worse. God did it for David; He will do it for you!

**Acknowledge** – Lord, one day You will judge all mankind. Let me find refuge in the redeeming blood of Jesus Christ.

**Confess** – Lord, I am ashamed of the way I handle conflict and misunderstandings. Forgive me when I try to take control and do things my way.

**Thanksgiving** – Lord, thank You for being our shield. You will gather Your faithful servants to assemble around Your throne.

**Prayer** – Lord, help me to remain faithful and confident that You hear and answer our prayers.

# Day 17

Psalm 7:17 I will give thanks to the Lord because of His righteousness; I will sing the praises of the name of the Lord most high.

David closes Psalm 7 by giving thanks to God because of His righteousness. Notice he is not thanking God for destroying his enemies or delivering him from trouble. Although in verses 15 and 16, David does say that his enemies have fallen into the very traps they set for him. David could have easily said 'I give thanks to the Lord for destroying my enemies. The traps they set for me have backfired and ensnared them.' No, David is thanking God for His righteousness. What is righteousness? Why should we give thanks to the Lord because of His righteousness? David said he would even 'sing praises of the name of the Lord most high' because of it. Simply put, righteousness is the quality of being morally right and just. God the Father, Jesus the Son, and the Holy Spirit, three in one, are perfect, holy and righteous. God, being a righteous and just God, cannot ignore sin. When Adam and Eve disobeyed His command in the garden by eating the fruit from the Tree of Life, sin entered the world and separated us from a perfect God. Their disobedience required punishment because for God to overlook or excuse their actions would not be just. As David points out, it is because of God's righteousness that we can worship Him. Could you trust a God who was not just, who didn't treat everyone the same? Could you trust a God who was lenient to some and strict towards others? Since Adam and Eve's disobedience, mankind has lived in a broken, evil world. If not for a loving, righteous God, who sent His Son to bridge the gap and make a way for us to become right with Him, we would forever be separated from God. Although David did not know how God's plan of salvation would unfold, he still recognized God for His righteousness and praised Him. Now that we know how God unfolded His plan, we should forever give thanks to Him and sing praises to Him.

**Acknowledge** – Lord, You are a righteous and holy God.

**Confess** – Lord, forgive me when I fail to worship You as I should.

**Thanksgiving** – Lord, thank You for Your plan of salvation.

**Prayer** – I give thanks to the Lord, who is my shield, my protector and my salvation. I worship You.

# Day 18

**Psalm 8:1** O Lord, our Lord, how majestic is Your name in all the earth! You have set Your glory above the heavens.

When I read this Psalm, I am reminded of a song written by Michael W. Smith and sung by Sandi Patti, entitled, 'How Majestic is Your Name.' I recommend that you 'YouTube' the song. It is a simple song of praise to a mighty God. I doubt David's version had the same melody, but it is a perfect song to recognize how great God is. When penning these words, David must have been sitting outside on a bright, clear night when the sky was littered with stars. When you have the opportunity, go outside on a clear night and watch the stars begin to show up. One by one they appear as the night sky grows darker. Suddenly the sky will be full of stars that are millions of miles away. As you look up, think about David and his words, 'God has set His glory above the heavens.' Imagine that, He has set His glory above the heavens far above the farthest star in the night sky. David also said that God's name was majestic in all the earth. In other words, His name has impressive beauty and dignity. At times, it is difficult to comprehend that God was already present, before the heavens and the earth were even created. Yet, in Genesis chapter 1, we read that God created the heavens and the earth. His creation defies our imagination. The more sophisticated science becomes the more amazing things we learn about God's creation. Yet, in its simplicity, His creation is beautiful. To quote another song, sung by Ray Stevens, 'Everything is Beautiful in its own way, like a starry summer night or a snow-covered winter's day.' There is beauty all around us. Take the time to enjoy God's creation like David. As my wife reminds me, 'take time to smell the roses.' Tomorrow, we will look further into God's creation. However, for today let's just recognize and praise Him for who He is. Praise Him for His majesty. Praise Him for His glory. Praise Him for His righteousness. Praise Him for His love for you.

**Acknowledge** – Lord, how majestic is Your name.

**Confess** – Lord, forgive me when I fail to recognize Your majesty.

**Thanksgiving** – Lord, thank You for Your creation.

**Prayer** – Praise the name of the Lord, who is above the earth, who has set His glory in the heavens.

# Day 19

Psalm 8:3-4 When I consider Your heavens, the work of Your fingers, the moon and the stars, which You have set in place, what is mankind that You are mindful of them, human beings that You care for them.

When you look into the night sky filled with stars, you may see a few thousand stars without a telescope. However, as we probe further into the heavens, we find there are millions of stars in the sky. According to www.scienceline.ucsb.edu there are approximately 10 billion galaxies in the observable universe. The number of stars in a galaxy varies, but it is estimated there are 100 billion stars per galaxy. Do the math. That would be 1 billion, trillion stars in the observable universe, all of which God set in place. I imagine as David sat out in the fields at night tending his father's flocks, he spent many hours gazing into the night sky causing him to wonder, what is it that causes God to think about us? Why does He care for us? Why should God care for you, one person out of the billions in the world? Job said it this way in Job 7:17-18, 'What is man that You make so much of him, that You give him so much attention, that You examine him every morning and test him every moment?' Secondly, why should God care about something that doesn't last very long? 1 Peter 1:24-25 tells us, 'For, all men are like grass, and all their glory is like the flowers of the field; the grass withers and the flowers fall, but the work the Lord stands forever.' No one knows how long they will live. James 4:14 says it this way, 'Why, you do not even know what will happen tomorrow. What is your life? You are a mist that appears for a little while and then vanishes.' The answer is very simple, He created you in His image and He loves you. He loved you so much that He sent His only Son to die for you, so that you might have eternal life. He loves you! Dwell on His love for you today.

**Acknowledge** – Lord, You created the heavens and the earth and set the stars in their place.

**Confess** – Lord, forgive me when I fail to care for Your creation.

**Thanksgiving** – Lord, thank You that You love and care for us.

**Prayer** – Lord, help me to stop and look up into the night sky to see Your handiwork and give You praise as David did.

# Day 20

**Psalm 9:1** I will give thanks to You, Lord, with all my heart; I will tell of all Your wonderful deeds.

What has God done that causes you to give Him thanks? What has He done that compels you to tell others? Has He healed you? Has He delivered you from a broken relationship? Has He seen you through a difficult financial situation? Has He shown up in your time of need? Has He opened doors for a new job? Don't forget to thank Him for what He has done. Luke 17 tells the story of Jesus healing ten lepers. Jesus healed them and told them to go show themselves to the priests. However, only one came back and thanked Jesus for healing him. Don't be like the nine who didn't think it was important to give God thanks for what He has done. Healing, deliverance, and restored relationships are the tangible things we can see God's hand working in. What about the intangible? Has there been a time when in the matter of only minutes you could have been part of a terrible accident? My mother, who is in her mid-eighties, lives next door. She is slow, but still mobile. Vivian and I had pulled into the driveway to pick up something from the house and head back out. My mother who was outside saw us and made her way into my yard as I was dashing into the house. I jumped back into the car and inadvertently dropped the keys when putting them into the ignition. I picked them up, cranked the car, and started backing. As soon as I started backing, I saw my mother standing by the passenger side of the car waving. Had I not dropped the keys, I would have backed over my mother who had walked behind the car to get to the passenger side. A matter of seconds made the difference. Was this a coincidence or was it God's handiwork? No question in my mind, I praise Him for this wonderful deed to protect my mother. Give thanks to God; tell others about the God coincidences in your life.

**Acknowledge** – Lord, You do miracles every day.

**Confess** – Lord, forgive me when I overlook the wonderful things You have done for me.

**Thanksgiving** – Lord, I give thanks with all my heart for all You have done for me.

**Prayer** – Lord, I acknowledge those so-called coincidences are really Your hand of providence in my life. Help me to tell all about Your wonderful deeds.

# Day 21

Psalm 9:9 The Lord is a refuge for the oppressed, a stronghold in times of trouble.

David refers to God as a refuge, a stronghold in times of trouble. What does being a refuge entail? It is a place of safety, a shelter from pursuit, danger or trouble. David may have possibly been thinking about the cities of refuge where a person who accidentally killed someone could flee to find protection. In those days, a close relative was supposed to avenge the murder of a family member, even if accidental. The avenger could not punish the accused if they made it to a City of Refuge. The accused remained protected until he or she could stand trial. This law was given to Moses. Isn't it wonderful that we have a God who cares for us; a God who is our place of safety and shelter that we can run to and not some city? It is very unlikely we would need protection for the reason the Cities of Refuge were established. However, as Christians, there are times when we may face persecution and oppression because of our faith. It is in those times we need a place of refuge where our souls can find rest. The Apostle Paul put it this way in 1 Corinthians 4:8-9, 'We are hard pressed on every side, but not crushed; perplexed, but not in despair; persecuted, but not abandoned; struck down, but not destroyed.' Paul is the epitome of someone who was persecuted. He later tells of his trials in 2Corinthians 11. To name a few, he was imprisoned on many occasions, flogged, he received 39 lashes five times, beaten with rods three times, stoned, and shipwrecked three times. While we have not had the same experiences as Paul, we need a stronghold and a refuge in times of trouble. During those times, seek shelter in the Savior who is our refuge. He is the place where the storms of life cannot harm you. He is the Savior who loved you enough to die for you.

**Acknowledge** – Lord, You are our shelter, a stronghold in times of trouble.

**Confess** – Lord, forgive me when I look to others for refuge.

**Thanksgiving** – Lord, thank You for Your hand of protection on me.

**Prayer** – Lord, as Paul said, we feel pressed on every side, perplexed, persecuted, and struck down. But because of Your love for us, we are not crushed, not in despair, not abandoned, and not destroyed. You are our place of refuge.

# Day 22

Psalm 9:18 But God will never forget the needy; the hope of the afflicted will never perish.

What is one date in history that will never be forgotten? The date that sticks with me is 9/11/2001, which will not be forgotten because of the terrorist attack that occurred on that day. This attack took approximately 3,500 lives and impacted thousands more. I can also remember the day and events when Vivian and I were married. I remember the details of when our children were born. I remember the Sunday night I gave my heart to Jesus. However, my memory of events and people seem to fade over the years if I am not reminded of them on a periodic basis. Sadly, most sermons and Sunday school lessons I have heard are fleeting memories as well. In Deuteronomy 11:18-20, God gives Moses very clear instructions for helping the people remember His commandments. He said, 'Fix these words of mine in your hearts and minds; tie them as symbols on your heads. Teach them to your children, talking about them when you sit at home and when you walk along the road, when you lie down and when you get up. Write them on the doorposts of your houses and your gates.' In other words, keep God's word in front of you all the time. Isn't it wonderful that we serve a God who doesn't forget anything or anyone, especially the needy, and the afflicted? These tend to be the lowest on the 'totem pole.' They are the forgotten ones of society who struggle to keep their heads above water. God cares for them, He cares for you. He does not forget them, He has not forgotten you. Jesus said in Matthew 10:29-31, 'Are not two sparrows sold for a penny? Yet not one of them will fall to the ground apart from the will of the Father. And even the very hairs on your head are all numbered. So don't be afraid; you are worth more than many sparrows.' Don't lose hope. You have a God who loves you and will never forget you!

**Acknowledge** – Lord, You never forget the needy.

**Confess** – Lord, forgive me when I worry and forget Your love for me.

**Thanksgiving** – Lord, thank You that we have hope in You.

**Prayer** – Lord, thank You that You never forget or forsake us. We are worth more than many sparrows in Your sight.

# Day 23

Psalm 10:4 In his pride the wicked man does not seek Him, in all his thoughts there is no room for God.

How true this is! I have heard it said that pride is actually idolatry. It causes us to worship ourselves instead of God. Pride comes when we have a deep pleasure or satisfaction from our own achievements. How quickly do we take credit for a big achievement or financial success? It is very easy to fall into the trap of being prideful, especially when there is someone on the sidelines cheering us on and giving us credit for something. In Philippians 2:3, Paul tells us, 'Do nothing out of selfish ambition or vain conceit, but in humility consider others better than yourselves.' What happens when we think too much of ourselves? We tend to take our eyes off God and seek attention for ourselves. Pretty soon our vocabulary is filled with the word 'I.' Solomon wrote several proverbs dealing with pride. He doesn't have anything positive to say about it. In Proverbs 11:2 he writes, 'When pride comes, then comes disgrace, but with humility comes wisdom.' He also writes in chapter 16, verse 18, 'Pride goes before destruction, a haughty spirit before a fall.' In my own life, I have had a few instances where pride has caught up with me and served a large helping of 'humble pie.' Where are you on the pride spectrum? Are you self-serving, worshiping the desires of your heart, and chasing after worldly fame and fortune? Or, are you self-giving, humble, seeking God and worshiping Him for the good things in your life? 1Peter 5:5 tells us, 'Young men, in the same way be submissive to those who are older. All you clothe yourselves with humility toward one another, because, God opposes the proud but gives grace to the humble.' If you are not sure where you are on the pride spectrum, it might be a good time to do a self-evaluation of the direction you are headed. Don't get caught up in the pride trap. I promise you, humble pie doesn't taste very good.

**Acknowledge** – Lord, pride causes me to put myself ahead of You.

**Confess** – Lord, forgive me when pride takes over and pushes You out of my life.

**Thanksgiving** – Lord, thank You for forgiveness when we put other things ahead of You.

**Prayer** – As Solomon wrote, "pride goes before destruction…' Lord, help me to avoid pride and its consequences.

# Day 24

Psalm 10:12 Arise, Lord! Lift up Your hand, O God. Do not forget the helpless.

Read Psalm 10 and ask yourself, have I said the same thing the Psalmist said in verse 1 or verse 10? 'Lord, why do You stand far off?' 'Arise, Lord, lift up Your hand.' Or in today's terminology, 'God, do something!' 'Lord, where are You?' 'Lord, isn't it time You did something to fix this?' We don't have to look too far to see tragedy, oppression, and hopelessness in the world around us. I have had the opportunity to travel to Nicaragua on several mission trips. Like many Third World countries, there is poverty and hopelessness in the communities of Nicaragua. We found people were living in the city dump, making a living by scratching around in the trash to find recyclables they could sell or use. In the United States, as prosperous as it is, there is still poverty and homelessness. As we see these things, do we ask, Lord, lift up your hand and do something? The good news is that He has done something. God sent his Son, to become one of us, one of the oppressed, one who experienced pain and persecution. He ministered to the poor, the sick, the needy, and the helpless. Jesus touched lepers. He ate with the hated tax collectors. He sat at the well with a Samaritan woman and asked her for a drink of water. Jesus rebuked the disciples for trying to keep the little children away. He had compassion on an old lady who had been sick for twelve years, whose only hope for healing was to touch the hem of His garment. He forgave a woman who had been caught in adultery and thrown before Him by a mob wanting to stone her. He healed the son of a Roman Officer, the very people who were oppressing the Jews. Jesus has called us to follow His example. What can you do? How can you help someone? It is time to step out of our comfort zone and be like Jesus.

**Acknowledge** – Lord, You never forget the helpless, in fact You came to save them.

**Confess** – Lord, forgive me when I fail to follow Your command to go.

**Thanksgiving** – Lord, thank You that You came to the earth and became one of us; to experience life and conquer death.

**Prayer** – Lord, arise, lift up Your hand and help me not forget the helpless.

# Day 25

Psalm 11:4 The Lord is in His holy temple; the Lord is on His heavenly throne. He observes the sons of men; His eyes examine them.

DAVID ANSWERS THE QUESTION WE OFTEN TIMES ASK, 'GOD WHERE are You?' His adversaries were closing in on him. They were so close, that he uses the analogy of 'shooting arrows from the shadows'. (v3) When life seems to be caving in, how often have you asked the same question? I admit that I have. When things are going good, we tend to forget about God and think we have everything under control. But, when the wheels come off, and they do, we begin to sing a different tune. God, I need You. God, where are You? Isn't it comforting to know that God knows what is going on in our lives? There are two truths we can glean from today's verse. 1) He has His eyes on you. He knows the problems you are facing. He knew them before they happened. He knows the outcome as well. In Luke 22:31-32, Jesus is talking to Simon Peter at the Last Supper before His betrayal. Jesus said, 'Simon, Simon, Satan has asked to sift you as wheat. But I have prayed for you, Simon that your faith may not fail. And when you have turned back, strengthen your brothers.' Jesus knew Simon was going to deny Him three times that night. But Jesus had prayed for his faith to remain strong because He knew the ministry Peter would have after His death. 2) The picture of God sitting on His heavenly throne gives us reassurance of God's omnipotence, which is His unlimited power and ability to do anything. Isaiah 6:1 gives us a great picture of God on His throne. 'In the year that King Uzziah died, I saw the Lord seated on a throne, high and exalted, and the train of His robe filled the temple.' God is in control, He is on His throne. Even when things are not going well for you, He is in control. Take time today to give Him praise for His plan for you and keeping watch over you.

**Acknowledge** – Lord, You are omnipotent, You are in control.

**Confess** – Lord, forgive me when I doubt Your hand working in my life.

**Thanksgiving** – Lord, thank You that You keep Your eyes on me.

**Prayer** – Lord, I pray that I will always put my faith and trust in You. You are in control.

# Day 26

**Psalm 11:7** For the Lord is righteous, He loves justice; the upright will see His face.

David closes Psalm 11 with three statements about God. First, the Lord is righteous. We learned that righteous means the quality of being morally right and just. Secondly, God is a Holy God who loves justice. God could not turn His back on man's sin, so Jesus had to pay the penalty once and for all for our sin to make us right with God. No longer would animal sacrifices be needed to pay the penalty for our sin. Those sacrifices were part of the old covenant God had made with His people. Thank God we have a way to be truly upright and able to see God's face because of the redeeming blood of Jesus Christ shed on the cross. Thank God we don't have to sacrifice a goat to cover our sins. Now we can claim the promise David closed this verse with, 'the upright will see His face.' When we see His face, we are in the presence of God. According to www.ancient-hebrew.org, the translation for the Hebrew word 'face' is 'presence.' There are several scriptures that command us to seek His face. 1 Chronicles 16:11 tells us, 'Look to the Lord and His strength; seek His face always.' What is so important about being in God's presence and seeking His face? Do we need God's presence in our lives each day? Can we get along without it? The answer to those questions is yes you can, but not very well. Hebrews 11:6 says it this way, 'And without faith it is impossible to please God, because anyone who comes to Him must believe that He exists and that He rewards those who earnestly seek Him.' What are those rewards? In my life, the reward of being in God's presence and seeking His face is the manifestation of the fruits of the spirit; love, joy, peace, patience, goodness, faithfulness, and self-control. I love that kind of fruit. It is very healthy for you. I hope you will taste of it well.

**Acknowledge** – Lord, the upright and the righteous will see Your face.

**Confess** – Lord, forgive me when I fail to seek Your presence in my life.

**Thanksgiving** – Lord, thank You for Your presence in our lives.

**Prayer** – Lord, I pray that I will seek Your presence in my life each day.

# Day 27

Psalm 12:6 And the words of the Lord are flawless, like silver purified in a crucible, like gold refined seven times.

Psalm 12 was written by David as a prayer for help when it appeared that no one around him was honest and upright. In verse two he writes, 'everyone lies to his neighbor; their flattering lips speak with deception.' According to David, you can't trust what these people utter because it is foolishness and worthless. Without God in their lives, the love of truth goes out the window. Deceit and flattery become the standard form of conversation. If I didn't know better, I would think David was writing about us today. It takes a discerning mind to weed out the fluff of what we are being told in order to get to the truth. Isn't it refreshing that the words of the Lord are flawless? He doesn't lie. He doesn't have to put a spin on a conversation to make it look right. No, His words are like purified silver and refined gold. They are truth, certainty, holiness, and faithfulness all wrapped into one. His words are free and clear of error and filled with integrity. So what type of words do you use? Do you spread lies, slander, and deception? Do you stretch the truth? Do you tell lies to cover up something you have done? Do you spread rumors and gossip about others? Do you try to justify yourself by coming up with a number of reasons and excuses for not telling the truth? Yesterday, we talked about being in God's presence and how that produces the fruits of the spirit. In Ephesians 5:8-9, Paul talks about the fruit of living in the light of the Lord. He says, 'For you were once darkness, but now you are light in the Lord. Live as children of light (for the fruit of the light consists in all goodness, righteous, and truth).' As a child of God, we should use words that are honest, true, few, wise, kind, and well-chosen. Start today, choose your words wisely.

**Acknowledge** – Lord, Your words are true and flawless.

**Confess** – Lord, forgive me when I fail to speak the truth and respond with sarcastic and hurtful words.

**Thanksgiving** – Lord, thank You for being truth.

**Prayer** – Lord, we live in a time when what is good is now bad, what was unacceptable is now acceptable, what was untrue is now truth. Help me to speak truth and discern between truth and lies.

# Day 28

**Psalm 12:8** The wicked freely strut about when what is vile is honored among men.

Yesterday, we closed our prayer with the thought that we live in a time when what is good is now bad, what was unacceptable is now acceptable, what was untrue is now truth. Unfortunately, this does not shock us anymore. David tells us that the wicked were proud of themselves and strutting about. Their actions were honored among men. To make matters worse, they were following the example of their leaders. Poor leadership will destroy a nation. That is why we need to elect leaders with high moral values who value the sanctity of life. To me, the most shocking practice in our day that is honored and protected by the government is abortion. According to www.now.org, there are approximately 46 million abortions performed each year in the world. Those who support abortion hold to the point that it is a woman's right to make decisions about her own body. Sadly, today as I am writing this thought, women across America are holding protests in favor of Pro-Choice, the right to have an abortion. To them, any arguments for the rights of the unborn child are old fashioned and outdated. They claim the unborn baby doesn't have any rights and its life can be terminated. Even more horrific is the selling of the body parts of the aborted children. We will see later in the Psalms how God feels about an unborn child. For now, we will visit Luke 1:44. Mary, the mother of Jesus, was pregnant and went to visit her relative, Elizabeth who was approximately six months pregnant with her child, John the Baptist. Luke tells us, 'As soon as the sound of your greeting reached my ears, the baby in my womb leaped for joy.' How awesome is that! An unborn child recognized the mother of Jesus and leap for joy. Don't let foolish arguments or pressure from friends sway your belief in the value and sanctity of life.

**Acknowledge** – Lord, we are living in a time when what is right is wrong and what is wrong is right.

**Confess** – Lord, forgive me when I fail to stand up for what is right.

**Thanksgiving** – Lord, thank You for Your word. It is still relevant today.

**Prayer** – Lord, help me to recognize what is right and true and not be ashamed to make a stand for it.

# Day 29

Psalm 13:1 How long, O Lord? Will You forget me forever? How long will You hide Your Face from me?

'How long,' is perhaps the most favorite question asked by a child, and least favorite a parent has to answer. David repeats it four times in the first two verses of Psalm 13. David even claims God is hiding His Face from him. David, because of his illness, feels God has left him. I confess that I have at times wondered if God has forgotten me. However, thank God I haven't experienced a long term illness or sickness that has had me in the hospital as David seemed to be experiencing. I have had routine illnesses and flu, but nothing major. My worst experience was a case of appendicitis that required surgery, a day in the hospital, and several weeks to recover. However, I have had problems that seemed to go from bad to worse that have led me to ask God, 'How long?' Perhaps you are facing something now or you know of someone else that might be going through a difficult time. It could be health-related, finance-related, a broken relationship, depression, or even racial persecution. Prayer works. It is okay to ask God, how long will this go on? How long before You answer my prayer? But trust Him to see you through whatever problem you are facing. If a friend is suffering, come alongside them and agree to pray and support them. God wants to hear our genuine feelings, even if they are doubt and anger at Him. Never stop praying. Never stop seeking God. As long as we continue to seek Him, we will end at a place of peace. As we will find out tomorrow, David turns his frustration with God to rejoicing.

**Acknowledge** – Lord, I know You hear me when I call upon Your name.

**Confess** – Lord, forgive me when I doubt Your love for me.

**Thanksgiving** – Lord, thank You for loving me and taking care of me.

**Prayer** – Lord, there have been times when I have felt like David, away from Your presence. But I know You were always there even though I didn't feel You were.

# Day 30

Psalm 13:5 But I trust in Your unfailing love; my heart rejoices in Your salvation.

Although David is sick and near death, as we learned in verse one, his faith and confidence in God is expressed in today's reading. He trusts in God's unfailing love, he rejoices in God's salvation. He may have remembered the words written by Moses in Deuteronomy 31:6 which said, 'Be strong and courageous. Do not be afraid or terrified because of them, for the Lord your God goes with you; He will never leave you nor forsake you.' Or he may have remembered the words of Joshua 1:5, 'No one will be able to stand up against you all the days of your life. As I was with Moses, so I will be with you; I will never leave you nor forsake you.' David is holding on to the promises of God. Let's look at what faith is. How strong is your faith? How should we express our faith? Hebrews 11:1 gives a great definition of faith, 'Now faith is confidence in what we hope for and assurance about what we do not see.' David didn't know if he was going to get better or not, but he puts his trust in God. His circumstances didn't change right away, but his outlook and perspective on his situation did. He had confidence that God was in control. So, how strong is our faith? 2 Corinthians 5:7 states, 'We live by faith, not by sight.' I don't know about you, but I would prefer to see the path ahead of me. However, God wants us to step out in faith; He wants us to trust Him in all circumstances. Just as David does here, we need to begin praising Him for an answer to our situation before the answer has arrived. How should we express our faith? The entire chapter of Hebrews 11 gives us example after example of how people who didn't have the Bible or resources we have today, demonstrated their faith in God. The key to each of their stories is obedience. As we stay obedient to God, we demonstrate our faith to follow Him, wherever He leads. Is it time for you to step out in faith?

**Acknowledge** – Lord, I trust in Your unfailing love.

**Confess** – Lord, forgive me when my faith is weak.

**Thanksgiving** – Lord, I rejoice in Your salvation.

**Prayer** – Lord, help me to be obedient to Your will in my life. I pray that my faith will be strong.

#  Day 31

### Psalm 13:6 I will sing the Lord's praise, for He has been good to me.

TODAY, DAVID HAS MOVED FROM A CRY OF DESPERATION AND HOPElessness to an expression of faith and trust in God's love. Notice David wasn't praising God because of his healing, in fact his condition had not improved, but his perspective and trust in God had been renewed. Where are you today? Are you crying out to God for help? Do you think He has forgotten or abandoned you? Do you feel He has hidden His face from you? Or have you trusted God for the answer to your prayer? Has your faith grown because of the situation you are facing? Have you moved to a place where you are now able to sing praises to the Lord for His goodness to you? Think back to a time when God intervened on your behalf to work out a situation in your life. Maybe He healed you from a sickness, or restored a relationship that went bad, or perhaps He delivered you from an addiction. God has a way of turning our trials into blessings. Isaiah 61:3 says, 'And provide for those who grieve in Zion – to bestow on them a crown of beauty instead of ashes, the oil of gladness instead of mourning, and a garment of praise instead of a spirit of despair. They will be called oaks of righteousness, a planting of the Lord for the display of His splendor.' If you are hurting today, meditate on Isaiah 61:3. Let Him give you a crown of beauty instead of ashes. Let Him anoint you with the oil of gladness. Let Him clothe you with the garment of praise. Give Him praise today for all He has done in your life and what He is going to do. If you are having a hard time praising God, begin singing this simple chorus. It will lift your spirits and put you in a place of worship with the Father. It goes, 'I sing praises to Your name, oh Lord, praises to Your name oh Lord, for Your name is great and worthy to be praised.' Lord, I thank You for Your goodness to me!

**Acknowledge** – Lord, You have been good to me.

**Confess** – Lord, forgive me when fail to praise You.

**Thanksgiving** – I sing praises to Your name, oh Lord.

**Prayer** – I will sing Your praises because You have been good to me. Thank You that Your goodness and mercy last forever.

# Day 32

Psalm 14:1 The fool says in his heart, there is no God. They are corrupt, their deeds are vile, there is no one who does good.

In this verse, David is not just referring to the atheist. David tells us that God is looking down on all mankind to search out the righteous. In the story of Sodom and Gomorrah found in Genesis 18 & 19, we learn that the Lord searched for any who were righteous before He destroyed the two cities. Genesis 18:20 tells us, 'Then the Lord said, "The outcry against Sodom and Gomorrah is so great and their sin so grievous that I will go down and see if what they have done is as bad as the outcry that has reached Me. If not, I will know." Abraham had pleaded with the Lord to spare the cities if He could find as few as 10 righteous people there. Out of the two cities, only Abraham's nephew, Lot, and his two daughters were spared. Where were we before we came to know Christ as our Savior? Were we like the fool who denied the existence of God? You may argue 'I am not as bad as the people of Sodom and Gomorrah.' Unfortunately, God doesn't compare us against a serial killer or even our neighbor who has a few more flaws than we do. Our lives are put up against His righteousness, of which we fall very short. Thank God that He sent His Son, Jesus, to cleanse us of our sin and unrighteousness. Our sins are covered in His bloodshed at the cross. His death and resurrection have made it possible to receive eternal life with a Holy God. Let's not be like the fool who continues to deny his condition and need for a Savior. If you have not accepted Christ as your Savior, now is the time. There is not a more perfect time to ask Him into your life.

**Acknowledge** – Lord, You are holy and righteous.

**Confess** – Lord, I was a sinner who denied You. Forgive me for denying You.

**Thanksgiving** – Thank You for Your love for us, by sending Your Son to offer salvation to all.

**Prayer** – Thank You for loving me, even when I didn't love You. Let Your love, Your words, and Your Spirit control my life.

Psalm 14:2 The Lord looks down from heaven on the sons of men to see if there are any who understand, any who seek God.

God watches over the earth and knows our every step. Job 28:24 speaking about God says, 'For He looks to the ends of the earth and sees everything under the heavens.' And Proverbs 5:21 tells us, 'For the ways of a man are before the eyes of the Lord, and He watches all his paths.' Today, David asks the question 'will God find anyone who is seeking Him?' If you continue to read the rest of Psalms 14, you will get the impression as David writes in verse 3, 'All have turned aside, they have together become corrupt; there is no one who does good, not even one.' David's summary of mankind is not very encouraging. He said, 'all have turned aside, they have become corrupt, there is no one who does good.' This reminds me of Paul's assessment in Romans 3:23, 'For all have sinned and fallen short of the glory of God.' Thank goodness that God sent His Son to cover our sins. Today we see a picture of a loving Father who is looking to find someone who is seeking Him; who wants to have fellowship with Him. How much are you seeking Him each day? Are you daily spending time in His word? Are you praying to Him each day? On a scale of 1 to 10, how would you rate your devotional life with the Father? When He is looking down, does He find you seeking Him? Or, does He find you putting Him on hold while you catch up on email, social media, television, and sporting events? I confess it is very easy to let the busyness of life crowd out my time with God. But those times when I earnestly seek Him, I have an inner peace and joy in the midst of the busyness, and turmoil of everyday life. Look for God, He wants you to find Him.

**Acknowledge** – Lord, You are looking to have a relationship with us.

**Confess** – Lord, forgive me when I put other things ahead of You.

**Thanksgiving** – Thank You for Your love for me and Your desire to have a relationship with me.

**Prayer** – Lord, help me to put aside distractions that keep me from having a relationship with You.

# Day 34

**Psalm 15:1** Lord, who may dwell in Your sacred tent? Who may live on Your holy mountain?

At the time David wrote this Psalm, the Temple was not a building, but an actual tent. In fact, from the time of Moses until Solomon, David's son, started construction, God's presence resided in a tent, not a permanent building. In Exodus 40:34, we find that the temple had just been completed and the glory of the Lord filled it. 'Then the cloud covered the Tent of Meeting, and the glory of the Lord filled the tabernacle.' Verse 38 says 'So the cloud of the Lord was over the tabernacle by day, and fire was in the cloud by night, in the sight of all the house of Israel during their travels.' David asks a good question, who can get close to God and enter into the presence of the Lord? In the following verses, David provides the answer. In verse two, 'those whose walk is blameless, and does what is righteous, who speaks truth from his heart.' In verse three; one who speaks words in love about others and does not slander. In verse four; one who honors those that fear the Lord, who keeps his promises, even when it hurts. In verse five; one who is generous and does not accept a bribe, one who is honest, and faithful to their word. David is saying that the words we use are important. If we go about telling lies, tearing down people with our words, and making empty promises then how can we expect God's presence in our lives? His nature is holy, righteous, and truthful. As hard as we may try, there will be times when we fall into doing the very things David is warning us about. No one but Jesus lived a perfect life. Thankfully, God made a way for us to be close to Him through His Son, Jesus Christ. He paid the penalty for our sin and offers forgiveness. If we confess our sins and ask forgiveness, He will cleanse you and make you right with the Father. Because He is now our Savior, we can have access to the Father through Him.

**Acknowledge** – Lord, You are holy, righteous, and truthful.

**Confess** – Lord, forgive me when I fail to speak words that are true.

**Thanksgiving** – Thank You for Your Son whose sacrifice atoned for my sin.

**Prayer** – Lord, no one is perfect other than Jesus, Your Son. Help me to live like Him.

# Day 35

Psalm 16:5 Lord, You alone are my portion and my cup; You make my lot secure.

Psalm 16 is a prayer of protection written by David. In what do you put your complete trust? Is it your bank account, your 401K? Is it a unique talent? Is it family? Is it a job? Is it your looks? How often do we find ourselves depending on something that is really temporary in the grand scheme of things? In one turn of events, a bank account or 401K can be quickly wiped out. Technology, a pandemic, and outsourcing can and have displaced many jobs. Relationships between family members can change. We spend billions of dollars each year on maintaining a youthful look, but our bodies continue to age. Nothing remains the same. When a major crisis hits, what are you going to do? For many years, David's life was in crisis mode. He was on the run from Saul and later his son Absalom. Through all the danger in his life, David understands the One who alone is his 'portion' and his 'cup', the One who 'makes my lot secure.' A 'portion' in those days was a part or share of an estate given to an heir; his 'cup', is a metaphor referring to what a host offers his guests. To the godly the Lord offers a cup of blessings. Our lot is secure in Him. In what is your hope and trust rooted in today? Is it the Lord? Or, is it an earthly fix that only provides temporary security? If that is the case, reach out to God today; let Him be your portion and your cup.

**Acknowledge** – Lord, You are my portion and my cup.

**Confess** – Lord, forgive me when I chase after the gift instead of the Giver.

**Thanksgiving** – Thank You for making my lot secure.

**Prayer** – Lord, You have created us with a desire to love and find fulfillment in Your presence. Without it, we try to fill in the void with many other things. Lord, let us seek You and find You each day.

# Day 36

**Psalm 16:8** I keep my eyes always on the Lord, with Him at my right hand, I will not be shaken.

DAVID IS EXPRESSING HIS CONFIDENCE IN GOD. NO MATTER HIS CIRcumstances, David was not going to be shaken by life's ups and downs because he knew that God was with him. In Ephesians 6:12, Paul tells us we are in a battle every day against Satan and his angels. 'For we wrestle not against flesh and blood, but against principalities, against powers, against the rulers of the darkness of this world, against spiritual wickedness in high places.' Satan and his workers know how to attack us at our weakest point. Daily we are faced with temptation. Who can help us in this daily struggle with temptation? Who is by our side, ready to go into battle with us? David answers, the Lord is 'at my right hand.' God is right beside us, giving us strength, encouragement, and guidance when we need it. He takes our hand and leads us when our faith has weakened. With God by our side, we will not be shaken. In verse nine, David writes, 'Therefore my heart is glad and my tongue rejoices; my body also will rest secure.' Notice the confidence David expresses as he keeps his eyes on the Lord. He will not be shaken when the troubles and trials of this life rage against him because he knows the Lord is with him. He rejoices and celebrates his confidence in God's presence beside him. Isaiah confirms what David is telling us today, that God holds our right hand. Isaiah 41:13; 'For I, the LORD your God, will hold your right hand, saying to you, Fear not, I will help you.' What a great assurance we have that God is with us. Are you struggling with the trials and temptations of life? Focus your attention on God. Let Him strengthen and encourage you. Allow Him to take your hand and lead you. As the old gospel hymn says, 'Turn your eyes upon Jesus, look full in His wonderful face, and the things of earth will grow strangely dim, in the light of His glory and grace.'

**Acknowledge** – Lord, You are with us each day.

**Confess** – Lord, forgive me when I doubt Your presence in my life.

**Thanksgiving** – Thank You for Your counsel, let my tongue rejoice and my body rest securely in Your presence.

**Prayer** – Lord, may I keep my eyes on You.

# Day 37

Psalm 16:11 You have made known the path of life; You will fill me with joy in Your presence, with eternal pleasures at Your right hand.

IS DAVID THE 'HOLY ONE' MENTIONED HERE OR IS HE PROPHESYING about his promised Son who would one day rule the earth? Peter, speaking in Acts 2:25-36, quotes Psalm 16 telling the people that David died and was buried, but that David was confident in God's promise of his descendant that would one day take the throne. Peter said in verses 31-32, 'Seeing what was ahead, he spoke of the resurrection of the Christ. God has raised this Jesus to life, and we are all witnesses of the fact.' David said he was filled with joy as he closed Psalm 16 with a statement that speaks of eternity with God. What path of life are you on? Do you have the confidence of David? Are you confident in God's promise of eternal life? Peter tells us how to have this confidence in Acts 2:38-39, 'Repent and be baptized, every one of you, in the name of Jesus Christ for the forgiveness of your sins. And you will receive the gift of the Holy Spirit. The promise is for you and your children and for all who are far off – for all whom the Lord our God will call.' Is your heart glad, does your tongue rejoice because of God's love for you? Have you repented of your sins and received Christ as your Savior? Or, is life just one day at a time? Do you lack hope? Do you feel like you are on the 'treadmill of life' with no way off? Take heart, there is hope. It starts with a daily walk with God. Ask Him into your life and let Him direct you. Start each day seeking the God who promises eternal life with Him. David knew the answer to eternal life; you can know Him as intimately as David did. It is worth the effort.

**Acknowledge** – Lord, You are the only one who offers eternal life.

**Confess** – Lord, forgive me when I fail to seek You.

**Thanksgiving** – Thank You for the joy of Your presence in my life.

**Prayer** – Lord, keep my eyes focused on You and Your promises, let me rest secure in Your love.

# Day 38

Psalm 17:5 My steps have held to Your paths; my feet have not slipped.

Psalm 17 was written by David as an appeal to God as judge of the earth. David opens the Psalm in verse one by saying 'Hear, O Lord, my righteous plea; listen to my cry.' By verse three he is asking God to examine his heart and test him to see what He might find. David said, 'I have resolved that my mouth will not sin.' By verse five, he is claiming that he has been faithful and followed God. I wish I could make the same claim as David does here. However, I have slipped and fallen many times. We have already learned from Paul in Romans 3:23, 'that all have sinned and fallen short of the glory of God.' So, let's take a look at David's life for just a moment. Didn't he commit adultery with Bathsheba and have her husband Uriah killed in battle? Didn't he try to cover up the whole affair by marrying Bathsheba? Wasn't David guilty of other sins as well? What is he really saying here? At this time in his life, David is under attack by ungodly foes. He makes his appeal for justice against those who are after him. He is not claiming to be sinless as it seems he is, but he is denying that he is as corrupt as those after him. He has not lied to his people (verse 3) or taken bribes (verse 4). He is being falsely accused but his conscience is clear. How do we keep our conscience clear before God? The first thing is to be like David, holding our feet to God's path by making right choices. The second is to repent. 1 John 1:9 says, 'If we confess our sins, He is faithful and just to forgive us our sins and to cleanse us from all unrighteousness.' Aren't you glad that we serve a God that doesn't hold our sins over us? He is faithful to forgive us when we seek Him in repentance. Take time today to confess your sins to Him.

**Acknowledge** – Lord, You have set a path for me to follow.

**Confess** – Lord, forgive me when I slip and fall, I am human.

**Thanksgiving** – Thank You for accepting our confession of sin in our lives and remembering them no more.

**Prayer** – Lord help me, like David, be able to say my steps have held to Your paths, my feet have not slipped.

# Day 39

Psalm 17:6 I call on You, my God, for You will answer me; turn Your ear to me and hear my prayer.

Today's verse is a good indication of how David felt about prayer. He had prayed enough to know God's character and God's love for him. David had confidence that God heard his prayers. He even asks God, 'turn your ear to me.' That confidence led him to expect an answer from God. No matter where you are in your walk with the Lord, isn't it wonderful to know that we have a God we can call on; a God that will answer us? While Jesus was on the earth, He recognized the importance of prayer. In Luke 6:12-13 we find that Jesus spent all night in prayer before choosing His disciples. 'One of those days, Jesus went out to a mountainside to pray, and spent the night praying to God. When morning came, He called His disciples to Him and chose twelve of them, whom He also designated Apostles.' Luke 5:16 also tells us, 'But Jesus often withdrew to lonely places and prayed.' Lastly, we know the night before His crucifixion, Jesus and the disciples went to the garden of Gethsemane to pray. Luke 22:41 states, 'And He withdrew from them about a stone's throw, and knelt down and prayed.' Unfortunately, while He was praying the disciples fell asleep. Are we following Jesus' example and making time to pray in all situations? Or, are we following the disciples' example by falling asleep instead of praying? I have to admit there have been some nights where I didn't make it to amen before falling asleep. A healthy prayer life takes discipline. There is power in prayer. James 5:16 tells us, 'Therefore confess your sins to each other and pray for each other so that you may be healed. The prayer of a righteous man is powerful and effective.' Let's give thanks to God who takes time to listen to you and to me. Let's also develop a habit of praying regularly to the God who answers our prayers according to His will.

**Acknowledge** – Lord, You are my God, the God who hears me when I call on You.

**Confess** – Lord, forgive me for not spending more time with You in prayer.

**Thanksgiving** – Thank You Lord that You are a God who hears us when we call out to You.

**Prayer** – Lord, I cry out to You for You are the only one who can heal, forgive, restore, and redeem.

# Day 40

Psalm 17:13 Rise up, Lord, confront them, bring them down; with Your sword rescue me from the wicked.

When I first read today's verse, I thought, I'm with David on this one. Lord, it is time You took action, confronted the wicked, and sent a few lightning bolts their way. Earlier in verse 10, David describes the wicked as having 'callous hearts', speaking with arrogance, and being selfish. But wait, I have acted like that as well. In God's eyes that makes me wicked too. However, we are quick to judge others and wish bad fortune on them. Several years ago, there was a situation that caused me to pray like David does here. I actually got very specific in my prayer, that God would send doubt, distrust, and dislike into someone's relationship that I didn't approve of. It took several months before I realized, it wasn't my place to judge this relationship. We live in a fallen world, and people make bad choices. However, if we look at Jesus' life, we find that He had compassion on the wicked. In Matthew 8:16 we see that Jesus even had compassion on the demon-possessed. 'When evening came, many who were demon-possessed were brought to Him, and He drove out the spirits with a word and healed all the sick.' Jesus had compassion on them and healed them. Later in Matthew 9:36, we see Jesus' compassion on display again, 'When He saw the crowds, He had compassion on them, because they were harassed and helpless, like sheep without a shepherd.' Because of my own sinfulness and God's compassion for all, I had to change my prayer about the person I mentioned and ask forgiveness. In the end, all wrongs will be made right when we face God. Thank God it is not up to me to be the judge. My job is to pray for the wicked whether I want to or not.

**Acknowledge** – Lord, You are in control. The wicked will not go unpunished.

**Confess** – Lord, forgive me for doubting You and Your sovereignty.

**Thanksgiving** – Lord, thank You for not letting the wicked win and in the end that all wrongs will be made right.

**Prayer** – Lord, help me to be faithful to You, help me to pray for my enemies.

# Day 41

Psalm 18:2 The Lord is my Rock, my Fortress and my Deliverer; my God is my Rock, in whom I take refuge, my Shield and the Horn of my Salvation, my Stronghold.

Before we dig into today's verse, I want to provide some background on Psalm 18. For years, David was pursued by Saul who led an all-out manhunt for David and his men. Psalm 18, is a song to the Lord when the Lord delivered him from the hand of all his enemies including Saul. Can you imagine David's relief and joy? His running was over. How does David respond? He begins with a declaration of faith. Look at the words he uses to describe God, (verse 1) my Strength, (verse 2) my Rock, my Fortress, my Deliverer, my Refuge, my Shield, the Horn or Strength of my Salvation, and my Stronghold. These are powerful words that describe God. Let's take a closer look at the words he used: 1. My Strength – In other words, I am weak but He is strong. 2. My Rock – An immovable force that can withstand storms of life. 3. My Fortress – A military stronghold, an especially strong and fortified place not easily attacked. 4. My Deliverer – One who rescues, one who saves. 5. My Refuge – A place or condition of safety and security from danger. 6. My Shield – The shield of faith, intercepting the darts and arrows of Satan. 7. The Horn or Strength of my Salvation – The power and force behind my salvation. 9. My Stronghold – A place that has been fortified to protect it from attack. David found refuge and strength in God. We are no different than David. There are times in our lives when we need to take refuge in God. Like David, we are being pursued by our enemies and have nowhere else to turn. However, as we turn to God, we learn He is the only real support we have in life. Are you able to call the Lord, your Rock, your Fortress, your Deliverer, your Shield, your Salvation and your Stronghold? Claim His protection over you and your family. As we have learned, He hears our prayers.

**Acknowledge** – Lord, You are my Strength, my Salvation, my Fortress.

**Confess** – Lord, forgive me for running to the things the world has to offer for comfort.

**Thanksgiving** – Lord, thank You for being our Strong Tower, our Rock, our Fortress, our Deliverer.

**Prayer** – Lord. thank You for opening my eyes each day to Your word. Let me run to You and the security You provide.

# Day 42

Psalm 18:6 In my distress I called to the Lord; I cried to my God for help. From His temple He heard my voice; my cry came before Him, into His ears.

WE KNOW FROM EXPERIENCE THAT LIFE PROVIDES MANY OPPORTUNITIES for us to call on God for help. Just a few verses earlier, David is confidently declaring that God is his Rock, his Fortress, his Deliverer. Now David is in trouble again. He writes, 'The cords of death entangle me; the torrents of destruction overwhelm me.' It seems as if David goes from one problem to the next. But isn't that like life? We hardly seem to get through one situation before another one arrives. Today's verse gives us insight into how David responded to his troubles and how he called on the Lord. First, David acknowledges that he is in distress. Isn't it reassuring to know that we don't have to wait until we calm down or cool off before we call out to God? Wherever you are, whatever your situation, call out to Him. He wants to hear from you. Are you mad, scared, lonely, in pain, or suffering? Call out to Him. Tell Him what you are feeling. Don't wait until you calm down and try to compose yourself. Like David, cry out in your distress. Also, notice how David addressed God in this verse. In the beginning, he said, 'I called out to the Lord,' and later he said, 'I cried out to my God.' Notice the progression, his prayer increases in intensity. As his prayer intensifies, so does his relationship with God. The use of the word 'Lord' depicts something of a more formal title for God, whereas 'my God' represents more of a personal relationship with Him. What is your relationship with God? Are you on a formal name basis or do you have a personal and intimate relationship with God and call Him, 'Abba Father?' God desires to have a personal relationship with you.

**Acknowledge** – Lord, You hear us when we call out to You.

**Confess** – Lord, forgive me for not getting to know You better.

**Thanksgiving** – Lord, thank You that we can have a personal relationship with the Creator of the universe.

**Prayer** – Lord, I pray that I will get to know You better, that I will call out to You in my distress.

# Day 43

Psalm 18:16 He reached down from on high and took hold of me; He drew me out of the deep waters.

Our grandchildren love to play in the water. When they were learning how to swim, we would make them wear a 'swimmie' or floatation device. They would hang around the steps of the pool, jump off, and float around. As they became more confident, they would venture further out into the pool. Occasionally, they would take off their 'swimmie' and stay on the steps. Invariably, each one has stepped off the last step without their 'swimmies' and went straight down. Someone has had to grab them and pull them out of the water. The memory of rescuing them relates very well to today's verse. The grandchildren were helpless and could have drowned if we had not pulled them out. Who comes to mind when David speaks of being drawn out of the deep waters? My first thought is Jonah. Jonah was a prophet called by God to go to the city of Nineveh to preach repentance because of the wickedness there. Did Jonah obey God and head off to Nineveh to hold a series of revivals? No, he boarded a ship for Tarshish headed in the opposite direction of Nineveh. God sent a terrible storm that threatened the life and safety of the ship Jonah was on. At the worst point of the storm, Jonah was below deck, asleep. The crew cast lots to see who was responsible for the storm. The lot fell to Jonah and to make a long story short, he was thrown overboard. A large fish swallows Jonah, and he survives three days inside the fish. On the third day, God commands the fish to vomit Jonah on dry land. This time Jonah heads straight to Nineveh in obedience to God. Are you running from God or His call in your life? Have you gotten yourself in such 'deep water' that you are drowning in the sea of life? God rescued David and Jonah even though he disobeyed him. He can rescue you. Ask Him to pull you out of the deep waters you are in.

**Acknowledge** – Lord, You rescue us even when we don't deserve it.

**Confess** – Lord, forgive me when I chose to disobey You and get myself in deep water.

**Thanksgiving** – Lord, thank You for keeping Your eye on me.

**Prayer** – Lord, I look to You for my salvation, my deliverance, let me grow in the knowledge that I am loved and accepted by You.

# Day 44

**Psalm 18:27** You save the humble, but bring low those whose eyes are haughty.

In today's verse, David describes what happens to the humble and to those whose eyes are haughty. Let's start with the latter part of the verse first and get an understanding of haughty eyes. Someone who is haughty is defined as being arrogant and full of pride. A haughty person acts superior and looks down on others. They are prideful and obnoxious. Have you met a person with haughty eyes? You would recognize them very quickly if you did. What does God have to say about a haughty person? Solomon writing in Proverbs 6:16-19 says, 'There are six things the Lord hates, seven that are detestable to Him: haughty eyes, a lying tongue, hands that shed innocent blood, a heart that devises wicked schemes, feet that are quick to rush into evil, a false witness who pours out lies and a man who stirs up dissension among brothers.' What about the fate of the humble? The Lord saves them. What is a humble person? Humbleness is defined as one who has a modest or low view of oneself, the absence of pride. (www.oxfordlearnersdictionay.com) Where are you on the pride scale? Do you think more highly of yourself than others? Paul writing in Philippians 2:3 tells us, 'Do nothing out of selfish ambition or vain conceit. Rather, in humility value others above yourselves.' Take an inventory of your life to determine where you are on the pride scale. If you find yourself leaning towards the haughty side, ask God to help you by replacing your pridefulness with more humility in your life. Proverbs 16:18 tells us, 'Pride goes before destruction, a haughty spirit before a fall.' I have found it true for my life, that God has a way of bringing us down if we don't humble ourselves. Humble yourself before Him.

**Acknowledge** – Lord, You save the humble and bring low the haughty.

**Confess** – Lord, forgive me for my pride. Help me to humble myself.

**Thanksgiving** – Lord, thank You for humbling Yourself to be born as a baby, to grow up, and submit to the Father's will by offering Yourself as a sacrifice for our sins.

**Prayer** – Lord, help me to do nothing out of selfish ambition or vain conceit, but let me value others more than myself.

# Day 45

Psalm 18:30 As for God, His way is perfect; the Lord's word is flawless, He shields all who take refuge in him.

David, who had a lot of trouble in his life, tells us that God's way is perfect. David who had been rightfully anointed King of Israel as a young boy, but waited 15 years before becoming king, claims God's way is perfect. David who hid in caves for fear of his life, still claimed God's way is perfect. David didn't allow his circumstances define who God is. He understood that God is sovereign. Paul writing in Romans 11:33 said, 'Oh, the depth of the riches of the wisdom and knowledge of God! How unsearchable His judgments, and His paths beyond tracing out!' God knows all things past, present, and future. There is no limit to His knowledge. John writing in Revelation 21:6 said, 'He said to me: It is done. I am the Alpha and the Omega, the Beginning and the End. To the thirsty I will give water without cost from the spring of the water of life.' God is the beginning and the end. He is present everywhere and everyone can know Him. We also serve a God who doesn't make mistakes. His word is flawless. You may be thinking 'but what about this terrible thing that has happened to me?' Or you might ask 'what about all the hatred and violence in the world? Why doesn't God do something about it?' These are questions that we may never know the answers to until we see God face to face. Do you trust God and His word? The writer of Hebrews tells us that God's word is a living word. It is as relevant today as it was thousands of years ago when it was written. Hebrews 4:12 says, 'For the word of God is living, and active. Sharper than any double-edged sword, it penetrates even to dividing soul and spirit, joints and marrow; it judges the thoughts and attitudes of the heart.' Take the time to read and study God's flawless word. There is much to learn about God and His plan for you. Dig deeper into His word.

**Acknowledge** – Lord, Your way is perfect, Your word is flawless.

**Confess** – Lord, forgive me when I neglect to read and study Your word.

**Thanksgiving** – Lord, thank You for loving us. You are our shield, our refuge.

**Prayer** – Lord, open my eyes to Your word so that I understand You better and share it share with others.

# Day 46

**Psalm 18:34** He trains my hands for battle; my arms can bend a bow of bronze.

DAVID IS TELLING US HOW GOD HAS PREPARED HIM FOR BATTLE. He didn't tell us that God helped him avoid life's battles. Nor did he tell us that God made the battles easy for him. David had to be pretty strong and have the proper training to bend a bow of bronze. We read that David is very capable of using the weapons God has given him. What life battles are you fighting now; sickness, depression, bullying, relational problems, family issues, discouragement, or financial problems? The list can be endless. I don't want to speak negativity in anyone's life, but if life is good right now, things will change. The question becomes, are you prepared for the battle? Where do you find your strength? As a Christian, our strength is found in God and His word. The first thing to remember is that we are in a spiritual war. Paul tells us in Ephesians 6:12, 'For our struggle is not against flesh and blood, but against the rulers, against the authorities, against the powers of this dark world and against spiritual forces of evil in the heavenly realms.' What does David tell us in today's verse? The Lord trains us for battle, He gives us strength. Are you using your training manual and the weapons God has given you to fight? Paul gives further instructions in Ephesians 6:13-18, to put on the full armor of God. Take time to read about God's armor. Put it on each day. As we close today's thought, I want to leave you with a song, sung by Michael W. Smith, "Surrounded." It goes, 'This is how I fight my battles, This is how I fight my battles, This is how I fight my battles, This is how I fight my battles, It may look like I'm surrounded, but I'm surrounded by You. It may look like I'm surrounded, but I'm surrounded by You. It may look like I'm surrounded, but I'm surrounded by You.' Let God surround You with His presence today.

**Acknowledge** – Lord, You prepare us for life's battles. You strengthen us.

**Confess** – Lord, forgive me for not trusting You through life's battles.

**Thanksgiving** – Lord, thank You for providing us armor to protect us from Satan and his spiritual forces.

**Prayer** – Lord, prepare me for life's battles, provide me the weapons to use, train my hands for battle, and give me the strength to continue to fight.

# Day 47

Psalm 18:46 The Lord lives! Praise be to my Rock! Exalted be God my Savior.

Today David begins to close Psalm 18 with a short hymn of praise. In verse 49, David states that not only will he praise God privately; he will praise God among the nations. In verse 50, he praises God for His unfailing kindness to him and to his descendants. Despite David's imperfect efforts, God through His grace and mercy saved David and elevated him to king. It took almost 15 years for David to receive what God had promised him. From defeating Goliath to running for his life, David had his ups and downs. Yet David made it a priority to give God praise. Today, David is giving praise to his Rock, his God, and Savior. Although our lives may not have had the drama and excitement of David's, hasn't God done the same for us? Hasn't He delivered us from sin and the grave, and elevated us to be an heir with Christ? Before knowing Christ, we were dead in our sins despite our best efforts to reach God. Paul writing in Ephesians 2:4-5 said, 'But because of His great love for us, God, who is rich in mercy, made us alive with Christ even when we were dead in transgressions, it is by grace you have been saved.' Not only has God saved us, He has trained us for battle, and has given us the weapons we need to live each day. It is only through God's great love for us that we are made alive and can live each day victoriously no matter our circumstances. Like David, we should praise God for His love, for being our Rock and our Savior. We should gladly sing praises that exalt Him. I am reminded of a praise chorus written by Michael O'Shields that fits in well with this Psalm. Sing it to the Lord today. 'I will call upon the Lord, Who is worthy to be praised, So shall I be saved from my enemies. The Lord liveth and blessed be the Rock, and let the God of my salvation be exalted.'

**Acknowledge** – Lord, You are our rock, our salvation.

**Confess** – Lord, forgive me for trying to earn my salvation. It is by Your grace we are saved.

**Thanksgiving** – The Lord lives, blessed be the Rock, the God of my salvation.

**Prayer** – Lord, help me to take time to praise You for Your plan of salvation, Your great mercy, and Your grace.

# Day 48

Psalm 19:1 The heavens declare the glory of God; the skies proclaim the work of His hands.

DAVID STARTS BY SAYING THE HEAVENS DECLARE THE GLORY OF God. Notice how he uses the plural word heavens instead of heaven. David isn't leaving anything out. I love to witness a beautiful sunset with the sun reflecting off the clouds, painting the sky orange. Or later, watch a full moon rise up over the ocean, sending beams of light shimmering off the ocean. As the night sky grows darker, thousands of stars begin to dot the sky. When a bad storm approaches, I can see the fierceness of the clouds, the flashes of lightning, and hear the roll of thunder. Or, early morning at daybreak observe the calmness of the sky, and the freshness of a new day. How can anyone observe these things and say there is not a God? How could something that beautiful, that complicated, that big, and that far away just happen? Do you give God praise when you witness something incredible in the sky? There is an old song that we used to sing, "He's Everything to Me", written by Ralph Carmichael that comes to mind when I read this verse. It goes, 'In the stars His handiwork I see, On the wind He speaks with majesty, Tho He ruleth over land and sea, What is that to me? The chorus answers, 'Till by faith I met Him face to face, And felt the wonder of His Grace, Then I knew that He was more than just a God who didn't care, That lived away out there, And now He walks beside me day by day, Ever watching o'er me lest I stray, Helping me to find the narrow way, He's everything to me.' We can observe the heavens and their beauty, but without a relationship with its Creator, they are just a pretty picture. Give God thanks for His creation. Also, give Him thanks for what He has prepared for you.

**Acknowledge** – Lord, the heavens declare Your glory, the work of Your hands.

**Confess** – Lord, forgive me when I worship the creation, not the Creator.

**Thanksgiving** – Lord, thank You for the beauty and majesty of Your creation that points us to You.

**Prayer** – Lord, help me to seek the Creator not the creation who desires to have a personal relationship with me.

# Day 49

Psalm 19:7 The law of the Lord is perfect, reviving the soul. The statues of the Lord are trustworthy, making wise the simple.

DAVID DECLARES THAT GOD'S LAW IS PERFECT. GOD HAD GIVEN THE Israelites a number of laws after they had left Egypt. They had been living in slavery under the rule of Pharaoh and didn't know how to live in a free society. So, it was important that God give them laws to govern themselves. The first and most important set of laws that was given to them by God through Moses on Mount Sinai was the Ten Commandments. These laws are still relevant today although many non-Christians are trying to have them removed from our society. As a quick reminder, they are: 1.You shall have no other gods before Me. 2.You shall not make for yourself a carved (graven) image. 3.You shall not take the name of the Lord your God in vain. 4.Remember the Sabbath day, to keep it holy. 5.Honor your father and your mother. 6.You shall not murder. 7.You shall not commit adultery. 8.You shall not steal. 9.You shall not bear false witness. 10.You shall not covet. Laws are good. They set boundaries, keep us safe and protect us. However, we can get caught up in trying to follow the letter of the law rather than the intent. When we do that, we can become like the Pharisees who were sticklers for following the rules at the expense of others. When Jesus came, He tore down their ritualistic system of religion. In John 13:34, Jesus gives a new law, 'I give you a new law. That law is, "Love each other." As I have loved you, so you also love each other.' Where do you fall on the law scale? Are you ritualistic or do you consider the intent? James 1:25, says, 'But the man who looks intently into the perfect law that gives freedom, and continues to do this, not forgetting what he has heard, but doing it – he will be blessed in what he does.' Enjoy God's blessing today, trust in His perfect law. Man-made laws will come and go and change with the tide. However, God's laws can be trusted, they are forever.

**Acknowledge** – Lord, Your law is perfect, it revives my soul.

**Confess** – Lord, forgive me when I fail to love others.

**Thanksgiving** – Lord, thank You for Your trustworthy statues and making the wise simple.

**Prayer** – Lord, help me to look intently into Your perfect law that gives freedom.

# Day 50

**Psalm 19:14** May these words of my mouth and this meditation of my heart be pleasing in Your sight, Lord, my Rock and my Redeemer.

DAVID CLOSES PSALMS 19 WITH THIS SHORT PRAISE OFFERING TO the Lord. Notice how he aligns his words with his thoughts. He not only wants his words to be pleasing to God, but his thoughts as well. Vivian and I have begun to incorporate Bible verses at the end of the blessing when our grandchildren are eating with us. It is amazing how fast they learn the verses and enjoy repeating them. Today's verse is one of the verses we have taught them. We want them to know that the words they use and the thoughts they have are important. Our prayer is that this verse will come to mind as they get older and begin to say something they shouldn't. We pray that God will check their spirit and guard their tongue. Carefully chosen words could save them a lot of misery and trouble. What about you? Do your words align with what is going on in your heart? In Matthew 12:34-36 we find where Jesus confronts the Pharisees about the condition of their hearts, 'You brood of vipers, how can you who are evil say anything good? For out of the overflow of the heart the mouth speaks. The good man brings good things out of the good stored up in him, and the evil man brings evil things out of the evil stored up in him. But I tell you that men will have to give account on the day of judgment for every careless word they have spoken.' What kind of words are you using in your conversations today? Are they pleasing to God? Would you be willing to have them played back before you in front of a Holy God? As we begin to align our heart and mind on God's Word and thoughts, then the words we use will be in sync with His. Lord, I pray that my words and my meditations are pleasing to You.

**Acknowledge** – Lord, You hear our words and know the thoughts of our hearts.

**Confess** – Lord as David prayed, forgive my hidden faults, keep me from willful sins, and don't let them rule over me.

**Thanksgiving** – Lord, thank You that You are our Rock and our Redeemer.

**Prayer** – Lord, thank You for Your Word. I pray that I will read it, learn it, meditate on it, follow it, live it, cherish it, and proclaim it.

# Day 51

**Psalm 20:4 May He give you the desire of your heart and make your plans succeed.**

Psalm 20 was written by David as a prayer for the king and his army just before they headed into battle. David is seeking God and His help to fight the battle. How easy would it be to look to their military strength, their advanced weaponry, and their well-trained commanders for victory and leave God out of the planning? We will look further into this aspect of preparing for the battle tomorrow. But today we are going to focus on having a successful strategy for winning a war. We might have the impression that wars fought in those days were pretty simple. Each army lined up in front of the other and ran towards each other trying to overpower the other side. In the Old Testament, we find several exciting stories of battles and the different strategies employed by the Israelites. For example, Joshua and the Israelites marched around the city of Jericho for seven days and shouted for the walls to come down. Later, Joshua used the tactic of setting up an ambush behind the City of Ai to defeat them. On another occasion, Joshua and his army marched all night and launched a surprise attack on the Amorite Kings. King Jehoshaphat sent the choir ahead of the army, singing praises to God. Strategy and plans were important for achieving victory. They are important for us as well. Do you make plans? Proverbs 19:2 gives us some advice, 'Ignorant desire isn't good; rushing feet make mistakes.' There is nothing wrong with planning for the future. However, you should include God in the planning process if you want them to be successful. Proverbs 16:3 tells us, 'Depend on the Lord in whatever you do, and your plans will succeed.' Make plans, and give them to God. Let Him mold them to His will and bless your future.

**Acknowledge** – Lord, You are interested in our life, our future, and our plans.

**Confess** – Lord, forgive me for leaving You out of my plans for the future.

**Thanksgiving** – Lord, thank for Your blessings on our plans.

**Prayer** – Lord, I depend on You in whatever I do. Guide my life and my future. I want to include You in all that I do.

# Day 52

Psalm 20:7 Some trust in chariots and some in horses, but we trust in the name of the Lord our God.

Today, we focus on the advantage of the military strength of an army, their advanced weaponry, and their well-trained commanders. First, I would like to thank anyone who may be serving or has served our country. In my opinion, the United States, without question, leads the world in military strength. Our weaponry, our troops, and our commanders are second to none. We are blessed to have such a strong military that has fought in a number of wars. However, history has shown that having the strongest military doesn't always guarantee a swift victory. The tactics of the enemy can negate military superiority and require an army to adapt its strategy. The military might of an army in David's day was measured by the number of troops, horses, and chariots they had. But David relied on something else. His trust was in the name of the Lord his God. We have spoken earlier about the battles we have faced. Do you try to rely on your own strength to get you through them? Or, do you put your trust in God? Satan will use every tactic available to him to separate us from God. All too often, our human wisdom, our talents, our resources, and our strength are no match for him. Who do you want to fight your battles? Who can you trust to expose the tactics of Satan? Put your trust in the name of the Lord. He is the only one who can protect you from Satan's schemes. As you begin to trust God more, you will be able to say like David in verse 5, 'We will shout for joy when you are victorious, and will lift up our banners in the name of our God.'

**Acknowledge** – Lord, You are the one we should put our faith and trust in, not our own wisdom, talents, or strength.

**Confess** – Lord, forgive me when I look to my own strength and my limited abilities to accomplish something.

**Thanksgiving** – Lord, let us shout for joy and raise our banner high for You have won the victory.

**Prayer** – Lord, may You give us the desires of our heart and make our plans succeed as we put them in Your hands.

# Day 53

Psalm 21:7 For the king trusts in the Lord; through the unfailing love of the most-High, he will not be shaken.

Psalm 21 is a celebration for the answered prayers of victory in Psalm 20. What a great blessing it is for a nation whose leaders trust in God. They set the example for the entire nation to follow. A great example of a godly leader is Nehemiah. During his life, the people of Judah had been in exile in Babylon for a number of years. Nehemiah, who was serving as a cupbearer in King Artaxerxes court, received an update from the Jews who had been left in Jerusalem. The people there were in great trouble. The walls of Jerusalem had been torn down and the gates burned. Upon hearing the news, Nehemiah wept, fasted, and prayed to God for a number of days. The king recognized his sadness which led to Nehemiah being commissioned to go back to Jerusalem to rebuild the wall. Nehemiah ran into many obstacles in the process of rebuilding the wall. Through every challenge, Nehemiah trusted in God. In Nehemiah 4:14-15 he tells the people, 'After I looked things over, I stood up and said to the nobles, the officials, and the rest of the people, "Don't be afraid of them. Remember the Lord who is great and awesome, and fight for your brothers, your sons and your daughters, your wives and your homes." When our enemies heard that we were aware of their plot and that God had frustrated it, we all returned to the wall, each to his own work.' Nehemiah's trust in God gave the people confidence. His leadership led to the wall being rebuilt and Jerusalem being restored. Are there any "Nehemiah's" in office today? If so, there are very few. Sadly, we now find that many of our elected leaders do not trust in God. However, in spite of who is in charge, we still serve a God whose 'unfailing love' surrounds us each day. Pray for our leaders. Ask God to change their hearts. God is in control, worship Him today for His unfailing love.

**Acknowledge** – Lord, You are the Lord of unfailing love.

**Confess** – Lord, forgive me, forgive our fathers, and forgive our leaders when we stop trusting and following You.

**Thanksgiving** – Lord, what a great blessing is the country whose leadership trusts in You.

**Prayer** – Lord, I am Yours forever, You are my strength, You are a God of grace and power.

# Day 54

Psalm 21:13 Be exalted in Your strength, Lord, we will sing and praise Your might.

Psalm 21 is a song of praise for victory granted to the king. In verse 1, David acknowledging the strength of the Lord writes, 'O Lord, the king rejoices in Your strength. How great is his joy in the victories You give.' Now as he closes the Psalm, David circles back to praising God for His strength and His might. Isaiah 40:29 tell us, 'He gives power to the weak and strength to the powerless.' Without God, aren't we powerless? He is the One who gives us power over sin and Satan. Jesus speaking in John 15:5 said, 'I am the vine; you are the branches. If a man remains in Me and I in him, he will bear much fruit; apart from Me you can do nothing.' Notice that Jesus is not talking about worldly accomplishments, He is referring to bearing fruit by living a Christ-like life, producing love, joy, peace, patience, kindness, goodness, faithfulness, and self-control. Do we give Him thanks and praise as David did for His strength? If so, how do we stand strong in the Lord and in the power of His might? God told Joshua in Joshua 1:6, 'Be strong and courageous, because you will lead these people to inherit the land I swore to their forefathers to give them.' What did God do for Joshua? He gave him victory after victory. Joshua didn't win those victories under his own power and might. He had help from God. God prepared Joshua and strengthened him. Paul tells us in Ephesians 6:10, 'Finally be strong in the Lord, and the strength of his might.' David learned long ago, Joshua before him, and Paul expressed it in his letter to the Ephesians that our human effort is inadequate to get us through life. We need to lean on God's strength and His might to carry us through. When your doubts become bigger than you are, look to God and His mighty strength. He will carry you through. And when you have made it, you will be able to sing like David, 'Be exalted in Your strength, Lord I sing and praise Your might.'

**Acknowledge** – Lord, You are the Lord of strength and might.

**Confess** – Lord, forgive me when I doubt You are bigger than my problems.

**Thanksgiving** – Lord, I exalt You. I praise Your strength and might.

**Prayer** – Lord, help me to follow Paul's encouragement, to be strong in the Lord, and His might.

# Day 55

Psalm 22:3 Yet You are enthroned as the Holy one; You are the One Israel praises.

DAVID IS ACKNOWLEDGING THE DEITY OF GOD AND AS THE ONE who Israel praises. This doesn't sound like someone who is being persecuted by his enemies, but more like someone who is confident in God's love for Him. Yet verses 1-2 tell a different story. There, David opens up his heart and cries out to God saying, 'My God, my God, why have You forsaken me? Why are You so far from saving me, so far from the words of my groaning? O my God, I cry out by day, but You do not answer, by night, and am not silent.' David doesn't mind pouring out what is on his heart to God. He doesn't start out with a 'flowery' introduction. Jesus even repeated this verse while He was on the cross. Matthew 27:46 says, 'About the ninth hour Jesus cried out in a loud voice, "Eloi, Eloi, lama sabachthani?" – Which means, My God, my God, why have You forsaken me?' I have cried out something similar in my prayers to God. I suspect you may have as well. We know that God loves us, He hears us, and will answer our cries to Him, in His perfect timing and way. We also know that God is our strength. David knew this when he wrote this Psalm. So after crying out to God for help, feeling all alone, and his prayers not yet answered, David expresses his unwavering confidence in God. Despite his trials, he knew God was in control. Can you do like David? In the midst of your pain and suffering, acknowledge God for who He is; that He is in control, and that He cares about you. It may not be easy at first, but begin to acknowledge God's sovereignty, His power, and His ability to change your circumstances. Thank Him for things He has done in your past, and then begin to thank Him for what He is going to do. Give him praise today, join in singing the children's hymn, 'Praise Him, Praise Him, all ye little children, God is Love, God is Love.'

**Acknowledge** – Lord, You are in control, You are enthroned as the Holy One.

**Confess** – Lord, forgive me when my cries for help are selfish and self-serving.

**Thanksgiving** – Lord, thank You that You hear our prayers and know our needs.

**Prayer** – Lord, in You we put our trust. You are the Holy One. You sit on Your throne.

# Day 56

**Psalm 22:11** Do not be far from me, for trouble is near and there is no one to help.

It is worth pointing out that nowhere in scripture does it record David having experienced the things he is writing about in this Psalm. David writes in verses 12-18, 'Many bulls surround me; strong bulls of Bashan encircle me. Roaring lions tearing at their prey open their mouths wide against me. I am poured out like water, and all my bones are out of joint. My heart has turned to wax; it has melted away within me. My strength is dried up like a potsherd, and my tongue sticks to the roof of my mouth; you lay me in the dust of death. Dogs have surrounded me; a band of evil men has encircled me, they have pierced my hands and my feet. I can count all my bones; people stare and gloat over me. They divide my garments among them and cast lots for my clothing.' It sounds like David is describing an execution. In fact, it reads very much like Jesus' execution, down to the piercing of His hands and the dividing up of His clothes. David, writing over a thousand years earlier, describes the very details of Jesus' crucifixion. It is also important to note that crucifixion was not even invented during David's lifetime, yet under the inspiration of the Holy Spirit, he accurately describes it. In Mark 14:36, Jesus is in the Garden of Gethsemane and praying, 'Abba, Father, everything is possible for You. Take this cup from Me. Yet not what I will, be what You will.' Yet Jesus was willing to be obedient and go to the cross for our sins. When you see trouble is just ahead, do you reach out to God to be near you? Do you ask Him for His presence in your life as you are headed through difficult times? Or, do you wait until things have gotten so bad, that the only thing to do is cry out to God and say 'my God, my God, why have You forsaken me? Don't delay, call out to God today. Ask Him to help you.

**Acknowledge** – Lord, even from the beginning of time, You knew the pain and suffering You would endure for us.

**Confess** – Lord, forgive me when I think You have abandoned me.

**Thanksgiving** – Lord, thank You for Your love and mercy that was poured out on Calvary for me.

**Prayer** – Lord, do not be far from me. I need Your help.

# Day 57

Psalm 22:19 But You, Lord, be not far from me. You are my strength; come quickly to help me.

Today's verse is very similar to yesterday's verse. However, David adds, "Lord," be not far from me. He recognizes the Lord as his strength where yesterday he felt alone. He also adds, 'come quickly,' escalating the urgency of his need. David is confident that God is not far from him and He is his strength. However, David needs God to come quickly. Isn't that exactly what we do? When God doesn't immediately answer our prayer or change our situation, don't we begin to increase the urgency of our prayers? Do we pray, Lord, I know You heard me, but I really need to hear from You? Have you been to the point as Paul when he wrote in Romans 8:26-27, 'In the same way, the Spirit helps us in our weakness. We do not know what we ought to pray for, but the Spirit Himself intercedes for us through wordless groans. And He who searches our hearts knows the mind of the Spirit, because the Spirit intercedes for God's people in accordance with the will of God.' Did you grasp what Paul is telling us? God's Holy Spirit that lives within us comes to our aid. He makes our prayers more real to God the Father. The Holy Spirit helps us because of our weaknesses, not in spite of them. He knows what our weaknesses are whether they be physical, emotional, or spiritual. He knows how to boost our prayers at our weakest point. The Holy Spirit also helps us because there are times when we just don't know what to pray for. Aren't you glad the Holy Spirit is there to help you when you pray? He knows what is best for you. Let Him intercede for you when you are in so much pain that you have run out of words to say. God is not far from you, He is your strength. He will come quickly to help you.

**Acknowledge** – Lord, thank You for Your Holy Spirit that intercedes for us in accordance to Your will.

**Confess** – Lord, forgive me when I doubt Your presence in my life.

**Thanksgiving** – Lord, thank You for being my strength, my shield, my portion, my deliverer.

**Prayer** – Lord, You are our strength, come quickly to help.

Psalm 22:27 All the ends of the earth will remember and turn to the Lord, and all the families of the nations will bow before Him.

THERE ARE TIMES WE FOCUS ON OUR OWN LITTLE WORLD, THAT WE fail to see the work of the Lord in many other places. While our nation has been blessed, the good news of the gospel of Jesus Christ is being spread all over the world. Isaiah 40:5 tells us, 'And the glory of the Lord will be revealed, and all mankind together will see it. For the mouth of the Lord has spoken.' Jesus, before He ascended into heaven, left us with His great commission in Matthew 28:19-20, 'Therefore go and make disciples of all nations, baptizing them in the name of the Father and of the Son, and of the Holy Spirit, and teaching them to obey everything I have commanded you. And surely I am with you always, to the very end of the age.' Jesus tells us that we are missionaries, we should think and live on mission. We should be sharing the good news of the gospel of Jesus Christ with our neighbors, our unsaved family members, and friends. Some people are called to go on the mission field. Their life's work is to go and serve in a foreign country. Is that your calling? If not, you can find ways to support them. You can also find missional opportunities right where you live. There is one thing you must know before you begin your missional work. It will cost you something. It will cost you time, money, and inconvenience. However, what you receive is worth far more than the effort. I can't explain the feeling you get from helping someone in Jesus' name, but it makes the work seem worthwhile. What is God calling you to do? Listen to His voice, respond to His call, so that one day you can rejoice and worship with families all over the world.

**Acknowledge** – One day every knee will bow and every tongue confess that You are Lord.

**Confess** – Lord, forgive me for not sharing the good news when I have had the opportunity.

**Thanksgiving** – Lord, thank You for those who respond to Your call to serve on the mission field.

**Prayer** – Lord, let me proclaim Your righteousness to the poor, the homeless, and the sick.

# Day 59

### Psalm 23:1 The Lord is my shepherd, I lack nothing.

TODAY WE LOOK AT VERSE ONE OF PERHAPS THE MOST FAMOUS Psalm written by David, Psalm 23. This short verse is packed with meaning. David reverses roles and now becomes one of the sheep. As a sheep, he had no worries about putting his life and future in the hands of the Great Shepherd. He had complete confidence in his Shepherd, because with the Lord as his Shepherd, he lacked nothing. In John 10, Jesus tells us that He is the Good Shepherd. He gives us several attributes of a good shepherd and the sheep He looks after. In verse 11 He says, 'I am the good Shepherd. The good Shepherd lays down His life for the sheep.' In this verse, we see that a good shepherd will defend his sheep and is willing to die for them if necessary. In verses 14-15 He said, 'I am the good Shepherd; I know My sheep and My sheep know Me–Just as the Father knows Me and I know the Father – And I lay down My life for the sheep.' Secondly, we see that the Good Shepherd knows each one of His sheep by name. Next, we know that He cares deeply for His sheep, because He repeats His pledge to lay down His life for His sheep. Jesus also teaches us that the sheep know their Shepherd. They recognize His voice. They hear Him calling them by name. They love Him, trust Him, and follow Him. Their shepherd provides for their every need. Verse 2 of Psalm 23 says, 'He makes me lie down in green pastures, He leads me beside quiet waters.' What more can a sheep want than to lie down in a secure, abundant, peaceful, and refreshing area? This is where our Good Shepherd wants to lead us. Is the Lord your Shepherd? Is He leading your life right now? If not, get to know the Good Shepherd today. Allow Him to lead you beside the still waters and to lie down in luscious green pastures. With the Lord as our Shepherd, we lack nothing. Seek the one who knows you by name.

**Acknowledge** – The Lord is my shepherd, I lack nothing.

**Confess** – Lord, forgive me for when I fail to trust in Your care.

**Thanksgiving** – Lord, thank You that You know your sheep, and Your sheep know You.

**Prayer** – Lord, help me to have a personal relationship with You, my Shepherd, and my soon coming King.

# Day 60

**Psalm 23:4** Even though I walk through the valley of the shadow of death, I will fear no evil, for You are with me.

This is likely one of the most recognized verses in the Psalms. It has also been misquoted as well. I remember seeing a T-shirt years ago using this verse. It read, 'Even though I walk through the valley of the shadow of death, I will fear no evil because I am the meanest person in the valley.' For those of us who are not so tough, I think having God beside us is more comforting and reassuring than relying on ourselves. You may be traveling through what seems like the valley of the shadow of death right now. Perhaps life has thrown you some unexpected news. Take heart, the Shepherd is with you. For those traveling on the mountain top, take heart because the Shepherd is also with you. The longer we live the more we realize there will be valleys to cross. There will be bad news we have to accept. Yet in the midst of all the uncertainty of life, the Shepherd is with us. And while it may seem like it, the valley you are going through is not a dead-end road. Jesus tells us in John 16:33, 'I have told you these things, so that in Me you may have peace. In this world you will have trouble. But take heart! I have overcome the world.' Isn't this what David is saying in today's verse. 'I will fear no evil, for You are with me.' At the end of the journey, hopefully you will discover that it is in the valleys of our lives that we find refreshment and comfort from God Himself. There have been several times in my life that I can see how God has walked with me through the valley. As you walk with Him, take a look back and see where the Good Shepherd has led you through as well. Thank Him for His goodness.

**Acknowledge** – I will fear no evil for You are with me.

**Confess** – Lord, forgive me when I doubt Your love for me when I am going through the valleys of life.

**Thanksgiving** – Lord, thank You for leading me to places of refreshment in the middle of my troubles.

**Prayer** – Lord, help me to have a personal relationship with You, my Shepherd, and my soon coming King, so that I can face the valleys before me.

# Day 61

**Psalm 23:6** Surely Your goodness and mercy will follow me all the days of my life, and I will dwell in the house of the Lord forever.

GOD'S GOODNESS AND MERCY NEVER TAKE A DAY OFF. THEY ARE FOLlowing us every day of our life. I'll never forget an illustration by our Pastor, Lavon Phillips, as he was preaching on Psalms 23. He was walking across the stage, looking back and saying, 'are you still with me? Come on goodness, come on mercy, let's go, stay with me.' Just like a good shepherd who never leaves his sheep, goodness and mercy are always there. What a great illustration to close this Psalm with and to cap it off, we will dwell in the house of the Lord forever. Let's define God's goodness. To start, goodness is part of the character of God. God is good. It is who He is. He is the original definition of good. Psalms 34:8 states, 'Taste and see that the Lord is good...' Whenever you need to remember that God is good, sing this simple chorus about His goodness that goes, 'God is so good, God is so good, God is so good, He's so good to me.' Mercy, on the other hand, is God not punishing us as our sins deserve, or deliverance from judgment. God has left something beneficial for us, His goodness and His mercy. He has also promised eternal life for His sheep and we will dwell in His house forever. Jesus speaking in John 14:2-3 said, 'In my Father's house are many rooms; if it were not so, I would have told you. I am going there to prepare a place for you. And if I go and prepare a place for you, I will come back and take you to be with me that you also may be where I am.' The question is what am I doing with His gifts of goodness and mercy that are following me? Am I leaving behind peace or turmoil; forgiveness or bitterness; contentment or conflict; joy or frustration? The choice is yours. You have God's goodness and mercy left for you, share it with someone else.

**Acknowledge** – Surely goodness and mercy will follow me all the days of my life.

**Confess** – Lord, forgive me when I leave behind bitterness, turmoil, and conflict.

**Thanksgiving** – Lord, thank You for Your goodness and mercy and providing a place in Your house forever.

**Prayer** – Lord, You are the great Shepherd who looks after His sheep. You are so good to me.

# Day 62

**Psalm 24:1** The earth is the Lord's and everything in it, the world, and all who live in it.

Psalm 24 was written by David and is thought to be part of the celebration of bringing the Ark into Jerusalem. He begins the Psalm by proclaiming that God is the creator, sustainer, and possessor of the entire earth. He reminds the Jewish people that God isn't only concerned about the land where they live, but the rest of the world and its inhabitants as well. Even today we need to be reminded that God cares just as much for a remote area in Siberia as He does for the town you live in. Genesis 1:1 says, 'In the beginning, God created the heavens and the earth.' So it would naturally follow that His creation would belong to Him. He created everything which includes you and me, nature, natural resources, wealth, talents, kingdoms, health, power, and pleasure. God gave Adam and Eve and their descendant's dominion over the earth. Genesis 1:28, tells us, 'God blessed them and said to them, be fruitful and increase in number, fill the earth and subdue it. Rule over the fish of the sea and the birds of the air and over every living creature that moves on the ground.' That places on us the responsibility to be caretakers of God's creation. Like with anything else, there are those who take their responsibility for taking care of nature to the extreme. Organizations, such as Greenpeace, are at the forefront of protecting the environment; however, at a tremendous cost to everyone. There are times when I think we place more emphasis on being caretakers of nature and things we can't control over the things we can; such as our talents, our wealth, our health, our time, our abilities. These are gifts from God and He has given us responsibility over them as well. What are you doing with your talents and time? Are you using them for His glory? Will people remember you for your faithfulness to God and His creation or for your selfishness and self-centeredness? Even worse, will no one remember you at all? Create a legacy.

**Acknowledge** – The earth is the Lord's and everything in it.

**Confess** – Lord, forgive me when I fail to take care of Your creation.

**Thanksgiving** – Lord, You created everything. You own the 'cattle on a thousand hills.' Thank You for Your creation.

**Prayer** – Lord, help me to seek the Creator not the creation. Your presence is more precious than any treasure.

# Day 63

Psalm 24:10 Who is He, this King of glory? The Lord almighty, He is the King of glory.

David writes in verse 9, 'Lift up your heads, O you gates; lift them up, you ancient doors, that the King of glory may come in.' This Psalm was written at a time of great celebration because the Ark which represented God's presence was brought to Jerusalem. The King of glory had just passed through the gates of Jerusalem and into the doors of the temple. As the Ark entered the city, David would call out, "Who is He, this King of glory?" And the people would shout back the answer, "The Lord almighty, He is the King of glory." The Hebrew word translated 'glory' in this verse is 'kabod,' which means heavy or weight. (www.wikipedia.org) Used in this context it means the most awesome, the most powerful, the most supreme king, one who should be taken very seriously. Sadly, years later the children of Israel missed the 'King of Glory' when he came to earth. Paul writing in 1 Corinthians 2:8 said, 'None of the rulers of this age understood it, for if they had, they would not have crucified the Lord of Glory.' So who is the King of Glory? It is Jesus Christ, our Lord and Savior. He is the King of Glory and one day He will return to reign as King here on earth. The contemporary Christian group, Third Day, answers this question in a song they sing entitled "King of Glory." In it the lyrics ask, 'Who is this King of glory that pursues me with His love?' The answer is found in the chorus, 'His name is Jesus, precious Jesus, The Lord Almighty, the King of my heart, the King of glory.' Do you serve this King of glory? Have you given Him your heart? If not, today reach out to the King of glory, the Lord almighty. He wants to save you. Worship the King of glory.

**Acknowledge** – The Lord almighty, He is the King of glory.

**Confess** – Lord, forgive me when I walk in disobedience to You, the King of glory.

**Thanksgiving** – Lord, we lift up our heads to behold Your glory, we lift up our hands and behold the beauty of Your presence.

**Prayer** – Praise Your name forever. All glory, honor, praise, worship, adoration are Yours. Holy, Holy, Holy is the Lord, God almighty. Worthy is the Lamb who was slain.

# Day 64

Psalm 25:4-5 Show me Your ways, Lord, teach me Your paths. Guide me in Your truth and teach me, for You are my God, my Savior, and my hope is in You all day long.

It appears that David is under attack by enemies who are trying to discredit him through false accusations. In verses 1-2, David writes, 'To You, Lord, I lift up my soul; in You I trust, O my God. Do not let me be put to shame nor let my enemies triumph over me.' Social media has opened 'Pandora's Box' when it comes to making public comments. If your comments are not 'politically correct' you are subject to a wave of persecution. For example, a local professor in our city has been publicly attacked and lost his job because of comments he made on Twitter that were perceived to be racist by social media followers. On the other hand, many comments posted on social media may be misleading at best, or outright lies at worst. Our news media today seems to be more focused on delivering unverified information and rumors rather than unbiased, verified stories. How do we sort out the truth from lies? Where can we find help? The answer is the same place that David found it. 'To You, Lord, I lift up my soul; in You I trust, O my God.' God has not changed. He helped David, He can help you. David asked God to show him His ways, His Paths, and to guide him in truth. We can find God's way and truth in His word, the Bible. Jesus said in John 14:6, 'I am the way the truth and the life, no one comes to the Father except through Me.' The Bible also points us to Jesus, our hope for salvation. Jesus tells us in Matthew 7:14, 'But small is the gate and narrow the road that leads to life, and only a few find it.' Have you found Jesus? He will guide and direct your paths. Do as David; put your hope in God. Share His word with others.

**Acknowledge** – You are my God, my Savior, my hope is in You.

**Confess** – Lord, forgive me when I don't walk with integrity, or live according to Your word.

**Thanksgiving** – Lord, thank You for being our guide to the truth. Thank You for teaching me Your ways through Your word.

**Prayer** – Lord, help me to live according to Your Word, rather than what will make me popular or powerful.

Psalm 25:14 The Lord confides in those who fear Him; He makes His covenant known to them.

God's word contains truth, life, and hope. Today we will focus on where to find these qualities. David tells us in today's verse that the 'Lord confides in those who fear Him.' I appreciate it when someone confides in me. It lets me know that the person trusts me with the information they share. They know I will not use it against them or tell someone else. A bond of trust is developed between us. I am also committed to bearing the burden they shared with me. David said the Lord confides in those who 'fear him.' So what does 'fear Him' mean? It is a sense of reverence, adoration, honor, respect, awe, love, and submission to God. We also need to understand how God communicates or confides in us. The first way God communicates with us is in an audible voice. However, before you think God will carry on a conversation with you, understand this is very rare and unusual. I don't know of anyone who has spoken audibly with God. Moses is perhaps one of the few people who has spoken with Him. The second way God speaks to us is through His Word. Hebrews 4:12 tells us, 'For the word of God is living and active. Sharper than any double-edged sword, it penetrates even to dividing soul and spirit, joints and marrow; it judges the thoughts and attitudes of the heart.' This tells me that God's Word is applicable today for answers to our daily lives. The third way God communicates with us is through the Holy Spirit which places deep inner convictions about God's will in our lives. Our verse tells us that the Lord confides with those who fear Him. Do you reverence, adore, honor, love and submit to God? Do you spend time with Him daily? Don't expect to hear from God if you put other things ahead of Him and His Word. Start today, get into His Word, pray and seek him. Allow His Holy Spirit to talk to you.

**Acknowledge** – You confide in those who love You and keep Your commands.

**Confess** – Lord, forgive me when I don't spend time reading and searching Your Word.

**Thanksgiving** – Lord, thank You for Your instruction, guidance, and for confiding in us, for making Your covenant known to us.

**Prayer** – Lord, help me to grow in wisdom, judgment, discernment, and prudence. However, keep me humble, not proud or haughty.

# Day 66

Psalm 25:21 May integrity and uprightness protect me, because my hope, Lord is in You.

DAVID CLAIMS HIS HOPE LIES IN THE LORD. HE ALSO REFERS TO protection through integrity and uprightness (the condition or quality of being honorable or honest). It is hard to discern if David is referring to his own integrity and uprightness, or that of God. David tried to live a life of integrity, but he certainly had his failures. Today we will focus on how God wants us to conduct ourselves with honesty and integrity. These attributes should be as important for us as they were to David. So, why are they important character traits? As a Christian, how do others first recognize Christ in our lives? Most importantly, they should recognize Christ by our love for others. Second, they should be able to see us live out a life of honesty and integrity each day. If our actions and behaviors are no different from those who are not saved, what is it about us that will attract someone to Christ? So how do I demonstrate these qualities in my daily life? I hope the following example helps. The coils in our HVAC unit blew-out which was going to be very costly to repair. The system should have been under warranty; however, when the HVAC Company checked, they found our system had been warranted under the builder's name instead of the homeowner resulting in a shorter warranty period. Instead of telling me 'sorry, the warranty has expired,' the company spent several days correcting the warranty so the cost would be covered. Instead of taking a short cut, they took the extra effort to do the right thing. Can you act with integrity and honesty and not be a Christian? The short answer is yes, but it would be very difficult to stay the course over time. Here are a few traits of someone of integrity: Humility, Goodness, Authenticity, Honesty, and Trustworthy. Try living up to those qualities each day without God's help. Seek Him each day and ask Him to mold your character into one of love, integrity and honesty.

**Acknowledge** – Lord, You are our hope.

**Confess** – Lord, forgive me when I fail to be honest or act with integrity.

**Thanksgiving** – Lord, I thank You for the hope I have in You.

**Prayer** – Lord, help me to seek You each day. I pray that I will live my life with integrity and honesty.

# Day 67

**Psalm 26:2** Test me, Lord, try me, examine my heart and my mind.

David is asking the Lord to examine his heart and mind. In verse 1, David says, 'Vindicate me O Lord, for I have led a blameless life; I have trusted in the Lord without wavering.' Notice that David didn't say he has lived a sinless life, but one of moral integrity. Are you ready to ask God to examine your heart and mind? I admit there are times when I would not be raising my hand for God to examine me. I would want someone else to go first to give me time to get prepared. However, David is confident in his request for God to examine him. Would it surprise you to learn that God already knows our hearts and minds better than we do ourselves? He is aware of our thoughts and feelings. He knows our internal battles, our struggles with addictions, our unclean thoughts, and our fears. Even if we think we are doing okay, there are things that likely need to be revealed and brought out. Proverbs 21:2 states, 'All a man's ways seem right to him, but the Lord weighs the heart.' 1 Samuel 16:7 tells us that God looks at our hearts, "But the Lord said to Samuel, 'Do not look at his appearance or at the height of his stature, because I have rejected him; for God sees not as man sees, for man looks at the outward appearance, but the LORD looks at the heart.'" God already knows what is going on in your life. Allow Him to expose things that are in your heart that you didn't even realize were there. After you have spent time with God examining your heart, confess and repent of the things He reveals to you. After you have repented, put a guard around your heart. Proverbs 4:23 tells us, 'Above all else, guard your heart for it is the wellspring of life.'

**Acknowledge** – Lord, You know our hearts and minds. You knew us when we were in our mother's womb.

**Confess** – Lord, I admit I am not sinless, I fall each day. Forgive my desire to satisfy self.

**Thanksgiving** – Lord, I thank You that You know our hearts and minds.

**Prayer** – Lord, examine my heart today. Expose the things that I didn't even realize were there. Cleanse me, and help me to put a guard around my heart.

# Day 68

Psalm 26:8 Lord, I love the house where You live, the place where Your glory dwells.

ONE OF THE JOYS OF HAVING GRANDCHILDREN IS WATCHING THEM grow and learn. I appreciate the experience more now with grandchildren than when our children were growing up because of the busyness of life at that time. One of the things you teach them at an early age is where they live. David proclaims that he loves the house where God lives. So that leads to the question, where does God dwell? Our first thought might be heaven. Which is correct, but He is omnipresent, so His glory is everywhere. In the Old Testament, the presence of the Lord appeared in the Holy of Holies in the tabernacle. 1 Kings 8:11 tells of God's glory filling the temple that Solomon built. 'And the priests could not perform their service because of the cloud, for the glory of the Lord filled His temple.' Years later we find reference to God's glory dwelling in Jesus. John 1:14 tells us, 'The Word became flesh and made His dwelling among us. We have seen His glory, the glory of the One and Only, who came from the Father, full of grace and truth.' After Jesus' death and resurrection, the Holy Spirit comes to indwell His people. In 1 Peter 2:5, Peter tells us, 'You also, like living stones, are being built into a spiritual house (or temple of the spirit) to be a holy priesthood, offering spiritual sacrifices acceptable to God through Jesus Christ.' You are His temple, His dwelling place. What type of temple are you? Are you always open and ready for His presence? If not, ask Him to fill your life with His presence today. What better way to end than with a song written by Lanny Wolfe called, "Surely the Presence of the Lord." The chorus goes, 'Surely the presence of the Lord is in this place, I can feel His mighty power and His grace, I can hear brush of angel's wings, I see glory on each face, Surely the presence of the Lord is in this place.' Experience His presence today.

**Acknowledge** – Lord, we are Your temple. We welcome Your Holy Spirit in our lives.

**Confess** – Lord, forgive me when I fail to seek Your presence, when I don't take time to seek You.

**Thanksgiving** – Lord, I love to be in Your presence, thank You for loving me.

**Prayer** – Lord, surely Your presence is in this place today. Let me feel Your mighty power and Your grace.

# Day 69

Psalm 27:1 The Lord is my light and my salvation, whom shall I fear? The Lord is the stronghold of my life, of whom shall I be afraid?

David was known as a 'man after God's own heart.' Today's reading gives us a glimpse of his character, devotion, and his love for God. In verse one, David is expressing his confidence in God as the source of his life and well-being. God is his light, his salvation, the stronghold of his life. Even though his enemies were conspiring to bring him down, David was confident of God's hand in his life. Paul said in Romans 8:31, 'What, then shall we say in response to this? If God is for us, who can be against us?' Let's look at the words David used to describe the Lord. David first describes God as His 'light.' Light is defined as something that makes vision possible. (www.merriam-webster.com) Isn't that so true of God? Doesn't He reveal things to us that we would not have realized on our own? Doesn't He light the way before us, showing us the way we should go? We will learn more in Psalms 119:105, about God's light. It says, 'Thy Word is a lamp unto my feet and a light to my path.' Can you, like David, say He is your light? Secondly, David said that the Lord was his salvation. Salvation for the Christian is the deliverance from sin and its consequences by our faith in Christ. Is Christ your salvation? Lastly, David said the Lord was the stronghold of his life. What is a stronghold? It is a place that has been fortified so as to protect it against attack. Ephesians 6:12 states that, 'For our struggle is not against flesh and blood, but against the rulers, against the authorities, and against the powers of this dark world and against spiritual forces of evil in the heavenly realms.' Is the Lord your stronghold, a place fortified against the attacks of Satan? Can you join David in saying, 'of whom shall I be afraid?' If not, ask Him to be your light, your salvation, and your stronghold.

**Acknowledge** – Lord, You are our light, our salvation and our stronghold. Of whom shall I be afraid?

**Confess** – Lord, forgive me when I doubt Your hand of protection on my life.

**Thanksgiving** – Lord, thank You for the confidence You give Your children.

**Prayer** – Lord, please be my light and my salvation, the stronghold of my life. Remove any doubt and fear I may have.

# Day 70

**Psalm 27:4** One thing I ask of the Lord, this is what I seek; that I may dwell in the house of the Lord and to seek Him in His temple.

IF YOU COULD ASK ONE THING OF THE LORD, WHAT WOULD IT BE? Would it be a million dollars? Would it be fame and fortune? Would it be healing? Would it be restoration of a relationship? David's list could have looked very similar to ours. However, in the midst of his troubles, he asks the Lord for one thing, to be in His presence. It is in His presence that David finds peace, contentment, and satisfaction. Are you searching for peace and contentment in your life? Does everything you try seem to fall short, leaving you searching for answers? Have you tried to get alone with God and get into His presence? Our troubles seem so small when we are in His presence. I want to leave you with a song written by Geron and Becky Davis entitled, 'In the Presence of Jehovah.' I hope it encourages you to find time to spend with God. It was a favorite at our church in Princeton, NC where Vivian's cousin, Ken, would sing it and lead us into the presence of the Lord. Let the words of this song sink into your spirit. 'In the presence of Jehovah, God Almighty, Prince of Peace, Troubles vanish, Hearts are mended, In the presence of the King. In and out of situations, That tug-a-war at me, For all day long I struggle, For answers that I need, Then I come into your presence, All my questions become clear, For a sacred moment, No doubt can interfere. Through His love the Lord provided, A place for us to rest, A place to find the answers, In hours of distress, There is never any reason, To give up in despair, Just slip away and breathe His name, He will surely find you there.' I hope that you will put a high priority on spending time with God each day. Get into His presence.

**Acknowledge** – Lord, there is an inner peace and joy that can be found in Your presence.

**Confess** – Lord, forgive me when I fail to seek Your presence.

**Thanksgiving** – Lord, thank You that we can dwell in Your house and seek You in Your temple.

**Prayer** – Lord, we are not promised a trouble-free life. Lord, help me seek Your presence, where there is peace in the storms of life.

# Day 71

Psalm 27:14 Wait for the Lord, be strong and take heart and wait for the Lord.

Earlier this year our family went to Disney. I hesitated on whether to invest the extra money in a 'Fast Pass.' After seeing how long the lines were, I am glad we bought them. There are more serious types of waiting; such as, waiting to hear back from a job interview, test results from your doctor, or sitting with a loved one who is extremely sick. Also, more times than not we have to wait on the Lord to answer our prayers. God's time schedule can be very different from ours. If He were to answer our every prayer immediately, that would put us in control instead of Him. Fortunately, He is always on time, never early, never late. David gives us instructions on how to wait. First, we should wait. That sounds very simple, but it is the key to victory in our lives. God can teach us so much in the seasons of life when we are waiting. Second, we should be strong and courageous. Joshua was about to undertake a dangerous and long assignment from God to lead the people of Israel into the Promised Land. God told Joshua in Joshua 1:9, 'Have I not commanded you? Be strong and courageous. Do not be terrified; do not be discouraged, for the Lord your God will be with you wherever you go.' Take heart, God is with you, don't be discouraged, be strong and courageous as you wait. Don't let your circumstances cause you to live in fear. Thirdly, we should have perseverance. James 1:4 tells us, 'Let perseverance finish its work so that you may be mature and complete, not lacking anything.' Waiting for God provides an opportunity for our faith to grow and mature. It is worth the wait. Isaiah 40:31 tells us, 'But they that wait upon the Lord shall renew their strength; they shall mount up with wings as eagles; they shall run and not be weary; and they shall walk, and not faint. Be strong and courageous as you wait on Him.

**Acknowledge** – Lord, there are times when all we can do is wait on You.

**Confess** – Lord, forgive me when I grow impatient and miss blessings You have in store for me during the wait.

**Thanksgiving** – Lord, thank You that those who wait on You can renew their strength.

**Prayer** – Lord, help me to wait for You and to be strong and courageous as I wait.

# Day 72

Psalm 28:2,6 Hear my cry for mercy as I call to You for help, as I lift my hands toward Your most Holy place. 6. Praise be to the Lord, for He has heard my cry for mercy.

Psalm 28 was written by David for deliverance from those who were out to harm him. David was desperate and in need of God's mercy. Do you have a special place where you pray? The good news is that you can enter into the presence of God anywhere, anytime, even in Managua, Nicaragua. On our mission trips there, the team would go to Ruby's house just outside the city dump to pray. It is amazing to witness the power of God answering prayers in that little upper room of her house. There is also no specific position to be in to reach out to God. How do you pray when you are desperately seeking the Father? Are you kneeling, crying, silent, sitting, standing, or hands in surrender? There are even times when I can't verbalize my prayers. Paul tells us in Romans 8:26, 'In the same way, the Spirit helps us in our weakness. We do not know what we ought to pray for, but the Spirit Himself intercedes for us with groans that words cannot express.' Isn't it wonderful in those times the Holy Spirit takes over and intercedes for us to help us with our prayer? Lifting our prayers to God is very important. He wants to hear from us. But are there times when you feel your prayers hit the ceiling? Thankfully David answered that question in verse six. 'Praise be to the Lord, for He has heard my cry for mercy.' God hears us when we cry out to Him. He knows what you are going through. 1 Peter 3:12 tells us, 'For the eyes of the Lord are on the righteous and His ears are attentive to their prayer, but the face of the Lord is against those who do evil.' God loves you and hears your prayers. As we have learned, we may have to wait patiently for His answer, but He hears and answers our prayers.

**Acknowledge** – Lord, You hear our prayers, You have heard our cries for mercy.

**Confess** – Lord, forgive me when I doubt Your love for me.

**Thanksgiving** – Lord, thank You that You know our needs before we even ask.

**Prayer** – Lord, I lift my hands to You, fill them with Your grace and mercy.

# Day 73

Psalm 29:11 The Lord gives strength to His people, the Lord blesses His people with peace.

IN PSALM 29, DAVID APPEARS TO BE DESCRIBING A TERRIBLE THUNDERstorm or hurricane. Living on the coast, I can attest to the power of a hurricane. In September 2018, Hurricane Florence sat over the east coast of North Carolina for a couple of days, with pounding winds, lightning and thunder, spawning tornados, and dumping over 30 inches of rain causing massive flooding in our area. In verse four, David describes the 'thunder over the mighty waters.' In verse five, he describes the cedars of Lebanon being torn into pieces. In verse seven, flashes of lightning are striking everywhere. In verse nine, the oaks are being twisted and the forests stripped bare. In verse ten, 'the Lord sits enthroned over the flood.' That sounds like the experience we had with Hurricane Florence. While David might be describing a weather event, perhaps you are going through what feels like a terrible storm in your life right now. Can you hear the thunder of hatred and see the lightning bolts of jabs crashing all around you? Are the winds of chaos buffeting your life? Are the floodwaters of turmoil about to overtake you? Take heart, 'the Lord sits enthroned over the flood, the Lord is enthroned as King forever.' He is in control, even when our world seems to be crashing in on us. He gives us strength to make it through the storms of life. Isaiah 41:10 tells us, 'So do not fear, for I am with you; do not be dismayed, for I am your God. I will strengthen you and help you; I will uphold you with My righteous right hand.' Speaking from experience I know this to be true. It may take weeks or months to get through the storm, but He will strengthen you and send moments of encouragement through the storm. Trust Him; let Him bless you with His peace today.

**Acknowledge** – Lord, You are our strength, You uphold us with Your righteous right hand.

**Confess** – Lord, forgive me when I doubt Your Word, when I don't seek Your Word for its truth, when I don't believe Your Word applies to me.

**Thanksgiving** – Lord, thank You that You are enthroned over the flood waters of our lives.

**Prayer** – Lord, be my strength, my portion, my peace, my strong tower.

# Day 74

Psalm 30:5 For His anger lasts only a moment, but His favor lasts a lifetime; weeping may stay for a night, but rejoicing comes in the morning.

We know that God gives us strength to make it through the storms of life. Yesterday, I mentioned Hurricane Florence and the fierceness of that storm. For me, the worst part of riding out the Hurricane was that it came ashore at night. The strong winds had taken out the power. In the middle of the night, still awake, we heard a loud crash near our house. It was too dark to tell what had fallen. About that same time, the sound of the wind changed from howling into more of a train sound. We later learned that a tornado had spawned off the storm clouds and passed near our house. It was a very long night. The next morning we could see the damage caused by the storm. The loud crash that we had heard was a huge oak tree that had fallen across our driveway. However, we had survived the storm. There is something about the morning after a storm that gives you a reason for rejoicing. Each morning brings new perspective and offers hope that things will be different today. You can look back and confidently say you have survived another day. As David tells us in this Psalm, 'rejoicing comes in the morning.' Some nights of 'weeping' may seem like they last forever. But the morning does come. Has pain and sorrow taken over your life? Have these twins left you with no hope? The good news is pain, sorrow, sickness and disease will not have the last word. How do we know this? Because of Jesus and the love He demonstrated for us on the cross. He is the One who gives us life, who gives us hope, who gives us salvation. Receive the blessing of joy that comes in the morning.

**Acknowledge** – Lord, our weeping may last through the night, but joy comes in the morning.

**Confess** – Lord, forgive me when I let troubles overwhelm me, when I fail to trust You, when I let circumstances in my life get me down.

**Thanksgiving** – Lord, thank You that Your anger lasts only a moment, that You offer us forgiveness and grace.

**Prayer** – Lord, help me to trust Your word in 2 Corinthians 4:17 that tells us, 'For our light and momentary troubles are achieving for us an eternal glory that far outweighs them all.'

# Day 75

Psalm 30:10 Hear Lord and be merciful to me; Lord be my help.

TODAY'S VERSE CONTAINS TWO VERY SIMPLE AND COMPACT PRAYERS. The first prayer was used by Jesus in the parable of the Pharisee and the Tax Collector in Luke 18:13. It says, 'But the tax collector stood at a distance. He would not even look up to heaven, but beat his breast and said, God, have mercy on me, a sinner.' While the Pharisee prayed, 'God, I thank You that I am not like other men–robbers, evildoers, adulterers – or even like this tax collector. I fast twice a week and give a tenth of all I get.' Jesus went on to say in verse 14 that the tax collector, not the Pharisee, was justified or made righteous in the sight of God. God is more concerned with our heart. While the Pharisee was bragging about his godly lifestyle, the tax collector was truly repentant for his. The Pharisee was more concerned about living a checklist of do's and don'ts rather than having his heart right with God. The tax collector's lifestyle was full of dishonesty, cheating, and greed, yet his heart was repentant and drawn to God. His simple prayer of confession was heard and honored by God because of its sincerity and earnestness. Be sincere in your prayer to Him. David's second prayer is even more succinct, 'Lord be my help.' When we ask God to help us, what is our motive? Is it for personal gain or heavenly gain? James 4:3 tells us, 'When you ask, you do not receive, because you ask with the wrong motives, that you may spend what you get on your pleasures.' When our prayer life becomes aligned with His will for us, our simple prayers will have power and can change our lives. Matthew 6:33 tells us, 'But seek first His kingdom and His righteousness, and all these things will be given to you as well.' Spend time with God, seek His kingdom, seek His righteousness, and His presence.

**Acknowledge** – Lord, You hear our simplest prayers, You are our help.

**Confess** – Lord, forgive me when I pray selfish prayers that are for personal gain, not in line with Your will for me.

**Thanksgiving** – Lord, thank You for access to Your throne of mercy and grace through prayer.

**Prayer** – Lord, help me to be as sincere as the tax collector when I ask You for mercy for my sins.

# Day 76

Psalm 30:11-12 You turned my wailing into dancing; that my heart may sing to You and not be silent. O Lord my God, I will give You thanks forever.

Today's reading lets us know that it is okay to celebrate and give praise to God. It takes us from the pain, suffering, and weeping that comes with difficult times to a season of rejoicing for God's deliverance. When the Egyptian army was drowned in the Red Sea, the children of Israel rejoiced. Miriam, Moses's sister, led the women in celebration before the Lord. Exodus 15:20-21 tells us, 'Then Miriam the prophet, Aaron's sister, took a timbrel in her hand, and all the women followed her, with timbrels and dancing. Miriam sang to them: 'Sing to the Lord, for He is highly exalted. Both the horse and driver He has hurled into the sea.' Have you come through a painful season where you have felt the presence of God in your life? Did your heart sing out to Him in thanksgiving and praise? Isaiah 61:1-3 prophesies about the coming of Jesus and His mission. It states, 'The Spirit of the Sovereign Lord is on Me, because the Lord has anointed Me to preach the good news to the poor. He has sent Me to bind up the brokenhearted, to proclaim freedom for the captives and release from darkness for the prisoners, to proclaim the year of the Lord's favor and the day of vengeance of our God, to comfort all who mourn, and provide for those who grieve in Zion – to bestow on them a crown of beauty instead of ashes, the oil of gladness instead of mourning and a garment of praise instead of a spirit of despair. They will be called oaks of righteousness, a planting of the Lord for the display of his splendor.' Has God set you free? Has He comforted you? Has He anointed you with the oil of gladness? If so, praise Him today. Thank Him for a garment of praise instead of despair.

**Acknowledge** – Lord, You turn our wailing to dancing, our cries to songs of praise.

**Confess** – Lord, forgive me when I become bitter and hard-hearted.

**Thanksgiving** – Lord, thank You for bestowing a crown of beauty instead of ashes, the oil of gladness instead of mourning, and a garment of praise instead of despair.

**Prayer** – Lord, my heart sings out to You, I will give You praise forever for all You have done for me.

# Day 77

**Psalm 31:1 In You, O Lord, I have taken refuge; let me never be put to shame; deliver me in Your righteousness.**

Psalm 31, written by David, expresses extreme confidence in the Lord when he was confronted by evil men. While on the cross, Jesus quoted verse five of this Psalm, 'Into your hands I commit My spirit…' Let's breakdown the key words in this verse to find application for our lives. The first is Refuge – A condition of being safe or sheltered from pursuit, danger or trouble. Days after Hurricane Florence our house became a refuge for several friends because we had food, a way to cook it, and running water. They were able to come over, take showers, get a hot cooked meal, and regroup from the storm. David points out that he found safety and security in the Lord. When you are being pursued by life's troubles, where do you turn? Do you try escaping by using drugs, alcohol, or things that numb you from your troubles? If so, do they seem to be working? If not, try taking refuge in the Lord. He will give you peace and rest. The second word is Shame – A painful feeling of humiliation or distress caused by the consciousness of wrong or foolish behavior. Sadly, the areas where we turn for refuge can lead us down the path of shame and humiliation. The good news is God can wipe away our guilt and shame and make us righteous before Him. 1 John 1:9 tells us, 'If we confess our sins, He is faithful and just and will forgive us our sins and purify us from all unrighteousness.' Ask and receive His forgiveness today. The last word is Righteousness – The quality of being morally right or justifiable. If we receive God's forgiveness, then we are delivered into His righteousness. In Romans 6:18 Paul tells us to become slaves of righteousness, 'And having been set free from sin, you become slaves of righteousness.' Once we have taken refuge in Christ our sin and shame are removed. Then we are able to pursue righteous living. Have you asked God to forgive you? He is faithful to forgive you and clean up your life.

**Acknowledge** – Lord, You are our refuge, a place of safety and security.

**Confess** – Lord, forgive me when I look to earthly solutions for safety from life's problems.

**Thanksgiving** – Lord, thank You for being faithful to forgive and cleanse me.

**Prayer** – Lord, in You I have taken refuge; deliver me in Your righteousness.

Psalm 31:2 Turn Your ear to me, come quickly to my rescue; be my rock of refuge, a strong fortress to save me.

DAVID ESCALATES HIS REQUEST BY ASKING THE LORD TO LISTEN TO him and quickly come to his rescue. Unfortunately, I am a little hard of hearing. Background noise can drown out a conversation with someone right next to me. When I think about the background noise and the number of prayers the Lord experiences 24 hours per day, every day, it amazes me that He can hear my specific prayer over the others that are coming in at the same time. There are occasions when my prayers may seem to be routine, but they are important, and I want God to hear and answer them. Isn't it wonderful we serve a God who does not put our prayers in a queue and operate on a first in – first out basis? God is omnipresent, meaning He is everywhere at the same time. He can hear and answer more than one prayer at a time. But there are occasions when, like David, I have to say, 'Lord please listen to my cry for help, and put Your ear to my feeble lips so that You can hear me.' 1 John 5:14 tells us, 'Now this is the confidence we have before Him: Whenever we ask anything according to His will, He hears us.' Not only does David ask God to listen to him, but he also asks Him to come quickly to his rescue. God has His own time schedule for answering our prayers. But like David, there are times when we just need to say, 'Lord come quickly to my rescue. I need a place of refuge; I need You to save me.' God knows your needs. In Matthew 6:8, Jesus teaching the disciples how to pray tells us, 'Do not be like them, for Your Father knows what you need before you ask Him.' Don't be afraid to ask God to hear you, to come quickly to your rescue. He loves you and will provide at the right moment.

**Acknowledge** – Lord, You know our needs before we even ask.

**Confess** – Lord, forgive me when I doubt Your ability to work things out according to Your good plan.

**Thanksgiving** – Lord, thank You for hearing my prayers and coming to my rescue.

**Prayer** – Lord, teach me how to pray in the spirit reaching Your heavenly throne.

Psalm 31:14 But I trust in You, Lord; I say You are my God.

The 19th Century Scottish Poet George McDonald wrote, 'To be trusted is a greater compliment than being loved.' (www.inspiration.rightattiudes.com) Trust is defined as 'a firm belief in the reliability, truth, ability, or strength of someone or something.' (www.oxfordlearnersdictionay.com) In what do you put your trust? Is it money? Money can disappear faster than you make it. Look at the back of a dollar bill, it tells you who to trust. There you will find the words, 'In God we Trust.' Perhaps you put your trust in the church or in the government? With nothing being secure why is it that we don't put our complete and total trust in God? Could it be that life's battles are hard and we look for immediate relief from our troubles? We think money will buy us out or a TV Evangelist's message of prosperity sounds pretty good. Whatever the reason, we tend to let our circumstances take our eyes off God and His faithfulness to us. Renew your faith in Him. Lauren Daigle, Paul Marbury, and Michael Farren, have written a song entitled, "I Trust in You Lord." Its message is very simple and relates to today's verse; when life doesn't go like we planned, trust in God. 'Letting go of every single dream, I lay each one down at Your feet, Every moment of my wandering, Never changes what You see, I try to win this war, I confess, my hands are weary, I need Your rest, Mighty warrior, king of the fight, No matter what I face You're by my side. When You don't move the mountains, I'm needing You to move, When You don't part the waters I wish I could walk through, When You don't give the answers as I cry out to You, I will trust, I will trust, I will trust in You. Truth is, You know what tomorrow brings, There's not a day ahead You have not seen, So let all things be my life and breath, I want what You want Lord, and nothing less.' When life doesn't make sense, trust in Him.

**Acknowledge** – Lord, You are my God, in You I place my trust.

**Confess** – Lord, forgive me when I let circumstances overwhelm me and cause me to take action to fix them without You.

**Thanksgiving** – Lord, thank You for knowing what tomorrow brings.

**Prayer** – Lord, teach me to trust in You for all things.

Psalm 31:16 Let Your face shine on Your servant; save me in Your unfailing love.

WHAT DOES THE PHRASE, 'LET YOUR FACE SHINE ON YOUR SERVANT' mean to you? Is it saying, Lord, keep your eye on me and keep me safe? Is it a request for material blessings such as good health, money, or a bigger house? While God can bless us with those things, that is not what David is seeking here. David is seeking God's presence and approval. When the face of God, 'shines on us,' it means that God takes pleasure in His people. I heard it described as a child playing in their first soccer game. They get in the game and happen to score a goal. After scoring the goal, they look immediately to their father or mother for their cheers of approval. Our children, Emily and Bren, were able to participate in sports through their high school years. I will always remember how they looked into the stands to make sure we were watching them. Playing sports was a good opportunity for Vivian and me to demonstrate our approval of their efforts. How often do we look for approval and acceptance from the people around us? We want to be loved and accepted by others. Unfortunately, we may experience rejection from the very people we are seeking acceptance from. But we, like David, can look to our heavenly Father for His approval. We can know that He loves us and is pleased with us. Do you want His presence and approval in your life each day? Give Him first place in your life. The Lord gave Moses a blessing to pray over the children of Israel. Pray this prayer over you and your family each day. It is found in Numbers 6:24-26, 'The Lord bless you and keep you; the Lord make His face shine upon you and be gracious to you; the Lord turn His face toward you and give you peace.'

**Acknowledge** – Lord, Your presence is all I need.

**Confess** – Lord, forgive me when I focus too much on acceptance from others that I compromise my devotion to You.

**Thanksgiving** – Lord, thank You for making Your face to shine upon me.

**Prayer** – The Lord bless you and keep you; the Lord make His face shine upon you and be gracious to you; the Lord turn His face toward you and give you peace.

# Day 81

**Psalm 31:24 Be strong and take heart, all you who hope in the Lord.**

To gain a better perspective on Psalm 31, let's read verse 22 which says, 'In my alarm I said, I am cut off from Your sight! Yet You heard my cry for mercy when I call to You for help.' Have you felt far away from His presence? The ironic thing is that we can experience this feeling of being away from God's sight in times of adversity or even prosperity. There have been times when I felt self-sufficient, that I could handle things on my own, but I learned very quickly that I needed God's presence. Being away from God's presence is similar to flying in an airplane through the thick cover of storm clouds. Have you flown through a strong storm? The flight can be terrifying. I recall a flight Vivian and I were on to NYC. Taking off from Wilmington, the skies were clear. However about half-way to NYC, we ran into a strong line of storms. The turbulence caused the plane to bounce up and down. The bouncing continued to grow worse. Several passengers even became nauseous. As we approached LGA, the plane was now bouncing up and down, and shifting sideways. You could feel the plane was in descent but couldn't see a thing. Still bouncing and shifting sideways, the plane miraculously touched down. The entire plane erupted in cheers for the pilot and crew because of the safe landing. The pilot had been trained to fly through such storms, using the plane's instruments to guide him to our destination. What word of encouragement did David give us when he felt cut off from God's presence? In verse 23 he tells us, 'Love the Lord…' In verse 24, 'Be strong and take heart…' Like passengers on an airplane, we have to be courageous and remain confident in our pilot when the flight gets bumpy. Where are you today? Are you in a season of prosperity or adversity? No matter our circumstances we need God's presence in our lives every day. Seek Him each day. Trust Him, He is in control.

**Acknowledge** – Lord, You hear our cries for mercy when we call out to You.

**Confess** – Lord, forgive me when I let the storms of life throw me off course.

**Thanksgiving** – Lord, thank You for being in control even when we don't feel like You are.

**Prayer** – Lord, help me to be strong and courageous, let my hope be in You.

# Day 82

**Psalm 32:1** Blessed is the one whose transgressions are forgiven, whose sins are covered.

HAVE YOU EVER DONE SOMETHING THAT WEIGHED SO HEAVILY ON you that you couldn't function normally? When my sister and I were young kids, we decided to trash our neighbor's garage. We didn't destroy anything, but made a good mess. We also decided to blame it on someone else. When our neighbors got home, we told them who we thought we saw leaving their yard. Feeling guilty we helped clean up the mess we made. That day my conscience was bothering me. I was miserable. My father investigated our story when he got home. Things weren't adding up, and my sister and I couldn't tell any more stories. We confessed, were punished, and apologized. It was probably one of the worst spankings I ever received. But surprisingly, I felt so much better after the punishment. Isn't this what David is saying today? The weight of our sins can overwhelm us. What joy and blessing it is when our sins are forgiven. Proverbs 28:13 tells us, 'Whoever conceals their sins does not prosper, but the one who confesses and renounces them finds mercy.' Unfortunately, the older we get the better we become at concealing, justifying, and living with our sins. Don't harbor sin in your life and let it weigh you down. Do as David expressed in verse five, 'Then I acknowledged my sin to You and did not cover up my iniquity. I said, I will confess my transgressions to the Lord, and You forgave the guilt of my sin.' Experience God's forgiveness and the joy of having your sins forgiven. Jesus has paid the price for your sins. Confess them to Him and He will forgive you. Paul speaking in Acts 13:38-39 tells us, 'Therefore my brothers, I want you to know that through Jesus the forgiveness of sins is proclaimed to you. Through Him everyone who believes is justified from everything you could not be justified from by the Law of Moses.' Do you want to feel blessed and pardoned? Then call on the Lord to forgive you.

**Acknowledge** – Lord, You offer grace and pardon for our sins.

**Confess** – Lord, unforgiven sin is a burden and it drains me of energy. I ask for forgiveness today.

**Thanksgiving** – Lord, thank You for the joy and peace I can experience through forgiveness of my sins.

**Prayer** – Lord, Your word tells us that whoever conceals their sins does not prosper, Lord I confess my sins to You.

# Day 83

**Psalm 32:8** I will instruct you and teach you in the way you should go; I will counsel you and watch over you.

Do you learn by reading and putting into practice what you read? Or, do you prefer an instructional setting with a teacher reviewing the information? Perhaps you are a hands-on learner? We are all different and have different learning styles. David tells us that God will teach us, instruct us, counsel us, and watch over us. He has provided a training manual called the Bible. There have been a multitude of books written to help us study and understand God's word. In every church, there are opportunities for us to meet and study God's word together. You can also find a wealth of information through Christian podcasts, web sites, and Christian television that teach God's word. 2 Timothy 3:16 tells us, 'All scripture is breathed out by God and profitable for teaching, for reproof, for correction, and for training in righteousness.' The question is, 'are you taking advantage of the opportunities God has given you to learn and mature in His word?' Are you using it to train you in how to live a righteous life? Hebrews 4:12 tells us, 'For the word of God is living and active...' That means it applies to us today as much as it did when it was written. Read Hebrews 5:12-14. These verses describe a believer who is not growing in God's word. He tells us they need teaching on elementary truths of God's word over and over again, needing milk, not solid food. There are a number of resources to help you grow in Christ. Get involved in a Bible study of some type and get to know God's word. As Tara-Leigh Cobble with the Bible Recap says, 'He is where the joy is.'

**Acknowledge** – Lord, You will instruct us and teach us the way we should go.

**Confess** – Lord, forgive me for being like the horse and mule needing a bridle to be led to study Your word.

**Thanksgiving** – Lord, thank You for the opportunities You have provided us to learn Your word.

**Prayer** – Lord, Your word is a lamp to my feet and a light to my path. Help me to use it daily to light my path.

# Day 84

Psalm 32:11 Rejoice in the Lord and be glad, you righteous; sing, all you who are upright in heart!

To better understand today's verse; we need to look back to the beginning of Psalm 32. David starts out by expressing joy that God had forgiven his sins. The weight of his sins was heavy upon him, and he couldn't function. But God was faithful to forgive him and lift the burden of guilt off his shoulders. We know that God will guide us, instruct us, and watch over us. Today, David rejoices in God's deliverance. It is very difficult to rejoice and show great joy when the guilt and shame of our sins weigh us down. There have been times when I attended church only to go through the motions. I couldn't sing, I couldn't concentrate, I was numb to God's presence. My prayers were insincere and shallow. Have you been there? I was carrying baggage that made it impossible to worship. After I confessed my sins to Him and received His forgiveness, my entire demeanor changed. My perspective on worship changed. Tears would stream down my face as I was singing and worshiping God. These were not tears of sorrow, but tears of joy and heartfelt love for the Father. My burden had been lifted. Paul tells us in Philippians 4:4, 'Rejoice in the Lord always. I will say it again: Rejoice.' What can you rejoice in the Lord for today? Has He forgiven your sins and saved your soul? Jesus tells us in Luke 10:20, 'However, do not rejoice that the spirits submit to you, but rejoice that your names are written in heaven.' Take time today to rejoice in the Lord. Worship Him for saving your soul and paying the penalty for your sin. Worship Him that He forgives your sin and remembers them no more. Worship Him that you are a child of God. Feel free to create your own list of reasons to worship God.

**Acknowledge** – Lord, You are worthy of our praise.

**Confess** – Lord, forgive me when I try to hold on to sin in my life and not confess it to You.

**Thanksgiving** – Lord, thank You for being our hiding place, for teaching us, for counseling us, with a loving eye.

**Prayer** – Lord, as Your word tells us 'rejoice in the Lord always, again I say rejoice. Help me to rejoice in You each day.

# Day 85

Psalm 33:4 For the word of the Lord is right and true; He is faithful in all He does.

Isn't it a blessing we have access to God's very words that can be trusted to be right and true? This verse reminds me of a Vacation Bible school song that speaks about the solid foundation of God's word. It goes, 'The B I B L E yes that's the book for me, I stand alone on the word of God, the B I B L E.' Because we can trust God's word, we can have full confidence that the Bible is the inspired, inerrant, authoritative record of God's plan and purpose for His creation. Do you read His word and know what it says? Take time each day to read His word and get to know God. As you do, you will also find as David did, that God is faithful. Throughout the scripture, God's faithfulness to His children is recorded. Hebrews, chapter 11 is dedicated to God's faithfulness in keeping His promises and the faithfulness of those who trusted God to keep His promise. Some, like Abraham, took years before God's promise was fulfilled. But yet, they were faithful and trusted God. Can you look back and see God's faithfulness in your life? Perhaps you are going through a struggle right now and can't see God working in your life. He is ever faithful, working on your behalf. Read the words of this song written by Carol Cymbala, that speaks to God's faithfulness. 'In my own suffering, Through every pain every tear, There's a God who's been faithful to me. When my strength was all gone, When my heart had no song, Still in love He's proved faithful to me. Every word He's promised is true, What I thought was impossible, I've seen my God do. He's been faithful, faithful to me, Looking back His love and mercy I see, Though in my heart I have questioned, And failed to believe, He's been faithful, faithful to me.' Has He been faithful to you? The answer is yes, look back and see His love and mercy at work in your life.

**Acknowledge** – Lord, Your word is right and true.

**Confess** – Lord, forgive me when I doubt Your faithfulness in my life.

**Thanksgiving** – Lord, thank You for being faithful to me.

**Prayer** – Lord, though in my heart I have questioned Your faithfulness, You have been faithful to me. Help me to recognize Your hand of mercy in my life.

# Day 86

Psalm 33:11 But the plans of the Lord stand firm forever, the purposes of His heart through all generations.

As the Psalmist points out today, God's plans have no beginning and no end. They span years, generations, and centuries. I am reminded of the story in the Old Testament of the family of Jacob who moved to Egypt during a great famine in the land. His son, Joseph had been sold into slavery in Egypt and had risen to second in command under Pharaoh to manage the crops in preparation for the great famine that was on the way. To make a long story short, Joseph recognized that it was God's plan for him to go ahead of his family into Egypt to save their lives. It was also God's plan for the Israelites to leave Egypt over 400 years after Joseph's death. Joseph trusted God's promise to Abraham, Isaac, and Jacob believing that He would take the Israelites out of Egypt one day by making them promise to take his bones with them when they left. All through the Bible we can read of God's plans. In Revelation, we can read of His plan to return to earth to set up His kingdom here. In the midst of all the plans for the world, God also has a plan for your life. Are you asking Him in prayer what His plans are for you? Are you following the commands He is putting in your heart? It is very unlikely you will hear the audible voice of God speaking to you. However, He plants thoughts, ideas, and plans in your spirit that give birth to His plans. Take time to listen to God and follow Him. This verse might be repeated several times this year, but it applies so well for today. Jeremiah 29:11, 'For I know the plans I have for you, declares the Lord, plans to prosper you and not to harm you, plans to give you hope and a future.' Trust in God's plan for your life.

**Acknowledge** – Lord, Your plans stand firm forever. They last from generation to generation.

**Confess** – Lord, forgive me when I fail to seek Your plans and make a mess of my life.

**Thanksgiving** – Lord, thank You for loving me enough to have a plan for my life.

**Prayer** – Lord, I want to know Your plans for my life. Teach me Your ways. Teach me Your will.

# Day 87

Psalm 33:12 Blessed is the nation whose God is the Lord, the people He chose for His inheritance.

WHAT NATION HAS GOD CHOSEN AS HIS PEOPLE? IT MAY OR MAY NOT surprise you to find out that it isn't the United States, but it is Israel. However, modern-day Israel wasn't even recognized as a nation until 1948 when Israel's Provisional Government proclaimed a new State of Israel, in the land given to them by God years ago. God, speaking to Abram in Genesis 12:2-3, said, 'I will make you into a great nation and I will bless you; I will make your name great, and you will be a blessing. I will bless those who bless you, and whoever curses you I will curse; and all the peoples on the earth will be blessed through you.' This promise God made to His chosen people continues today; however, you and I now have a place in His inheritance. Through the death and resurrection of Jesus Christ we have been made a part of the family of God. Galatians 4:4-7 tells us, 'But when the time had fully come, God sent His Son, born of a woman, born under the law, to redeem those under the law, that we might receive the full rights of sons. Because you are sons, God sent the Spirit of His Son into our hearts, the Spirit who calls out, Abba, Father. So you are no longer a slave, but a son; and since you are a son, God has made you also an heir.' And as Paul wrote in Colossians 1:12, we share in His inheritance; 'Giving thanks to the Father, who has qualified you to share in the inheritance of the saints in the kingdom of light.' Give thanks to God for making a way for us to become a part of His family. The sacrifice was His only Son. Isn't it wonderful that we are members of the family of God?

**Acknowledge** – Lord, blessed is the nation whose God is the Lord.

**Confess** – Lord, forgive me when I turn away from following You as Your children the Israelites did many times.

**Thanksgiving** – Lord, thank You for blessing our nation who has continued to support the nation of Israel.

**Prayer** – Lord, You have blessed our nation beyond measure. Please forgive our sins. May we as a nation, worship and acknowledge You as our God.

# Day 88

Psalm 33:20 We wait in hope for the Lord; He is our help and our shield.

I'll never forget October 20, 1984. It was one of the longest, but most rewarding days of my life. Our first child, Emily, was born on that day. The 20th of October that year happened to be a beautiful fall Saturday. Vivian started having labor pains very early in the morning. To burn off some nervous energy, I went outside and raked the yard. After finishing the yard, the contractions were still far apart. So we waited and waited. North Carolina State and UNC were playing football that day, so I tried to watch the game. By mid-afternoon, Vivian's contractions were getting closer together. Being the good husband, I asked her how far apart were the contractions. She wasn't sure, so I gave her my watch so she could time them. (A note to future fathers, this is not a good idea. Do not hand a watch to a pregnant woman in labor. Be there with her and help time the contractions. Your day will be stressful enough without having to repeatedly apologize for being insensitive.) We headed for the hospital and Vivian was prepped and taken to the delivery room. After an hour or two of labor and a few tense moments when the baby's heart rate dropped, the doctor said a cesarean section would be necessary. After more waiting and a few more nervous moments that seemed like hours, our first child, a healthy baby girl was put in my arms. There are times when we may have a very long day, but things work themselves out. Other times our problems may last weeks, months, or even years. When that happens, can we wait in hope for the Lord? Can you wait in quiet expectation, knowing God already knows your tomorrow? Are you single-minded in the confidence of God's love for you even when the storms of life rage around you? As the Psalmist reminds us, God is our help and our shield. Hold fast to Him. Trust in His love for you.

**Acknowledge** – The Lord is our help and our shield.

**Confess** – Lord, forgive me when I take my eyes off of You and get impatient for my circumstances to change.

**Thanksgiving** – Lord, thank You for knowing my tomorrow.

**Prayer** – Lord, waiting is hard sometimes. Help me to wait in hope for You, and to learn what You want me to know as I go through life's trials.

# Day 89

Psalm 34:8 Taste and see that the Lord is good; blessed is the man who takes refuge in Him.

WHEN YOU WERE A CHILD, DID YOUR PARENTS INTRODUCE YOU TO new foods? Mine would say 'try this, it is good.' Or 'eat your green beans, they are good for you.' My tastes have changed and foods that I would never eat as a child, I now like. Our grandchildren, even before trying something new, will say, 'I don't like it, it is yucky.' Then we go through a painful process of trying to convince them to try it. Occasionally we get them to try something and like it. Unfortunately, the healthier the food, the less likely they are to like it. David tells us in today's study, to 'taste and see.' To taste involves testing or sampling something such as a new food. To see involves understanding or perceiving or to experience something first hand. David doesn't want us to take his word for it, but wants us to experience His goodness for ourselves. Like trying new foods, we need to taste and see the Lord is good. Finally, we have something that is good for us that is also pleasant to taste. 1 Peter 2:1-3 tells us, 'Therefore rid yourselves of all malice and all deceit, hypocrisy, envy, slander of every kind. Like newborn babies, crave pure spiritual milk, so that by it you may grow up in your salvation, now that you have tasted the Lord is good.' Take time to reflect on your life. Have you personally experienced the goodness of the Lord? Can you look back and specifically say it was His hand that got you through a difficult time in your life or, do you think it was simply by chance? Take time to taste and see the Lord's goodness. When you do, you will burst out in praise as David did in verse 1, 'I will extol the Lord at all times; His praise will always be on my lips.' The beautiful part is that as you get closer to Him, the more you take refuge in Him, the more you will discover the blessings of God in your life.

**Acknowledge** – Taste and see that the Lord is good.

**Confess** – Lord, forgive me when I doubt Your goodness and fail to give You praise.

**Thanksgiving** – Lord, as David said, I will enthusiastically praise You at all times.

**Prayer** – Lord, thank You for the bread of life, let me taste and see that it is good.

# Day 90

Psalm 34:17 The righteous cry out, and the Lord hears them; He delivers them from all their troubles.

TODAY'S VERSE ALMOST SOUNDS LIKE DAVID IS SAYING THAT GOD offers the righteous a 'get out of jail free' card. In other words, the Lord will deliver us immediately from our troubles. But that is not what he is saying at all. Look at verse 18, 'The Lord is close to the brokenhearted and saves those who are crushed in spirit.' There are times when our troubles overwhelm us. They can be complicated with no end in sight. When we reach that point, God can use these situations to show us His power, His glory, and to show Himself strong on our behalf. David opened the verse by saying, 'the righteous cry out...' The first thing our troubles do is lead us to pray. How often do you pray? How do you express your need for Him? We are using a very simple prayer model in our daily devotional. It can be a good starting point for reaching out to the Father. However, make time to expand your prayers to more than what is provided and make them your own. I would recommend adding 'Supplication' or asking earnestly and humbly after giving thanks to God. Tell Him your needs and the needs of others. Next, David tells us that our prayers bring us to the Lord's hearing ear. He hears our prayers. 1 John 5:14-15 states, 'This is the confidence we have in approaching God: that if we ask anything according to His will, He hears us. And if we know that He hears us – whatever we ask – we know that we have what we asked of Him.' Lastly, our prayers prepare us for the joyful experience of having them answered. David said, 'He delivers them from all their troubles.' One day you will be able to look back and see how God has delivered you. It may not be the way you had intended, but God will have brought you through to the other side. My prayer is that you will daily recognize God's hand in your life.

**Acknowledge** – Thank You for hearing my prayers.

**Confess** – Lord, forgive me when I let troubles and trials take over and overwhelm me.

**Thanksgiving** – Lord, thank You for Your deliverance that comes at the right time.

**Prayer** – Lord, everyone faces troubles in their lives, help me to keep my eyes on You during those times.

# Day 91

Psalm 34:19 A righteous man may have many troubles, but the Lord delivers him from them all.

TODAY WE LEARN THAT OUR TROUBLES CAN BE NUMEROUS AND complicated. Jesus, speaking in John 16:33 tells us, 'I have told you these things, so that in Me you may have peace. In this world you will have trouble. But take heart! I have overcome the world.' We are not guaranteed a trouble-free life as a Christian. You have probably figured this out by now. In fact, you may feel your problems couldn't get any worse. They keep mounting up until it feels like someone being tackled in football and the players keep piling on until the bottom person is about to suffocate. There is a small three-letter word in today's verse and it is also found in John 16:33 that offers hope, the word 'but'. What a powerful word. It can be found in many other places in the Bible. Here we find it contrasting our troubles against the deliverance of them by the Lord. Perhaps though, one of the most important times it is found in the Bible is in Romans 5:8, '**But God** demonstrates His own love for us in this: While we were still sinners, Christ died for us.' Notice that Paul uses the word 'demonstrates' which implies that God's love for us is ongoing and never ending and uses the word 'died' which is a one-time, once and for all action that will not be repeated. What is the significance here? God wants us to know that His love is not just a one-time event. Nothing can separate us from His everlasting love. Through Him we have the hope of eternal life. Be strong, God will see you through the tough times and you will reign with Him forever.

**Acknowledge** – God, You demonstrate Your love for us each day.

**Confess** – Lord, forgive me when I doubt Your love for me.

**Thanksgiving** – Lord, thank You for sending Your Son to die for my sins.

**Prayer** – Lord, thank You that I can have hope in the face of trials and tribulations because of Your love for me.

# Day 92

Psalm 35:18 I will give You thanks in the great assembly; among the throngs I will praise You.

WHERE DOES IT SOUND LIKE DAVID IS OFFERING HIS PRAISE TO GOD? Obviously, he is in the temple or a place of worship with fellow believers giving thanks. It is important to offer God praise throughout the day expressing your love to Him. In fact, 1 Thessalonians 5:16-17 states, 'Be joyful always; pray continually; give thanks in all circumstances, for this is God's will for you in Christ Jesus.' Philippians 4:6 tells us, 'Do not be anxious about anything, but in everything, by prayer and petition, with thanksgiving, present your requests to God.' However, there is something powerful when praising God with other believers. You might say I don't have anything to praise God for right now or I don't feel like going to church. I can get just as much from watching a sermon online or on TV. Yes, you may receive the word of God, but you are missing out on the power that comes from a room full of people worshiping God. The energy and excitement in the air can make a great difference in the experience. We have had the opportunity of worshiping at Brooklyn Tabernacle in New York. We have also downloaded the Brooklyn tabernacle app and have watched many of Pastor Cymbala's sermons. There is no comparison to sitting among several thousand people singing and worshiping God. Tears were streaming down my face as we sang praises to God. I could sense the power of the Holy Spirit moving in the congregation. I have witnessed the same presence of the Holy Spirit in my own church. The good news is that this same experience is taking place in hundreds of thousands of churches across the world. People are gathering together to worship and give thanks to God. Matthew 18:20 assures us, 'For where two or three gather in My name, there am I with them.' Get together with other believers. Give thanks and sing praises to His name in the sanctuary. When you worship with others, enjoy His presence and the peace that surpasses all understanding.

**Acknowledge** – God, You desire our worship.

**Confess** – Lord, forgive me when I don't feel like worshiping with others.

**Thanksgiving** – Lord, thank You that we have the freedom to worship You freely without fear of persecution.

**Prayer** – Lord, don't let Your church become a social gathering, let it be a place of worship.

# Day 93

Psalm 35:28 My tongue will proclaim Your righteousness, Your praises all day long.

WE GENERALLY LIKE TO TALK ABOUT THINGS WE KNOW ABOUT OR have interest in. I have to admit, talking about the Lord's righteousness and goodness doesn't flow in my conversations as it should. I don't find myself proclaiming His praises either. How much better my conversations might go if I did. There are some who have the ability to speak about the goodness of the Lord in any type of situation. What a blessing to be able to do so. When something good happens to us, how hard would it be to tell someone how God blessed you? When a friend is going through a difficult situation, can you tell them how God brought you through something similar? As you proclaim His goodness to others, your eyes will be opened even more of His work in your life. You will come to realize the little things you once may have thought were just coincidence, are His hand of providence in your life. Our first grandson, Walker, was born several weeks early and his lungs had not fully developed. He spent two weeks in the NICU Unit and had several touch and go moments. We spent many hours praying for his recovery and God was faithful. He is now a healthy young boy. Was his healing just coincidence or was God at work in his life? We know that God brought him through and it was something we could confidently share with others. Open your eyes to see His righteousness and His goodness working in your life. Once you do, you will want to tell others about Him. We didn't have a hard time sharing about God's goodness when our grandson was healed. Let the words of the chorus of Bethel Music's song, 'Goodness of God' speak to you today. "And all my life You have been faithful, And all my life You have been so, so good, With every breath that I am able, Oh, I will sing of the goodness of God." He has been faithful to you, proclaim His goodness to others.

**Acknowledge** – God, You are righteous and holy.

**Confess** – Lord, forgive me when I don't speak of Your goodness and righteousness as I should.

**Thanksgiving** – Lord, thank You for Your faithfulness to me, I will sing of Your goodness to me.

**Prayer** – Lord, I pray that the words of my mouth and the meditation of my heart will be acceptable in Your sight.

# Day 94

**Psalm 36:1** I have a message from God in my heart concerning the sinfulness of the wicked. There is no fear of God before their eyes.

David makes it clear that the wicked have no love or respect for God. The story of Jesus' crucifixion found in Luke 22:39-43 tells of two criminals who were crucified on either side of Jesus. One of the criminals hurled insults at Jesus saying, 'Aren't You the Christ? Save Yourself and us!' Think about the pain and agony this man was in. Yet, he mocked Jesus right along with the others who were attending the crucifixion. Verses 36-37 tell us, 'The soldiers also came up and mocked Him. They offered Him wine vinegar and said, 'He saved others; let Him save Himself if He is the Christ of God, the Chosen One.' Obviously, they didn't believe Jesus was the Messiah. They had no fear of God or remorse for their sins. If they had, their attitude would have been like the other criminal who rebuked the first criminal saying, 'Don't you fear God, since you are under the same sentence? We are punished justly, for we are getting what we deserve. But this man has done nothing wrong. Jesus, remember me when You come into Your kingdom.' What a contrast of two people sentenced to die for their crimes. One went to his grave defiant, unconcerned about his sin, and its consequences. The other repented of his sins, put his faith and trust in Jesus, and received eternal life with the Father. We are all sinners, condemned to die. If not for the cruel death suffered by our Savior, Jesus Christ, and His resurrection our fate would have been the same as the first criminal. Have you confessed your sins and asked for forgiveness? Have you asked Him into your life to change you and fill you with His Spirit? Don't go to your grave facing the consequences of your sin. It is never too late, your sin is not too great for God to forgive you and make you His child. He loves you!

**Acknowledge** – Lord, Your message to the wicked is forgiveness and grace for those who seek it.

**Confess** – Lord, forgive me when I, like the criminal on the cross, mock You with my actions and my words.

**Thanksgiving** – Lord, thank You that no sin is too great to separate me from Your love.

**Prayer** – Lord, I pray that I will love, honor, respect, and obey You.

# Day 95

Psalm 36:5 Your love, Lord reaches to the heavens, Your faithfulness to the skies.

How do you measure the love of God? David attempted by saying it reaches to the heavens. How far is it to the heavens? In David's day, it would have been an impossible journey. Even today, space travel is difficult and takes a lot of time to reach the closest of planets to the earth. The contemporary Christian group, Third Day, wrote about the vastness of God's love. The song is entitled 'Your Love, Oh Lord.' The lyrics go, 'Your love, oh Lord, Reaches to the heavens, Your faithfulness stretches to the sky, Your righteousness is like the mighty mountains, Your justice flows like the ocean's tide. I will lift my voice, To worship You, my King, I will find my strength in the shadows of Your wings.' In Ephesians 3:14-21, Paul writes a prayer to the Ephesians for their understanding of God's love. It is a beautiful prayer, full of power and promise. Let this be your prayer today. 'For this reason I kneel before the Father, from whom this whole family in heaven and on earth derives its name. I pray that out of His glorious riches He may strengthen you with power through His Spirit in your inner being, so that Christ may dwell in your hearts through faith. And I pray that you, being rooted and established in love, may have power, together with all the saints to grasp how wide and long and high and deep is the love of Christ, and to know this love that surpasses knowledge – that you may be filled to the measure of all the fullness of God. Now to Him who is able to do immeasurably more than all we ask or imagine, according to His power that is at work within us, to Him be the glory in the church and in Christ Jesus throughout all generations, for ever and ever! Amen.' Start trying to grasp how wide and long and high and deep is the love of Christ.

**Acknowledge** – Lord, Your love reaches to the heavens, Your faithfulness to the skies.

**Confess** – Lord, forgive me when I worry about the insignificant things of life and forget about Your love and faithfulness to me.

**Thanksgiving** – Lord, thank You that Your love has no boundaries.

**Prayer** – Lord, I put my delight in You. Help me grasp how long, how wide, how high, how deep is Your love for me.

# Day 96

Psalm 37:7 Be still before the Lord and wait patiently for Him; do not fret when people succeed in their ways, when they carry out their wicked schemes.

PSALMS 37 IS PACKED WITH GODLY WISDOM ABOUT THE GREAT riddle of life, the prosperity of the wicked and the affliction of the righteous. Today we are told by David to wait patiently for the Lord, while the wicked seem to be prospering around us. Patience is a virtue that we have very little of these days. Sitting in traffic or drive-through window lines can be exhausting. When we look around today, doesn't it seem like the ungodly are winning. Maybe it is someone who got the promotion you were hoping for. Or is it the family who doesn't go to church that has the big house, nice boat, and expensive vehicles? Maybe it is the politician who has accumulated great wealth and power while seemingly doing nothing to benefit the people. The list goes on of the people who don't seem to love or follow God, but seem to be doing well. Verse eight tells us, 'Refrain from anger and turn from wrath; do not fret – it only leads to evil.' In Exodus, the children of Israel are leaving Egypt and the bondage they suffered after 400 years of slavery. They are trapped between the Red Sea and the Egyptians who are in hot pursuit. Did they fret and complain? Of course. Did they want to wait? Of course not. What did Moses tell them, 'Do not be afraid. Stand firm and you will see the deliverance of the Lord will bring you today. The Egyptians you see today, you will never see again. The Lord will fight for you; you need only to be still.' (Exodus 14:13-14) What areas of your life are you fretting and complaining about? Do you need to stand firm, be still, and wait patiently and trust God? You can trust Him to see you through difficult seasons of your life. Wait on Him.

**Acknowledge** – Lord, You are in control, I need to wait patiently for You.

**Confess** – Lord, forgive me when I try to take matters into my own hands. Forgive me for fretting when evil people succeed.

**Thanksgiving** – Lord, thank You that You are there, that You love me.

**Prayer** – Lord, help me to be patient, to learn to wait on You, to be still, and allow You to lead me.

# Day 97

**Psalm 37:16** Better the little that the righteous have than the wealth of many wicked.

In today's world, we tend to associate happiness with wealth and possessions. I have had the privilege to go on several mission trips to Nicaragua. Our family has partnered with a ministry that supports a small community outside of Managua called Los Brasiles. This small community is home to several hundred families. The streets are unpaved, and many of the houses are constructed out of any scrap material that can be found. Food is prepared over a wood fire. There are very few bathrooms with sewer and running water. However, in the middle of this community is a preschool and after school facility started by our friend Coburn Murray. It is a refuge for over a hundred children where they are taught about Jesus, receive tutoring and a meal. The children we have met are always smiling and happy. They can pick up a flat soccer ball and play with it for hours. They have rice and beans every day for lunch, and do not complain and are happy to get it. They wear uniforms to school which consists of a white shirt and navy-blue pants. No matter how hard they play and how dirty they get, their clothes are clean and fresh the next day. Their lives really put into perspective the vast wealth that we have. They are very satisfied with what they have and are not putting themselves deep in debt to accumulate worldly possessions. As today's verse points out, we are better off with what we have rather than chasing after the wealth of others. Do you have peace and contentment in your life today? Are you investing in the kingdom of God? Or, are you chasing after things you really can't afford? Be careful, listen, and follow God's instructions. This is not to say having nice things is a sin, but allow God to bless you with them instead of chasing after them. Don't miss out on God's blessings.

**Acknowledge** – Lord, our inheritance will endure forever. You will uphold the righteous.

**Confess** – Lord, forgive me when I worry about money and possessions. Everything I have is Yours.

**Thanksgiving** – Lord, thank You for Your provision in my life.

**Prayer** – Lord, we can't take anything with us when we die. Let me invest in Your kingdom and Your work where my future lies.

# Day 98

**Psalm 37:23** The Lord makes firm the steps of the one who delights in Him.

WHAT DOES DAVID MEAN BY THE WORD 'STEPS'? HERE HE IS TALKING about the path of life. God didn't plan for us to drift aimlessly through life, without a purpose. When we accepted Christ as our Savior, He not only saved us, but had a plan for our lives. Paul writes in Romans 8:14, 'For all who are led by the Spirit of God are children of God.' He leads us, He opens doors for us. I can attest to God's faithfulness in directing steps. In the early 1980's I was working as an Accounting Supervisor for CP&L in Garner, NC. An Area Manager position had come open in the Fuquay Varina Office. I interviewed for the job and was very disappointed when I didn't get the position. However, little did I know that God was working on a plan that would work out much better for our family. Six months later I was offered the Area Manager position in Johnston County. This put Vivian and I near her family. It was a much better place for us. As David tells us, His plans are 'firm' and they are 'directed.' He loves you enough to plan out every step of your life. If you read the next verse, you will discover that our steps will likely take us through some rocky ground. However, He is there to steady us and to hold us with His strong hand. Jeremiah 29:11 tells us about God's plan for us, 'For I know the plans I have for you, declares the Lord, plans to prosper and not harm you, plans to give you hope and a future.' What is your hope and future? Is your hope based on God's plans for you? Or, are you wandering aimlessly through life? I hope you are relying on the One who makes our steps firm. Solomon in Proverbs 3:5-6 tells us, 'Trust in the Lord with all your heart and lean not on your own understanding, in all your ways submit to Him, and He will make your paths straight.' Ask God to order your steps each day.

**Acknowledge** – Lord, You order our steps, You direct our paths.

**Confess** – Lord, forgive me for straying off Your path, Your plan for my life.

**Thanksgiving** – Lord, thank You for your plan for my life.

**Prayer** – Lord, help me to look forward, not backward. Help me to trust Your plan for my life.

# Day 99

Psalm 37:30 The mouths of the righteous utter wisdom, and his tongue speaks what is just.

WHAT TYPE OF WORDS COMES FROM YOUR MOUTH? DO YOU SPEAK negatively of things in your life such as your family, your job, your friends, and your appearance? Or do you use positive words, words that heal or that encourage? Words are very powerful. They have the power to restore, heal and inspire. They also have the power to hurt, to destroy, and to curse. Do you wish you could redo a conversation? In Proverbs 15:2, Solomon speaking about the tongue says, 'The tongue of the wise adorns knowledge, but the mouth of the fool gushes folly.' The wise and the righteous apply wisdom and knowledge before speaking. The foolish just seem to babble on about anything and everything. Where do our words come from? Luke 6:45 tells us, 'The good person out of the good treasure of the heart produces good, and the evil person out of the evil treasure produces evil; for it is out of the abundance of the heart that the mouth speaks.' What is in your heart? Are you harboring bitterness, envy, or hatred from your past? Are these past experiences driving your conversations? Are you stuck in a cycle of negativity? Give your past to God. Ask Him to remove those feelings you are harboring. Ask Him to replace those feelings with love, joy, peace, patience, goodness, kindness, gentleness, faithfulness, and self-control. Ask Him to guard your conversations, as Paul told the Ephesians in chapter 4 verse 29, 'Do not let any unwholesome talk come out of your mouths, but only what is helpful for building others up according to their needs, that it might benefit those who listen.' Use your words to speak wisdom and speak justly. Use your words to build rather than destroy. Use your words to encourage rather than to tear down. Choose your words wisely. Your friends and family will notice the difference.

**Acknowledge** – Lord, our words are powerful.

**Confess** – Lord, forgive me for allowing negative thoughts to influence my conversations and saying something hastily in anger.

**Thanksgiving** – Lord, thank You for giving us wisdom to choose the right words to say.

**Prayer** – Lord, please fill my heart with love, joy, peace, patience, goodness, kindness, gentleness, faithfulness, and self-control. I want my conversations to be filled with words that encourage and build.

# Day 100

Psalm 37:39 The salvation of the righteous comes from the Lord; He is their stronghold in time of trouble.

Psalms 37 assures us of our salvation. If I were to ask you, 'Are you saved?' How would you respond? Would you answer by saying, 'yes'? Or perhaps, 'I think so or I don't know for sure,' or maybe 'no'. Do you want to confidently say, 'yes'? 1 John 5:13 tells us, 'I write these things to you who believe in the name of the Son of God so that you may know that you have eternal life.' John tells us that it is possible to know we are saved. Questioning our faith can help serve as a checkpoint in our lives. Our salvation begins when we, by faith, accept Jesus Christ as our Lord and Savior. We acknowledge that Jesus Christ, the Son of God, was crucified, died, buried, and rose on the third day to purchase our salvation. John 3:16, "For God so loved the world, that He gave His one and only Son, that whoever believes in Him shall not perish but have eternal life.' The true test of our salvation is whether we have been transformed into God's image. 1 John 2:3-6 tells us, 'We know that we have come to know Him if we obey His commands. The man who says I know Him, but does not do what He commands is a liar, and the truth is not in him. But if anyone obeys His word, God's love is truly made complete in him: Whoever claims to live in Him must walk as Jesus did.' The goal should be to live as God commanded. We will stray from time to time, but our desire should be to live as He commanded. Secondly, we should love others. 1 John 3:14 tells us, 'We know that we have passed from death to life, because we love our brothers. Anyone who does not love remains in death.' Do you love others? 1 John 3:10 says, 'Anyone who believes in the Son of God has this testimony in his heart. Anyone who does not believe God has made Him out to be a liar.' Are you living for God each day?

**Acknowledge** – Lord, You are our salvation and our stronghold.

**Confess** – Lord, forgive me when I fall away and fail to keep Your commands.

**Thanksgiving** – Lord, thank You for being our salvation.

**Prayer** – Lord, help me to live for You each day. Help me to share Your love.

# Day 101

**Psalm 38:1** Lord, do not rebuke me in Your anger or discipline me in Your wrath.

I RECALL A TIME WHEN MY YOUNGER SISTER AND I HAD GOTTEN INTO trouble. My mother was getting her switch ready to spank us. My sister, full of wisdom said, 'run Charlie, she can't catch you.' Two steps later, my feet were dangling from the ground with a switch connecting with my bottom. I learned the hard way that my mother was much faster than we thought. I was blessed to have parents who loved me enough to correct my behavior when I got off track. We have a heavenly Father who loves us and disciplines us. Proverbs 3:11-12 tells us, 'My son, do not despise the Lord's discipline and do not resent His rebuke, because the Lord disciplines those He loves, as a father the son He delights in.' Why would a loving God discipline us? Would it surprise you that He uses discipline as a last resort? Could it be that He is trying to get us to listen to Him, to repent of sin in our life, or to prevent us from hurting ourselves? The writer of Hebrews addresses the Lord's discipline in more detail in chapter 12:7-11. 'Endure hardship as discipline; God is treating you as sons. For what son is not disciplined by his father? If you are not disciplined (and everyone undergoes discipline), then you are illegitimate children and not true sons. Moreover, we have all had human fathers who disciplined us and we respected them for it. How much more should we submit to the Father of our spirits and live. Our fathers disciplined us for a little while as they thought best; but God disciplines us for our good, that we may share in His holiness. No discipline seems pleasant at the time, but painful. Later on, however, it produces a harvest of righteousness and peace for those who have been trained by it.' The Lord's discipline is to make us more like Him. Thankfully, His discipline is done in love.

**Acknowledge** – Lord, You discipline Your children.

**Confess** – Lord, forgive me for when I have strayed away and need Your loving discipline to bring me back.

**Thanksgiving** – Lord, thank You that Your punishment is not out of anger or wrath, but that of a loving Father.

**Prayer** – Lord, help me to avoid the sin that so easily entangles my life and run with perseverance the race You have marked out for me.

# Day 102

Psalm 38:9 All my longings lie open before You Lord; my sighing is not hidden from You.

We have gotten very good at hiding our feelings and emotions from those around us. We pass by people and when asked, 'How's it going?' our typical response is 'Things are good, thanks for asking.' While on the inside things are not so good. We tend to hide our feelings and problems that are overwhelming us on the inside. Why? The reason is because we think we have everything under control and can manage the situation. Or, it might be that we are embarrassed. Or, perhaps the person asking is just trying to be nice and really doesn't care to hear our troubles because they have enough of their own. No matter the reason, we tend to keep things to ourselves until we can't hold them in any longer. We wait until things get so bad; we have no other choice but to tell someone else. But wait, what does today's verse tell us? All the emotions, the worries, the disappointments are an open book to the Lord. He knows what you are going through. He hears the cries of your heart, the ones that don't even make it out of your mouth. He understands the pain, the sorrow, and the anguish of your situation. In fact, He knew you in your mother's womb, He watches over you every day. Your entire life is known to Him. The good news is that He loves you and wants to heal you. He is not waiting for you to find the right words, the perfect prayer, or the right moment to talk to Him. Open your heart to Him. Even if the words don't come, your groaning and sighing are known to Him. He can interpret your tears. Open your heart and let the prayers flow to Him. He wants to hear from you today.

**Acknowledge** – Lord, my inner most thoughts are known by You.

**Confess** – Lord, forgive me for when I try to fix things on my own, when I try to keep my problems all bottled up inside.

**Thanksgiving** – Lord, I thank You that my cries for help are not hidden from You.

**Prayer** – We are frail creatures who need a Lord and Savior. You are our strength, our shield, our fortress.

# Day 103

Psalm 38:15 Lord, I wait for You; You will answer, Lord my God.

David seems to be all about waiting. As a young boy, he spent many hours in the fields tending his father's sheep. First, David would have to move the sheep to the right pasture, and wait hours for them to graze. After eating he would move the flock to a slow-moving stream for them to drink. Later, he would move the flock to a safe place to stay the evening. David had time to think, to plan, and to wonder about God and His creation. Although he had distractions, his life wasn't filled with the clutter and noise we have added to our lives today. I am referring to the demand of our time brought on by the use of technology. Technology has so permeated our lives that we can't function without it. Almost everyone has a smartphone. I read a statistic that there are 3.5 billion smartphone users in the world. (www.oberlo.com) I was surprised to find on our mission trips to Nicaragua that many Nicaraguans, even the poorest, had cell phones. I also read where the average American adult spends nearly three hours a day on their mobile device. This small device that fits in your pocket can be a blessing or a curse. It is a great tool for keeping your Bible at your fingertips. However, if you allow it, it can consume you and make you its slave. How much time are you spending on your phone each day? Is your prayer time competing with Facebook? Are you replacing the time you used to spend reading God's word with reading emails and tweets? Would you be able to hear God answer when He speaks to you? Has your device drowned out the voice of God? If so, you need to make some changes in your lifestyle. Give God first place in your life, not brief moments in between text messages and SnapChat. Commit to spending uninterrupted time with Him. Wait for Him, He will show up.

**Acknowledge** – Lord, You always answer our prayers.

**Confess** – Lord, forgive me for allowing technology to crowd out the time I should be spending with You.

**Thanksgiving** – Lord, I thank You for answering our prayers. Sometimes You seem far away or slow to respond, but You are always on time.

**Prayer** – Lord, You are always with us, slow to anger, abounding in love. Help me to wait patiently for Your answer to my prayers.

# Day 104

Psalm 39:12 Hear my prayer, Lord, listen to my cry for help; be not deaf to my weeping, I dwell with You as a foreigner, a stranger, as all my ancestors were.

HAVE YOU BEEN WHERE DAVID IS TODAY? HAVE YOU STARTED OUT by offering up a simple prayer for God to do something in your life? Then as the days go by, nothing seems to be happening so your prayers intensify to a cry for help. I have been there. Each day brought about new twists and complications to my situation. The more I seemed to pray, the opposite of what I was praying for happened. Things seemed to get worse instead of better. The more difficult and complicated they got, the more intense my prayers. It took almost a year for God to calm my fears and answer my prayers. We reach out to the Lord to tell Him our pain. We start out, 'Lord, hear my prayer.' Quickly our prayer changes to 'Lord, listen to my cry for help.' When the pain doesn't stop or the healing doesn't take place, weeping overtakes us and we pray 'Lord, please do not be deaf to my weeping. Hear me Lord, please help me.' Cling to Him through the pain. Hold on to Him as you travel this path of grief and heartache. He may feel like a thousand miles away, but He is with you. Earlier in Psalm 30:5, David writes, '...weeping may last for a night, but rejoicing comes in the morning.' You may be going through a long, dark, cold night right now. Hold on, because rejoicing will come in the morning. Even though you feel like a stranger to God, a foreigner in a strange land where you don't know the language, He hears you and knows what is hurting your heart right now. One day you will be able to look back and tell everyone what God has done for you. So, hold fast, joy comes in the morning because He is our hope, He is our answer.

**Acknowledge** – Lord, You hear our prayers and listen to our cries to You.

**Confess** – Lord, forgive me when I doubt your love for me. Forgive me when I feel far away from You.

**Thanksgiving** – Lord, I thank You for hearing and answering our prayers.

**Prayer** – Lord, help me to trust You and Your timing for I know that joy comes in the morning.

# Day 105

Psalm 40:3 He put a new song in my mouth, a hymn of praise to our God. Many will see and fear the Lord and put their trust in Him.

When I was a child, the only Christian music I heard or sang was from the Broadman Hymnal and children's choruses like, 'This Little Light of Mine.' We sang a lot of great hymns that I can still remember. As I got older, contemporary Christian music started to blossom with artists such as Dallas Holmes and Amy Grant. Now there is a wide variety of Christian music and artists. I am amazed at the new songs that continually come out. Just when I think the music has plateaued, another song will be released that speaks to my heart. These are songs that after hearing them, replay in my mind. When I am down, a song will come to mind and lift my spirits. When I get frustrated or angry, a song will come to mind and calm me down. When I am feeling good, a song will come to mind and take me to a place of worship. I love to worship God through song with others. Have you ever wondered why there is always singing before the pastor shares the word of God? Why do we invest so much time in worship through song? There are several reasons; the first is that music unites us. Secondly, it changes our perspective on things, shifting our focus to God's faithfulness to us. Lastly, it prepares us to hear the word of God. And as David points out in this Psalm, those who witness a congregation full of people praising and worshiping God through song will be drawn to Him. They will want the freedom, the peace, and the joy that accompanies worship. Has God put a new song in your heart today? Do you find yourself singing to Him? I hope that you can find the comfort, the peace, and the joy that comes with singing a new song to your Creator.

**Acknowledge** – Lord, You put a new song in our heart when we gave our life to You.

**Confess** – Lord, forgive me when I don't feel like worshiping You in song.

**Thanksgiving** – Lord, I thank You for creating music and giving people the talent to write and produce music.

**Prayer** – Lord, help me worship You through music. Put a new song in my heart each day.

# Day 106

**Psalm 40:6** Sacrifice and offering You did not desire. But my ears You have opened; burnt offerings and sin offerings You did not require.

IN OLD TESTAMENT TIMES, GOD SET UP A SYSTEM OF SACRIFICES AND offerings for the people to follow. This same system of sacrifices was still being followed by David. Ultimately, the sacrifices in the Old Testament lead us to the perfect and final sacrifice of Jesus Christ. However, until Jesus died for our sins, the sacrificial system remained in place. Why do you think David said that God did not desire his sacrifice and offerings? Was God changing the rules? The answer can be found in 1 Samuel 15:22. We find Saul, who was King of Israel before David, had just defeated the Amalekites. Saul was told to destroy everything that belonged to the Amalekites, but he kept some of the best sheep and cattle. Samuel arrives at Saul's camp and asks about the animals. Saul tells him they were kept to offer as sacrifices to the Lord for the victory. Samuel's reply is in verse 22, 'Does the Lord delight in burnt offerings and sacrifices as much as in obeying the voice of the Lord? To obey is better than sacrifice, and to heed is better than the fat of rams.' What do you think the Lord would rather have: our obedience or our sacrifices? He wants our obedience. In Psalm 40:8, David said, 'I desire to do Your will, O my God; Your law is written on my heart.' We may not offer up animal or grain sacrifices today, but there are other ways in which we offer sacrifices. Are we like Saul thinking we are doing a good thing with the sacrifice we are making, but find out that is not what God wants of us? We may put too much emphasis on our service to God, rather than our obedience to Him. Ask God to show you those areas and move towards obedience.

**Acknowledge** – Lord, You desire our obedience over sacrifices and offerings.

**Confess** – Lord, forgive me when I become selfish with my time and resources and when my service to You comes more out of duty rather than love for You.

**Thanksgiving** – Lord, thank You for making the ultimate sacrifice to pay the penalty for my sin.

**Prayer** – Lord, help me to walk in obedience to Your will for my life.

# Day 107

Psalm 40:16 But may all who seek You rejoice and be glad in You; may those who love Your saving help always say, "The Lord is great."

How great is the Lord? Jeremiah 10:6 says, 'There is none like You, O Lord; You are great, and great is Your name in might.' 1 Chronicles 16:25 states, 'For great is the Lord, and greatly to be praised; He also is to be feared above all gods.' And later in 1 Chronicles 29:11, 'Yours, O Lord, is the greatness and the power and the glory and the victory and the majesty, indeed everything that is in the heavens and the earth; Yours is the dominion, O Lord, and You exalt Yourself as head over all.' In these verses we learn that God's name contains great power and is to be reverenced above all things. He has sovereignty over the heavens and the earth including every aspect of your life. He knows every detail about you. He even knows the number of hairs on your head. Luke 12:7, 'Indeed, the very hairs of your head are all numbered. Don't be afraid; you are worth more than many sparrows.' This great and mighty God loves you. We should rejoice and praise Him all day long. Soak in the words of this old hymn written by Fanny J. Crosby, "Praise Him! Praise Him! Jesus, our Blessed Redeemer." 'Praise Him! Praise Him! Jesus, our blessed Redeemer! Sing, ye saints! His wonderful love proclaim! Hail Him! Hail Him! Mightiest angels in glory; Strength and honor give to His holy name! Like a shepherd, Jesus will feed His people, In His arms He carries them all day long; O ye saints that live in the light of His presence, Praise Him! Praise Him! Ever in joyful song! (V2) Praise Him, Praise Him, Jesus our blessed Redeemer, for our sins He suffered and bled and died; He our rock, our hope of eternal salvation, Hail Him! Hail Him! Jesus the Crucified. Loving Savior, meekly enduring sorrow, Crowned with thorns that cruelly pierced His brow; Once for us rejected, despised and forsaken, Prince of Glory, ever triumphant now.' Give God praise today because of His greatness.

**Acknowledge** – Lord, You are great and greatly to be praised.

**Confess** – Lord, forgive me when I fail to see Your hand working in my life.

**Thanksgiving** – Lord, thank You for Your love and faithfulness to us.

**Prayer** – Lord, You have numbered the very hairs on my head. I am in awe of Your love for me.

# Day 108

Psalm 41:1 Blessed are those who have regard for the weak; the Lord delivers them in times of trouble.

As you read this verse, substitute the word 'poor' in place of 'weak' as some translations do. The following are a few verses from Proverbs on the subject of helping the poor. Proverbs 22:9, 'The generous will themselves be blessed, for they share their food with the poor.' 14:31, 'Whoever oppresses the poor shows contempt for their Maker, but whoever is kind to the needy honors God.' 28:27, 'Those who give to the poor will lack nothing, but those who close their eyes to them receive many curses.' 21:13, 'Whoever shuts their ears to the cry of the poor will also cry out and not be answered.' This sample should be enough verses for us to get the message. God makes it very clear that we should help the poor. So, how do we know who to help and how to help them? There is no set answer on how to know who to help. My recommendation on who and how to help is simple. Listen to God. Ask Him to show you who to help and how you can help them. He will open a door for you to help someone. It could be something simple as providing a gift card, a meal, transportation, or even buying some groceries. God will bless you for your faithfulness in helping the poor. Also, as today's verse points out, we may later find ourselves in a similar situation. When we are, God will carry us through those hard times. Listen to God, act on His leading. You will enjoy the blessing of helping someone. I close with Acts 20:35, 'In everything I did, I showed you that by this kind of hard work we must help the weak, remembering the words the Lord Jesus himself said: "It is more blessed to give than to receive." Find someone you can help.

**Acknowledge** – Blessed are those who have regard for the poor.

**Confess** – Lord, forgive me for being selfish and not wanting to help someone in need.

**Thanksgiving** – Lord, thank You for Your example of giving. You gave Your only Son.

**Prayer** – Lord, thank You for allowing me to be in a position to help the poor. I pray that my heart will be like Yours toward the poor and that I will be faithful to Your leading.

# Day 109

Psalm 41:6 When one of them comes to see me, he speaks falsely, while his heart gathers slander; he then goes out and spreads it around.

DAVID IS TALKING ABOUT HIS SO-CALLED FRIENDS WHO TELL HIM one thing while they are with him and then make up untrue stories and lies about him to others. The words of his so-called friends would lead him to believe they were compassionate and loving. However, their actions while away from David are completely opposite. Do you know someone like that? Are they friendly and nice to you in person, but spread gossip and lies about you to others? Do you feel like they have stabbed you in the back? What do you do when this happens? Do you confront the person or do you ignore the gossip and lies being told? Do you take steps to avoid being around that type of person? These are difficult questions with no right or wrong answers. Paul gives us some insight into this type of situation in 1 Corinthians 4:12-13, 'We work hard with our own hands. When we are cursed, we bless; when we are persecuted, we endure it; when we are slandered, we answer kindly. Up to this moment we have become the scum of the earth, the refuse of the world.' Ask God for wisdom on how to deal with a situation you may be facing. Ask Him to give you the confidence and courage to keep a positive and healthy self-image. Ask Him to lead you to conversations that allow you to answer kindly when correcting the lies being told. Ask Him for the strength to handle the gossip and lies and not let them control you. We live in an imperfect world with imperfect people who may take every opportunity to make us look bad in order to make themselves look good. Seek God and ask for His guidance when you find yourself the object of someone's gossip. Ask yourself, 'What Would Jesus Do' and allow Him to direct your paths.

**Acknowledge** –Lord, You faced the lies and gossip about Yourself when You were here on earth.

**Confess** – Lord, forgive me when I spread rumors and false stories about someone else.

**Thanksgiving** – Lord, thank You for Your word about human nature and Your example of how to deal with those who hate You.

**Prayer** – Lord, let the words of my mouth and the meditation of my heart be acceptable in Your sight, oh Lord, my Rock and my Redeemer.

# Day 110

Psalm 41:12 Because of my integrity You will uphold me and set me in Your presence forever.

DAVID GIVES US INSIGHT INTO HOW HE RESPONDED TO THE LIES being told about him. Notice that he didn't go on the attack against those who were speaking untruths about him, or worry if others believed the lies or not. David speaks of his integrity. What is integrity? It is defined as the quality of being honest and having strong moral principles; moral uprightness. David lets his character and his actions speak for him. He is confident that God will uphold him because of the way he has handled himself. 1 Peter 3:16 tells us, 'Keeping a clear conscience, so that those who speak maliciously against your good behavior in Christ may be ashamed of their slander.' David wasn't perfect; however, he always turned to God and trusted Him. In 1 Samuel 24 we find a story that speaks of David's integrity. Saul was chasing after David to kill him. Saul had gone into a cave by himself where David and his men were hiding. David had the opportunity to kill Saul, but didn't. David's men even urged him to kill Saul. Instead of attacking, David snuck up and cut off a piece of Saul's robe. Why didn't David kill Saul? He answers that question in 1 Samuel 24:6, 'The Lord forbid that I should do such a thing to my master, the Lord's anointed, or lift my hand against him; for he is the anointed of the Lord.' David had several opportunities to take Saul's life but didn't. Even in the toughest of times, David's character didn't waver. He put in trust in God to take care of him and to protect him from Saul. He does the same with those who were spreading lies about him. Where do you stand on the integrity scale? Do you stick to your beliefs and moral principles when difficult times arrive? Would you have taken a shortcut? These questions may only be answered when the opportunity arises. I hope you can find the confidence in God that David had to trust Him through every situation you may face.

**Acknowledge** –Lord, You will uphold me and place me in Your presence.

**Confess** – Lord, forgive me when I hold a grudge against someone or try to fix things on my own.

**Thanksgiving** – Lord, thank You that our actions can speak louder than words.

**Prayer** – Lord, let me look to You for justice when someone is telling lies about me.

# Day 111

Psalm 42:1 As the deer pants for streams of water, so my soul pants for You my God.

You may recognize today's verse as the praise and worship song written by Martin Nystrom. The lyrics go, 'As the deer panteth for the water, so my soul longs after You, You alone are my heart's desire, And I long to worship You. You alone are my strength my, shield. To You alone may my spirit yield. You alone are my heart's desire and I long to worship You.' Have you ever been so thirsty that a sip of cool water is the best thing you have ever tasted? How did your body respond when you took that sip of water? Did it refresh and renew you? What is the longest you have gone without something to drink? The human body can only last about three to four days without water. We need water to survive. As the Psalmist is saying today, we also need God's presence in our lives to survive. Have you ever been thirsty for God's presence? Have you panted for God's presence as the deer pants for water, or do you just want a sip every now and then? Our lives have become so crowded with activities, that we run from here to there and never stop long enough to enjoy the moment. We let our activities control us. How do we stop the madness and slow down the world? While easier said than done, it becomes a matter of priorities. Deep down, does your soul long to know God and spend more time with Him? If so, make time for Him. Give up something else that has no lasting value to spend time with God. What does Jesus teach us in Matthew 5:6? 'Blessed are those who hunger and thirst for righteousness, for they will be filled.' Jesus promises you will not regret it, for you will be filled. He will replace the emptiness, the hopelessness, and the frustration with His joy and peace. Start panting for God today.

**Acknowledge** –Lord, my priority should be seeking You each day.

**Confess** – Lord, forgive me when I let the busyness of life prevent me from seeking You.

**Thanksgiving** – Lord, thank You for being a living God, one who is real, one who will meet with us.

**Prayer** – Lord, my prayer is that I will hunger and thirst after You each day as the deer pants for the water.

# Day 112

Psalm 43:4 Then I will go to the altar of God, to God, my joy and delight. I will praise You with the lyre O God, my God.

To better understand where David is, we need to start at verse one where he is asking God to vindicate him. He goes on to ask God to guide him and bring him to His Holy mountain where the temple is located. Despite his troubles, David would prefer to be where God is rather than have help solving his problems. Why? Because David knows that being in the presence of God makes his problems seem small and insignificant. He acknowledges this is where his joy and delight reside. Several days ago, we learned about the types of sacrifices commanded by God that were offered on the altar at the temple. These sacrifices were replaced by the sacrifice of Jesus Christ on the cross, whose blood has covered our sins. He has become our altar, our place of worship. Isn't it wonderful to know that we don't have to travel thousands of miles to an altar to be in the presence of God? Because of Jesus' sacrifice, we can come to Him no matter where we are. Why is this so important? Consider David's desire to be in God's presence. First, being in God's presence brought him great joy and delight. Have you experienced the joy and delight of being in God's presence? If not, stop today and seek Him. Start at the foot of the cross where Jesus died. Secondly, when David's problems overwhelmed him, they were made insignificant in God's presence. Have you found peace from this world's problems? Paul writes in Philippians 4:7, 'And the peace of God, which transcends all understanding, will guard your hearts and minds in Christ Jesus.' The only place you can find peace is through Jesus Christ. He promises to guard your heart and mind. Ask Him to fill you with His presence and replace your problems with His peace.

**Acknowledge** – Lord, You are my joy and my delight.

**Confess** – Lord, forgive me when I seek after other things to give me relief from my problems instead of seeking after You.

**Thanksgiving** – Lord, thank You for guarding my heart and mind in Christ Jesus.

**Prayer** – Lord, my problems become insignificant when I enter into Your presence. Help me to seek You each day and ask You to guard my heart and mind.

# Day 113

Psalm 44:8 In God we make our boast all day long, and we will praise Your name forever.

WHAT IS BOASTING? IT IS EXCESSIVE PRIDE AND SELF-SATISFACTION about one's accomplishments. (www.oxfordlearnersdictionay.com) What does the Bible have to say about boasting? Jeremiah 9:23 tells us, 'This is what the Lord says: Don't let the wise boast in their wisdom, or the powerful boast in their power, or the rich boast in their riches.' And in James 4:16-17, 'As it is, you boast in your arrogant schemes. All such boasting is evil. If anyone, then, knows the good they ought to do and doesn't do it, it is sin for them.' Boasting about ourselves, our accomplishments, or our plans is sin. It takes the glory away from God and focuses it on us. It is only by God's grace and His power that we were able to accomplish the things we are boasting about. If it is a sin to boast, why is it okay for David to boast? Let's look at what David is boasting about. He is acknowledging God and giving Him the credit for the good things in his life. Paul writes in 1 Corinthians 1:31, 'Therefore, as it is written: Let him who boasts, boast in the Lord.' Later in 2 Corinthians 11:30 he writes, 'If I must boast, I will boast of the things that show my weakness.' In other words, we should act with humility, giving God the credit for the good things in our lives. Where are you today? Do you spend time boasting and drawing attention to yourself or do you give God the glory for His favor and provision? Think about the words you use. Are your conversations tempered with humility or pride? Try using words that encourage, approve, and affirm others. Are you following Jesus' example of humbly following God's plan for your life? At the end of the day can you, like David, say 'In God we make our boast all day long and we will praise Your name forever'?

**Acknowledge** –Lord, in You we make our boast every day.

**Confess** – Lord, forgive me for boasting about accomplishments that would not be possible without You.

**Thanksgiving** – Lord, thank You that we can boast in You all day long and praise Your name forever.

**Prayer** – Lord, let me not boast in myself, but boast in You.

# Day 114

**Psalm 44:13** You have made us a reproach to our neighbors, the scorn and derision of those around us.

Why would the Psalmist write that we are a reproach to our neighbors? Could our belief in God cause some people to not like us or even hate us? Unfortunately, this could very well happen. It is nothing new and will become more prevalent the closer we get to Jesus' return. Jesus, talking to his disciples in Mark 13, tells them what to look for at the end of the age. In verses 9-13 He tells us, 'Be on your guard. You will be handed over the local councils and flogged in the synagogues. On account of Me you will stand before governors and kings as witnesses to them. And the gospel must first be preached to all nations. Whenever you are arrested and brought to trial, do not worry beforehand about what to say. Just say whatever is given to you at the time, for it is not you speaking, but the Holy Spirit. Brother will betray brother to death, and a father his child. Children will rebel against their parents and have them put to death. All men will hate you because of Me, but he who stands firm to the end will be saved.' You might be thinking this is not a pleasant thought for today. Take heart, Jesus promised that your reward will be great and that you are blessed. Matthew 5:20-12 tells us, 'Blessed are those who are persecuted because of righteousness, for theirs is the kingdom of heaven. Blessed are you when people insult you, persecute you and falsely say all kinds of evil against you because of Me. Rejoice and be glad, because great is your reward in heaven, for in the same way they persecuted the prophets who were before you.' Be strong, stand firm in your belief, don't waver when things get tough or friends turn their back on you. Pray for them. Ask God to turn their hearts toward Him through your actions. Your life may be the only Bible they read.

**Acknowledge** –Lord, You were persecuted and hated by the world.

**Confess** – Lord, forgive me for wanting to be liked by the crowd more than I want to live for You.

**Thanksgiving** – Lord, thank You for showing us the way to endure to the end and sending Your Holy Spirit to guide and support us.

**Prayer** – Lord, help me to stand strong in Your word in the face of adversity and persecution.

# Day 115

Psalm 44:26 Rise up and help us; rescue us because of Your unfailing love.

WHAT A SIMPLE, SHORT, AND ALL-ENCOMPASSING PRAYER FOR US today when we need God's mercy in our life. David takes our 'Lord help me' prayer further by asking God to stand up and help us. I think he wanted to make sure the Lord was paying attention to his prayer. I don't think it was necessary for David to remind God of His love, but rather he, himself needed to be reminded of God's unfailing love. Thankfully, we have a Bible that is filled with verses which remind us of God's love. 1 John 3:1, 'See what great love the Father has lavished on us, that we should be called the children of God! And that is what we are! The reason the world does not know us is that it did not know Him.' Ephesians 2:4-5 tells us, 'But because of His great love for us, God, who is rich in mercy, made us alive with Christ even when we were dead in our transgressions – it is by grace you have been saved.' Romans 5:8, 'But God demonstrates His own love for us in this: While we were still sinners, Christ died for us.' God loves us and hears our prayers no matter how short or simple. He doesn't require words such as 'thee' or 'thou' from the King James Version of the Bible to gain His favor. Nor does He require us to go through some ritualistic chant to get His attention. Jesus gave us a model prayer in Matthew 6:9-13. 'Our Father, in heaven, hallowed be Your name, Your kingdom come, Your will be done, on earth as it is in heaven. Give us today our daily bread. Forgive us our debts as we forgive our debtors. And lead us not into temptation, but deliver us from the evil one.' Take time to pray each day. Ask God to energize your prayer life. Use the model He gave us and fill in more details where you feel it is needed. He loves you and wants to hear from you.

**Acknowledge** –Lord, You love us and hear our prayers, even the short ones.

**Confess** – Lord, forgive me when I don't trust Your love for me, when I fail to lift my burdens to You.

**Thanksgiving** – Lord, thank You for teaching us how to pray and giving us a model to follow.

**Prayer** – Lord, rise up and help us; rescue us because of Your unfailing love.

## Day 116

Psalm 45:4 In Your majesty ride forth victoriously in the cause of truth, humility and justice; let Your right hand achieve awesome deeds.

Today's verse sounds like an inaugural charge to a king. For their well-being, the people would want a king who excelled in the areas of truth, humility and justice. Today's verse is a great example of scripture pointing us to Christ our King. Let's look at the three attributes of our victorious King. **Truth** – When Jesus was on trial before Pilate, He tells Pilate that He came into the world to testify to the truth. John 18:37, 'You are a king, then! Said Pilate. Jesus answered, You are right in saying I am a king. In fact for this reason I was born, and for this I came into the world, to testify to the truth. Everyone on the side of truth listens to Me.' In John 14:6, 'Jesus answered, I am the way and the truth and the life. No one comes to the Father except through Me.' Truth is not what I believe to be true, Jesus is truth. **Humility** – Philippians 2:7:8, 'But made Himself nothing, taking the very nature of a servant, being made in human likeness, and being found in appearance as a man, He humbled Himself and became obedient to death – even death on a cross.' Jesus humbled Himself to be born as a baby to later die on the cross for our sins. **Justice** – My first thought of justice is when Jesus cleared the temple of merchants who had taken over the courtyard. Luke 19:45-46 tells us, 'Then He entered the temple area and began driving out those who were selling. It is written, He said to them, My house will be a house of prayer, but you have made it a den of robbers.' Jesus ran the merchants out of the temple, returning it to its proper use. Later in Revelation, we find Jesus at the Great White Throne of Judgement. There He will judge all who have died without accepting Jesus as their Savior. One day Jesus will return to the earth to reign as King. He will rule with truth, humility and justice.

**Acknowledge** – Lord, You are the way, the truth and the life.

**Confess** – Lord, forgive me when I doubt, when I think Satan has the upper hand, because You are victorious.

**Thanksgiving** – Lord, thank You for teaching us truth, humility, and justice.

**Prayer** – Lord, Your reign will last forever and Your right hand has achieved awesome deeds.

## Day 117

Psalm 45:17 I will perpetuate Your memory through all generations; therefore the nations will praise You forever and ever.

Who was the MVP of the 1973 World Series? Who was the 20th President of the United States? If you are a trivia person, you may be able to name these. However, throughout history there have only been a handful of names that are remembered. There is one name that will never be lost in the annals of time. That name is Jesus. Paul writes in Philippians 2:9-11, 'Therefore God exalted Him to the highest place and gave Him the name that is above every name, that at the name of Jesus every knee should bow, in heaven and on earth and under the earth, and every tongue confess that Jesus Christ is Lord, to the glory of God the Father.' Although Satan has tried everything to block us from hearing about Jesus, His name is magnified. His name is being shared all around the world. Even in places like Communist China where it is illegal, the name of Jesus is being spread. Why? Because there is power, there is healing, there is salvation, there is joy, there is peace, and there is deliverance in the name of Jesus. There is just something about that name. This brings to mind a song by that title written by Bill and Gloria Gaither. Soak in the words of their song, 'Jesus, Jesus, Jesus; there's just something about that name. Master, Savior, Jesus, like the fragrance after the rain; Jesus, Jesus, Jesus, let all Heaven and earth proclaim, Kings and kingdoms will all pass away, but there's something about that name. Kings, and kingdoms will all pass away, but there's something about that name.' How well do you know Jesus? Is He your Master, your Savior? One day, everyone will bow before Him. Don't wait until it is too late to acknowledge Him as Lord and Savior. Worship Jesus and receive the joy that comes in His name. There's just something about that name.

**Acknowledge** –Lord, there is something special about Your name.

**Confess** – Lord, forgive me when I fail to praise You and to lift Your name on high.

**Thanksgiving** – Lord, thank You for the healing, the power, the salvation, the peace, the joy that comes in Your name.

**Prayer** – Lord, let me perpetuate Your memory to the next generation. Let me show others Your love and compassion, mercy and grace so that it may be passed from generation to generation.

# Day 118

> Psalm 46:1 God is our refuge and strength, an ever-present help in trouble.

In Psalms 20, we read that, 'Some trust in chariots and some in horses, but we trust in the name of our Lord.' I think it is easy to say God is our refuge, but how well do we fully trust Him? The story of Shadrach, Meshach, and Abednego found in Daniel chapter 3 is a great example of fully trusting God. King Nebuchadnezzar had made a golden image and required everyone to bow and worship it. Anyone failing to worship the image would be thrown into a fiery furnace. When Shadrach, Meshach, and Abednego failed to worship the golden image, King Nebuchadnezzar gave them a second chance to change their mind. They refused, which made the king furious. He had the furnace heated seven times hotter and ordered the three to be thrown in. Their reply to King Nebuchadnezzar when offered a second chance to worship the image shows us how they fully trusted God. It is found in Daniel 3:17-18, 'If we are thrown into the blazing furnace, the God we serve is able to save us from it, and He will rescue us from your hand, O king. But even if He does not, we want you to know, O king, that we will not serve your gods or worship the image of gold you have set up.' For all they knew, in a few minutes they were going to be toast. Yet they trusted God to save them from the furnace, but didn't know how God would intervene. As today's verse points out, we are going to face trouble. So how do we make God our refuge and strength when we are facing difficulty? We do like Shadrach, Meshach, and Abednego; we put our trust in God. We turn to God for help and protection. Each day our faith in Him will grow stronger as we see His hand moving and working on our behalf. We learn that no matter what our circumstances, the safest place to be is in the center of God's will.

**Acknowledge** –Lord, in You we find our refuge and strength.

**Confess** – Lord, forgive me when I ask You to take away the storms of my life instead of being my refuge and strength.

**Thanksgiving** – Lord, thank You for being my refuge and my strength.

**Prayer** – Lord, troubles will come, disasters will occur, yet You are with me. There is calmness and security knowing that You are my refuge.

# Day 119

> Psalm 46:10 Be still, and know that I am God; I will be exalted among the nations, I will be exalted in the earth.

When Moses and the children of Israel were backed up to the Red Sea and the Egyptians in pursuit, God tells them in Exodus 14:14, 'The Lord will fight for you: you need only to be still.' In Ecclesiastes 3:7 Solomon writes, 'A time to tear and a time to mend, a time to be silent and a time to speak.' There are times when God wants us to be still. Even God took time to be still. After He created the heavens and the earth, He rested on the seventh day. While the children of Israel were slaves in Egypt, they were forced to work seven days a week. God changed their work habits from Egypt in the Ten Commandments. The eighth commandment reads, 'Remember the Sabbath day by keeping it holy. Six days you shall labor and do all your work, but the seventh day is a Sabbath to the Lord your God. On it you shall not do any work.' In the New Testament, we find the disciples on the Sea of Galilee caught up in a terrible storm fighting the raging sea. The story is in Mark 4:35-40. While the disciples were frantic and fearing for their lives, Jesus simply spoke to the wind and the waves, telling them, 'Quiet! Be still.' So, how do we find this stillness and peace in our lives? Spend time with God. He would rather you spend time with Him than doing things for Him. He desires your company over your accomplishments. We get too caught up in thinking I need to get this done, before I can spend time with God. We may even feel guilty for not doing something. Once you get beyond the guilt for not working, then you can begin to experience a stillness in your heart. That is where you begin to know God and come to understand Him better. Ask Him to help you prioritize and get rid of the things that are preventing you from having a relationship with Him. Be still and know God.

**Acknowledge** –Lord, Your name will be exalted among the nations.

**Confess** – Lord, forgive me for not being still. Forgive me for not taking time to know You.

**Thanksgiving** – Lord, thank You for peace and quiet. Thank You for calming the storms of life.

**Prayer** – Lord, help me to give my problems great or small to You.

# Day 120

Psalm 47:1 Clap your hands, all you nations, shout to God with cries of joy.

I'll never forget the first Sunday I attended a Pentecostal worship service. Coming from a traditional Baptist Church, I was not prepared for the experience. There was a lot of clapping, shouting, and dancing. I was standing near one man whose shout sounded like a train whistle. We called it a white-knuckle Sunday, because I had gripped the back of the pew so hard, that my knuckles had turned white. The ironic thing is that service did not scare Vivian and me away. In fact, we kept attending and later joined the church. I think the reason we joined was because the worship was real, not fake, and we felt the presence of God at that church. Even in many non-Pentecostal churches today, you will find a more expressive worship. This is not to say that traditional, reverent worship is dry, dull, and void of the presence of God. That is not the case at all. God created and ordains all types of worship that honor and glorify Him. However, there are times just like David when we need to praise the Lord. Why shouldn't we praise our God with clapping and shouting? In Luke 19:40, Jesus, speaking to the Pharisees after they had told Him to tell the crowd to be quiet, told them, 'I tell you, He replied, if they keep quiet, the stones will cry out.' Do you want the 'rocks' to take your place in praising God? Isn't there something you can praise Him for? If you are having trouble, start small. At dinner time, we go around the table doing our "Thankful's." Our grandchildren love to participate in telling one thing they are thankful for. It doesn't matter how big or how small; we all have something we can be thankful for. Take time each day to give God praise for something He has done for you. As you begin to praise Him for the little things, you will find yourself shouting with cries of joy when He does something big in your life. Praise Him!

**Acknowledge** –Lord, if I don't praise You the rocks will cry out.

**Confess** – Lord, forgive me when I don't feel like praising You. You are worthy of my praise.

**Thanksgiving** – Lord, thank You allowing me the privilege of being able to praise You.

**Prayer** – Lord, open my heart and my tongue that I might speak of Your goodness, Your mercy, and Your love for me.

# Day 121

Psalm 47:7 For God is the king of all the earth; sing to Him a psalm of praise.

As of May 2020, the coronavirus had spread around the world causing confusion and panic. The virus was first reported in Wuhan, China in December 2019. In just five short months, it spread around the world with cases reported on every continent. Here in the United States, items such as hand sanitizer, disinfectant wipes, and surgical masks were in short supply because of the demand. Instead of shaking hands, men are now fist and elbow bumping. Most sporting events were canceled and contingency plans made for others if the virus continued to worsen. The stock market plunged due to the impact of the coronavirus on businesses across the world. Airlines experienced a significant decline in global and domestic air travel. However, in the midst of all the anxiety and disruption caused by the coronavirus, God is still King of the earth. In the midst of conflicts taking place in the world today, God is still King of the earth. Even when your world is crashing in on you, God is still King of the earth. No matter the situation, no matter the outcome, God is still King of the earth. Are you worried about these or other events? Don't worry; He is still King of the earth. He is in control. Do you know the King? Do you trust Him? 1 Peter 5:7 says, 'Cast all your anxiety on Him because He cares for you.' God loves you. He doesn't want you to worry about world events, conflicts, viruses, the stock market, health, relationships, or finances. Give them to Him, because He cares for you. He loves you. Take time today to tell God, the King of the earth, how you feel and what you fear the most. Let Him take it off your shoulders.

**Acknowledge** –Lord, You are King of the earth, we give You praise.

**Confess** – Lord, forgive me when I worry about events or circumstances that are out of my control.

**Thanksgiving** – Lord, You are great and greatly to be praised.

**Prayer** – Lord, You reign over all the earth. Nothing that happens is a surprise to You. Help me to cast my cares on You and not carry them around.

# Day 122

**Psalm 48:1** Great is the Lord, and most worthy of praise, in the city of our God, His Holy mountain.

No one can truly understand just how great Jehovah God is. However, we can see His greatness displayed in His creation. We can see His greatness in the lives He has transformed. We can see His greatness by looking into the night sky and marveling at the vastness of the universe. We can see His greatness through the miracles of healing that take place. We can see His greatness in the power of nature. We can see His greatness in His word and His promises to us. I could give more examples of God's greatness, but let's see what His Word tells us about His greatness. 1 Chronicles 29:11, 'Yours, O Lord, is the greatness and the power and the glory and the victory and the majesty, indeed everything that is in the heavens and the earth; Yours is the dominion, O Lord, and You exalt yourself as head over all.' The writer of Chronicles tells us that God is head over all. In Jeremiah 10:6 we read, 'There is none like You, O Lord; You are great, and great is Your name in might.' Jeremiah says there is none like our God, He is great and His name is great. Ephesians 2:4 tells us about His riches, 'But God, being rich in mercy, because of His great love with which He has loved us.' God is rich in mercy because of His great love. How can we not praise this great God who loved us enough to send His Son to die in our place? The One like no other, the One who is in control. The One who knew you when you were in your mother's womb. Worship the greatness of our loving and merciful God today.

**Acknowledge** – Great are You Lord and worthy of praise.

**Confess** – Lord, forgive me for not worshiping You as I should.

**Thanksgiving** – Lord, thank You for being a great God, rich in love and mercy to me, a sinner who does not deserve it.

**Prayer** – Lord, one day we will worship You in the New Jerusalem. It will be the center of worship and government, a city of peace, joy, and happiness. Lord help me to share Your greatness to a lost and dying world.

# Day 123

Psalm 48:14 For this God is our God forever and ever, He will be our guide even to the end.

Have you ever heard the phrase, 'nothing lasts forever?' However, isn't it wonderful that we have a God who is with us forever? One who has promised to be with us. Jesus, speaking in John 14:15-17, tells us that His Spirit will be with us, 'If you love Me, you will obey what I command. And I will ask the Father, and He will give you another Counselor to be with you forever – The Spirit of truth. The world cannot accept Him, because it neither sees Him nor knows Him. But you know Him, for He lives with you and will be in you.' Jesus speaking just before He ascended to heaven, said in Matthew 28:18-20, 'Then Jesus came to them and said, All authority in heaven and on earth has been given to Me. Therefore go and make disciples of all nations, baptizing them in the name of the Father, and of the Son, and of the Holy Spirit, and teaching them to obey everything I have commanded you. And surely I am with you always, to the very end of the age.' God promises to always be with us. Even when you are going through some of the most difficult trials, He is with you. It is in those times Satan wants you to think that God has abandoned you. He wants you to doubt God's promises. He wants you to question God's love for you. Have you ever asked God, 'If you love me, then why am I going through this right now?' Or, 'why me God?' It is in those times we need to hold fast to His promise that He is with us. He knows what we are going through and on the other side of the trial we will be made stronger in Him. He will work out the situation for our good. Romans 8:28 tells us, 'And we know that in all things God works for the good of those who love Him, who have been called according to His purpose.' Trust God and His word that He will always be with us.

**Acknowledge** –Lord, You are with us forever and ever.

**Confess** – Lord, forgive me for doubting Your presence in my life.

**Thanksgiving** – Lord, thank You for being our guide to the end.

**Prayer** – Lord, I know that all things work together for my good, help me to trust You when times are difficult.

# Day 124

**Psalm 49:3** My mouth will speak words of wisdom; the meditation of my heart will give understanding.

THE PSALMIST GIVES US INSIGHT TO SPEAKING WITH WISDOM. Notice the last half of the verse where he says 'the meditation of my heart will give understanding.' We should think before we speak. Words matter. Tone matters. At work when I had to correct an employee's behavior, I would typically plan the conversation. I didn't want the employee to interpret my message as if they were incapable, but wanted them to learn from their mistakes. The same goes for disciplining our children. Words like, 'can't you do anything right?' Or, 'I am ashamed of you,' have a lasting impact on our children. In the heat of the moment, these words can easily roll off our lips and never be taken back. In Proverbs, Solomon gives us some advice on the words we use. Proverbs 15:1, 'A gentle answer turns away wrath, but a harsh word stirs up anger.' Proverbs 18:4, 'The words of a man's mouth are deep waters, but the fountain of wisdom is a bubbling brook.' Proverbs 18:7 tells us, 'A fool's mouth is his undoing, and his lips are a snare to his soul.' So how do we avoid using words and tone that put someone down? First, realize the words we use are important. Choose them carefully. Secondly, the instant we speak in haste, the wrong words are more likely to come out. Pause before you speak. James 1:19 tells us, 'My dear brothers and sisters, take note of this: Everyone should be quick to listen, slow to speak and slow to become angry.' Third, ask God to give you understanding about the situation you may be speaking about. Ask Him to guard your words. Colossians 4:6 tells us, 'Let your conversations be always full of grace, seasoned with salt, so that you may know how to answer everyone.' Ask God today to give you words of wisdom even in the routine conversations. Let what comes out of your mouth today build and encourage someone.

**Acknowledge** – Lord, You provide understanding and wisdom to guide my conversations.

**Confess** – Lord, forgive me when I speak in haste saying things that hurt others.

**Thanksgiving** – Lord, thank You for your word and instruction on how to use our words wisely.

**Prayer** – Lord, I ask that the words of my mouth and the meditations of my heart will be pleasing in Your sight.

# Day 125

Psalm 49:5 Why should I fear when evil days come, when wicked deceivers surround me.

I HAVE HEARD IT SAID THAT 'FEAR NOT' OR SOME FORM OF IT APPEARS in the Bible 365 times, one for each day of the year. It is very clear God does not want us to live in fear. We have already read in Psalm 23, 'Even though I walk through the valley of the shadow of death, I will fear no evil.' Why wasn't David afraid? Because he goes on to say, 'For You are with me; Your rod and Your staff, they comfort me.' David acknowledged God's presence in his life which helped him to overcome his fears. However, one of Satan's most popular weapons is fear. He tries to create doubt and fear in every area of our lives. Because of his attacks, we can't prevent from having thoughts of fear and doubt coming to our minds. So, how do we combat those types of thoughts when they do come to mind? The answer is very simple, rely on God's Word. His Word is full of promises to help us overcome fear. Read His word, memorize them, and pray over them. These are a few of the many verses that remind us we do not have to fear. Isaiah 41:10, 'So do not fear, for I am with you; do not be dismayed, for I am your God. I will strengthen you and help you; I will uphold you with My righteous right hand.' Isaiah said that God promises to be with us and strengthen us. 2 Timothy 1:7, 'For God hath not given us a spirit of fear but of power and of love and of a sound mind.' Paul writing to Timothy tells us that God gives us a sound mind, not one filled with fear. Mark 5:36, 'Jesus told him, "Don't be afraid; just believe."' Jesus tells us, to trust Him. We might still feel afraid, but we can know that God is with us. He is in control. He knows our future. Trust God, fear not.

**Acknowledge** –Lord, I don't need to fear when evil days come. You are with me.

**Confess** – Lord, forgive me when I allow fearful scenarios to take over my thoughts.

**Thanksgiving** – Lord, thank You for being with me, for upholding me when evil days come.

**Prayer** – Lord, help me to seek You and the comfort of Your Word when fearful thoughts start to creep in my mind.

# Day 126

Psalm 49:15 But God will redeem me from the realm of the dead; He will surely take me to himself.

ALMOST 1,000 YEARS BEFORE THE BIRTH OF JESUS, GOD SHARED HIS plan of salvation through the words of this Psalm. He promises a hope and a future with Him in heaven. It is sad to see people who do not believe in God. No wonder they are seeking all the happiness they can find in this world. Unfortunately, the things they are working towards only provide temporary pleasure. Jesus, talking to the disciples about heaven, said in John 14:1-3, 'Do not let your hearts be troubled. Trust in God, trust also in Me. In My Father's house are many rooms; if it were not so, I would have told you. I am going there to prepare a place for you. And if I go and prepare a place for you, I will come back and take you to be with Me that you also may be where I am.' Jesus promised that one day we will live with Him in a place especially prepared for us. How do we claim this promise from God? Jesus tells us a few verses later, in John 14:6, 'I am the way, the truth and the life. No one comes to the Father except through Me.' It is through our belief and trust in Jesus Christ that we have eternal life with Him. Jesus speaking in John 3:16 said, 'For God so loved the world that He gave His one and only Son, that whoever believes in Him shall not perish but have eternal life.' The Bible makes it very clear that our hope, our redemption, our salvation comes through Jesus Christ, who was crucified and buried, and rose to life on the third day. Do you know Jesus Christ as your personal Lord and Savior? If so, rejoice in the knowledge that you will be with Him one day in heaven. If not, take time today to repent of your sins and ask Him to come into your heart. Ask Him to be your Lord and Savior.

**Acknowledge** –Lord, You have prepared a place for those who trust in You.

**Confess** – Lord, forgive me when I am shortsighted and fail to see the big picture of Your plan for us.

**Thanksgiving** – Lord, thank You for Your plan of salvation.

**Prayer** – Lord, there is comfort in Your words to us. Help me to walk in confident assurance of Your word.

# Day 127

Psalm 50:1 The mighty one, God, the Lord, speaks and summons the earth from the rising of the sun to where it sets.

Today's verse reminds us of God's dominion over the entire earth as He has summoned everyone from the east to the west to be His audience. I can pretty confidently say that such a gathering has not yet taken place, but there will be one in the future. In Revelation 20:11-13, John writes of such a gathering, 'Then I saw a great white throne and Him who was seated on it. Earth and sky fled from His presence, and there was no place for them. And I saw the dead, great and small, standing before the throne, and books were opened. Another book was opened, which is the book of life. The dead were judged according to what they had done as recorded in the books. The sea gave up the dead that were in it, and death and Hades gave up the dead that were in them, and each person was judged according to what he had done.' Also, in Philippians 2:10-11 Paul writes, 'that at the name of Jesus every knee will bow, of those in heaven, and of those on earth, and of those under the earth, and that every tongue should confess that Jesus Christ is Lord, to the glory of God the Father.' Is your name written in God's Book of Life? If not, it is important that you have every opportunity to make that decision. Today is the second day in a row where our scripture is leading us to make a decision for Christ. Don't put that decision off. One day, we will all stand before God in a great assembly. My prayer is that your name will be found in the Book of Life. It will be too late to confess Jesus is Lord, once we stand before Him at the judgement.

**Acknowledge** –Lord, one day every knee will bow and every tongue confess that Jesus Christ is Lord.

**Confess** – Lord, forgive me for not sharing Your plan of salvation with others.

**Thanksgiving** – Lord, thank you that You are our judge, the mighty one. One day Your glory will be displayed for the entire world to see.

**Prayer** – Lord, help me to be prepared and to prepare as many people as I can for the day of Your return.

# Day 128

Psalm 50:14-15 Sacrifice thank offering to God, fulfill your vows to the most-High, and call on Me in the day of trouble, I will deliver you, and you will honor Me.

OUR GOD TELLS US TO CALL ON HIM IN THE DAY OF TROUBLE. If ever there was a day of trouble, now is the time. COVID-19 continues to spread across the world. The President, in an unprecedented move, declared Sunday, March 15th as a National Day of Prayer for the nation to call out to God for His divine help in combating the virus. The following is a portion of the Proclamation issued by the President. 'In times of greatest need, Americans have always turned to prayer to help guide us through trials and periods of uncertainty. As we continue to face the unique challenges posed by the coronavirus pandemic, millions of Americans are unable to gather in their churches, temples, synagogues, mosques, and other houses of worship. But in this time we must not cease asking God for added wisdom, comfort, and strength, and we must especially pray for those who have suffered harm or who have lost loved ones. I ask you to join me in a day of prayer for all people who have been affected by the coronavirus pandemic and to pray for God's healing hand to be placed on the people of our Nation.' (www.whitehouse.gov) By the time you are reading this, hopefully the coronavirus is history. Several more 'days of trouble' may have come and gone. What are you facing today? John 16:33 tells us, 'I have said these things to you, that in Me you may have peace. In the world you will have tribulation. But take heart; I have overcome the world.' Jesus tells us that we are going to have troubles. Today's verse gives us some practical steps in calling to God when we experience trouble. First, give thanks to God. Secondly, walk in obedience to Him. Next be patient and call out to Him. If you are struggling to believe God will help you, look back. Think on how God has brought you through difficult times before. Give Him thanks, obey and trust Him.

**Acknowledge** – Lord, You will deliver us in our day of trouble.

**Confess** – Lord, forgive me for doubting Your love for me.

**Thanksgiving** – Lord, I give thanks in all circumstances for this is Your will for me.

**Prayer** – Lord, show me the gaps between my faith and my practical living. Empower me to live by faith alone.

# Day 129

Psalm 51:1 Have mercy on me, O God, according to Your unfailing love, according to Your great compassion blot out my transgressions.

IN PSALMS 51, WE FIND DAVID'S HUMBLE PRAYER FOR FORGIVENESS and cleansing. Nathan the prophet had confronted David about his adulterous affair with Bathsheba and the murder of her husband, Uriah. While David never mentions the details of his sin, his sincere words of repentance can serve as a guide to repentance for us. He is humbly and honestly pouring out his heart to God for forgiveness. One day we will have to give an account for our lives before God. Like David, I want God's forgiveness for my sins. In Psalms 103:12, David writes, 'as far as the east is from the west, so far has He removed our transgressions from us.' David was confident that God could and would blot out his sin. However, in seeking God's forgiveness, David immediately appeals to God's mercy even before mentioning his sin. Let's look at God's mercy. In Exodus 34:6, God tells us a lot about His character. Moses is headed back up Mount Sinai to meet with God to receive the Ten Commandments. The Lord comes down in a cloud and passes in front of Moses proclaiming, '...The Lord, the Lord, a God merciful and gracious, slow to anger, and abounding in steadfast love and faithfulness.' In the New Testament, we find example after example of God's mercy in those who came to Jesus for healing. They didn't walk up and simply ask Jesus to heal them. No, their words were, 'Have mercy on me.' Not only did Jesus have mercy on them and healed them, He offered them eternal life. Paul writes in Ephesians 2:4-5 writes, 'But because of His great love for us, God, who is rich in mercy, made us alive with Christ even when we were dead in transgressions, it is by grace you have been saved.' Have you experienced God's mercy and forgiveness? Maybe you have an unconfessed sin in your life that is weighing heavily on you right now? Appeal to God's mercy. He will forgive you.

**Acknowledge** –Lord, have mercy on me according to Your great love.

**Confess** – Lord, blot out my transgressions.

**Thanksgiving** – Lord, I thank You that You are rich in mercy and grace.

**Prayer** – Lord, through the blood of Jesus we are set free, our sins are forgiven. Help me to experience freedom from guilt and shame through Your love and mercy.

# Day 130

**Psalm 51:7,9** Cleanse me with hyssop, and I will be clean; wash me, and I will be whiter than snow. Hide Your face from my sins and blot out all my iniquity.

David begins this verse with, 'cleanse me with hyssop.' It might be helpful to understand the significance of hyssop and why David would use it for cleansing. Hyssop is an herb used for cleansing, medicinal, and flavoring purposes. It is first mentioned in the Bible when it was used as a paintbrush to mark the doorposts of the Israelites in Egypt when the angel of death was to pass over. In Leviticus, hyssop was used in the ceremonial cleansing of people and houses. We also find hyssop at the crucifixion of Christ. It was a hyssop stalk that was used by the Roman Soldier who dipped the sponge in wine vinegar and gave to Jesus to drink. Not only has David asked God to cleanse him with hyssop, he asks God to wash him. In Numbers 19, the Lord gave Moses and Aaron instructions for cleansing anyone who has become 'unclean.' The instructions included washing and sprinkling of cleansing water with a hyssop plant. However, David didn't rely on a symbolic ritual to cleanse his sins. He called on God to perform the cleansing. The beauty of David's prayer is that he had confidence that God would cleanse him of his sins. In Isaiah 1:18 God is telling the rebellious nation of Israel their sins can be forgiven and made white as snow: 'Come now, let us reason together, says the Lord. Though your sins are like scarlet, they shall be as white as snow; though they are red as crimson, they shall be like wool.' Yesterday we sought God's mercy, today we ask for God's cleansing. Hebrews 8:12 tells us, 'For I will forgive their wickedness and will remember their sins no more.' Our sins are forgiven through the cleansing blood of Jesus. It is His sacrifice on the cross that eliminates the animal sacrifices and cleansing rituals set up in the Old Testament. Ask Him to cleanse you and remember your sins no more.

**Acknowledge** –Lord, wash me and I will be whiter than snow.

**Confess** – Lord, my sins are many, cleanse Me with Your hyssop.

**Thanksgiving** – Lord, thank You for remembering our sins no more.

**Prayer** – Lord, we are born with a sinful nature which has been passed down from generation to generation. It is through Your Son that we have forgiveness and eternal life.

# Day 131

Psalm 51:10,15 Create in me a pure heart, O God, and renew a steadfast spirit within me. Open my lips, Lord, and my mouth will declare Your praise.

DAVID HAS RECEIVED GOD'S MERCY AND HIS SINS FORGIVEN, NOW he is asking God to create something new in him, a pure heart. How often do we go back and commit the same sin over and over? I ask for forgiveness and no sooner than the words are off my lips, I stumble right back into doing the same thing I asked God to forgive me for. Paul said it best in Romans 7:19, 'For what I do is not the good I want to do; no, the evil I do not want to do – this I keep on doing.' Why do we keep falling back into the sins we know are wrong, but can't stop doing? It is in our DNA; we were born with a sinful nature. Although our sins have been forgiven by the blood of Jesus Christ, we will continue to sin and disobey as long as we live. Repentance is defined as deep sorrow, or contrition for a past sin or wrongdoing. (www.dictionary.com) Repentance is also accompanied by a commitment for our actions to show a change for the better. However, our sinful nature wants to draw us back into the very sins we have asked repentance for. That is why we need to ask God to instill in us a right and pure heart like David did. He asked God for a radical change in his life. We need God's help in changing our heart too. We need a renewed spirit that becomes more steadfast, remaining strong to resist temptation. Paul wrote in 1 Corinthians 10:13, 'No temptation has seized you except what is common to man. And God is faithful; He will not let you be tempted beyond what you can bear. But when you are tempted, He will also provide a way out so that you can stand up under it.' As we put to use our newly created heart and steadfast spirit, we are able to hold fast in the face of temptation and declare His praise.

**Acknowledge** –Lord, You can change our hearts.

**Confess** – Lord, forgive me when I jump back into the sins I have just asked forgiveness for.

**Thanksgiving** – Lord, thank You for providing a way out of the temptations we face each day.

**Prayer** – Lord, I ask that You create in me a pure heart and a steadfast spirit.

# Day 132

**Psalm 51:17** The sacrifices of God are a broken spirit; a broken and contrite heart, O God, You will not despise.

TO BETTER UNDERSTAND WHAT DAVID IS SAYING, LET'S READ VERSE 16, 'You do not delight in sacrifice, or I would bring it; You do not take pleasure in burnt offerings.' The repentance for sin in David's day would have been some type of animal sacrifice. However, David realizes there is nothing he can offer God to appease Him for his sin. Another animal sacrifice wouldn't change David's heart or restore his relationship with God. God desires true repentance, the type we talked about yesterday that requires a pure heart and a renewed spirit. We spend a lot of time trying to make ourselves right with God, when all He wants is our heartfelt contrition. We may even have regret for our sins, but that is no substitution for repentance. To keep us from repenting, Satan will put thoughts in our heads that cause us to justify our actions. He knows as long as we remain unforgiven, we will live in bondage to sin. Our prayer life and our fellowship with God will not be the same. Don't be like the Pharisee in the parable of the Pharisee and the Tax Collector found in Luke 18:9-14. The Pharisee prayed that he was glad he wasn't like other men, robbers, adulterers, or even the tax collector. He was comparing himself to everyone around him and felt pretty good about his life. While the Tax Collector humbled himself before God and cried out, 'God have mercy on me a sinner.' Jesus summarized the parable in verse 14, 'I tell you this man, (the Tax Collector) rather than the other, (the Pharisee) went home justified before God. For everyone who exalts himself will be humbled, and he who humbles himself will be exalted.' Humble yourself before God today. Come before Him with a broken spirit and a broken and contrite heart. Confess your sins to Him. Receive His forgiveness and love.

**Acknowledge** – Lord, You want us to humble ourselves before You and confess our sins.

**Confess** – Lord, forgive me when I begin to compare myself to someone else and fail to acknowledge my shortcomings.

**Thanksgiving** – Lord, thank You for forgiving our sins.

**Prayer** – Lord, create in me a true brokenness and humbleness.

# Day 133

**Psalm 52:1** Why do you boast of evil, you mighty hero? Why do you boast all day long, you who are a disgrace in the eyes of God?

Psalm 52 was written by David after Doeg the Edomite slaughtered the people in the village of Nob, while David was on the run from Saul. The priests had innocently helped David by giving him and his men food and the sword of Goliath. The story can be found in 1 Samuel 21 -22. Psalm 52 talks about the attributes of an evil person and their outcome in comparison to the righteous person. David claims evil people love to do evil. In verse 1, David asks why do you boast all day long about what you are doing? In verse 2 he says, the tongue plots destruction. But behind that evil tongue was an evil heart, an evil mind, and an evil life directing that tongue. That person's tongue caused death and destruction. Do you know of someone who twists words and crafts lies to get their way? They have no concern for anyone who gets hurt in the process. When I read today's verse, my first thought was the argument for abortion. Many have stood and proclaimed the right of women to make decisions about their own body, while ignoring the life and rights of the unborn child. Just recently, a Senator threatened conservative members of the Supreme Court if they revisited the Roe v. Wade decision. He called out two of the conservative members of the Court by name. After facing criticism from all sides, the Senator later apologized for his comments. However, one day as David writes in verse 5, 'Surely God will bring you down to everlasting ruin; He will snatch you up and tear you from your tent; He will uproot you from the land of the living.' Take heart, God is in control. He does not let evil go unpunished. However, our response to evil people should be as Jesus tells us in Matthew 5:44, 'But I tell you: Love your enemies and pray for those who persecute you.' This is not an easy command, but one we need to take to heart.

**Acknowledge** –Lord, there is evil all around us.

**Confess** – Lord, forgive me when my heart seeks to do evil and put myself on the throne of my life.

**Thanksgiving** – Lord, thank You for knowing our heart and innermost thoughts. Let them be pleasing in Your sight.

**Prayer** – Lord, help me to pray for my enemies.

# Day 134

Psalm 52:8 But I am like an olive tree flourishing in the house of God; I trust in God's unfailing love forever and ever.

Our focus today is on the righteous person who David describes as an olive tree. Earlier in Psalms 1, we learned about a tree that was planted by the streams of water that produced fruit and prospered. Today's verse is very similar. Where does David tell us he prospers? He describes himself like a flourishing olive tree in the house of God. Proverbs 12:12 tells us, 'The wicked desire the plunder of evil men, but the root of the righteous flourish.' Both David and Solomon tell us that the righteous should be flourishing. Our flourishing should be manifested in a desire to produce fruit in service to Him. How do we produce fruit? We do it by showing love towards others. Jesus tells us in John 13:35, 'By this all men will know that you are My disciples, if you love one another.' What are some ways we can show love to one another? The list is endless but it takes time and effort on our part. One of the top ways to show you love someone is to listen to them. Take interest in their lives and the things they are going through. You may not have an answer for them, but you can empathize with them. As you develop the relationship, that person will be more willing to listen to you about Christ. People don't care what you have to say, until they know you care about them. Paul writes in Galatians 5:13, 'You, my brothers and sisters, were called to be free. But do not use your freedom to indulge the flesh; rather, serve one another humbly in love.' You are a flourishing tree. Go forth and bear fruit today. Find someone you can show the love of God to by getting to know them and offering your help.

**Acknowledge** –Lord, I trust in Your unfailing love forever.

**Confess** – Lord, forgive me when I fail to show love to those around me.

**Thanksgiving** – Lord, thank You for loving us and planting us in Your House.

**Prayer** – Lord, help me to be like the olive tree, planted by the river, whose roots run deep and who is not bothered by the heat or drought. Help me produce fruit in all seasons.

Psalm 53:1 The fool says in his heart, 'There is no God.' They are corrupt, and their ways are vile; there is no one who does good.

How do you define good? What we consider good may not be by someone else. Good is a relative term. God does not grade or judge us on the 'curve.' Either we have accepted Christ as Savior and received forgiveness of our sins or we are lost and bound for eternal punishment. There is no in-between. We do not receive merits for our good behavior and work our way into heaven. In God's eyes, we are still foolish and our ways are vile if we haven't accepted Him as Lord and Savior. Paul writes in Romans 3:9-12, 'What shall we conclude then? Are we any better? Not at all! We have already made the charge that Jews and Gentiles alike are all under sin. As it is written: There is no one righteous, not even one; there is no one who seeks God, All have turned away, they have together become worthless; there is no one who does good, not even one.' Paul confirms that we are all under sin. He also tells us that we are under God's wrath because of our sin in Romans 1:18, 'The wrath of God is being revealed from heaven against all the godlessness and wickedness of men who suppress the truth by their wickedness.' How do we escape God's wrath? God had a plan; Romans 5:8-9 says 'But God demonstrates His own love for us in this: While we were still sinners, Christ died for us. Since we have now been justified by His blood, how much more shall we be saved from God's wrath through Him.' Aren't you glad you don't have to complete so many good acts to receive salvation? Aren't you glad that one slip up doesn't erase all the good things you have done? Give God praise today for His marvelous plan of salvation that doesn't require you and me to walk around doing good deeds to receive eternal life.

**Acknowledge** –Lord, without Christ, we are all fools.

**Confess** – Lord, forgive me when I try to rely on good works to gain Your favor.

**Thanksgiving** – Lord, thank You that we do not have to work our way into heaven. Salvation is a free gift.

**Prayer** – Lord, help me to share Your plan of salvation with others. Being a good person is not enough. We must surrender our lives to You.

# Day 136

Psalm 54:1-2 Save me, O God, by Your name; vindicate me by Your might. Hear my prayer, O God, listen to the words of my mouth.

I HAVE NEVER BEEN IN THE POSITION AS DAVID WHERE SOMEONE WAS out to physically harm me or destroy my reputation with false accusations and slander. David experienced both. I can't imagine how stressful and painful that might have been. The stress and uncertainty may have been the reason for David's choice of words in this short prayer. They are very straightforward to God. Unfortunately, people are no different today as they were in the days of David. 2 Timothy 3:1-5 tells us, 'But mark this: There will be terrible times in the last days. People will be lovers of themselves, lovers of money, boastful, proud, abusive, disobedient to their parents, ungrateful, unholy, without love, unforgiving, slanderous, without self-control, brutal, not lovers of the good, treacherous, rash, conceited, lovers of pleasure rather than lovers of God – having a form of Godliness but denying its power. Have nothing to do with them.' The most recent example where an all-out campaign to destroy someone's reputation occurred during a recent Supreme Court Justice Confirmation hearing. Because of his conservative background and fear that he might in the future vote to repeal the Roe v. Wade decision, it was alleged that the nominee sexually assaulted a woman in 1982. His character and reputation were under attack before the entire world. The accusations were proven to be false and the Justice was later appointed. When confronted with his situation, David reaches out to God and starts his prayer with four short commands to God, 1. Save me, O God, 2. Vindicate me, 3. Hear my prayer, 4. Listen to me. How often have you and I done the same thing? Although David knew that God could hear his prayer, twice he asked God to hear him. Isn't that what we want most when we pray? Don't we want to make sure that God is listening to us and hears our prayer? What are you going through today that makes you want to cry out to God, 'save me?' He heard David's prayers. He hears yours.

**Acknowledge** –Lord, You have the power to save.

**Confess** – Lord, forgive me when I want to take matters into my own hands and not give them to You.

**Thanksgiving** – Lord, thank You that You hear our prayers.

**Prayer** – Lord, I look to You. You are my light and my salvation. In whom shall I fear?

# Day 137

Psalm 55:1-2 Listen to my prayer, O God, do not ignore my plea. Hear me and answer me. My thoughts trouble me and I am distraught.

Today's verse implies that David is in between the time he has first reached out to God and to receiving an answer to his prayer. We have all been there. Depending upon God's timing, it could be weeks, months, or even years before God's answer is fully revealed to us. As hard as these moments are, they provide us with an incredible opportunity for growth as we wait on God to answer our prayer. It is during these times we tend to draw closer to Him and dig deeper into His word. The wait can also weigh us down when our faith is tested during these times. When that happens, rely on God's word. Don't try to take matters into your own hands and solve the problem yourself. Continue to pray and seek God's answer. It is also important to be strong when our faith begins to waver. In Joshua 1, the Lord told Joshua to be 'strong and courageous.' He also told Joshua, '…I will be with you; I will never leave you or forsake you.' The Lord was preparing Joshua and the Israelites to cross the Jordan River into the Promised Land. He knew the journey was going to be long and difficult. Joshua 23:1 summarizes the journey, 'After a long time had passed and the Lord had given Israel rest from their all their enemies around them, Joshua, by then old and well advanced in years.' Notice it was a long time between the time the Israelites first entered the Promised Land and finally took possession of it. They also had to fight a number of battles to take it. Their journey was not easy. Just like the Israelites, our journey is not easy. There are times when we are going to have to face life's battles. We will face discouragement and trouble. Hold fast to God's word during those times. Be strong and courageous. He will never leave you or forsake you.

**Acknowledge** –Lord, there are times when my thoughts trouble me and I am distraught.

**Confess** – Lord, forgive me when I doubt Your love for me while I am waiting for You to answer my prayer.

**Thanksgiving** – Lord, thank You that You hear and answer our prayers.

**Prayer** – Lord, help me to be strong and courageous. Help me to fight life's battles knowing You will never leave me or forsake me.

# Day 138

Psalm 55:17 Evening, morning and noon I cry out in distress, and He hears my voice.

Seasons of great distress require the call for fervent seasons of prayer and devotion. David did not shy away from reaching out to God when things were not going well for him. If ever there was a time when we needed to cry out to God evening, morning, and noon, the year 2020 was it. A friend of mine described this time as a generation-defining moment. It is a time when our generation will tell our grandchildren about the deadly coronavirus and its impact on our lives. But my friend goes on to say that our generation will also be able to tell of the great victories God provided and how God sustained us through this turbulent time. We will be able to tell how, as with all the other great calamities, God saw us through. We will be able to tell how we cried out to God morning, noon, and night. We will share how many people across the nation prayed Psalm 91 over their families each day. We will say as David said in verse two of Psalms 91, 'I will say of the Lord, He is my refuge and my fortress, my God, in whom I trust.' Why were we confident in God's deliverance? Because David was confident that God heard him. So much so, he concludes this verse by saying, 'he hears my voice.' God hears our cry of distress. He loves us. What calamity are you facing today? It may not be a deadly virus, but whatever you are going through is just as serious and threatening to you. Are you living in fear and doubt or are you relying on God? Is He your refuge and your fortress? Reach out to him, evening, morning, and noon. Tell Him your fears, your doubts, and your troubles. He heard David and He will hear you.

**Acknowledge** – Lord, You hear our voice when we cry out to You.

**Confess** – Lord, forgive me when I fail to cry out to You. Forgive me when I forget Your mighty works in the past and doubt You can do it again.

**Thanksgiving** – Lord, thank You that we can call out to You at any time and that You hear our voice.

**Prayer** – Lord, You are my source of strength, my direction, my comfort, my counselor, my refuge, and my fortress. You are the one I trust.

# Day 139

Psalm 55:22 Cast your cares on the Lord and He will sustain you; He will never let the righteous be shaken.

THE APOSTLE PETER, WRITING TO THE BELIEVERS SCATTERED throughout Asia Minor, in 1 Peter 5:7 tells them, 'Cast all your anxiety on Him because He cares for you.' I wonder if Peter had ever read or heard Psalm 55 and remembered David's words in today's verse. Both tell us to cast our cares on the Lord. This is great advice; however, it is not quite as easy to put into practice. The devil is a master at creating fear and confusion in our lives. A missionary friend who lives in Nicaragua faced some difficult times in 2018. Because of political unrest, a number of mission teams canceled their trips to Nicaragua that year. My friend provided housing and meals to the mission teams and employed local Nicaraguans to help look after them. Because of the cancellations, the income he counted on to pay his employees and maintain the property dried up. The political unrest settled down and it became safe to travel to Nicaragua. In February 2019, I had the opportunity to travel to Nicaragua with a small mission team from Asheville. While there, we spent time together in prayer. Someone who had prayed often for me and my family needed prayer. 1 Peter 5:7 kept coming to mind. I prayed that verse over my friend. I told him to put all his cares into 'God's Big Care Bucket.' Take his financial problems, his family problems, his ministry problems and throw them in the 'Care Bucket.' I also told him that God cares for him. I wasn't surprised to hear him say that the most important thing to him was that 'God loves him and cares for him.' He could deal with the financial, family, and ministry problems as long as he knew that God loved him. Take heart, God loves you too! He will sustain you. Even though the storms rage around you and it feels as if everything is crashing in, God loves you.

**Acknowledge** –Lord, You want us to cast our cares and fears on You.

**Confess** – Lord, forgive me for worrying about things and letting my imagination run wild with fear.

**Thanksgiving** – Lord, thank You that You love us and sustain us in times of trouble.

**Prayer** – Lord, help me to focus on You and not worry about the future. I know You will sustain me, and hold me up in times of trouble.

# Day 140

**Psalm 56:4** In God, whose word I praise. In God, I trust and am not afraid. What can mere mortals do to me?

DAVID ASKS A VERY GOOD QUESTION IN TODAY'S VERSE. WHAT CAN anyone do to me? In the following two verses, he gives a summary as to what is going on in his life. He said people are twisting his words and plotting to harm him. They conspire with each other, watching his every move and are eager to take his life. At some time in our lives, we are going to experience hurtful and untrue comments about us. The old saying, 'sticks and stones may break my bones, but words will never harm me,' is comforting, but much harder to put into practice. Often times, words do hurt. They can cut deep into our soul. Satan wants nothing more than to keep us upset with others and fearful of what they might do. Paul, writing in Romans 8:31 said, 'What, then, shall we say in response to this? If God is for us, who can be against us.' Like with David, if God is for him, Paul is not worried about what anyone can say or do to harm him. He knows that God has him in His hands no matter the outcome. In His word, God encourages us to be strong, to trust Him, and to be secure in His love and protection. God didn't insulate David or Paul from verbal or physical attack. As a Christian, it is very likely we will face persecution of some type for our faith. Don't lose hope or think you are on your own when persecution comes. Trust God and do not be afraid. Allow Him to lead you through that season of your life. If you are facing some type of attack today, bring your situation before the Lord. Let Him be your protection and your guide.

**Acknowledge** –Lord, if You are for me, what can mere man do to me.

**Confess** – Lord, forgive me when I worry and fret over what other people have said about me.

**Thanksgiving** – Lord, thank You for being with me and giving me peace during the middle of the storm.

**Prayer** – Lord, no matter the circumstances, You are with me. Help me to rely on You to fight my battles.

# Day 141

Psalm 56:13 For You have delivered me from death and my feet from stumbling, that I may walk before God in the light of life.

DAVID CLOSES PSALM 56, EXPRESSING HIS GRATITUDE, HIS FAITH, and his hope in God. David's gratitude is found in his acknowledgment that God delivered him from death. David didn't say that he was lucky or he did it through his own power. Do we give God credit for bringing us through a challenging season of our life, or do we take credit for our success? Do we believe our hard work, perseverance, and intuition made us successful? If so, who gave you the ability to work hard? Who instilled within you the desire to persevere? Who plants the thoughts and ideas in our minds that lead us out of the trials we are facing? Be careful to take credit for things God has done in your life. Secondly, David expressed his faith in God. David had faith that God would steady his feet and keep him from stumbling into the traps set by his enemies. In Psalms 40:2, David wrote, 'He lifted me out of the slimy pit, out of the mud and mire; He set my feet on a rock and gave me a firm place to stand.' David knew that God would place him on solid ground and keep him from stumbling into trouble. God will do the same for you if you trust Him to guide you. Lastly, David has hope that one day he will walk before God. We find this reference of walking before God in Genesis 17:1, 'When Abram was ninety-nine years old, the Lord appeared to him, and said, "I am God Almighty, walk before Me and be blameless.' When we walk before God, we are walking in reverence and fear of Him. David's hope was that his life would be blameless so that he could be in God's presence. Shouldn't that be our ultimate goal; to walk in holiness before God our Savior and seek His presence? Let's begin today by expressing our gratitude to God for what He has done in our lives, and to walk daily with and before our Savior.

**Acknowledge** –Lord, You keep my feet from stumbling.

**Confess** – Lord, forgive me when I wander off the path You have set before me.

**Thanksgiving** – Lord, thank You for lifting me out of the mud and mire and setting me on solid ground.

**Prayer** – Lord, I pray that I can walk humbly before You each day.

# Day 142

**Psalm 57:5** Be exalted, O God, above the heavens, let Your glory be over all the earth.

WHENEVER DAVID WAS IN TROUBLE OR FELT THREATENED, HE WENT to God. In verse one of Psalm 57, David cries out for mercy from God and seeks refuge in the shadow of God's wings. In verse two, he makes it clear that his cries are for God only, the God Most High, who finishes everything He begins. In verse three, he recognizes that God sends His help from heaven. Just as God sent manna from heaven to the Israelites who were wandering in the desert, God will send help to David for protection from his enemies. Even better, God sends His love and faithfulness to comfort him. In verse four, David describes his enemies as ravenous beasts, whose tongues are sharp as swords which can be more deadly and painful than physical blows. David had experienced both physical and verbal threats. Yet in the middle of this Psalm, he takes time to exalt God, his Deliverer. As a reminder, to exalt someone is to raise high or elevate them by praise. He recognizes God as being higher than the heavens and that His glory fills the entire earth. David understood that God was greater than his problems and He isn't limited by time and space. Have you been where David is today? Have you wanted to take refuge and get away from your troubles even for just a short while under the protection of God's wings? Maybe you have experienced His help in a time of trouble. Did you, like David, give a shout of praise to God for being greater than your problems? You may be stuck at verse one, only able to cry out for God's mercy and refuge. Your problems seem insurmountable and you don't know where to go, but to God. There is nothing wrong with that. Keep praying, the right words will come. He knows what you are going through. He will answer your prayer. Then, when God answers your prayers, exalt Him. Give Him the praise and adoration due Him.

**Acknowledge** –Lord, I exalt You above the heavens.

**Confess** – Lord, forgive me when I doubt You and let my fears overtake my faith.

**Thanksgiving** – Lord, thank You for allowing me to take refuge under the shadow of Your wings.

**Prayer** – Lord, be glorified in my life. I look to You for my strength and my help.

# Day 143

Psalm 57:10 For great is Your love, reaching to the heavens; Your faithfulness reaches to the skies.

No matter his situation, David is confident of God's love and protection. In verse six, he says his enemies have fallen into the very trap they set for him. God used the very traps set by David's enemies to stop them. Proverbs 26:27 says, 'If a man digs a pit, he will fall into it; if a man rolls a stone, it will roll back on him.' David recognizing God's hand of protection, said in verse nine, 'My heart is steadfast O God...I will sing and make music...' We find the song on David's heart in verse ten, 'For great is Your love, it reaches to the heavens; Your faithfulness to the skies.' Paul, writing in Ephesians 3:17-18 said, 'So that Christ may dwell in your hearts through faith. And I pray that you, being rooted and established in love, may have power, together with all the saints, to grasp how wide and long and high and deep is the love of Christ.' David described God's love as reaching to the heavens and His faithfulness to the skies. Paul describes the love of God as an imaginary box that has no end. I have no idea how high the heavens are. Yet His love reaches there. Not only does it reach high, Paul tells us that God's love surrounds us. His love is as wide and as long and as high as it is deep. His love is much bigger than the problems you are facing. It reaches far beyond your current circumstances and goes back before your problems existed. It reaches down to where you are and then keeps going. Like David, in the midst of your problems stop to praise God for His love for you. Thank Him for His faithfulness that reaches to the skies. Focus your attention on Him. As you continue to focus your praise on God, your problems will begin to seem insignificant. Allow your praise to drown out your problems and enjoy the presence of the Father.

**Acknowledge** –Lord, Your love reaches to the heavens, Your faithfulness to the skies.

**Confess** – Lord, forgive me when I fail to offer my praise to You.

**Thanksgiving** – Lord, thank You that your love is much wider, much longer, much higher, and much deeper than my problems.

**Prayer** – Lord, help me to realize You love me even when I struggle to see it.

# Day 144

**Psalms 58:1** Do you rulers indeed speak justly? Do you judge people with equity?

I really like the way the Message Bible translates today's verse. 'Is this any way to run a country? Is there an honest politician in the house?' David points to the source of the matter very quickly in verse two, 'No, in your heart you devise injustice, and your hands mete out violence on the earth.' The world has a heart problem. A blog in the Association of Biblical Counselors, written in 2015 by Leslie Vernick, describes five indicators of someone with a heart problem. "1. Evil hearts are experts at creating confusion and contention. They twist the facts, mislead, lie, avoid taking responsibility, and withhold information. 2. Evil hearts are experts at fooling others with their smooth speech and flattering words. 3. Evil hearts crave and demand control, and their highest authority is their own self-reference. They make up their own rules to live by. 4. Evil hearts play on the sympathies of good-willed people. They demand mercy, but give none themselves. 5. Evil hearts have no conscience, no remorse." People with these characteristics have permeated their way throughout society and into places of leadership. Paul, writing in 2 Timothy 3:1-5, warns, 'But mark this: There will be terrible times in the last days. People will be lovers of themselves, lovers of money, boastful, proud, abusive, disobedient to their parent, ungrateful. Unholy, without love, unforgiving, slanderous, without self-control, brutal not lovers of the good, treacherous, rash conceited, lovers of pleasure rather than lovers of God – having a form of godliness but denying its power. Have nothing to do with them.' Be careful not to follow their example. Do not be drawn into their behavior because of their apparent success. Keep your heart focused on God and produce the good fruit God wants you to. Ephesians 5:11 tells us, 'Have nothing to do with the fruitless deeds of darkness, but rather expose them,' and in Ephesians 5:1, 'Be imitators of God, therefore, as dearly loved children.' Walk in the light of God's love. Be honest and fair in your dealings with others.

**Acknowledge** –Lord, You desire us to walk in holiness.

**Confess** – Lord, forgive me for not taking a stand for You in times of difficulty.

**Thanksgiving** – Lord, thank You for honest, fair, and wise leaders. They are few and far between.

**Prayer** – Lord, help me to imitate You in my speech and interactions with others.

# Day 145

> Psalm 58:11 The people will say, 'Surely the righteous still are rewarded; surely there is a God who judges the earth.'

David isn't the only one who wants God to judge the ungodly. The prophet Jeremiah in Jeremiah 12:1 speaks about it, 'You are always righteous, O Lord, when I bring a case before You. Yet I would speak with You about Your justice: Why does the way of the wicked prosper? Why do all the faithless live at ease?' In my words, O Lord, when are You going to bring judgment on the wicked? When I look at how the wicked seem to prosper, I, like Jeremiah, selfishly want God to take action on the wicked. However, there is an issue with my idea of judgment. In my selfishness, I want to see someone suffer for their wickedness. I have a lack of sympathy and concern for them. God on the other hand is completely different. He judges according to His principles, not ours. He holds us to the highest standards, His perfect and Holy character. Yet God knew and understood from the beginning of time that we couldn't live up to His standards. That is why long ago, He planned a way for us to be made right with Him, and avoid His judgment and wrath. His plan was to send His Son, Jesus, to die for our sins. Without the blood of Christ atoning for our sins, our judgment would be just as deserving as those we want God to judge. Instead of wishing God's judgment on someone, we should be praying that their hearts and lives would be changed by God's saving grace. God did that for you and me; shouldn't we want Him to do the same for others? Do you have a list of people you want God to punish or do you have a list of people you are praying for God to rescue? One day God will return and judge each of us for how we responded to Him. My prayer is that your heart will be in tune with His, caring for those around you, including those with wicked hearts.

**Acknowledge** – Lord, one day every knee will bow and every tongue confess You are Lord.

**Confess** – Lord, forgive me for wishing judgment on the wicked and not praying for them.

**Thanksgiving** – Lord, thank You that You are in charge and I am not.

**Prayer** – Lord, give me a spirit of reconciliation, forgiving others, praying for them, and sharing Your love and mercy with them.

# Day 146

> Psalm 59:1 Deliver me from my enemies, O God; be my fortress against those who are attacking me.

DAVID ASKS GOD TO BE HIS FORTRESS AGAINST THOSE WHO WERE attacking him. Note that David made his request personal. Whenever we seek God, we need to make our requests personal and relevant to our needs. On one of our mission trips to Nicaragua, we had fasted and specifically prayed for God's protection over our Team and the resources we were taking. We claimed the words of protection found in Ezra 8:21, 'There, by the Ahava Canal, I proclaimed a fast, so that we might humble ourselves before our God and ask Him for a safe journey for us and our children, with all our possessions.' We put our trust in God for protection. In Nicaragua, our Team's money, passports, and other valuables were kept in a safe place at the compound we were staying. Little did we know the compound would be robbed at gunpoint; however, God did. He had led us to pray specifically for our Team's protection. He had directed us to this obscure scripture found in the Old Testament to pray over our Team. He was our fortress against those who would try to harm us. We were blessed that no one was hurt in the robbery, and by God's hand, our Team's money and passports were not taken. We could say like Ezra in Ezra 8:31, 'On the twelfth day of the first month, we set out from the Ahava Canal to go to Jerusalem. The hand of our God was on us, and He protected us from enemies and bandits along the way.' God had protected us by making sure we had left the compound before the robbery and kept our valuables secure. After we had time to recover from the shock of the robbery, we gave God the glory and praise for His protection. Each new day holds something different for us. We don't know what lies ahead. God may be leading you to a particular scripture to pray and meditate on specifically for that day. Listen to His voice and trust Him to deliver you.

**Acknowledge** –Lord, You are our fortress and our defender.

**Confess** – Lord, forgive me for not trusting You and Your love when things get difficult for me.

**Thanksgiving** – Lord, thank You for Your hand of protection that shows up at the right time.

**Prayer** – Lord, remind me to humble myself before You and seek Your protection over the life of my family.

# Day 147

**Psalm 59:9** You are my strength, I watch for You; You God, are my fortress.

DAVID EXPRESSES HIS CONFIDENCE IN GOD WHILE HE IS STILL waiting on God's protection. He claims God to be his strength and his fortress, even as 'I watch for You.' David learned through his trials that God's answer to prayer was not instantaneous. He had to wait and trust God. He had faith that God was working out the details even though there was no visible evidence of anything happening. Have you waited in prayer hoping for something to happen right away? How do we wait patiently and expectantly for God to move in our lives? First, we should not stop praying. Don't quit on your prayer. You may be one day away from God's deliverance. Secondly, get into God's word. Your answer may be found in a verse of scripture that God leads you to. You may also find reassurance from God that He loves you, cares for you, and has your best interest at heart. Third, keep watching. Often His answers are falling into place, little by little as the pieces come together. Some answers to prayers can happen overnight, but many come together over time. Fourth, look inward and make sure your prayers are in line with God's will. Are you carrying any unconfessed sin? If so, you need to repent and align your life with His plan and purpose. Lastly, keep living your life. Don't let fear and doubt keep you from getting out of bed each morning. Allow God to direct your paths each day and continue to trust Him. He is leading you to your answer. Lamentations 3:24-26 tells us, 'I say to myself, "The Lord is my portion; therefore I will wait for Him." The Lord is good to those whose hope is in Him, to the one who seeks Him; it is good to wait quietly for the salvation of the Lord.' And Paul, writing in Romans 12:12, tells us, 'Be joyful in hope, patient in affliction, faithful in prayer. So as David wrote today, acknowledge God as your strength and your fortress. Eagerly wait for God to answer your prayer, and ask Him to lead you each day.

**Acknowledge** –Lord, You are our strength and our fortress.

**Confess** – Lord, forgive me for allowing fear and doubt to rule my life.

**Thanksgiving** – Lord, thank You that You answer our prayers.

**Prayer** – Lord, help me to wait expectantly for Your answer to my prayers.

# Day 148

Psalm 59:16 But I will sing of Your strength, in the morning I will sing of Your love; for You are my fortress, my refuge in times of trouble.

DAVID REJOICES WHEN THE MORNING DAWNS AND GOD HAS answered his prayers. I am reminded of Psalms 30:5 that tells us, 'For His anger lasts only a moment, but His favor lasts a lifetime; weeping may remain for a night, but rejoicing comes in the morning.' Where are you today? Are you still in the dark night of despair and hopelessness waiting for God to answer your cry for help? Or, has the morning come and you can see God's hand working in your life? How do you respond when morning comes? Do you give God praise for His unfailing love for you? Do you sing of His love, His strength, His faithfulness, and His protection over you? Can you declare that God is your refuge in times of trouble? Or, have you taken refuge in alcohol or drugs to dull your senses? Perhaps you have taken refuge by withdrawing and becoming a loner? Let God be your refuge. Sing praises to Him for all He has done and what He is going to do in your life. Don't let fear and doubt drive you away from the shelter of His wings. Don't let your current circumstances weaken your faith in Him, for He is your fortress and refuge. There is an old praise and worship song that fits today's verse very well. Let the words of this song, "I Could Sing of Your Love Forever' written by Martin Smith, become your song of praise today. 'Over the mountains and the sea, Your river runs with love for me, And I will open up my heart, And let the healer set me free. I'm happy to be in the truth, And I will daily lift my hands: For I will always sing of when, Your love came down. I could sing of Your love forever, I could sing of Your love forever, I could sing of Your love forever...' Join David in singing of His love forever.

**Acknowledge** –Lord, You are our refuge in times of trouble.

**Confess** – Lord, forgive me when I take refuge in things that are harmful.

**Thanksgiving** – Lord, thank You for carrying us through the dark nights into the light of a beautiful morning.

**Prayer** – Lord, let me sing of Your love forever. Teach me a new song to sing to You in worship.

# Day 149

Psalm 60:5 Save us and help us with Your right hand, that those You love may be delivered.

Today's verse reminds me of the story in Matthew 8:23-27, where Jesus and the disciples had been at Capernaum and got in a boat to cross over the Sea of Galilee to Gadarenes. Without warning, a terrible storm came up and sent waves crashing over the boat. The disciples, many of whom were experienced fishermen, were afraid for their lives. While the storm was raging, Jesus was asleep in the boat. The disciples woke Him up saying, 'Lord save us! We are going to drown! What was Jesus' response to the disciples? Did He calm the storm and give them an object lesson? He may have, but not in that order. His first response was to speak to the disciples, 'You of little faith, why are you so afraid?' Then Jesus got up and rebuked the storm and immediately the waters were calm. There are a couple of things we can take hold of in today's verse and the story of Jesus calming the storm. The first is that we have someone we can call on to save us. We have a God who cares for us and has the power to deliver us from any storm. Secondly, our Lord is in the boat with us. He knows what we are going through and is with us. He is not bothered by the storm; in fact, He can sleep while the storm is raging. Thirdly, our Lord has the power to calm the storm. He can speak healing, deliverance, and peace to any storm we are facing. Lastly, our Lord loves and cares for us. Yet He wants us to have faith in Him and to trust Him while we are going through the storm. Where is your faith level today? Has it been shaken by storms that never seem to end? Or, do you trust Him to bring you through the storm? Call out to Him today as David did and as the disciples did. He loves you.

**Acknowledge** –Lord, You save us with Your right hand.

**Confess** – Lord, forgive me when my faith starts to waver and doubt Your love for me.

**Thanksgiving** – Lord, thank You for calming storms in my life.

**Prayer** – Lord, hear my cry of help during the storms of life. Deliver me from them in Your time frame and according to Your will.

# Day 150

**Psalm 60:12 With God we will gain the victory, and He will trample down our enemies.**

I don't have the experience of fighting in a war. David has and knows the commitment, the planning and the trust in his army it takes to win a battle. But most importantly, he knows that with God on his side, the victory is his. Even as a young man, David realized that it was God who delivered him from the bear and lion as he protected his father's sheep. In 1 Samuel 17:36-37, David, talking to Saul, said, 'Your servant has killed both the lion and the bear; this uncircumcised Philistine will be like one of them, because he has defied the armies of the living God. The Lord who delivered me from the paw of the lion and the paw of the bear will deliver me from the hand of this Philistine.' Later as David was standing in front of the 9'9" Goliath, covered in armor, David is not afraid. He tells Goliath in verses 45-46, '....You come against me with sword and spear and javelin, but I come against you in the name of the Lord Almighty, the God of the armies of Israel, whom you have defied. This day the Lord will hand you over to me, and I will strike you down and cut off your head. Today I will give the carcasses of the Philistine army to the birds of the air and the beasts of the earth, and the whole world will know that there is a God in Israel.' What giant are you facing today? Be bold and use the weapons God has provided. For David, it was five smooth stones, not the conventional weapons of Saul. Then call upon God to go before you and give you victory over your giant. Lastly, step out in faith and courage, trusting God as you take on your giant. Some giants will fall easier than others. Goliath fell when struck by the stone, but David had to finish the job. This is a good reminder for us, as you see your giant fall, finish the job. Remove it completely from your life and give God the praise.

**Acknowledge** –Lord, You go before me in battle.

**Confess** – Lord, forgive me when I let the size and the taunts of the giant intimidate me.

**Thanksgiving** – Lord, thank You for trampling down our enemies.

**Prayer** – Lord, it is only by Your power, Your strength, Your provision that we can have victory over spiritual darkness.

# Day 151

> Psalm 61:3 For You have been my refuge, a strong tower against the foe.

DAVID IS REFLECTING ON HOW GOD HAS HELPED HIM IN THE PAST. He recognizes God as having been a refuge and a strong tower when he was under attack. In verse two, David said, 'lead me to the rock that is higher than I.' This is not the first time David has called God his place of refuge and his rock. In my daily Bible reading with the Bible Recap, Tara Leigh-Cobble, made the point that David might have been hiding from Saul at Masada, when he was writing about God being his refuge and strong tower. Masada is a massive rock structure that rises out of the desert resembling a tower. It is located on the eastern edge of the Judean Desert, overlooking the Dead Sea. David could have had this picture of Masada in his mind when he called God his refuge and strong tower. What imagery do you use in your prayers? Have you, like David, referred to Him as your strong tower? Have you used other words to describe and honor God in your prayers? I sometimes like to use phrases that represent God in my worship to honor Him. Phrases such as; 'Lamb of God, Rose of Sharon, Lily of Valley, the Bright and Morning Star, the Prince of Peace, the King of Kings, Lord of Lords, the Lord God Almighty, the Rock of Ages, the Rock of my Salvation, and our Soon Coming King.' The words to describe Him are endless. The point is that He desires our worship and wants us to put our faith and trust in Him. Paint a picture of God in your mind that represents your true praise. For David, it was a place of refuge, a rock, a strong tower because he was on the run. For you, it may be something totally different. Let the descriptive words of praise flow from your lips.

**Acknowledge** –Lord, You are the Rock of Ages, let me hide myself in Thee.

**Confess** – Lord, forgive me when I fail to praise You as I should.

**Thanksgiving** – Lord, thank You that as David cried out to You and You heard his prayers, You also hear ours.

**Prayer** – Lord, today I lift up my praise to You. You are the Lily of the Valley, the Bright and Morning Star, the Prince of Peace, the Lord of Lords, the Rock of Ages. In You, I place my trust.

# Day 152

Psalm 62:1 Truly my soul finds rest in God; my salvation comes from Him.

DAVID HAD HIS SHARE OF PROBLEMS. HOWEVER, HE LEARNED HOW to calm down in the midst of his troubles to claim the promises of God. He also sought the presence of God where he found rest and peace. Like David, you can have rest in the midst of your problems. Jesus tells us in Matthew 11:28-29, 'Come to Me, all you who are weary and burdened, and I will give you rest. Take My yoke upon you and learn from Me, for I am gentle and humble in heart, and you will find rest for your souls.' Jesus tells us that rest is found in Him. In Exodus 33:14, we find the same promise of rest given to Moses. This promise applies to us as well. It says 'The Lord replied, "My presence will go with you, and I will give you rest."' The Bible tells us that rest comes from being in God's presence. How do we claim the rest promised by God? The first step is to do as David and tell Him, 'my soul finds rest in You alone.' Secondly, put aside the things that are crowding out your time with God and seek His presence each day. You can start by daily reading His word and spending time in prayer. After you have declared rest comes from God and have committed to spending time with Him, you will begin to experience the rest and peace that comes over your life. Lastly, as your problems begin to fade away while in His Presence, declare His grace to others. Your circumstances may not have changed. The world may still be spinning out of control all around you, but your outlook towards life will be changed. In David's case, it took years before things settled down in his life; however, he trusted in God to find rest. You can have the same peace David had. Trust the words of Jesus, 'Come to Me, all you who are weary and burdened. I will give you rest.'

**Acknowledge** –Lord, only in You can my soul find rest.

**Confess** – Lord, forgive me when I try to find rest and peace in things that only provide temporary relief from my problems.

**Thanksgiving** – Lord, thank You for Your promise of rest.

**Prayer** – Lord, all too often I let the burdens of this life overwhelm me and take my eyes off Your promise of rest. Please help me seek your presence each day.

Psalm 62:5 Yes, my soul, find rest in God; My hope comes from Him.

DAVID IS CONFIRMING WHAT HE DECLARED IN VERSE ONE, THERE IS rest in God. He goes on to say, God is his source of hope. However, there are some people who prefer the noisiness of life to help block out the emptiness that is inside them. The busier they are, the less time they have to focus on themselves and the lack of purpose or meaning in their lives. They tend to keep their minds occupied and hands busy. Eventually burnout occurs, turning their energy and enthusiasm into exhaustion, frustration, and the emptiness they are trying to avoid. Are you this person? God longs to fill that empty spot in your life. However, you must come to a place of rest and peace where you can hear God. You cannot hear Him or receive the hope He provides while you are filling your time with busyness. Psalms 46:10 says, 'Be still, and know that I am God; I will be exalted among the nations, I will be exalted in the earth.' The first step is to take time to be still long enough to hear from God. Stop what you are doing, and schedule a time to reach out to Him. You need to give God your undivided attention and allow Him to speak into your spirit. Second, trust that God will replace the emptiness you are running from. Solomon wrote in Proverbs 3:5-6, 'Trust in the Lord with all your heart and lean not on your own understanding; in all your ways submit to Him, and He will make your paths straight.' The more you trust Him, the more He will work in your life. You will not likely have an overnight transformation, but as time goes on you will find yourself desiring to spend more time with God. God will open doors and straighten your path to allow you to find real purpose in your life. As you receive God's blessing and favor you, like David, will be able to say my soul finds rest in God.

**Acknowledge** –Lord, my soul finds rest in You. You are my hope.

**Confess** – Lord, forgive me when I try to use busyness to replace the emptiness in my life.

**Thanksgiving** – Lord, thank You for making my paths straight.

**Prayer** – Lord, help me to fully trust in You, to submit to You, and lean on Your understanding.

# Day 154

Psalm 62:11 One thing God has spoken, two things I have heard: 'Power belongs to You, God, and with You, Lord, is unfailing love'; and, 'You reward everyone according to what they have done.'

HAVE YOU EVER BEEN IN A SITUATION WHERE YOU WERE TRYING TO convince someone of your arguments and found yourself repeating the same points over and over? Wouldn't it be nice if everyone understood where we are coming from and actually listened to us? Unfortunately, that doesn't always happen. However, God doesn't have to repeat Himself when He speaks. Because of His unchanging character, His perfect will, and His promises that are true; He has no need to repeat Himself. With simple words, He spoke life and light into the world. In Genesis 1:3 God said, 'Let there be light and there was light.' There are at least nine other instances where the scripture tells us, 'God said,' and what He spoke came into being. His words are powerful. That is how David describes what God has spoken. He said power belongs to You, God. We know God's words are powerful, but they also offer hope, salvation, forgiveness, and eternal life. Have you heard God speak those words into your life? Do you have the hope of His salvation and forgiveness? Hebrews 1:1-2, tells us that God speaks to us through His Son, Jesus Christ. We can read of His unfailing love for us in John 3:16 that tells us He sent His only Son to die for us. Later in John 14:1-3, Jesus said, 'Do not let your hearts be troubled. Trust in God, trust also in Me. In My Father's house are many rooms; if it were not so, I would have told you. I am going there to prepare a place for you. And if I go and prepare a place for you, I will come back and take you to be with Me that you also may be where I am.' Experience His love for you through His Word, and enjoy the rewards of putting His Word into practice.

**Acknowledge** –Lord, Your words are powerful, they offer eternal life.

**Confess** – Lord, forgive me when I allow sharp and hurting words to come out of my mouth.

**Thanksgiving** – Lord, thank You for Your unfailing love for us.

**Prayer** – Lord, help me to read and learn Your word. I want to follow You.

# Day 155

Psalm 63:1 You, God, are my God, earnestly I seek You; I thirst for You, my whole being longs for You, in a dry and parched land where there is no water.

HAVE YOU EVER THIRSTED FOR GOD'S PRESENCE AND DELIVERANCE from a difficult situation in your life? Did the more you search, the further away God seemed? Perhaps you are going through a wilderness right now. What do we do when we find ourselves in those situations? First, we shouldn't think God has abandoned us. James 1:2-4 tells us, 'Consider it pure joy, my brothers, whenever you face trials of many kinds, because you know that the testing of your faith develops perseverance. Perseverance must finish its work so that you may be mature and complete, not lacking anything.' James tells us our trials could be developing our faith. However, it is possible to wind up in a 'wilderness' because of bad choices. If your 'wilderness' is a result of unconfessed sin, get right with God by asking forgiveness. No matter the reason for your wilderness experience, Jesus has been there. After He was baptized by John the Baptist, He spent 40 days and nights, fasting and praying in the wilderness preparing for ministry. Near the end of the 40 days when Jesus was at His weakest, Satan tried three times to tempt Jesus. Quoting scripture, Jesus resisted the temptation. Like Jesus, when in our 'wilderness', we need to rely on God's word to sustain us through the dry times and Satan's attacks. We can lean on verses like, Romans 8:35 that tell us, 'Who shall separate us from the love of Christ? Shall trouble or hardship or persecution or famine or nakedness or danger or sword?' No matter what we are going through, God loves us. Continue to pray as David did, with complete faith in God. Thirst for God; let your spirit long for Him. Trust Him to carry you through the 'wilderness' you may be in.

**Acknowledge** –Lord, You are my God, I earnestly seek You.

**Confess** – Lord, forgive me when I doubt Your love for me when I am going through the wilderness.

**Thanksgiving** – Lord, thank You that nothing can separate us from Your love.

**Prayer** – Lord, help me like James to consider it pure joy when I face trials because I know that they are helping me to grow closer to You.

# Day 156

**Psalm 63:11** But the King will rejoice in God, all who swear by God will glory in Him, while the mouths of liars will be silenced.

DAVID CONTRASTS TWO TYPES OF PEOPLE; THOSE WHO FOLLOW God with those who speak lies and have no fear of Him. According to David, those who follow God will glory in Him, while those who speak lies will be silenced. I think it would be difficult to find anyone who has never told a lie. There are a number of reasons why we might lie. The most obvious is to avoid punishment or exposing something we are embarrassed about. Lying can also be used to ruin someone's reputation. For some, lying has become as easy as telling the truth. Even at an early age, we have the propensity for not telling the truth. I'll never forget asking our five-year-old granddaughter about something she had done. She had no problem telling a convincing story that was completely untrue. The Bible has a lot to say about lying. Perhaps the most direct statement about lying is found in the ninth Commandment, 'You shall not give false testimony against your neighbor,' or 'Thou shall not lie.' In Proverbs 12:22, Solomon writes, 'The Lord detests lying lips, but He delights in people who are trustworthy. And Paul writing to the believers in Colossians 3:9 says, 'Do not lie to each other, since you have taken off your old self with its practices.' We know as Christians we should not lie; however, the opportunity is always there. We need to resist the temptation when it arises. I have heard it said you only have to tell the truth once, while one lie requires another. Lying can destroy trust in a relationship. One day, we will be held accountable for every word we speak. Jesus speaking in Matthew 12:36 said, 'But I tell you that men will have to give account on the day of judgement for every careless word they have spoken.' Guard your words. Let your words be truthful and honest. As the old saying goes, 'Honesty is the best policy.'

**Acknowledge** – Lord, as Your word tells us, 'You detest lying lips.'

**Confess** – Lord, forgive me when I use lies to make myself look better than someone else.

**Thanksgiving** – Lord, thank You for silencing those who do not tell the truth.

**Prayer** – Lord, it is very easy to make up a lie to get out of trouble. Put the desire to tell the truth in my spirit.

# Day 157

Psalm 64:1 Hear me, my God, as I voice my complaint; protect my life from the threat of the enemy.

THIS IS NOT THE FIRST TIME WE HAVE SEEN DAVID CALLING ON GOD for protection. If you were to read about David in 1 & 2 Samuel, you will find his life was constantly threatened. Whether being chased by Saul, fighting the Philistines, leading raiding parties, or nearly being overthrown by his son Absalom, David's life was filled with danger. Yet in every instance, God protected David and kept His promise to him. However, David did not take God's promises or His protection for granted. In every trial, David reached out to God for help. In the same way, we should not assume God's favor upon our lives and our family will just happen. It requires faith, prayer, and action on our part. God wants us to let Him know what we are going through and that we want Him to direct our lives. We learned a couple of days ago, God allows trials and troubles in our lives to help us grow. If we don't really know God and have an intimate relationship with Him, how can we have faith that He is listening to us when we call on Him? How do our prayers become more real and in line with His will rather than just a plea for help when we get into trouble? Jesus speaking in Matthew 7:21 said, 'Not everyone who says to Me, "Lord, Lord," will enter the kingdom of heaven, but only he who does the will of My Father who is in heaven.' This is an eye-opening statement from Jesus and speaks to our relationship with Him. What type of relationship do you have with God? Are you doing His will and bearing good fruit? How is your prayer life? Are you spending time in His word? Take the time to evaluate your relationship with Him. Ask God to reveal the areas in your life that need to change for you to have a deeper relationship with Him. Then pray as David, Lord protect my life from the threat of the enemy.

**Acknowledge** –Lord, You hear us when we pray.

**Confess** – Lord, forgive me when I allow the enemy's attacks to affect my relationship with You.

**Thanksgiving** – Lord, thank You for Your hand of protection on my life.

**Prayer** – Lord, I want to be one who does Your will and produces good fruit. Protect me from the enemy.

# Day 158

**Psalm 64:10** The righteous will rejoice in the Lord and take refuge in Him; all the upright in heart will glory in Him.

DAVID REALIZES THAT THOSE WHO TRUST IN THE LORD REJOICE AND take refuge in Him. He also introduces a couple of terms we may have heard, but perhaps have forgotten their importance. The first is righteous, which is having a high moral character, or doing what is right. The word righteous appears over 500 times in the Bible. (www.carm.org) As Christians we should pursue righteousness every day. Jesus speaking in Matthew 5:6 says 'Blessed are those who hunger and thirst for righteousness, for they shall be filled.' How do I pursue righteous living? Micah 6:8 tells us, 'He has shown you, O man, what is good; and what does the Lord require of you, but to act justly, to love mercy, and to walk humbly with your God.' It takes a conscious effort to live a righteous life because we are constantly fighting against the sin nature that we are born with. Paul explains this constant battle in Romans 7:19, 'For what I do is not the good I want to do; no the evil I do not want to do – this I keep doing.' Each morning as we prepare for the day, we should put on the 'breastplate of righteousness' which protects our heart. The second term David uses is the righteous will 'glory in Him.' 'To glory in Him' is when we recognize God for what He has done. Revelation 4:11 tells us, 'Worthy are You, our Lord and God, to receive glory and honor and power, for You created all things, and by Your will they existed and were created.' Also, in Revelation 5:13 we find who will be giving God the glory, 'And I heard every creature under the earth and in the sea, and all that is in them, saying, "To Him who sits on the throne and to the Lamb be blessing and honor and glory and might forever and ever!" As David wrote, 'all the upright in heart will glory in Him.' If you know God, have had your sins forgiven, and promised eternal life with Him, you should be giving Him glory every day.

**Acknowledge** – Lord, I take refuge in You.

**Confess** – Lord, forgive me for not giving You the glory and honor You deserve.

**Thanksgiving** – Lord, thank You for teaching us how to live a righteous life.

**Prayer** – Lord, You are worthy to receive glory, honor, and praise.

# Day 159

**Psalm 65:1** Praise awaits You, our God, in Zion; to You our vows be fulfilled.

David writes that his praise awaited God. It sounds as if he is telling God that he has stored up praise in his soul waiting for the right moment to be in His presence, the moment when God appears in Zion to express it to Him. Have you had that feeling of anticipation like David of entering into the presence of God with your heart bursting to praise Him? Maybe you never have, or it has been a long time since you have been there. How do we find our way to being in the presence of God? David provides the answer in Psalm 100. He tells us in verse four, 'Enter His gates with thanksgiving and His courts with praise; give thanks to Him and praise His name.' As we begin to give God thanks in all things, He opens the door of our heart to His presence. Thanksgiving gets us through the gate; however, praise begins to take over and ushers us into his courts or further into His presence. Thanksgiving is expressing our gratitude to God for what He has done for us. Praise on the other hand is worshiping God for who He is. Once in His presence we find joy, peace, comfort and forgiveness. Our requests are laid out before Him. It is there we renew our hearts to serve Him and to obey His commandments. It is there we determine, as David wrote in the last part of this verse, that our promises to God be fulfilled. Take time today to enter His gates with thanksgiving and into His courts with praise. As the chorus of the praise song, 'Jesus Paid it All', reminds us, 'O praise the one who paid my debt, and raised this life up from the dead.' Block out the noise and busyness of the day and enjoy His presence. Your outlook on today will be totally different.

**Acknowledge** –Lord, my praise awaits You.

**Confess** – Lord, forgive me when I fail to give You thanks because that is the door to Your presence.

**Thanksgiving** – Lord, thank You for being a God that loves us and allows us to enter into Your presence.

**Prayer** – Lord, my life should be about praise and worship to You because You paid my debt, and raised my life up from the dead.

# Day 160

Psalm 65:9 You care for the land and water it; You enrich it abundantly. The streams of God are filled with water to provide the people with grain, for so You have ordained it.

FARMERS WORK HARD. THEY HAVE LONG DAYS OF PLOWING, FERTILizing, planting, irrigating, fighting insects, maintaining equipment, and harvesting their crops. One season of drought can devastate a farmer and set them back years. Yet, they tirelessly and faithfully plant and harvest year after year to feed us. Today's verse tells us about God's love for the land. Tending the land was part of God's plan for mankind right from the beginning. Genesis 2:8 says, 'Now the Lord God had planted a garden in the east, in Eden; and there He put the man He had formed.' In verse 15, man was given the responsibility of taking care of the garden, 'The Lord God took the man and put him in the Garden of Eden to work it and take care of it.' God's plan was for us to work the land and grow our own food. Yet, this would not be possible without God enriching the land. It is not by happenstance that the soil in various parts of the world is more suitable for growing certain crops. For example, potatoes are grown in every state; however, over half the crop comes from just nine states. Corn is grown in most states as well; however, most of the corn produced comes from an area called the Heartland region. (www.ers.usda.gov) Year after year, crops are harvested and food is produced because God has ordained it. There are times when it is not easy to grow crops and produce food. In the Bible, we read about times of famine, drought, and pestilence. Whatever the reason, we know that God can and does open up the heavens with rain to water and enrich the land. Give Him thanks today for His provision of rain and goodness to the land. Thank Him for those who work the land to feed us.

**Acknowledge** –Lord, You make provision for us to have our daily bread.

**Confess** – Lord, forgive me when I take Your blessing of rain for granted.

**Thanksgiving** – Lord, thank You for those who work the earth to provide food for everyone.

**Prayer** – Lord, I pray that You will send rain to areas that need it. I ask that You water the crops at the right time so Your people can be fed.

# Day 161

**Psalm 66:1-2** Shout for joy to God, all the earth! Sing the glory of His name; make His praise glorious!

Psalm 66 is a Psalm of praise for God's great works, His gracious benefits, and His faithful deliverances. The Psalmist begins with the word 'shout.' He wants everyone to hear. Have you been in a worship service where the leader wants you to verbally proclaim God's goodness? Even participating in on-line services during the Covid-19 pandemic, I am a little uneasy about saying something out loud when the pastor asks us to. I know I shouldn't be, because there is power in our spoken words to Him. After his shout for joy, the Psalmist breaks out into singing because of God's glory. He says, 'Sing the glory of His name.' Or, sing to the honor and renown of His name. A name that, in Old Testament days, was so holy and reverent the Jews refused to speak the name at all. The Hebrew name for God was four letters, YHWH. Later vowels were added, YAHWEH or translated Jehovah. The Hebrews would substitute the word Adonai, or Lord, for God's name to ensure they did not break the 4th Commandment which says, 'You shall not misuse the name of the Lord your God, for the Lord will not hold anyone guiltless who misuses his name.' A name so powerful and reverent that when Moses asked God 'who should I tell the Israelites sent me to deliver you from the hand Pharaoh?' that God told him, 'I AM, WHO I AM.' Do you have reverence for God's name? Or do you use His name loosely in your conversations? Does the phrase, 'OMG', or 'Oh my God' roll off your lips when something unexpected happens? Or does the name, 'Jesus Christ', fly out of your mouth when you get frustrated? If so, take a moment to really consider the impact of your words. Our reverence and awe of Him should include respect for His name. His command about misusing His name hasn't changed. My prayer is that you will really grasp the holiness of His name and the reverence it deserves.

**Acknowledge** –Lord, I shout for joy to the glory of Your name.

**Confess** – Lord, forgive me when I use Your name flippantly and don't give You the reverence You deserve.

**Thanksgiving** – Lord, thank You that I can sing praises to You for You are my God.

**Prayer** – Lord, help me to understand the holiness of Your name and to choose my words carefully.

# Day 162

Psalm 66:8,16 Praise our God, all peoples, let the sound of His praise be heard. Come and hear, all you who fear God; let me tell you what He has done for me.

WHAT HAS GOD DONE FOR YOU? HAVE YOU TOLD SOMEONE? THE Psalmist was telling anyone who would listen what God has done for him. In Mark 5:1-20, we find the story of a demon-possessed man. He was naked and lived in a cemetery. Every day, he would cry out and cut himself with stones. One day as Jesus passed by, the demon-possessed man ran and fell on his knees before Jesus and shouted, 'What do you want with me, Jesus Son of the Most-High God?' Jesus then commanded the evil spirits to come out of the man. They left him and went into a large, nearby herd of pigs. The pigs rushed down a steep bank into a lake and were drowned. After the demons had left the man, he put on clothes and was in his right mind. He wanted to follow Jesus, but Jesus told him to go home to his family and tell them what the Lord had done for him. Verse 20 tells us, 'So the man went away and began to tell in the Decapolis how much Jesus had done for him. And all the people were amazed.' Our story may not be as dramatic as the demon-possessed man. We may not have been living in a cemetery, naked, cutting ourselves with stones. But maybe it is. Without Christ in our lives, aren't we living among the dead without hope of eternal life? Haven't we done crazy things to our bodies, to dull the pain of life? Although we may not be literally naked, He can see right through us. Yet, He loved us enough to save us. The price was much more than 2,000 pigs. The price was His Son, who sacrificed Himself on the cross. Because of His love for us, we are clothed in His righteousness and have a hope and a future. Isn't that worth telling someone else about? Tell someone today what God has done for you.

**Acknowledge** –Lord, You have done great things for me.

**Confess** – Lord, forgive me when I fail to tell others about Your love and mercy.

**Thanksgiving** – Lord, thank You for saving me.

**Prayer** – Lord, like the demon-possessed man, I was naked, lost, and afraid until You stopped by and rescued me. Help me to share my story with someone else.

# Day 163

Psalm 66:20 Praise be to God, who has not rejected my prayer or withheld His love for me!

The Psalmist concludes this Psalm by proclaiming that God has not rejected his prayer or withheld His love. God has been faithful to him throughout his entire life. Where are you today? Have you come through a struggle and can now look back to see how God has worked things out for you? Can you rejoice and give God praise because you know that God loves you and has guided you to where you are? Or are you in a valley of despair right now? Does life seem like it is caving in on you? Can you identify with the Psalmist as he writes in verses 10-12, 'For you, O God, tested us; you refined us like silver. You brought us into prison, and laid burdens on our backs. You let men ride over our heads; we went through fire and water.' Take heart, because He concludes verse 12 by saying, 'but You brought us to a place of abundance.' That 'but' changes everything. God doesn't allow trials and trouble in our lives to let us sink and drown in our misery. What the enemy means for evil, God uses for His good. Are you waiting for your 'but God' moment? Be patient, keep praying, and be confident because God has heard your prayer. The phrase 'but God' appears in the Bible over 30 times. I think the story of Joseph fits well here. He was sold into slavery by his brothers but ended up being next to Pharaoh in charge of Egypt and food distribution during a great famine. In Genesis 50:20, Joseph told his brothers, 'You intended harm to me, **but God** intended it for good to accomplish what is now being done, the saving of many lives.' Give God praise today because He will not withhold His love from you. He hears your prayers and will bring you through this difficult time. What others may have meant for harm to you, will turn out to be a blessing to you.

**Acknowledge** –Lord, You never withhold Your love for me.

**Confess** – Lord, forgive me when I begin to doubt Your love for me when I am facing trials in my life.

**Thanksgiving** – Lord, thank You for not rejecting my prayers.

**Prayer** – Lord, I am waiting for my 'but God' moment to appear in my life. Help me to be patient and faithful while I wait.

# Day 164

**Psalm 67:1** May God be gracious to us and bless us and make His face shine on us.

Psalm 67 is a short prayer seeking God's blessing. Notice how the Psalmist begins today's verse with a cry for God's mercy. Although our translation uses the phrase, 'be gracious to us;' others use, 'be merciful to us.' In either case, God's blessing starts with His mercy. God is rich in mercy. Ephesians 2:4-5 tells us, 'But God is so rich in mercy, and He loved us so much, that even though we were dead because of our sins, He gave us life when He raised Christ from the dead. (It is only by God's grace that you have been saved.)' God sent His Son to die on the cross to pay for our sins and give us eternal life with Him. We did nothing to deserve His mercy and forgiveness. It is only by His grace that we have eternal life. Like the Psalmist, Lord, be merciful to us, forgive us, and be gracious to us. Next, the Psalmist asks for God's blessing. God's blessing comes in both spiritual and material form. His spiritual blessings are eternal while His material blessings are temporary. When we ask for God's blessing, we are asking God to restore His favor on us and on others. Lastly, God's mercy and blessings are incomplete without His approval in our lives. So, we ask God to make His face to shine on us and be gracious to us. Why is the Psalmist seeking God's blessing? The answer lies in verse two, 'that Your ways may be known on earth, Your salvation among all nations.' In other words, God's mercy and favor will be so evident that the entire world will take note and seek Him. Because of God's mercy and favor on us, we will want to share it so that salvation will come to many others. Are you asking God's favor on you so you can share it with others? Or, are you looking simply for material blessings to get you through the day? Go deeper in your prayer life and ask God to help you share your blessings with others.

**Acknowledge** – Lord, You are rich in mercy and give us eternal life.

**Confess** – Lord, forgive me when I fail to share Your blessings with others.

**Thanksgiving** – Lord, thank You for shining Your face on us.

**Prayer** – Lord, draw me close to You so that I will serve and reach others.

# Day 165

*Psalm 68:4 Sing to God, sing in praise of His name, extol Him who rides on the clouds; rejoice before Him—His name is the Lord.*

DID YOU KNOW THAT GOD RIDES ON THE CLOUDS? ISN'T IT AWEsome we serve a God whose mode of transportation is in the clouds? Acts 1:9 captures Jesus' last moments on earth after He had been crucified and resurrected. 'After He said this, He was taken up before their very eyes, and a cloud hid Him from their sight.' Two verses later it says, 'Men of Galilee, they said, "Why do you stand here looking into the sky? This same Jesus, who has been taken from you into heaven, will come back in the same way you have seen him go into heaven." Jesus was caught up in the clouds and taken back to heaven. Later in 1 Thessalonians 4:17, we learn that the believers who are still alive will also ride in the clouds to meet the Lord when He calls us to meet Him. 'Then we who are alive and remain will be caught up together with them in the clouds to meet the Lord in the air, and so we shall always be with the Lord.' John, writing in Revelation 1:7, tells us, 'Look, He is coming with the clouds, and every eye will see Him, even those who pierced Him; and all the peoples of the earth will mourn because of Him. So shall it be. Amen.' Doesn't that give you a reason to sing praises to Him? Doesn't that inspire hope and confidence in our Lord and Savior? His return will not be a secret. Everyone will see Him coming in the clouds. Jesus said in Luke 21:28, 'When these things begin to take place, stand up and lift your heads, because your redemption is drawing near.' Keep looking for His return. Be expectant. Rejoice and sing praises to Him for your redemption is getting closer each day.

**Acknowledge** –Lord, You will return as You left the earth many years ago, riding on the clouds.

**Confess** – Lord, forgive me when I fail to rejoice and give You praise.

**Thanksgiving** – Lord, thank You for Your promise of calling all believers who are alive to meet You in the clouds when You return.

**Prayer** – Lord, help me to be prepared for Your return and tell others so they will be ready too.

# Day 166

Psalm 68:19 Praise be to the Lord, to God our Savior, who daily bears our burdens.

DAVID GIVES PRAISE TO GOD HIS SAVIOR, THE ONE WHO DAILY BEARS his burdens. Or as one translation puts it, 'For each day He carries us in His arms.' What burdens are you carrying right now? Are they heavy and seem to keep piling up? Today, many are facing severe financial trouble due to the shutdown of the nation resulting from the Corona Virus. Others are experiencing loneliness and isolation. Whatever burden you are facing, our God is there daily to take them off your shoulders. I like the way the King James Version interprets today's verse, 'Our God, daily loads us with benefits.' His benefits are not just a shovel full they are a dump truck load full. They are not for a select few but for everyone who trusts Him. As David tells us, it is '...God **our** Savior, who daily bears **our** burdens.' We may not see the dump truck coming down the road to our house. But it is there every morning when we rise. It is there every evening as we go to bed, dropping off a load of His love and mercy and picking up the heavy burdens of the day and taking them off our hands. He is never too early nor is He ever late in showing up. He is faithful to provide what we need to make it through that day. Each day we should praise Him and trust Him to bear our burdens. Tell Him your burdens and your cares. Ask Him to take those burdens and cares and drop off a load of His love and mercy on you. If He is your Lord and your Savior, trust Him. He is the only one who can make your burdens seem light. Jesus speaking in Matthew 11:30 said, 'For My yoke is easy and My burden is light.' Now give Him praise! Worship the One who loves you enough to ask you to give Him your burdens. Not only that, He is the only one who can replace them with joy, hope, and peace.

**Acknowledge** –Lord, You daily bear our burdens and lighten our load.

**Confess** – Lord, forgive me when I don't trust You to relieve me from the weight of my burdens and cares.

**Thanksgiving** – Lord, thank You for daily loading us with Your benefits.

**Prayer** – Lord, I praise You because You are my Lord and my Savior, the one who daily bears my burdens.

# Day 167

Psalm 68:26 Praise God in the great congregation, praise the Lord in the assembly of Israel.

David offered praises to God in the 'great congregation.' Meeting together to worship God with other believers is powerful. Matthew 18:20 tells us, 'For where two or three gather in My name, there am I with them.' We also learned in Psalm 22:3 that God inhabits the praise of His people. 'But Thou are Holy, O Thou that inhabitest the praises of Israel.'(KJV) I love the harmony and the sound of hundreds as they raise their voice in worship. David wrote in verse 25, 'In front are the singers, after them the musicians; and with them are the maidens playing tambourines.' It doesn't sound as if praise and worship hasn't changed much over thousands of years. For years we have been able to worship freely together as a congregation in the US. However due to the pandemic, in a matter of weeks corporate gatherings of ten or more were suspended indefinitely. The church has adapted and provided many creative ways to share God's word. However, none compare to meeting together in worship. David wrote in Psalm 122:1, 'I rejoiced with those who said to me, "Let us go to the house of the Lord." There are many lessons to be learned from our experience with Covid-19. However, the most significant seems to be how easily the freedoms, given to us by the Constitution, can be taken away in the name of public safety. The First Amendment protects several basic freedoms, including the freedom of religion, freedom of speech, freedom of the press, the right to assemble, and the right to petition the government. Do not take your basic rights for granted. When you go to worship, give God praise for the freedoms you have been bestowed. Give Him praise for allowing you to meet with others to join in worship with them.

**Acknowledge** –Lord, You inhabit the praise of Your people.

**Confess** – Lord, forgive me when I put limits on who I worship with and how worship is conducted.

**Thanksgiving** – Lord, thank You for the freedom to worship You in spirit and in truth.

**Prayer** – Lord, like David, I rejoice with those who said to me, let us go to the house of the Lord. Never let me take the freedom to worship You for granted.

# Day 168

**Psalm 68:35** You, God, are awesome in Your sanctuary; the God of Israel gives power and strength to His people. Praise be to God.

WE END OUR TIME IN PSALM 68 WITH DAVID ACKNOWLEDGING THE awesomeness of God and His great power. Notice that God bestows His strength and power to His people. In Joshua 23:10, we see how God's strength and power gave the Israelites supernatural strength to fight their enemies. 'One of you routs a thousand, because the Lord your God fights for you, just as He promised.' God still bestows His strength and power on us today to accomplish His will. If God wants you to accomplish something, He will give you the power to do it. I think of the Reverend Billy Graham whose ministry touched millions of lives. He could not have accomplished all that he did through his own abilities. God gave him the strength to carry the gospel across the world. Isaiah 41:9-10 says, 'I took you from the ends of the earth, from its farthest corners I called you. I said, 'You are My servant'; I have chosen you and have not rejected you. So do not fear, for I am with you; do not be dismayed, for I am your God. I will strengthen you and help you; I will uphold you with My righteous right hand.' What is God calling you to do? Are you ready to give up before you get started? When those thoughts arise, fall back on God's promises. Hold fast to His word and keep pressing on because God is about to send a breakthrough. Trust Him to 'strengthen you and uphold you with His righteous right hand.' Ask Him to renew your strength. Pray Isaiah 40:31, 'But those who hope in the Lord will renew their strength. They will soar on wings like eagles; they will run and not grow weary, they will walk and not grow faint.' When God takes over, things begin to fall into place. You wake up with renewed energy and determination. Praise Him for seeing you through the difficult days and renewing your strength.

**Acknowledge** –Lord, You provide us with the strength and power to accomplish Your plan for our lives.

**Confess** – Lord, forgive me when I want to give up.

**Thanksgiving** – Lord, thank You for choosing me to be Your servant.

**Prayer** – Lord, I give You praise because You are awesome. I give You praise because You strengthen me. Lord, help me to soar on wings like eagles.

# Day 169

Psalm 69:1 Save me, O God, for the waters have come up to my neck.

Psalm 69 was written by David in response to his troubles. But more importantly it foreshadows the crucifixion of Christ. Today's verse is one we can easily relate to when our problems continue to pile up. Just as David cries out to God, 'Save me,' there have been times in my life when I felt the same way. Do you tend to hold on to things until the way out seems impossible? It would be much less worry for us to hand all our problems, big and small to Him. This reminds me of a cartoon my grandchildren love to watch called, 'Paw Patrol.' It is about a group of puppies that go about rescuing people from various situations they find themselves in. The story line always includes a phrase which fits in with today's verse. It goes, 'No job is too big, no pup is too small, Paw Patrol on a roll.' David knew there was no problem too big or too small that his God couldn't handle. He knew God was greater than all his problems. As his problems continued to mount up, David cries out to the only one who could rescue him. David knew that God would not abandon him and that He would come to his aid. Why did David have that confidence? How can we have that same confidence? It is because His word tells us to give our problems to Him. Paul, writing in Philippians 4:6 said, 'Do not be anxious about anything, but in everything, by prayer and petition, with thanksgiving, present your requests to God.' Isn't it reassuring to know that our God wants us to call on Him? Our God is a way maker. He makes a way when there is no way. As the chorus from the song "Way Maker" goes, 'You are a way maker, miracle worker, promise keeper, light in the darkness, my God, that is who You are.' Trust Him today. Don't wait; call out to God today to save you. Give your problems to Him.

**Acknowledge** –Lord, You are a way maker, miracle worker, promise keeper and a light in the darkness.

**Confess** – Lord, forgive me when I lack faith to trust You with all my problems.

**Thanksgiving** – Lord, thank You for allowing me to present my prayers and petitions to You.

**Prayer** – Lord, save me for the waters have come up to my neck.

# Day 170

Psalm 69:6 Lord, the God of Israel the Lord almighty, may those who hope in You not be disgraced because of me; God of Israel, may those who seek You not be put to shame because of me.

DAVID SPEAKS OF HIS CONCERN ABOUT HOW THE CIRCUMSTANCES of his life may have influenced others. He was not perfect, nor did he always make good choices. For starters, he faced persecution from Saul and his son, Absalom. He had an affair with Bathsheba and had her husband Uriah killed in battle. But today's verse also provides a view of the crucifixion of Christ. Christ's followers had visions of Him setting up an earthly kingdom. Even as He was being nailed to the cross, they thought He would call for the angels to rescue Him. As they watched Him die, the chief priests and others mocked Him. He was beaten and spit upon. He was taken down from the cross and buried in a borrowed tomb. His disciples went into hiding thinking Jesus' life was over and so was His earthly kingdom. Their hopes of Jesus being the one to redeem Israel had died with Him on the cross. However, Jesus' story did not end with His humiliating and painful death on the cross. Jesus rose from the grave, defeating death, and establishing a heavenly kingdom. It is through His resurrection that we can have eternal life and share His kingdom. Just as David's life was not defined by one specific incident, neither are our lives. You may have done something that you feel can't be forgiven. Your actions may have caused others a great deal of pain. It doesn't matter. God loves you and wants to heal and restore you. Jesus' death on the cross covered your sins. Call out to Jesus today. Tell Him your sins and ask Him to forgive you. The good news is that He will! He will turn your life around. Like David, you may have to suffer the consequences of your actions, but your conscience will be healed. In the process, your life will become a shining example for Christ, not one that causes shame.

**Acknowledge** –Lord, no one is perfect except Jesus Christ.

**Confess** – Lord, forgive me when my actions do not reflect You and bring shame to myself and others.

**Thanksgiving** – Lord, thank You for taking my sins with You on the cross.

**Prayer** – Lord, my life is not perfect. Please forgive my sins and replace them with Your joy and peace.

# Day 171

Psalm 69:7 For I endure scorn for Your safety, and shame covers my face.

DAVID FORESHADOWS THE REPROACH AND SHAME JESUS FACED during His life and death on the cross. Jesus spoke truth, healing, and salvation. For that, He was hated and killed. In John 18:37, Jesus speaking to Pilate during His trial said, 'You are right in saying I am a king. In fact, for this reason I was born, and for this I came into the world, to testify to the truth. Everyone on the side of truth listens to me.' Yet, Jesus' primary mission was to provide all a way to forgiveness, redemption, a right standing with God, and eternal life. Because His mission interfered with the religious leader's status and power, they hated Him. They devised a plan to kill Him, although they couldn't find any fault in Him. They tried to trip Jesus up with trick questions. They put Jesus in a situation where He had to decide the guilt or innocence of a woman caught in adultery. All the attempts to discredit Jesus backfired and made them hate Him even more. Jesus could have easily called down His angels to turn those who hated Him to dust. Yet He endured their scorn for you and me. Their scorn led to a mock trial, complete with false accusations, that contradicted each other. Despite a complete lack of evidence, Jesus was found guilty in their eyes and sent to Pilate to get the death penalty. Given a choice by Pilate, the people chose to release Barabbas, a convicted murderer, instead of Jesus. He had Jesus flogged, ripping his back open, and placed a crown of thorns on His head. The soldiers mocked Him, spit on Him, and beat Him with a rod. He was led up the road to a place called Golgotha, and hung on a cross. There He died for you and me. Praise God that is not the end of the story, because He rose triumphantly from the grave on the third day. Today we need to praise Him for all He endured to make us right with Him.

**Acknowledge** – Lord, You endured the scorn on many for my salvation.

**Confess** – Lord, forgive me when I take for granted the sacrifice You made.

**Thanksgiving** – Lord, thank You for enduring all that You went through to make me right with You.

**Prayer** – Lord, one day I may face persecution and scorn for following You. Help me to face it with confidence and humility.

# Day 172

Psalm 69:13 But I pray to You, Lord, in the time of Your favor; in Your great love, O God, answer me with Your sure salvation.

When David says, 'I pray to you, Lord, in the time of your favor...' what does he mean? I think David is saying, Lord I lift up my problems to You, work them out in your timing. He is not seeking an immediate solution to his problems. He wants the Lord to work them out according to His plan. David is patient and understands God's timing is not always the same as his. He also knows that God's favor upon the answer will make the answer that much better. Next, David prays, 'in your great love, O God...' How much does God love us? John 3:16 explains it very well, 'For God so loved the world that He gave His only begotten Son, that whoever believes in Him should not perish but have everlasting life.' We have read about God's love for us over the last two days and how He endured the cross and all that came before it for our salvation. If God loves us that much, certainly His answer to our prayers will be covered with His love. In Exodus 20:6 we read, 'But I lavish unfailing love for a thousand generations on those who love Me and keep My commands.' A thousand generations is a long time for God to show His love towards us. We simply need to walk in obedience to Him. Which takes us to the last part of David's prayer, '...answer me with Your sure salvation.' David did not have the New Testament to read and learn about God's salvation. Yet he knew that God's salvation is sure, undeniable, unchangeable, and available to all who receive it. Have you experienced God's salvation? Have you trusted Him to be your Savior? If not, today is the day. If you have trusted God as your Lord and Savior, you can trust that He will answer your prayer.

**Acknowledge** –Lord, Your answer to my prayers are as sure as Your salvation.

**Confess** – Lord, forgive me when I become impatient, struggling to wait for You to answer my prayers.

**Thanksgiving** – Lord, I thank You that You answer my prayers with Your sure salvation.

**Prayer** – Lord, I trust You to answer my prayers in Your time because I know Your answer will be covered in Your love for me.

# Day 173

Psalm 69:30 I will praise God's name in song and glorify Him with thanksgiving.

Confident the Lord has heard and will answer his prayer, David begins to praise God in song, giving Him the glory and thanks for what He is going to do. How confident are you that God will answer your prayer? Are you confident enough to close your prayer in song and thanksgiving? Or, do you continue to focus more on your problems and not the problem solver? Do you begin a wish list of misfortune and God's punishment on those who are mistreating you? If so, you are not alone. Read Psalm 69, where you will find some pretty specific ideas from David of the punishment he wanted for his enemies. In verses 23-27, he said, 'May their eyes be darkened so they cannot see. Their backs bent forever. Pour out your wrath on them. May their place be deserted. Charge them with crime upon crime.' God allowed David to vent, but it is not our place to give God advice on how to deal with our enemies. What did Jesus tell us about our enemies? In Matthew 5:43-44 He said, 'You have heard that it was said, Love your neighbor and hate your enemy. But I tell you: Love your enemies and pray for those who persecute you.' We should show love towards those who don't like us. After David finishes venting, he closes his prayer in verse 29 with, 'I am in pain and distress; may Your salvation, O God, protect me.' All this leads up to David giving praise to God through song. Paul, writing in Philippians in 4:4, says, 'Rejoice in the Lord always. I will say it again: Rejoice!' After pouring your heart out to God, begin to praise Him. Rejoice in Him! It may be difficult when bad times are surrounding us, but we are not rejoicing in our circumstances, we are rejoicing in the one who has our lives in the palm of His hands. Give Him praise today.

**Acknowledge** –Lord, You inhabit the praises of Your people.

**Confess** – Lord, forgive me for trying to solve my problems my own way. Give me patience to allow You to work on my behalf.

**Thanksgiving** – Lord, I will glorify You with thanksgiving in my heart, I will enter Your gates with praise. I will rejoice because You have made me glad.

**Prayer** – Lord, as David wrote many years ago, 'Lord, I am in pain and distress; may Your salvation, O God, protect me.'

# Day 174

**Psalm 69:34** Let heaven and earth praise Him, the seas and all that move in them.

David is bringing this Psalm to a close, and in so doing expands his praise to God by encouraging heaven and earth, the seas, and anything that moves in them to praise God. That would include the stones Jesus talked about in Luke 19:28-40. There we read about the entry of Jesus into Jerusalem the week before His crucifixion. As He was entering the city, the people were shouting and praising God, saying, 'Blessed is the king who comes in the name of the Lord! Peace in heaven and glory in the highest!' The Pharisees were furious that the people would be praising Jesus and told Him to quiet the crowd. Jesus told them 'I tell you He replied, if they keep quiet, the stones will cry out.' If we look carefully enough, we are able to see how God's creation gives Him praise. Have you witnessed a colorful sunset or peaceful sunrise? How about a beautiful rainbow after a storm? Have you looked into the heavens on a cloudless night, observing millions of stars? I could go on how nature offers its praise to God. However, it would be a shame if nature took over what you and I are supposed to do. God created us in His image, gave us a physical body and a soul that is immortal to be in fellowship with Him forever. However, when Adam and Eve sinned, our fellowship with God was broken. It took the sacrifice of Jesus on the cross to bridge the gap between God and mankind to restore that relationship. He died so we could have eternal life with Him. That alone should give you plenty to praise God about. Like the old praise song from the 80's says, 'Ain't no rock gonna cry in my place; as long as I'm alive I'll glorify His Holy Name.' Don't let the rocks cry out in your place.

**Acknowledge** –Lord, we were created in Your image to have fellowship with You.

**Confess** – Lord, forgive me for not taking the time to praise You in spite of my circumstances. You sacrificed Your Son for me.

**Thanksgiving** – Lord, 'ain't no rock gonna cry out in my place. As long as I am alive, I'll glorify Your name.'

**Prayer** – Lord, my inheritance is in You. My life is in You, not worldly things. I ask the heavens and earth to join me in praising You, and not the other way around.

# Day 175

*Psalm 70:4 But may all who seek You rejoice and be glad in You; may those who love Your saving help always say, 'the Lord is great.'*

Throughout our lives, we spend a lot of time searching for happiness, peace of mind, financial security, a nice home, and an expensive car. How many of these things, remain constant throughout our lives? Sadly, none of these last forever. Even sadder is the time we invest chasing after things that only bring temporary satisfaction. Where does our passion for God fit into our schedule? Do we try to squeeze some time in for God on Sunday morning for an hour or two? Or perhaps we give Him a few minutes before going to bed, after watching our favorite TV shows or reading our favorite book? Better yet, do we reach out to God while running out the door each morning on the way to work? However, our priorities quickly change when we receive bad news from the doctor, or our job has been outsourced to another country, or our spouse decides they don't love us anymore. We humble ourselves before God and earnestly seek Him when trouble comes our way. Wouldn't it be more satisfying if we had that type of relationship with the Father before our world started caving in? Our foundation would be strong because of our relationship with Him. God's word tells us that we will find Him, if we seek Him. Proverbs 8:17 says, 'I love those who love Me, and those who diligently seek Me will find Me.' Also, Jeremiah 29:13 tells us, 'You will seek Me and find Me when you search for Me with all your heart.' Start seeking Him today. Change your schedule, get up earlier, or block out time to meet with Him. Jesus, speaking in John 6:35 said, 'I am the bread of life. He who comes to Me will never go hungry, and he who believes in Me will never be thirsty.' No wonder David said, 'may all who seek You rejoice and be glad in You.' There is peace, joy, happiness, and fulfillment for those who seek God.

**Acknowledge** –Lord, those who diligently seek You will find You.

**Confess** – Lord, forgive me for allowing my pursuit of worldly treasures to take the place of seeking You.

**Thanksgiving** – Lord, thank You for filling us with Your joy, peace, happiness, and fulfillment. My cup is running over.

**Prayer** – Lord, teach me to fervently seek and pursue You more than worldly treasure.

# Day 176

Psalm 71:1 In You, Lord I have taken refuge; let me never be put to shame.

Psalm 71 is a prayer for God's help from someone in their old age. So, as we study this verse, we want to do so from the perspective of someone who has trusted God for many years. Throughout his life, David made his share of mistakes but didn't waver in his faith and trust in God. He can look back on his life and say, Lord I have taken refuge in you. As I reflect back on my life, I wish I could say the Lord has always been my refuge. I accepted Christ at an early age, and have tried to serve Him. I never had a 'wild stage' but did my share of things I wish I could do over. There have also been times when life got difficult and instead of taking refuge in God, I would withdraw to myself. They didn't last long, but I wish I had taken my burdens straight to God instead of holding on to them. To grow my relationship with God, I committed to reading through the Bible each year. Each time I read His word, something new, and pertinent to my current situation jumps off the page. Are you taking the time to read God's word? God's word can be a refuge and source of strength. Proverbs 30:5 says, 'Every word of God is flawless; He is a shield to those who take refuge in Him.' From someone who has made his share of mistakes, my recommendation would be for you to get to know God better by digging deeper into His word. When the storms of life come, you will be equipped to handle them and have a strong foundation to stand on. Isaiah 33:6 says, 'He will be the sure foundation for your time, a rich stone of salvation and wisdom and knowledge; the fear of the Lord is the key to this treasure.' As you grow older, you can say as David, 'I have taken refuge in you.' What a great treasure to find early in life.

**Acknowledge** –Lord, You are a shield to those who take refuge in You.

**Confess** – Lord, forgive me for falling back on worldly ideas for refuge from life's storms.

**Thanksgiving** – Lord, thank You for being my sure foundation, a rich stone of salvation, wisdom, and knowledge.

**Prayer** – Lord, Your word is a shield and refuge. Help me to take time to read it each day and learn from it.

# Day 177

Psalm 71:18 Even when I am old and gray, do not forsake me, my God, till I declare Your power to the next generation, Your mighty acts to all who are to come.

DAVID RECOGNIZED THAT HE HAD A RESPONSIBILITY OF TEACHING the next generation about God. He wanted to acquaint them with God's power, forgiveness, mercy, grace, provision, and love. If anyone could speak from experience about God's hand on his life, it was David. In his day there were very few methods for passing on his knowledge and experiences with God. However, David was gifted in writing music and used the Psalms to record much of his relationship with Him. I continue to learn more about God each day through the written words of David. I also realize that just as the generation before me passed down a legacy of worshiping God, I have the same obligation. I want to pass down something to my children and grandchildren other than a savings account and a few worldly possessions. I want them to remember the time their 'Ya Ya' and 'Pa' spent with them. I want them to remember that worshiping God, reading His word, and prayer were a priority in our home. I want them to remember the Bible verses we taught them around the dinner table; such as, 'May the Lord bless you and keep you, may the Lord make His face to shine upon you and be gracious to you, may the Lord lift up His countenance upon you and give you peace.' Several years ago, Family Life Publishing printed prayer guides entitled, 'Lifting My Wife / Husband Through Prayer.' The prayer guide included 14 individual prayers, backed by scripture, to help your spouse grow spiritually. I close today's thought with one of those prayers, 'Increase his/her desire to teach and model Godliness as a father/mother, that the next generation might know…and not forget the works of God.' (Psalm 78:5-7) Think about your family. What legacy are you building for your family? What are you teaching your children and grandchildren? I pray that you are modeling Godliness as the foundation of your home.

**Acknowledge** –Lord, Your word is as relevant today as it was thousands of years ago.

**Confess** – Lord, forgive me when I begin thinking I have grown too old to serve You.

**Thanksgiving** – Lord, thank you for being with me throughout the many stages of life.

**Prayer** – Lord, help me to model Godliness so that the next generation might know and not forget the works of God.

# Day 178

Psalm 71:19 Your righteousness, God, reaches to the heavens, You who have done great things. Who is like You, God?

We close Psalm 71 with the question, 'Who is like You, God?' This is not the first time we find this question in the Bible. When the Israelites were backed up against the Red Sea with the Egyptians in hot pursuit, God parted the waters and they walked across on dry ground. Recorded in Exodus 15 is a song by Moses about that event. Verse 11 says, 'Who among the gods is like You, O Lord? Who is like You – majestic in holiness, awesome in glory, and working wonders?' Like Moses, David recalls the great things God has done in his life. God chose him, a lowly shepherd to be king. God delivered him from the hand of a giant and gave him victories over his enemies. God forgave his sins. What great things has God done in your life? For starters, He created you, and had a plan for you before you were born. He sent His Son to redeem you and make you His child. The God whose righteousness reaches to the heavens, loves and cares for you. He doesn't think and react to things as we do because nothing surprises Him. Isaiah 55:8-9 says, 'For My thoughts are not your thoughts, neither are your ways My ways, declares the Lord, As the heavens are higher than the earth, so are My ways higher than your ways and My thoughts than your thoughts.' There is no one who compares to our God. There is an old praise song that fits well with today's verse entitled, "There is None Like You," written by Lenny Leblanc. It goes, 'There is none like You, No one else can touch my heart like You do, I can search for all eternity Lord and find, there is none like You.' The answer to the question we started out with 'Who is like You, God?' is no one. Reflect back on your life and think about the great things He has done for you, and ask, who is like You, God?

**Acknowledge** –Lord, there is no one like You.

**Confess** – Lord, forgive me when I begin to doubt Your love and mercy for me.

**Thanksgiving** – Lord, thank You for doing great things in my life.

**Prayer** – Lord, Your thoughts are not my thoughts, nor Your ways my ways. They are much higher and greater than any I could ever have.

# Day 179

Psalm 72:14 He will rescue them from oppression and violence, for precious is their blood in His sight.

Psalm 72 is thought to be written by Solomon as a prayer for the king, but has strong references to Christ when He returns to rule the earth. The verses leading up to today's verse, describe a king who takes pity on the weak and needy. In verse 14, the king rescues them from oppression and violence. Isn't this like Jesus? Jesus healed the sick and restored sight to the blind. He had compassion on the poor and needy. Matthew 8:1-4 tells the story of Jesus healing a man with leprosy. People with leprosy were considered very contagious and unclean. They lived away from others and were reduced to being beggars. Jesus had gone up on a mountainside to preach to the large crowds that were following Him. As He was leaving, a man with leprosy came running up to Jesus and knelt before Him and said, 'Lord, if You are willing, You can make me clean.' The man had broken the rules for those with leprosy. He was supposed to walk around calling out 'unclean, unclean' to warn people not to get near him. Jesus also broke the rules because of His compassion for the man by reaching out and touching him. Jesus said to the man, 'Be clean!' and immediately he was cured of his leprosy. What can we learn from Jesus' example? First, God's word speaks pretty clearly about helping those in need. Proverbs 19:17 says, 'Whoever is kind to the poor lends to the Lord, and He will reward them for what they have done.' Also, Romans 12:13 tells us, 'Share with the Lord's people who are in need. Practice hospitality.' We should have compassion on those in need and offer help to them. We are to share our time, money, food, and clothing. You may not be able to solve world hunger, but you can make a difference in someone's life. Matthew 25:40, tells us, 'The King will reply,' "I tell you the truth, whatever you did for one of the least of these brothers of Mine, you did for Me." Take time to help someone today.

**Acknowledge** –Lord, You have compassion on the poor and needy.

**Confess** – Lord, forgive me when I am selfish and fail to help someone in need.

**Thanksgiving** – Lord, thank You for Your example on how to love others.

**Prayer** – Lord, help me to make a difference to the people I encounter each day.

# Day 180

Psalm 72:18-19 Praise be to the Lord God, the God of Israel, who alone does marvelous deeds. Praise be to His glorious name forever, may the whole earth be filled with His glory. Amen and Amen.

VERSES 18 AND 19 GIVE PRAISE TO GOD FOR HIS BLESSING ON THE king. Notice how the writer closes verse 19 by using the phrase 'Amen and Amen' sealing his prayer for him. The word amen in Hebrew means certainty, truth, and verily. (www.wikipedia.org) When we close our prayers with amen, we agree with what was said, or so be it. However, none of the kings measured up to the king described in this Psalm. Years later though, we read about a priest named Zechariah and his wife Elizabeth who were unable to have children. The Angel, Gabriel appeared to Zechariah and told him they were going to have a child that would bring back many to the Lord and prepare them for His coming. Because Zechariah didn't believe Gabriel, he was unable to speak until the child was born. Typically, the boy would have been named after his father, Zachariah; however, they named him John. After Zechariah confirmed that his name was John, he began to speak and praise God. We find the words he spoke in Luke 1:68-79. 'Praise be to the Lord, the God of Israel, because He has come and has redeemed His people. He has raised up a horn of salvation for us in the house of His servant David…' Notice the similarity in Zechariah's praise and today's verse. Zechariah goes on to describe a King that would save them from their enemies, show mercy to the people, and make it easy for the people to serve Him without fear and in holiness and righteousness. Zechariah knew that the Savior of the world was on the way. His son would prepare the way for the King of Kings. Thousands of years later, we have the privilege of serving this same King. Join with the Psalmist and say 'let the whole earth be filled with His glory.' Close your praise as the Psalmist did, Amen and Amen, so be it Lord.

**Acknowledge** –Lord, You have come to redeem Your people.

**Confess** – Lord, forgive me when I, like Zechariah, doubt Your word and plan for me.

**Thanksgiving** – Lord, You are the King of Kings, Lord of Lords, I give You praise today.

**Prayer** – Lord, You are our soon coming King. Help me to prepare the way for Your return so that others will know You.

# Day 181

> Psalm 73:1 Surely God is good to Israel, to those who are pure in heart.

Psalm 73 is attributed to Asaph, who was appointed to minister before the Ark of the Lord. Asaph claims, 'surely God is good to Israel, to those who are pure in heart.' Where have we heard the phrase 'pure in heart' before? In Matthew chapter five, we find Jesus speaking to a great crowd that was following Him. His sermon became known as the Sermon on the Mount. In verse 8 Jesus said, 'Blessed are the pure in heart, for they will see God.' What does it mean to be 'pure in heart?' Psalm 73 and Matthew 5:8 say they are blessed. The word 'pure,' translated from the Greek word 'katharos,' means to be clean, blameless, and free from guilt. (www.biblestudytools.com) The heart refers to our spirit which is our inner being where our thoughts, desires, will, and character are formed. To have a pure heart is to align our motives with our actions in such a way that both are pleasing to God. This is impossible without giving our lives to Jesus and allowing His Holy Spirit to work in us. Then the process of sanctification, or our growth towards Christlikeness, takes over. The Holy Spirit continuously works inside us, to clean out our sinful nature to replace it with a pure heart. If you are like me, your heart doesn't feel like it is completely pure yet. Don't worry, this is a lifelong process of God working within us. The key is that we continually grow our faith by turning away from sin. Paul writes in Galatians 5:16, 'So I say, live by the Spirit, and you will not gratify the desires of your sinful nature.' Will I ever achieve a 'pure heart?' The answer is yes. 1 John 3:2-3 tells us, 'Dear friends, now we are children of God, and what we will be has not yet been made known. But we know that when He appears, we shall be like Him, for we shall see Him as He is. Everyone who has this hope in Him purifies himself, just as He is pure.' Make it your goal to grow more Christ-like each day.

**Acknowledge** –Lord, blessed are the pure in heart, for they shall see You.

**Confess** – Lord, forgive me for having impure motives and thoughts.

**Thanksgiving** – Lord, thank You for sending Your Holy Spirit to teach us how to become pure in heart.

**Prayer** – Lord, my goal is to grow more like You each day.

# Day 182

Psalm 73:4 They have no struggles; their bodies are healthy and strong.

CONGRATULATIONS, YOU HAVE MADE IT HALFWAY THROUGH THE year. Today, we continue in Psalm 73 and read that the wicked seemingly have no struggles nor do they experience sickness and disease. Because of their excellent health they have no fear of death. According to the Psalmist, life is all good for the wicked. Of course, we know this is not true, but when others who are not Christians are prospering while we are struggling it can be easy to come to this conclusion. We don't have to look too hard to see celebrities, sports stars, even politicians who don't seem to follow God living extravagant lifestyles, appearing to be the picture of health. According to the American Society of Plastic Surgeons, in 2018 Americans spent more than $16.5 billion dollars on cosmetic plastic surgery. (www.plasticsurgery.org) These surgeries were primarily done to enhance features of our bodies we don't like. Additionally, Boston Medical Center reported an estimated 45 million Americans go on a diet each year and spend over $33 billion on weight loss products. (www.bmc.org) Yet the National Center for Health Statistics estimates that in 2019 in the U.S. almost 40% of adults aged 20 and over were obese. (www.cdc.gov) Our lifestyles and food choices can quickly catch up with us and affect our health. 1 Corinthians 6:19 tells us, 'Do you not know that your body is a temple of the Holy Spirit, who is in you, whom you have received from God? You are not your own; you were bought at a price. Therefore honor God with your body.' Do you honor God with your body? Do you try to eat and live a healthy lifestyle? It takes time, planning, and perseverance to make healthy choices. Eating healthy and regular exercise will make you feel better, have more energy, and help keep the weight off. It is difficult to serve others when we don't feel well. Take care of your body; treat it as a temple, so you can honor God.

**Acknowledge** –Lord, our bodies are Your temple.

**Confess** – Lord, forgive me for not taking care of my body and letting my health go.

**Thanksgiving** – Lord, thank You for my health. Help me to not take it for granted.

**Prayer** – Lord, I pray that You will strengthen me and motivate me to take care of my body so I can better serve You.

# Day 183

> Psalm 73:14 All day long I have been afflicted, and every morning brings new punishments.

THERE ARE TIMES WHEN OUR FAITH CAN WAVER AND LIKE ASAPH have the attitude that every morning brings new punishments not a new start. You can see his frustration begin to mount in verse 13 where he says, 'Surely in vain have I kept my heart pure; in vain have I washed my hands in innocence.' Asaph was bitter because the wicked seemed to prosper while he was suffering. No matter how much he did to stay pure and live a righteous life, his troubles continued to grow while the wicked seemed to live trouble-free. I have to admit, I have wondered what the use of trying to live right is. Have you felt the same way? Yet if we look carefully, Asaph actually didn't keep his heart as pure as he thought. He allowed bitter thoughts into his mind that left him brewing and unsure of God's love for him. The more we 'peel back the onion' in our own lives it reveals our true motives and thoughts. How pure are they? Inside are you mad at God for allowing things to happen in your life? Do you dread waking up each morning afraid of what is going to happen that day? Instead of focusing on the negative, begin each morning by giving God praise for the new day. Don't let the dark clouds of bitterness and anger be the reason you miss out on the opportunities God has for you. Paul was in prison when he wrote the book of Philippians. Yet in spite of his circumstances, he was always thinking of others and lifting them up in prayer. Paul writes in Philippians 1:4, 'In all my prayers for all you, I always pray with joy.' Are your prayers filled with joy? If not, maybe you should evaluate your prayer life. The storms you are going through could be the opportunity God is giving you to share the grace and love of Jesus Christ with someone.

**Acknowledge** –Lord, You allow storms in our lives to sharpen our faith in You.

**Confess** – Lord, forgive me for allowing my circumstances to dictate how I start out each new day.

**Thanksgiving** – Lord, thank You for the storms of life that shape us into the vessels You want us to be.

**Prayer** – Lord, help me to pray with joy no matter my circumstances. Guide me through the storms of life so I can be a blessing to someone.

# Day 184

Psalm 73:17 Till I entered the sanctuary of God; then I understood their final destiny.

When Asaph began to look at his circumstances through a broader view, his attitude changed. His 'Aha' moment came when his mind entered eternity where God dwells. Once he realized that the disorder in this world is temporary and that God is eternal, his doubts were erased. Just like Asaph, when we view our circumstances in the narrow scope of what we can see and not from God's eternal view, our life will seem chaotic at best. What we are going through right now is shaping our future. Jeremiah 29:11 tells us, 'For I know the plans I have for you declares the Lord, plans to prosper you and not harm you, plans to give you a hope and a future.' But what about the destiny of the wicked? Sadly, their destiny is hell if they have not repented of their sins and accepted Jesus as their Lord and Savior. Regrettably, there will always be wicked people in the world. Satan has blinded their eyes to the love of Jesus and His salvation. In Luke 16:19-31, Jesus tells the parable of the Rich Man and Lazarus. Lazarus was a beggar who lived at the rich man's gate, 'longing for to eat what fell from the rich man's table.' In the parable, both the rich man and Lazarus died around the same time. Lazarus went to heaven. The rich man was condemned to hell. Verse 23-24 says, 'In hell, where he was in torment, he looked up and saw Abraham far away, with Lazarus by his side. So he called to him, "Father Abraham, have pity on me and send Lazarus to dip the tip of his finger in water and cool my tongue, because I am in agony in this fire." In this parable we see that hell is a real place, a place of torment, agony, fire, and extreme heat. In God's eyes, we are all wicked and deserve the punishment of our sins. Praise God today for sending His only Son to die on the cross to pay the penalty for our sins.

**Acknowledge** –Lord, You know our final destiny.

**Confess** – Lord, forgive me for getting caught up in my daily problems and taking my eyes off You and Your plan for my life.

**Thanksgiving** – Lord, thank You for the plans You have for me.

**Prayer** – Lord, help me care about the destiny of the wicked, and share the good news of Jesus Christ with them.

# Day 185

Psalm 73:26 My flesh and my heart may fail, but God is the strength of my heart and my portion forever.

As the old saying goes, 'getting older is not fun but it sure beats the alternative.' In what seems like a few short years, I have witnessed six generations from my great-grandparents to my grandchildren. While growing older, our bodies begin to fail us. It is no wonder people try all types of fads and gimmicks to stay young. Trying to stay young is nothing new. Our history books tell us about Ponce de Leon, a Spanish explorer in the 1500's who searched for the 'Fountain of Youth' in the newly discovered America's. At some point we must face the facts of growing older. While growing older can bring us aches and pains, I would also like to say that aging can be fun and rewarding. In today's verse, Asaph recognized the aging process and knew that he would not live forever and set his sights on God. However, aging is not the only reason our flesh and hearts may fail. Our hearts can fail because we allow fear, doubt, sorrow, discouragement, worry, and stress take over our mind. Asaph also recognized his heart and flesh may fail, but that God was the strength of his heart. Not his human heart, but his soul. We have already looked at a number of verses about worry. We know that God is the Source of our life, joy, love, peace, and comfort. As Asaph puts it, God is our portion forever. God knows more about what we need than we do. He walks with us through life's difficulties instead of bailing us out. He wants us to trust Him and let His comforting presence in our lives strengthen us for our journey. I will leave you with a word from Lamentations 3:22-24, 'Because of the Lord's great love we are not consumed, for His compassions never fail. They are new every morning; great is your faithfulness. I say to myself, "The Lord is my portion, therefore I will wait for Him." Are you growing older with Him by your side? Is He your portion today?

**Acknowledge** –Lord, You are the strength of my heart and my portion.

**Confess** – Lord, forgive me for allowing doubt, sorrow, discouragement, worry and stress take over my mind.

**Thanksgiving** – Lord, thank You for Your faithfulness to me and my family.

**Prayer** – Lord, help me to age gracefully, giving You thanks for each new day.

# Day 186

**Psalm 74:22** Rise up, O God and defend Your cause; remember how fools mock You all day long.

Psalm 74 was written by Asaph after Israel had been destroyed and taken into exile by the Babylonians. He begins the Psalm by asking, 'Why have You rejected us forever, O God? Why does Your anger smolder against the sheep of Your pasture?' He goes on to remind God what the Babylonians did to them and to the temple. By verse 22, Asaph reminds God how the enemies of Israel had mocked Him and wanted God to take action. Israel had been exiled because of their disobedience to God although they had been warned by many prophets to repent. It would be easy for us to judge the Israelites and say they got what they deserved. But don't we have the same thoughts as Asaph? Have we reminded God of what others have done to us and ask God to punish them? I can recall reminding God what someone did in my life and praying that He would rain down the three 'D's (Doubt, Distrust, and Dislike) in that person's life. This was not a picture of love and forgiveness. God showed me that my behavior was just as bad and deserved His punishment. I repented and asked God for forgiveness and to replace the three D's with H, G, M (His Grace and Mercy). God doesn't need us to remind Him what other people have done. He knows our every thought and action. While we may want to take action and do something to correct a wrong, our best response is to pray. Pray that God will change their hearts and use you to open doors for His word to go forth. Pray that those who are in opposition to Him will be transformed to serving Him. Like the Apostle Paul who persecuted Christians by having them imprisoned and killed, no one is beyond the love of God. God transformed his life on the Road to Damascus and Paul became a champion for Christ. When you see someone mocking God, lift them up in prayer. Ask God to change their hearts as He did Paul's.

**Acknowledge** –Lord, You know our hearts and minds.

**Confess** – Lord, forgive me for telling You how to punish someone else.

**Thanksgiving** – Lord, thank You that we don't have to be perfect to be used for Your kingdom.

**Prayer** – Lord, I pray that You will break down barriers so that Your word will spread to all who need it.

# Day 187

**Psalm 75:1** We praise You, God, we praise You, for Your name is near; people tell of Your wonderful deeds.

Psalm 75 is a short Psalm of reassurance that God is in control and will not fail to call the arrogant to account. Asaph begins this Psalm by giving praise to God instead of calling out his enemies. First, he praises God because His Name is near. While the arrogant may be nearby and causing trouble, God is closer. Perhaps Asaph remembered the words of Moses in Deuteronomy 4:7, 'For what great nation is there that has a god so near to it as the Lord our God is to us, whenever we call upon Him?' Asaph had confidence that God would hear him when he called upon Him. Asaph also praises God because of His wonderful deeds. He doesn't recount the deeds God has done in his own life, but the deeds that have been told by others. The children of Israel had a rich history of God honoring His promises and performing miracle after miracle. These stories were handed down from generation to generation. While God did wonderful things back then, what wonderful deeds can we talk about? In Romans 8:28, Paul writes, 'We know that God causes everything to work together for the good of those who love God and are called according to His purpose for them.' Is Paul saying that God will make every event in my life good? I am afraid not. But he is saying that when you put your whole life together, every part of it works together for good. At times it can be difficult to see how things will work out for good, but trust God's word, they do. Because God is working in our lives and because He is near, we can have hope. Regardless how messy our life looks right now God can make something good out of it. Shouldn't that be reason enough to praise Him? Give Him praise today. Thank Him for all His wonderful deeds.

**Acknowledge** –Lord, You cause everything to work together for the good of those who love You.

**Confess** – Lord, forgive me when I fail to praise You.

**Thanksgiving** – Lord, we praise You simply because You are near. Praise You for the wonderful deeds You do.

**Prayer** – Lord, help me to trust You in all situations and circumstances of life. Help me to tell others of Your wonderful deeds so they will know and praise You as well.

# Day 188

**Psalm 76:4** You are radiant with light, more majestic than mountains rich with game.

Psalm 76, written by Asaph, is a celebration of God's deliverance from their enemy. In verse three he writes that God broke the flashing arrows, the shields and weapons of war. Today's verse is about recognizing God for what He has done for His people. Asaph begins by describing God as radiant with light. John writing in the Book of Revelation describes God in the same manner. Revelation 4:2-3 tell us, 'At once I was in the Spirit, and there before me was a throne in heaven, with someone sitting on it. And the One who sat there had the appearance of jasper and carnelian. A rainbow, resembling an emerald, encircled the throne.' Also, in Revelation 22:5 John writes, 'There will be no more night. They will not need the light of a lamp or the light of the sun, for the Lord God will give them light. And they will reign forever and ever.' God's radiance is almost indescribable. Asaph goes on to say that God is more majestic than the mountains rich with game. Charles Spurgeon in his commentary described the mountains rich with game as mountains of plunder taken from the defeated enemy.[2] In Ezekiel 39, we find a prophecy about the end of time and the collection of plunder. Verses 9-10 says, 'Then those who live in the towns of Israel will go out and use the weapons for fuel and burn them up – the small and large shields, the bows and arrows, the war clubs and spears. For seven years they will use them for fuel. They will not need to gather wood from the fields or cut it from the forests, because they will use the weapons for fuel. And they will plunder those who plundered them and loot those who looted them, declares the Sovereign Lord.' What should we take away from today's verse? God provides for His children and His radiant light illuminates our path. Praise Him for lighting our way.

**Acknowledge** – Lord, You are radiant with light. There is no darkness near You.

**Confess** – Lord, forgive me when I am impressed by human power and beauty, help me to focus on Your power and beauty.

**Thanksgiving** – Lord, we give praise to You, the 'Bright and Morning Star.'

**Prayer** – Lord, let my life be a reflection of You. Help me to share Your light with others.

# Day 189

Psalm 76:7 It is You alone who are to be feared. Who can stand before You when You are angry?

Asaph describes God as one who is to be reverently feared. He makes the obvious argument that no one can stand before God's judgment. Everyone will fall at His feet and worship Him. Even the angels worship God. We find a glimpse of their worship in Revelation 4:8 which says, '...they rest not day and night, saying, Holy, Holy, Holy, Lord God Almighty, who was, and is, and is to come.' Lucifer, whose name means Morning Star (www.wikipedia.com), chose to rebel against God and seek the glory belonging to Him. After his rebellion, Lucifer's name was changed to Satan which means adversary and was cast down to earth with his followers where they introduced rebellion against God to man. Adam and Eve were the first to fall for Satan's lies. However, Revelation 20:10 tells us of Satan's fate, 'And the devil, who deceived them, was thrown into the lake of burning sulfur, where the beast and the false prophet had been thrown. They will be tormented day and night for ever and ever.' But God had a plan to redeem us. His plan included the sacrifice of His only Son, Jesus Christ, to pay the penalty of our sin to avoid His judgment. Because of the blood shed by Jesus Christ, we do not have to hear the words spoken in Matthew 25:41, 'Then He will say to those on His left, "Depart from Me, you who are cursed, into the eternal fire prepared for the devil and his angels." If you have accepted Jesus Christ as your Savior, your sins have been forgiven. The punishment for your sins has been paid. Rejoice, because you will hear the words in Matthew 25:34, 'Then the King will say to those on His right, "Come, you who are blessed by My Father; take your inheritance, the kingdom prepared for you since the creation of the world."' Do you know Christ as your Savior? If not, today can be the day your entire future can change.

**Acknowledge** –Lord, You alone are to be feared because You hold the keys to eternal life.

**Confess** – Lord, forgive me when I allow Satan to deceive me and lead me into sin against You.

**Thanksgiving** – Lord, thank You that all efforts to rebel against You will be turned into Your glory.

**Prayer** – Lord, I long to hear the words, 'Well done my good and faithful servant' when I face You in eternity.

# Day 190

**Psalm 77:1** I cried out to God for help; I cried out to God to hear me.

Psalm 77, written by Asaph, reflects back to a time when he was in great distress. Asaph cried out to God twice, stressing the importance of the trouble he was facing. This was not a silent cry between his spirit and God, but a loud, verbal plea for help. Have you felt like crying out loud to the Lord? There is nothing wrong with crying out to God. He is the only one who has the ability to help you. Our cries also remind us that we are dependent on God. In Mark 10, we find the story of Blind Bartimaeus. Jesus and His disciples were leaving Jericho where Bartimaeus was sitting by the road begging. When he heard Jesus coming by, Bartimaeus began shouting, 'Jesus, Son of David, have mercy on me!' Verse 48 says, 'Many rebuked him and told him to be quiet, but he shouted all the more, "Son of David, have mercy on me!"' Bartimaeus' only hope for receiving his sight was Jesus. Even though many were trying to shut him up, he wasn't going to let Jesus pass by without healing him. Jesus stopped and called Bartimaeus to come over. Jesus asked Bartimaeus, 'What do you want me to do for you?' Bartimaeus replied, 'Rabbi, I want to see.' Jesus told him, 'Go, your faith has healed you.' Bartimaeus was immediately healed and began to follow Jesus. What a great story of faith and desperation. Had Bartimaeus not cried out for Jesus to heal him, he would have been sitting by the road the rest of his life. It took faith on his part to believe that Jesus would restore his sight. Like Bartimaeus, there are times when we need for God to hear us. We read in Psalm 50:15 which tells us to 'call on the Lord in the day of trouble.' But it goes on to say, 'I will deliver you and you will honor Me.' Are there obstacles in your life that are too big for you to handle? Cry out to God, give your burdens to Him.

**Acknowledge** –Lord, You hear us when we cry out to You.

**Confess** – Lord, forgive me for trying to solve my problems and not giving them to You.

**Thanksgiving** – Lord, thank You that we can cry out to You and that You hear our cries.

**Prayer** – Lord, my trust is in You. Hear my cries of desperation.

# Day 191

Psalm 77:6-7 I remembered my songs in the night. My heart meditated and my spirit asked; 'Will the Lord reject forever? Will He never show His favor again?'

Asaph is waiting for God to answer his cry for help. While he is waiting, Asaph recalls the songs he used to sing. I can recall a difficult time in the life of our family. During that time, falling to sleep seemed impossible. As soon as my head hit the pillow, thoughts began racing through my mind. The only thing that would calm my spirit and allow me to sleep was singing the worship song, 'Wonderful Peace' written by Don Moen. I would sing the chorus which goes, "Peace, peace, wonderful peace, Coming down from the Father above! Sweep over my spirit forever I pray, In fathomless billows of love!" Do you have a song to sing when things are difficult in your life? It helps having a reassuring song of God's love tucked away in your spirit for difficult times. But Asaph goes on to ask, 'Will the Lord reject forever?' Are there times when it feels like God has forgotten you. Perhaps He is using that time to grow your faith. I think about the Israelites who God had delivered from the hand of Pharaoh. Instead of leading them straight to the Promised Land, He took them down to the Red Sea. In Exodus 13:17, we read, 'When Pharaoh let the people go, God didn't lead them on the road through the Philistine country, though that was shorter. For God said, "If they face war, they might change their minds and return to Egypt." But didn't the Israelites have to fight to take possession of their Promised Land? Yes, they had to fight a number of battles. The difference is they were prepared and ready for the battles. They had wandered through the desert for 40 years and witnessed God miraculously provide water and food. Has God led you into the desert? Is He preparing you for something later that you can't see? Take heart for God has not forgotten or rejected you. He knows what you are going through.

**Acknowledge** –Lord, You have not forgotten or rejected me.

**Confess** – Lord, forgive me when I wonder where You are and for doubting that You care.

**Thanksgiving** – Lord, thank You that I can look back and see Your hand of mercy at work in my life.

**Prayer** – Lord, give me insight into Your word so that I will be prepared for life's battles.

# Day 192

Psalm 77:13 Your ways, God, are Holy. What god is as great as our God?

ASAPH ACKNOWLEDGES THAT WHILE WE MAY NOT UNDERSTAND God's ways, they are Holy. In verse 19 he writes, 'Your path led through the sea, Your way through the mighty waters, though Your footprints were never seen.' Yesterday, the children of Israel were at the shore of the Red Sea. There were mountains to either side and Pharaoh with his army in hot pursuit. Exodus 14:10 tells us, 'As Pharaoh approached, the Israelites looked up, and there were the Egyptians, marching after them. They were terrified and cried out to the Lord.' The Israelites were trapped. Pharaoh and his army were going to slaughter them right there in the desert. But God had a different plan. God's plan led the children of Israel through the Red Sea. He parted the waters and the Israelites crossed through on dry land. Exodus 14:22 tells us, 'and the Israelites went through the sea on dry ground, with a wall of water on their right and on their left.' That had to be a scary journey with walls of water on either side that could come crashing down at any time. However, that is the route God had provided. The same path the Israelites took became the graves for Pharaoh and his army. Exodus 14:28 says, 'The water flowed back and covered the chariots and horsemen – the entire army of Pharaoh that had followed the Israelites into the sea. Not one of them survived.' What path had God led you to? Are you at a place where there is nowhere else to turn but to trust Him? Is the enemy in hot pursuit? God has a great plan for your life. His plan may be taking you into the desert where you have nowhere to go, but to trust Him. Are you willing to take the first step into the parted waters of the sea in front of you? What He did to the Egyptians, He can do to the troubles that pursue you. He can wash them away, never more to be seen. He is a Great God.

**Acknowledge** – Lord, Your ways are Holy.

**Confess** – Lord, forgive me when I doubt Your greatness, when I look to my own power to solve my problems.

**Thanksgiving** – Lord, You are an awesome God that reigns from heaven above with wisdom, power and love.

**Prayer** – Lord, give me boldness to step out into the sea You have parted in front of me.

# Day 193

Psalm 77:14 You are the God who performs miracles; You display Your power among the peoples.

Asaph proclaims that God is the one who performs miracles. Our story of the Israelites doesn't end on the other side of the Red Sea. The first city they encountered in the Promised Land was Jericho. Joshua had sent two spies to Jericho to scout out the city. There they entered the house of Rahab, a prostitute, who assisted the spies and hid them from the King's soldiers. In Joshua 2:9-10, Rahab tells the spies, 'We have heard how the Lord dried up the water of the Red Sea for you when you came out of Egypt, and what you did to Sihon and Og, the two Kings of the Amorites east of the Jordan, whom you completely destroyed. When we heard of it, our hearts melted and everyone's courage failed because of you, for the Lord your God is God in heaven above and on the earth below.' The people of Jericho were terrified of the Israelites and of the miracles God had performed forty years earlier. However, that wasn't God's last miracle the people of Jericho would learn about. Between the Israelites and the people of Jericho stood a huge wall that was approximately 13' high and 4' thick. The people of Jericho were safely behind their wall hurling insults at the Israelites as they marched around the city for seven days. However, on the seventh day, the walls came crashing down and the Israelites conquered the city. God did not stop performing miracles that day. God continues to perform miracles today. We may not recognize His miracles because they are often times explained away as being something that happens by chance or just plain luck. We may also fail to see God's hand at work when we pray for a miracle and nothing seems to happen. We become discouraged and begin to wonder if God still performs miracles. At times, it is hard to wait on God. But as we have learned, God's timing is perfect and He is a God who performs miracles.

**Acknowledge** –Lord, You do miracles so great, there is no one like You.

**Confess** – Lord, forgive me when I become discouraged and doubt Your love for me.

**Thanksgiving** – Lord, thank You for performing miracles today.

**Prayer** – Lord, help me to wait patiently for You to provide the miracle that I am reaching out to You for.

# Day 194

> Psalm 78:4 We will not hide them from their descendants; we will tell the next generation the praise worthy deeds of the Lord, His power, and the wonders He has done.

Psalm 78 was written by Asaph as an instruction not to repeat past sins and to remember God's saving grace. He stresses the need of teaching our children about God. In verse two, he foreshadows the ministry of Jesus and the use of parables. He writes, 'I will open my mouth in parables, I will utter hidden things, things from old.' Asaph stresses the importance of passing down the Lord's saving acts and the laws God had given their forefathers. Both of these go hand in hand as we teach our children about God. Perhaps you have used everyday stories and other resources to teach your children about God. For smaller children, bedtime is a great time to read stories from a children's Bible and say prayers. Teach your children how to pray. The dinner table is another excellent place to teach your children. However, getting families to sit down for a meal together has become a challenge in today's world. Even if you are able to get the family to the table, everyone is more focused on technology than each other. Make a rule, no phones are allowed at the table. Second, make sure everyone is settled before saying the blessing. Give everyone a turn to say the blessing or say one together. Third, introduce a short Bible verse the family can learn together. Fourth, give everyone a chance to say what they are thankful for that day. The idea is to begin at an early age, talking to your children about God. Be creative and find ways to teach them about God and His word. Proverbs 22:6 says, 'Train up a child in the way he/she should go, and when he/she is old he/she will not turn from it.' As our children grow older, they may make some wrong turns. However, they will have God's word as a foundation in their life and with God's help one day get back on the right path. Teach the next generation about the works of God.

**Acknowledge** – Lord, Your deeds are praise worthy, they should be passed down.

**Confess** – Lord, forgive me when I fail to teach my children and grandchildren about You.

**Thanksgiving** – Lord, thank You for the greatest gift of Your Son, Jesus Christ.

**Prayer** – Lord, help me to teach the next generation so they will know You.

# Day 195

Psalm 78:24 He rained down manna for the people to eat, He gave them the grain of heaven.

Exodus 16:4,31 tells us, 'Then the Lord said to Moses, "I will rain down bread from heaven for you. The people are to go out each day and gather enough for that day. In this way I will test them and see whether they will follow My instructions." The people of Israel called the bread manna. It was white like coriander seed and tasted like wafers made with honey.' The Israelites had camped at a place called Elim, which was an oasis with twelve springs and seventy palm trees. They had no complaints while at Elim, but just as soon as they headed into the hot, dry desert, they began to grumble and complain about not having food. So the Lord provided manna and quail for the people to eat. Every day, except the Sabbath, God provided manna for the people. All they had to do was get up each morning and gather enough to feed themselves and their families for the day. Once the sun grew hot, the excess manna melted away, only to appear the next day. Imagine having delicious food right outside your door each day that you didn't have to plant, cultivate and harvest. That would be a story worthy of passing down from generation to generation. However, God continues to provide manna for His people. Jesus said in John 6:32-33, 'I tell you the truth, it is not Moses who has given you the bread from heaven, but it is My Father who gives you the true bread from heaven. For the bread of God is He who comes down from heaven and gives life to the world.' He goes on to say in verse 35, 'I am the Bread of Life. He who comes to Me will never go hungry, and he who believes in Me will never be thirsty.' Have you tasted the 'Bread of Life?' Psalm 34:8 says, 'Taste and see that the Lord is good; blessed is the man who takes refuge in Him.' Take time to share the good news of Jesus, the Bread of Life, with your family.

**Acknowledge** –Lord, You are the Bread of Life, life giving manna from above.

**Confess** – Lord, forgive me when I fail to recognize Your sacrifice for me.

**Thanksgiving** – Lord, thank You for being our provider.

**Prayer** – Lord, help me to share the good news of Your plan of salvation with my family.

# Day 196

Psalm 78:26 He let loose the east wind from the heavens and by His power made the south wind blow.

Asaph continues to speak of the experiences the Israelites faced while in the desert. One year later, the people began to crave food besides manna. The Bible says that every family started wailing for meat to eat. God became exceedingly angry at the people because the manna was also to be a test of their obedience. Moses was panicking. In Numbers 11:3 he asks God, 'Where can I get meat for all these people? They keep wailing at me, 'Give us meat to eat.'' God answered Moses in verse 19, 'Tell the people: Consecrate yourselves in preparation for tomorrow, when you will eat meat. The Lord heard you when you wailed, 'If only we had meat to eat! We were better off in Egypt!' Now the Lord will give you meat, and you will eat it.' He provided what they asked for. However, there is more to the story. Numbers 11:31 tells us, 'Now a wind went out from the Lord and drove quail in from the sea. It brought them down all around the camp to about three feet above the ground, as far as a day's walk in any direction.' God used a mighty wind to provide meat for the Israelites. In the New Testament, we also find reference of a mighty wind. Acts 2:1-2, describes the Day of Pentecost. The disciples had gathered together to pray. 'When the day of Pentecost came, they were all together in one place. Suddenly a sound like the blowing of a violent wind came from heaven and filled the whole house where they were sitting.' That wind brought an outpouring of God's Holy Spirit upon the disciples. Afterwards, Peter stood up with boldness and spoke about repentance. The Bible tells us that 3,000 people received the message and were saved. What is your prayer life like? Are you whining and complaining for material things or are you craving an outpouring of God's Holy Spirit? What has more lasting value, a bucket full of quail or the empowerment of the Holy Spirit? God can use the wind to send both. Choose wisely.

**Acknowledge** – Lord, the winds You send have power.

**Confess** – Lord, forgive me when I selfishly whine and complain for material things.

**Thanksgiving** – Lord, thank You for sending Your Holy Spirit to enable us to serve You.

**Prayer** – Lord, help me to seek You each day to receive a fresh wind of Your power.

# Day 197

Psalm 78:35 They remembered that God was their rock, that God most high was their Redeemer.

We have learned quite a bit about the Israelites journey to the Promised Land. Their journey lasted for 40 years and was filled with many spiritual highs and lows. Their attitudes towards God changed with the wind. They were doubtful of God's power to deliver them from the Egyptians. They also doubted God's ability to provide for them. On many occasions they talked of going back to Egypt into slavery. They whined about the manna God provided. They begged Aaron to make an idol in the form of a golden calf for them to worship. They listened to the report of the ten spies who said the Promised Land couldn't be taken. Many times, God's anger burned against the people. Each time, Moses would intercede and God would forgive them. They don't sound like a group of people deserving of God's love and deliverance. Yet there were times when they remembered that God was their Rock and Redeemer. As they were boldly marching out of Egypt after being there 430 years, they remembered who God was. When they stood on the other side of the Red Sea witnessing the destruction of Pharaoh and his army, or as they woke up each morning to a fresh delivery of manna, or as they watched God pour out water from a rock, they remembered who He was. What has God done in your life to remind you that He is your Rock and your Redeemer? Are you like the Israelites who at the first sign of trouble have doubts of God's ability to see you through? We need to acknowledge and understand that God alone is our Redeemer. He sent His only Son to bear the full weight of our sins. He offers forgiveness for our sins and gives us eternal life. Romans 8:32 tells us, 'He who did not spare His own Son, but gave Him up for us all – how will He not also, along with Him graciously give us all things?' God's plan is covered in love for us. Can you call Him your Rock and Redeemer today?

**Acknowledge** –Lord, You are our Rock and our Redeemer.

**Confess** – Lord, forgive me when I doubt Your love for me.

**Thanksgiving** – Lord, thank You for being the Rock of my salvation.

**Prayer** – Lord, help me to see You more clearly and know who You are.

# Day 198

**Psalm 78:38** Yet He was merciful; He forgave their iniquities and did not destroy them. Time after time He restrained His anger and did not stir up His full wrath.

TODAY, ASAPH SUMS UP THE CHARACTER OF GOD IN FOUR SHORT words, 'Yet He was merciful...' For all the times the Israelites disobeyed Him, He forgave them. Time after time He restrained His anger and did not punish them as they deserved. Regrettably our character and behavior are not any different today. We whine and complain when things don't go our way. We grumble when others have more than we do. We might not worship a golden calf, but we have created our own idols to take the place of God. Although we have seen God work in our lives before, we lack the faith that He can get us through our current circumstances. We fail to step out in faith to what God has promised us because someone tells us that we can't do it. That is why we need a God who is merciful and slow to anger, a God who doesn't punish us as we deserve. Lamentations 3:22-23 tells us, 'Because of the Lord's great love we are not consumed, for His compassions never fail. They are new every morning; great is Your faithfulness.' While on earth, Jesus exhibited the Father's love and mercy to those He ministered to. When an adulteress was brought before Jesus to pronounce judgment, He told her accusers, that the one without sin should throw the first stone. One by one, her accusers left. Jesus then told the woman, 'Neither do I condemn you. Go and sin no more.' He forgave her iniquities and did not stone her as the law required. However, He did tell her to, 'Go and sin no more.' He wasn't expecting her to go and start living a sinless life, but He was warning her against returning to her sinful lifestyle choices. Jesus was merciful, but He also demanded holiness. When He forgives us, He demands holiness from us as well. Thank Him for forgiving you of your sins and not punishing you as you deserved. Now follow Christ and 'go and sin no more.'

**Acknowledge** – Lord, You are merciful.

**Confess** – Lord, forgive me of my rebellion, my stubbornness, and my unwilling spirit to obey Your word.

**Thanksgiving** – Lord, thank You that you are merciful, slow to anger, and abounding in love.

**Prayer** – Lord, help me to seek repentance when I fall short, and to go and sin no more.

# Day 199

Psalm 78:52 But He brought His people out like a flock; He led them like sheep through the desert.

ASAPH CONTINUES TO RECOUNT THE STORY OF HOW GOD LED THE Israelites through the desert. Shepherds from that area never walked behind their sheep, they always walked ahead with the sheep following close behind. Exodus 13:21-22 tells us how God led the Israelites the entire 40 years they were in the desert. 'By day the Lord went ahead of them in a pillar of cloud to guide them on their way and by night in a pillar of fire to give them light, so that they could travel by day or night. Neither the pillar of cloud by day nor the pillar of fire by night left its place in front of the people.' God led the people to some interesting places. We have read where they camped in a beautiful oasis, while other times, they stopped in the middle of the desert with no apparent water supply. They camped at Mount Sinai where Moses received the Ten Commandments. Each stop in their journey was an opportunity to grow their faith and trust in God. Sadly, we find that for most of their journey they grumbled and complained. Fast forward several thousand years and we see that God is still shepherding His sheep. Jesus speaking in John 10:14-16 tells us, 'I am the good shepherd; I know My sheep and My sheep know Me – just as the Father knows Me and I know the Father – and I lay down My life for the sheep. I have other sheep that are not of this sheep pen. I must bring them also. They too will listen to My voice, and there shall be one flock and one shepherd.' By declaring himself the good shepherd, Jesus is claiming to be the Messiah the scriptures foretold. Notice in John 10, that Jesus said He had other sheep that He must bring in. Those sheep are you and I. Not only did He come to save Israel, He came to save anyone who would listen to His voice. Do you know the Good Shepherd? Are you following Him? Trust God to be your Good Shepherd.

**Acknowledge** –Lord, You are the Good Shepherd.

**Confess** – Lord, forgive me for wandering away from You.

**Thanksgiving** – Lord, thank You for being the Good Shepherd who searches after the one lost sheep.

**Prayer** – Lord, help me to follow You wherever You lead me. I know that You are the Good Shepherd who loves His sheep.

## Day 200

Psalm 78:70 He chose David His servant and took him from the sheep pens.

Asaph has taken us on a journey with the Israelites and concludes with a story about David. David was the youngest of eight brothers. His job was to tend the family sheep and wasn't even present when Samuel arrived to anoint him as King. As Samuel was preparing to anoint one of David's brothers; God said, 'Do not consider his appearance or his height, for I have rejected him. The Lord does not look at the things man looks at. Man looks at the outward appearance, but the Lord looks at the heart.' David wasn't perfect, but he had a deep love for God. God doesn't make mistakes when He calls someone to do something for Him. When He calls us, we might run the opposite way as Jonah did or be faithful like John the Baptist who prepared the way for Jesus. I'm thankful that God chose Vivian and me to lead teams to Nicaragua from 2010 to 2014. Those were some of the most rewarding trips we have been on. It all began when our son had a 'wild hair' after graduating from college to take a trip. His first choice fell through, and he heard about a young man from Raleigh who had started a ministry in a small community of Los Brasiles, Nicaragua. He spent the summer in Nicaragua and came back a changed person. Because of his experience and the needs there, we decided to take a team to help the ministry. We were shocked when over 25 people signed up to go. I had never traveled out of the country nor had the experience to book travel for that many people. However, God faithfully guided and protected us the years we traveled there. What is God calling you to do? Are you trying to avoid God and His plans for you? Maybe you are following God's plan, but things don't seem to be working the way you thought they would. Speaking from experience, you will face trouble and hardship if you are following God. However, He will see you through those times and make your relationship with Him much stronger.

**Acknowledge** –Lord, You call us from many different places to serve You.

**Confess** – Lord, forgive me when I try to run from Your plan for me.

**Thanksgiving** – Lord, thank You for seeing me through the difficult times.

**Prayer** – Lord, help me to be faithful to the task You have called me to do.

# Day 201

Psalm 79:5 How long Lord? Will You be angry forever? How long will Your jealousy burn like fire?

Psalm 79 is a prayer of forgiveness and a plea for help from God. Asaph is venting and expressing his anger to God about the circumstances Israel finds itself in. Like Israel, we have our own struggles and times when it seems as if God has closed the 'windows of heaven.' Our disappointments can turn into resentment which leads to anger and we cry out the same words to God, 'How long Lord? Will You be angry at me forever?' I recall a season in my life that I felt that way. I worked for a utility company and served as the Area Manager of one of our local business offices. Life was going well until our company reorganized and closed the local business offices, going to a centralized customer service model. Many of my peers lost their jobs. I was fortunate to be offered a job at our new Customer Service Center. However, that was the most stressful job I have ever had. The Center had just opened and there were a number of issues associated with operating a new call center. Every time the phone rang, there was a problem on the other end. The days were long and stressful with seemingly no end in sight. After 25 years with this company, I wasn't sure I was going to make it. I would cry out to God each night, 'Lord, how long will this go on? I can't take any more of this.' A year later, another job opened up in project management. What I didn't understand at the time, was that the experiences I had in the call center, directly led to my success in project management. I understood the problems I was trying to solve. All the time God was listening to my cries, but was training me for another job that I thoroughly enjoyed. What are you going through today? Are you at the point where you don't think you can make it another day? Cry out to God today and tell Him your problems. Then, wait on God to answer your prayer.

**Acknowledge** –Lord, You hear us when we cry out to You.

**Confess** – Lord, there are times when I don't like Your training methods, please forgive me when I get frustrated.

**Thanksgiving** – Lord, thank You for knowing what is best for us.

**Prayer** – Lord, help me to better understand Your ways and to wait patiently on You.

# Day 202

Psalm 79:9 Help us, O God our Savior, for the glory of Your name; deliver us and forgive our sins for Your name's sake.

Israel had sinned by turning away from God and worshipping idols. God's presence had left them and they were on their own against nations who were much stronger. Asaph realizes that the first step to seeking God's help is by reconciling with Him by seeking His forgiveness. How often do we fail to recognize the very reason we are facing the difficult circumstances is because of our sin in our lives? We make bad choices that go against God's Word and find ourselves facing the consequences. John 5:1-15 tells the story of Jesus healing an invalid who had been sitting at the Pool of Bethesda. Whenever the water was stirred by an angel, the first person in the pool was healed. The man who had been an invalid for 38 years tried to be the first in the water but never made it. Jesus walks by the man one day and asks him, 'Do you want to get well?' I would have quickly said, yes sir. But the invalid didn't, he goes into detail how he doesn't have anyone to help him get into the water. He doesn't realize that Jesus could heal him. Jesus tells the man to pick up his mat and walk and the man was instantly healed. Later, Jesus said to him, 'See, you are well again. Stop sinning or something worse may happen to you.' The man had been given a second chance at life, and Jesus warns him not to fall back into the same mistakes he had made earlier in his life. Our bad choices may not lead us to become a physical invalid, but can easily turn us into spiritual invalids. They can lead us into an addiction that can destroy our lives. Families have been destroyed, jobs lost, reputations ruined because of bad choices. Yet God is a God of second chances. Ask God to deliver you from the bad choices you have made. Ask Him to forgive your sins and restore the things you have lost. Take the first step to forgiveness and restoration.

**Acknowledge** –Lord, You offer forgiveness and restoration.

**Confess** – Lord, forgive me when I allow an addiction to take over my life and control my actions.

**Thanksgiving** – Lord, I thank You for Your restoration power.

**Prayer** – Lord, for the glory of Your name and for Your name's sake, deliver me from my sins.

# Day 203

Psalm 80:7 Restore us, God almighty; make Your face shine upon us, that we may be saved.

Psalm 80 was written by Asaph as a prayer of restoration. Today's verse is repeated three times in this Psalm. Today we are focusing on God's restoration power. Restoration is the process of healing, repairing, and returning to a previous state of being. God is a God of second chances and a God of restoration. He can restore families that have been split apart, He can replace a lost job, He can repair a reputation ruined because of bad choices, and He can replace financial loss. Better yet, God can restore the years our bad choices have wasted. God speaking in Joel 2:25-26 tells us, 'I will repay you for the years the locusts have eaten – the great locust and the young locust, the other locusts and the locust swarm – My great army that I sent among you. You will have plenty to eat, until you are full, and you will praise the name of the Lord your God, who has worked wonders for you; never again will My people be shamed.' The people of Israel had suffered the complete destruction of their harvests for four years. Every type of locust imaginable swarmed in and ate their crops. Locusts are devastating and relentless. What types of locusts are eating away your life? How many times have the locusts driven you to say 'if only?' These two words are fitting for all the missed opportunities in our lives 'if only I had not gotten involved with that crowd, if only I had spent more time with my family, if only I had accepted Christ.' We all have had our share of 'if only' moments. The good news is that God can replace those moments of regret with moments of joy and fulfillment. Isaiah 61:7 says, 'Instead of your shame you will receive a double portion, and instead of disgrace you will rejoice in your inheritance. And so you will inherit a double portion in your land, and everlasting joy will be yours.' Ask God to restore your relationship with Him and to restore the years the locusts have taken away.

**Acknowledge** –Lord, You promised You will repay the years the locusts ate.

**Confess** – Lord, forgive me for my actions that make me have 'if only' thoughts.

**Thanksgiving** – Lord, I thank You for double portions of Your love and mercy.

**Prayer** – Lord, I ask that You restore the years the locusts of taken away from me.

# Day 204

Psalm 80:19 Restore us, Lord God Almighty; make Your face shine upon us, that we may be saved.

Asaph repeats his cry for restoration to the 'Lord God Almighty.' Today our focus will be on worshiping the Lord God Almighty, the God who restores us and shines His face upon us. Isaiah 6:1-3 gives us a glimpse of the worship of God in heaven, 'In the year that King Uzziah died, I saw the Lord seated on a throne, high and exalted, and the train of His robe filled the temple. Above Him were seraphs, each with six wings: With two wings they covered their faces, with two they covered their feet, and with two they were flying. And they were calling to one another: "Holy, holy, holy is the Lord Almighty; the whole earth is full of His glory."' Being in God's holy presence brought Isaiah to his knees. In verse five he says, 'Woe to me! I cried. I am ruined! For I am a man of unclean lips, and I live among a people of unclean lips, and my eyes have seen the King, the Lord Almighty.' When we come into the presence of God, we see how perfect and Holy He is and how imperfect and sinful we are. Like Isaiah we cry out, 'I am ruined,' because I am such a sinner. However, God in His perfection and holiness is also merciful and full of grace. He sent His Son to pay the penalty for our sin. That is why we worship Him. Worship takes on many forms. It can be very formal and reverent, a great celebration, or somewhere in between. There is no right or wrong way to worship God. Most importantly we should take time to worship our Lord and Savior, the Lord God Almighty. Corporate worship is important. Find a local church that you feel comfortable with and begin attending. Matthew 18:20 says, 'For where two or three gather in my name, there am I with them.' Join with them in worshiping the Lord God Almighty.

**Acknowledge** –Lord, You are the Lord God Almighty.

**Confess** – Lord, forgive me when my mind attaches to worthless things and not on worshiping You.

**Thanksgiving** – Lord, I thank You for the local church where I can meet to worship with other believers.

**Prayer** – Lord, help me to spend time worshiping You each day.

# Day 205

Psalm 81:8 Hear me, My people, and I will warn you if you would only listen to Me, Israel.

Sadly, the people did not listen to God and His warnings. Instead of listening, they turned to worshiping idols, and disregarding God's laws. We are no different from the Israelites of Asaph's day. Haven't we allowed the culture of our day to influence our lives to the point that Christians do not look or behave any differently than the people around us? Have we tuned in to the world and its noise rather than listening to God? Perhaps God is warning us today. Let's turn to God's Word to find His warning to us. Although Isaiah 5:8-25 was written to the Israelites, God's warning of judgment is just as appropriate to us today. In those verses, Isaiah describes their behavior and speaks of six specific sins and warnings of imminent judgment: 1st, The sin of materialism. Once the Israelites were secure with land and houses, the people turned their backs on God. Do we chase after prosperity more than we do God? 2nd, The sin of partying and wild living. The people were consumed with chasing after drunken parties. Is our culture of alcoholism, drug addiction, and partying comparable to the Israelites? 3rd, The sin of promoting sin and evil without regard for God. Are our television and computer screens filled with videos and shows of sinful behavior that are promoted as normal? 4th, The sin of moral relativism. Isaiah wrote there are those who call evil good and good evil. We have tossed out the Ten Commandments, redefined marriage, and celebrate the murder of unborn children. Are there any moral standards left? 5th, The sin of arrogance and corruption. People thought themselves to be wise in their own eyes. 6th, The sin of corrupted leadership. Their leaders were champions at drinking and taking bribes. Can you identify any corruption in our leadership today? Because of their sin and disobedience, God promised to take away His hedge of protection and favor from the Israelites. He will do the same for us, unless we repent and turn to Him. Listen to God, hear the warnings He is giving us.

**Acknowledge** –Lord, Your words are truth.

**Confess** – Lord, forgive me for not listening to and following Your word.

**Thanksgiving** – Lord, I thank You for warning us of impending danger and punishment.

**Prayer** – Lord, I pray that revival will sweep across America. Let it start with me.

# Day 206

**Psalm 81:16** But you would be fed with the finest of wheat, with honey from the rock I would satisfy you.

God is telling the Israelites about the blessings they could have, had they trusted Him. Verse 11 says, 'But My people would not listen to Me; Israel would not submit to Me.' They chose to be disobedient and missed out on God's blessings. In Luke 5:1-11 we find a great example of how Peter's obedience led to God's blessing. Jesus was on the shore of Lake Gennesaret with people crowding around Him. He asked Peter to push his boat out a little further into the Lake so He could teach the people. Peter had been fishing all night and was cleaning the nets. He could have easily told Jesus he was tired and use someone else's boat. But Peter obeyed and the people were blessed by hearing the word of God. The story doesn't end there. Jesus tells Peter to head out to deep water and put the nets he had just cleaned into the water. Peter was hesitant, saying, 'Master, we've worked hard all night and haven't caught anything. But because you say so, I will let down the nets.' No sooner than the nets hit the water, they were filled with fish. There were so many fish that they had to call for help from a second boat. Verse 7 tells us that both boats were so full, they began to sink. Peter's obedience turned a fruitless all-night fishing trip into the greatest catch he had ever had. Not only that, it transformed his life. Verse 11 tells us, 'So they pulled their boats up on the shore, left everything and followed Him.' God can also turn our emptiness in to something amazing, when we choose to obey Him. What is God asking you to do today? Are you being hesitant like Peter, weighing out the pros and cons? We may not understand why God is asking us to do something, but one thing is certain, that if we obey Him, He will reward us with peace and joy. Trust God, enjoy the finest wheat and honey from the rocks.

**Acknowledge** –Lord, You want to feed us the finest wheat and honey from the rocks.

**Confess** – Lord, forgive me when I seek You solely for my selfish benefit and comfort.

**Thanksgiving** – Lord, I thank You for providing us with Your blessings.

**Prayer** – Lord, over and over Your word tells us that good things come from listening to You.

# Day 207

Psalm 82:8 Rise up, O God, judge the earth, for all the nations are Your inheritance.

PSALM 82 IS A WORD OF JUDGMENT AGAINST UNJUST RULERS AND judges. Asaph is looking for the time when God will come and rule the earth and the rights of the poor and needy are not trampled on. No longer would those in power oppress those who are less fortunate. However, it is God who puts the governments and leaders in place. What do I mean by this? Paul tells us in Romans 13:1 'Let everyone be subject to the governing authorities, for there is no authority except that which God has established. The authorities that exist have been established by God.' Daniel 2:21 also tells us, 'It is He who changes the times and the epochs; He removes kings and establishes kings; He gives wisdom to wise men and knowledge to men of understanding.' Jesus speaking to Pilate at His trial said in John 19:11, 'You would have no authority over Me, unless it had been given you from above; for this reason he who delivered Me to you has the greater sin.' God is the sovereign ruler of the universe. He has all power and authority, yet He entrusts leadership roles to us, starting in the family, the church, the workplace, and in government. Everyone is accountable to God for their actions whether they are in leadership or under someone's authority. In Asaph's day, the moral character of those in charge was not very strong. We can see this theme playing out throughout history and even today. When the moral character of a leader in the family, the workplace, the church, and the government is weak the people will suffer. Decisions will be made that benefit those in charge, hurting those under them. No leader is perfect. However, those that take their responsibility serious and seek God's guidance will do things that are beneficial to all who are under them. Are you in leadership? What type of moral compass are you using to guide your decisions? Are you seeking God and His wisdom? Ask God today to make you a better leader.

**Acknowledge** –Lord, You put leaders and governments in place.

**Confess** – Lord, forgive me when I forget the weak, the poor, and the homeless.

**Thanksgiving** – Lord, I thank You for being the sovereign God of the Universe. You are in control.

**Prayer** – Lord, help me to hate injustice, to love those whom You love, and to submit to the authority above me.

# Day 208

**Psalm 83:1** O God, do not remain silent; do not turn a deaf ear, do not stand aloof, O God.

Asaph is calling out to God for His help against the enemies of Israel. I have heard it said that we should only ask God one time, and then begin giving Him thanks for the answer that is to come. I don't know which approach is correct, but I know that I am more like Asaph who keeps calling out to God to answer his prayer. I recall a time when Vivian and I were at the airport, headed to NYC to visit our son and his family. Vivian's blood pressure dropped and she passed out at the airport. She was admitted to the hospital where she spent several days. I prayed continuously for her healing and recovery. I didn't pray once and hope for the best. I wanted to make sure God heard and answered my prayers. Jesus tells the parable in Luke 18:1-8 of the widow who kept coming to a judge over and over again seeking justice. Jesus describes the judge as one that 'neither feared God nor cared about man.' The judge kept refusing to grant the woman's request. However, after a period of time the judge relented and said, 'Even though I don't fear God or care about men, yet because this widow keeps bothering me, I will see that she gets justice, so that she won't eventually wear me out with her coming.' Jesus in verses 7-8 said, 'And will not God bring about justice for His chosen ones, who cry out to Him day and night? Will He keep putting them off? I tell you, He will see that they get justice, and quickly. However, when the Son of Man comes, will He find faith on the earth?' This parable is telling me that if an ungodly judge who really didn't care about right or wrong is driven to justice by the persistence of a helpless widow, how much more will God respond to our tireless efforts to reach Him. God hears us and knows our needs. We can rest assured He wants what is best for us. Keep praying, help is on the way.

**Acknowledge** –Lord, You hear our prayers.

**Confess** – Lord, forgive me when I think You are not listening to my prayers.

**Thanksgiving** – Lord, thank You for the good and perfect gifts You send from above.

**Prayer** – Lord, I pray that my prayers will be consistent, persistent, and aligned with Your will.

# Day 209

> Psalm 84:1-2 How lovely is Your dwelling place, Lord Almighty! My soul yearns, evens faints, for the courts of the Lord; my heart and my flesh cry out for the living God.

Psalm 84 is attributed to the sons of Korah, a descendent of Levi. As a Levite, Korah was assigned by Moses to work at the tabernacle and minister to the people. He and several other Levite leaders started a rebellion against Moses and Aaron. God became very angry with Korah and the others who had rebelled, so Moses set up a test to see who's offering God would accept; his and Aarons or Korah's. Moses told the people that if Korah and those following him died a natural death, then the Lord had not chosen him. But on the other hand, if they died an unnatural death then the people would know that Korah and the others had treated God with contempt. As soon as Moses finished speaking, the earth opened up and swallowed Korah and the others with all their households and possessions. The earth closed back up, burying them alive. The good news is that God doesn't hold us accountable for the sins of our ancestors. If so, we wouldn't find some of Korah descendants serving in the temple and writing Psalms. Ezekiel 18:20 says, 'The soul who sins is the one who will die. The son will not share the guilt of the father, nor will the father share the guilt of the son. The righteousness of the righteous man will be credited to him, and the wickedness of the wicked will be charged against him.' If you are counting on the salvation of your parents to get you to heaven, you will be very disappointed. Everyone must make their own decision whether or not to follow Christ. Being a good person doesn't get you to heaven. You must repent of your sins and ask Jesus Christ to come into your life, accepting Him as your Lord and Savior. Once you do, you can join in singing the song written by the sons of Korah, 'my heart and my flesh cry out for the living God.'

**Acknowledge** –Lord, how lovely is Your dwelling place.

**Confess** – Lord, forgive me when I take for granted the privilege of worshiping You in Your house.

**Thanksgiving** – Lord, thank You for the places where we can assemble to worship You.

**Prayer** – Lord, my soul cries out for the living God, the one who died for me.

# Day 210

Psalm 84:10 Better is one day in Your courts than a thousand elsewhere; I would rather be a door keeper in the house of my God than dwell in the tents of the wicked.

In that day, the work at the temple was assigned by family group. It is thought that Korah's descendants were the door keepers for the temple. Here they proclaim that they would rather be a door keeper than dwell in the tents of the wicked. Maybe they were thinking back on their ancestors who were buried alive. Or perhaps, they wanted to serve in the House of God. Let's look at the role of a door keeper and its importance to worship. In our trips to NYC, we have gotten to know several doormen. These men and women faithfully stand at the door, day and night, ready to greet and assist anyone by opening doors, helping with bags, and hailing rides. They stay alert and are the first line of security for the building. While it may seem the job is routine, their role is very important. It was the same for the door keeper of the temple. It was a job that was typically given to the most capable and loyal priests. They were to make sure that no one who was 'unclean' or 'undeserving' entered the temple. They had to be very careful in making sure that whoever entered the temple did so properly and reverently. You may be asking, what does being a door keeper have to do with me? Revelation 3:20 says, 'Here I am! I stand at the door and knock. If anyone hears My voice and opens the door, I will come in and eat with him, and he with Me.' You are the door keeper to your heart. Jesus is standing at the door and knocking. Have you invited Him into your life? If you have already invited Him in, you still have a role as door keeper. As a door keeper you have to be careful what you allow into your heart and mind. My prayer is that you would be a faithful door keeper.

**Acknowledge** –Lord, one day in Your presence is better than a thousand elsewhere.

**Confess** – Lord, forgive me when I allow things to enter my life that should not be there.

**Thanksgiving** – Lord, thank You for knocking on the door of my heart.

**Prayer** – Lord, I pray that I would have fellowship with You each day. Help me to be a faithful door keeper of my heart.

# Day 211

Psalm 85:7 Show us Your unfailing love, Lord, and grant us Your salvation.

Did you know that God's love for you is unfailing, enduring, and eternal? There is nothing you can do or say that will stop Him from loving you. Despite your sin, your flaws, your tendency to drift away, He still loves you. His love is unconditional. Even if you don't love Him, He loves you. Paul writing in Romans 5:8 tells us, 'But God demonstrated His own love for us in this; while we were still sinners, Christ died for us.' And in Romans 8:39 he writes, 'Neither height nor depth, nor anything else in all creation, will be able to separate us from the love of God that is Christ Jesus our Lord.' God loved us enough to die for us and nothing can separate us from His love. The parable of the Prodigal Son found in Luke 15:11-32 is a great illustration of God's love. A father had two sons. The younger son asks to be given his share of the family estate and sets out on a wild adventure, spending his entire inheritance partying. Before long, his money runs out and a famine hits the land. He was destitute and the only job he could find was feeding pigs. He became so hungry that he ate the slop he was feeding the pigs. The Bible doesn't say how long it took, but the son came to his senses and realized that his father's workers were much better off than him. So, he got up and headed back to ask forgiveness from his father to be one of the hired hands. While he was still a long way, his father who had been looking for him day after day, saw him and was filled with compassion. The father ran to meet his son, hugged him, and kissed him. He forgave his son, restored his place in the family and had a huge celebration. In the same way, God rejoices when one sinner repents and returns home. Have you wandered away from God like the Prodigal Son? No matter how far away you have drifted, God still loves you. Like him, start the journey back home. God will welcome you with open arms.

**Acknowledge** –Lord, Your love for us is unfailing.

**Confess** – Lord, forgive me when I wander away from You like the Prodigal Son.

**Thanksgiving** – Lord, thank You for loving me even when I didn't love myself.

**Prayer** – Lord, help me to share Your unfailing love with others.

# Day 212

Psalm 85:10 Love and faithfulness meet together; righteousness and peace kiss each other.

Today we read that God's unfailing love and His faithfulness merge together. Faithfulness defined by Dictionary.com means reliable, trusted, believed, true to one's word and promises. Because of God's love and faithfulness, He will not overlook even the smallest of His promises. Think about the promise God made to Abraham in Genesis chapter 13. In verses 15-16, God said, 'All the land that you see I will give to you and your offspring forever. I will make your offspring like the dust of the earth, so that if anyone could count the dust, then your offspring could be counted.' Or the promise God made to Noah in Genesis 9:11, 'I establish my covenant with you; Never again will all life be cut off by the waters of a flood; never again will there be a flood to destroy the earth.' These are two of the promises we know He has kept. God has promised us as well. Philippians 4:9 says, 'And my God will meet all your needs according to the riches of His glory in Christ Jesus.' Or, Revelation 3:5 which says, 'The one who is victorious will, like them, be dressed in white. I will never blot out the name of that person from the Book of Life, but will acknowledge that name before My Father and His angels.' But the Psalmist goes further to say that righteousness and peace kiss each other. I remember the first kiss Vivian and I had. It wasn't the 'aha' moment when many say 'that is the person I am going to marry.' However, it didn't take many more before I knew that she was the one I wanted to spend my life with. Although the Psalmist alludes to it, righteousness and peace come together in Christ. 1 Corinthians 1:30 tells us, 'But by His doing you are in Christ Jesus, who became to us wisdom from God, and righteousness, and sanctification, and redemption. Later he wrote in Philippians 4:7, 'And the peace of God, which transcends all understanding, will guard your hearts and your minds in Christ Jesus.' Have you experienced that 'kiss of peace and righteousness' in your life? Trust Him and His promises.

**Acknowledge** – Lord, You are where love and faithfulness meet.

**Confess** – Lord, forgive me for not trusting Your faithfulness.

**Thanksgiving** – Lord, thank You for the promises You have given us in Your word.

**Prayer** – Lord, help me to seek out and claim the promises found in Your word.

# Day 213

Psalm 86:10 For You are great and do marvelous deeds; You alone are God.

Today, David declares the greatness of God. Not only is God good (verse 5), He is also great (verse 7). What a perfect combination. To be good and not great would make God ordinary like us. Then to be great and not good would overlook God's character. The Bible repeatedly speaks to God's goodness. Exodus 34:6 tells us, 'The Lord, the Lord God, merciful and gracious, longsuffering, and abounding in goodness and truth.' Also, in 1 Chronicles 16:34 we read, 'Oh, give thanks to the Lord, for He is good! For His mercy endures forever.' Lastly in James 1:17 we read, 'Every good gift and every perfect gift is from above, and comes down from the Father of lights, with whom there is no variation or shadow of turning.' Out of God's goodness we have forgiveness of our sins. Out of God's greatness, He does marvelous deeds. Note that David said God continues to do marvelous deeds. 1 Chronicles 16:24 tells us to, 'Declare His glory among the nations, His marvelous works among the peoples.' Can you name some of God's marvelous deeds? For starters, He created the heavens and the earth, and everything in it. He provides the things we need to live, such as air, water, and food. He sent His Son, Jesus to die on the cross for our sins and make a way for us to have eternal life with Him. He has prepared a place for His children. These are just a start, I'm sure you can name many other marvelous works of God. However, David closes this verse by claiming that God is God alone. There is no other god like Him. In David's day, the pagan nations around Israel worshipped idols such as Baal, Asherah, or Dagon. Unfortunately, the Israelites allowed their neighbors to influence them and lead them into worshipping these false gods. However, as David declares, God is not to be worshipped as one among many gods, but as God alone. He is the one true God. He is our Creator, our Sustainer, and our Savior. Like David, declare God to be good, declare Him to be great, declare Him to be God alone.

**Acknowledge** – Lord, You alone are God.

**Confess** – Lord, forgive me for not recognizing Your marvelous deeds in my life.

**Thanksgiving** – Lord, thank You for the wonderful combination of Your goodness and greatness.

**Prayer** – Lord, help me to declare Your goodness and greatness to others.

# Day 214

**Psalm 89:1** I will sing of the Lord's great love forever; with my mouth I will make Your faithfulness known through all generations.

Psalm 89 was written by Ethan the Ezrahite as a prayer mourning the downfall of David's kingdom. A recurring theme we see in the Psalms is God's love and faithfulness to His children. Despite our rebellious and sinful lifestyle, God still loves us and is faithful to us. This doesn't mean that God approves or protects us from the consequences of bad choices. Even as we repent of our sins, we have to live with their consequences. For example, I drive 85 mph in a 70 mph zone. Other drivers are going faster so I am comfortable with speeding. However, several miles down the highway, a patrolman pulls me over and asks, "do you know how fast you were going?" I tell him I was just keeping up with the traffic, and may have been going a little over the speed limit. He replies, sir you were doing 15 miles over the speed limit, 85 mph in a 70 mph zone. I promise him that I will slow down and not speed any more. I tell him I respect law enforcement, and fully support the job they do. Unfortunately, my confession and promise to do better doesn't help. He tells me Mr. Hall, step back to my vehicle. A few minutes later, I am handed a speeding ticket. The patrolman doing his job rightfully gave me a fine for breaking the law. I had to pay the consequences of my actions. No amount of repentance, remorse, patronization, or blaming others could get me out of the fine. Today, we see that God's love for us is great and lasts forever. His love for us is constant and always there. No matter how great our sin, or how painful their consequences, His love for us has not changed. According to Ethan, that is reason enough to break out into song. He may have been the first to pen the words, 'I could sing of Your love forever.' Have you experienced God's love in your life? His love never changes nor fails. Sing of God's love and mercy just as Ethan did.

**Acknowledge** – Lord, Your love for me lasts throughout eternity.

**Confess** – Lord, forgive me when I question Your love for me because of my circumstances.

**Thanksgiving** – Lord, I could sing of Your love forever.

**Prayer** – Lord, give me boldness to make known Your faithfulness to those around me.

# Day 215

Psalm 89:15 Blessed are those who have learned to acclaim You, who walk in the light of Your presence, Lord.

Ethan writes that those who have a firsthand experience of God's love are blessed. In other words, blessings follow those who walk in obedience to God. Not only that, they have the privilege of living each day in His presence. How many truly know God and have experienced His blessings compared to those who hear the word of God, but have no relationship with Him? Jesus speaking in Matthew 7:21 tells us, 'Not everyone who says to Me, Lord, Lord, will enter the kingdom of heaven, but only he who does the will of My Father who is in heaven.' In 2020, the Covid-19 pandemic among many other things has separated those who truly love God from those who simply attended church for social reasons. I heard a pastor share some information about church attendance during the pandemic. Approximately 30% of church members have been faithful to their church by regularly watching on-line and continuing to give. Another 30% are 'church shopping' or visiting other churches online. The rest have dropped out and have not participated in any type of service. According to a 2019 Survey from Statista.com, those who describe themselves as having no religious beliefs are up from 2% in 1955 to 21% in 2019. What has happened to cause so many to lose interest in God? Is it our worship services? Have we watered down the gospel so much, and made it a feel good about ourselves gospel? Are we living in the last days where people in great numbers turn away from God? Paul writing to Timothy in 2 Timothy 3:1-2,5 said, 'But mark this: There will be terrible times in the last days. People will be lovers of themselves, lovers of money, boastful, proud, abusive, disobedient to their parents, ungrateful, unholy…having a form of godliness but denying its power. Have nothing to do with them.' Where do you fall in these statistics? Are you walking daily with God, seeking His presence, and giving Him praise? Or have you checked out of church and your relationship with Him? If the latter, it is never too late to renew your relationship with your loving Father.

**Acknowledge** –Lord, Your blessings follow those who have learned to acclaim You.

**Confess** – Lord, forgive me for walking away from You.

**Thanksgiving** – Lord, thank You for Your blessings on my life.

**Prayer** – Lord, restore my relationship with You. Help me to love and worship You.

# Day 216

**Psalm 89:38** But You have rejected, You have spurned, You have been very angry with Your anointed one.

TODAY THE PSALMIST EXPOSES GOD'S JUDGMENT AND WRATH towards David and his family because of their sins. God had promised David that someone from his lineage would always rule Israel. Yet we find the actions of his son Solomon, and grandson, Rehoboam, led to the splitting of the kingdom. Later, because of Israel's disobedience, the entire nation was exiled Babylon for 70 years. Despite their behavior, it appeared that God's actions were the opposite of His promise to David. It may have seemed to Ethan that God went a little too far in His discipline of the people of Israel, and felt led to put the matter plainly and boldly before God. God listened to Ethan voice his concerns. What can we learn from this? When you run into obstacle after obstacle following God, it is okay to voice your concerns to Him. However, it should be done humbly and in faith believing that God's ultimate plan is at work. We can only see how things are going, not how they will end. For example, in 2 Corinthians 12:7-9, the Apostle Paul writes about an affliction or 'thorn in the flesh'. 'To keep me from becoming conceited because of these surpassingly great revelations, there was given to me a thorn in my flesh, a messenger of Satan, to torment me. Three times I pleaded with the Lord to take it away from me. But He said to me, "My grace is sufficient for you, for My power is made perfect in weakness." Therefore I will boast all the more gladly about my weaknesses, so that Christ's power may rest on me.' Notice Paul pleaded three times for God to take away this affliction, but God chose not to heal him. However, with his 'thorn in the flesh', Paul wrote thirteen powerful letters that are recorded in the New Testament. God wants you to bring your doubts, your fears, your concerns, and your requests to Him. His answer may be like the one Paul received, or it may be healing and restoration. He loves you and only wants the best for you.

**Acknowledge** –Lord, there are times when Your actions seem to be the reverse of Your promises.

**Confess** – Lord, forgive me for doubting Your love for me.

**Thanksgiving** – Lord, thank You that I can come boldly before You with my doubts, fears, concerns, and requests.

**Prayer** – Lord, today I pray for healing.

# Day 217

*Psalm 89:47-48 Remember how fleeting is my life, for what futility You have created in all humanity. Who can live and not see death, or who can escape the power of the grave?*

Today's verses remind us how short life is. They pose some simple questions that we ask the older we get, 'What have I accomplished?' or 'What legacy am I leaving behind?' Solomon said it this way in Ecclesiastes 1:2-4, 'Meaningless! Meaningless! Says the Teacher. Utterly meaningless! Everything is meaningless. What do people gain from all their labors at which they toil under the sun? Generations come and generations go, but the earth remains forever.' In verse 11 he said, 'No one remembers the former generations, and even those yet to come will not be remembered by those who follow them.' Solomon calls life meaningless. His perception is that we live, work hard, and then we die, never to be remembered. James 4:14 tells us, 'Why you do not even know what will happen tomorrow. What is your life? You are just a mist that appears for a little while and then vanishes.' What do we do with the short time that we call our life? How do we beat the odds of living a meaningless and futile life? Sadly, anyone who has not surrendered their life to Jesus Christ is going to have a meaningless life. Without Him, there is something missing that has people searching for all their lives. They may find temporary pleasure in gaining wealth, their job, or in other earthly pursuits. However, once you have achieved those things, the thrill wears off. Having Christ in our lives gives us purpose, hope, joy, and a future with Him. When we surrender our lives to Him and walk in obedience to His word, our lives become more about others than ourselves. Paul writing in Ephesians 2:10 tells us, 'For we are God's handiwork, created in Christ Jesus to do good works, which God prepared in advance for us to do.' Do you want to live a life with purpose and meaning? If so, turn it over to God today. Ask Him to direct you to the good works He prepared for you even before you were born.

**Acknowledge** –Lord, life is very short.

**Confess** – Lord, forgive me for chasing after worldly pleasure that doesn't provide everlasting satisfaction.

**Thanksgiving** – Lord, thank You for preparing good works for me before I was even born.

**Prayer** – Lord, I want to live a life with purpose and meaning, help me to follow You.

# Day 218

**Psalm 90:4** A thousand years in Your sight are like a day that has just gone by, or like a watch in the night.

Today, we get a perspective of time from God's viewpoint. Psalm 90 was written by Moses and contrasts the shortness of life with an eternal God. In verse two, Moses writes, 'Before the mountains were born or You brought forth the earth and the world, from everlasting to everlasting You are God.' God was God before the heavens and the earth were created and He is God throughout all eternity. Moses goes on to say that to God, a thousand years is like a day that has just passed. Whether that is a literal or figurative declaration, when compared to eternity, a thousand years is like the blink of an eye to God. However, as we look back a thousand years, it is mind-boggling to see what has taken place during that time. To God, it will be just another day in His eternal timeline. What does this tell us about ourselves and God? First, it is difficult for the human mind to understand and comprehend a God who is eternal. Everything we see and touch has either died, will die, or will end, compared to God who never ends. Our earthly perspective is one where nothing lasts forever. However, through God's grace and mercy, doesn't God offer us eternal life with Him? Romans 5:21 tells us, 'So that, just as sin reigned in death, so also grace might reign through righteousness to bring eternal life through Jesus Christ our Lord.' Also, in Galatians 6:8 Paul writes, 'The one who sows to please his sinful nature, from that nature will reap destruction; the one who sows to please the Spirit, from the Spirit will reap eternal life.' Although our earthly lives will soon end, we are promised eternal life with God. He can deliver on His promise to us because He is already eternal. Are you concerned about your future? If so, put your trust in the Eternal One and let Him give you peace.

**Acknowledge** –Lord, a thousand years is like unto a day to You.

**Confess** – Lord, forgive me trying to sow to please my earthly sin nature, one that will reap destruction.

**Thanksgiving** – Lord, thank You for Your promise of eternal life with You.

**Prayer** – Lord, I know that life is short and that You are eternal. Help me to focus on sowing to please Your Spirit and reap eternal life.

# Day 219

Psalm 90:12 Teach us to number our days, that we may gain a heart of wisdom.

Moses tells us to count or number our days so we may gain a heart of wisdom. But how do we count our days when we don't know how many we may have? That is a very good question. In Luke 12:13-21, Jesus gives us the parable of the 'Rich Fool.' A person in the crowd asked Jesus to tell his brother to divide the family inheritance with him. Jesus replied to the man, 'Man, who appointed me a judge or an arbiter between you?' Then Jesus goes on to say, 'Watch out! Be on your guard against all kinds of greed; a man's life does not consist in the abundance of his possessions.' Then Jesus tells them the parable. A person, who was already rich, had an exceptional crop. It was so large, that he didn't have the space to store all the crops that had been produced. So, he thought, I will tear down my existing barns and build bigger ones so I can store up all my stuff. Then he says, 'And I'll say to myself, "you have plenty of good things laid up for many years. Take life easy; eat, drink and be merry."' But God had a different plan. Verse 20 states, 'But God said to him, "You fool! This very night your life will be demanded from you. Then who will get what you have prepared for yourself?"' In the parable, the rich man died suddenly without warning. He didn't have a long illness or appear to be very old. In fact, he said he planned to live off his savings for many years. Moses is telling us that we should not take life for granted. Our days are numbered and we don't know the exact number that we have. Therefore, we should wisely use the days we have been given. We really don't have time to waste. What are doing with your time? Seek God today and ask Him to give you a heart of wisdom as you begin to number your days. Ask Him to reset your priorities to align with His will and His purpose for your life.

**Acknowledge** –Lord, our days are numbered.

**Confess** – Lord, forgive me for not using my time wisely.

**Thanksgiving** – Lord, thank You for life and a heart of wisdom to use it wisely.

**Prayer** – Lord, help me reset my priorities to align with Your will and purpose.

# Day 220

Psalm 90:17 May the favor of the Lord our God rest upon us; establish the work of our hands for us. Yes establish the work of our hands.

TODAY WE CONCLUDE PSALM 90 BY SEEKING GOD'S FAVOR AND blessing on the work of our hands. From the very beginning, God's plan was for man to work. Genesis 2:15 tells us, 'The Lord God took the man and put him in the Garden of Eden to work it and take care of it.' Things were going along pretty well until Adam and Eve disrupted God's plan by eating fruit from the 'Tree of Life' which God had forbidden. As a result, God introduced three curses, one to Satan, one to Eve, and one to Adam. Adam's curse is found in Genesis 3:17-19. It reads, 'To Adam, He said, 'Because you listened to your wife and ate from the tree about which I commanded you, you must not eat of it. Cursed is the ground because of you; through painful toil you will eat of it all the days of your life. It will produce thorns and thistles for you, and you will eat the plants of the field. By the sweat of your brow you will eat your food until you return to the ground, since from it you were taken; for dust you are and to dust you will return.'" That is when work became real work. Work that requires effort and produces sweat. Additionally, God has given each person special abilities to do certain work. Exodus 35:10 says, 'Let every skillful craftsman among you come and make all that the Lord has commanded.' 1 Peter 4:10 tells us, 'Each one should use whatever gift he has received to serve others, faithfully, administering God's grace in its various forms.' What skills and talents have God given you? Are you using them as you should? He is interested in what you do and wants you to be successful no matter what type of work you do. Every day before starting work, I would always pray Proverbs 16:3 which says, 'Commit your work to the Lord, and then your plans will succeed.' Start involving God in your work today. Allow Him to establish the work of your hands.

**Acknowledge** – Lord, You created work.

**Confess** – Lord, forgive me when I fail to seek Your blessing on my work.

**Thanksgiving** – Lord, thank You for Your favor and blessing on my work.

**Prayer** – Lord, I commit my work to You this day, please make my plans succeed.

# Day 221

Psalm 91:1 He who dwells in the shelter of the Most-High will rest in the shadow of the Almighty.

Psalm 91 is a testimony to the reward of those who trust in the Lord. In its simplicity, it is total and complete faith in God. It also became a national anthem of sorts for many Christians during the COVID-19 pandemic. Vivian and I have prayed this Psalm over our family many times. You would have thought it was written in 2020 because of the relevancy of the verses to what we experienced that year. Verses 3-6 say, 'Surely He will save you from the fowler's snare and from the deadly pestilence. He will cover you with His feathers, and under His wings you will find refuge; His faithfulness will be your shield and rampart. You will not fear the terror of night, nor the arrow that flies by day, nor the pestilence that stalks in the darkness, nor the plague that destroys at midday.' The looming question becomes, does praying this prayer protect you from any and all potential harm? My answer, based on what I have read in scripture and heard from the pulpit is yes and no. God does protect us. Our prayers of protection are answered daily. On several occasions I have avoided a serious automobile accident by seconds due to God's intervention. Yet on the other hand, I have been in a couple of automobile accidents. To God's glory I wasn't seriously hurt. I have been sick and hospitalized with appendicitis. God's people experience life and difficult times. However, we have His promise that He is with us. Romans 8:38-39 tell us, 'For I am sure that neither death nor life, nor angels nor rulers, nor things present nor things to come, nor powers, nor height nor depth, nor anything else in all creation, will be able to separate us from the love of God in Christ Jesus our Lord.' I have peace and the confidence that God is with me, no matter what I may be going through. Whether I am sick or well, I can rest under the shadow of His wings.

**Acknowledge** –Lord, You provide rest and shelter underneath Your wings.

**Confess** – Lord, forgive me when I doubt Your love and faithfulness for me.

**Thanksgiving** – Lord, thank You for Your hand of protection in my life.

**Prayer** – Lord, help me to walk daily with You, dwelling in the shelter of the Most-High.

# Day 222

Psalm 91:15 He will call on Me, and I will answer him; I will be with him in trouble; I will deliver him and honor him.

We close Psalm 91 with a reminder to pray and given the assurance that God hears and answers our prayers. The Psalmist writes, 'He will call on me.' God's blessings do not come without prayer. James 4:2-3 says, 'You want something but don't get it. You kill and covet, but you cannot have what you want. You quarrel and fight. You do not have, because you do not ask God. When you ask, you do not receive, because you ask with the wrong motives, that you may spend what you get on your pleasures.' James has added a new dimension to our prayer life, motive. After telling us that we should pray, the Psalmist gives us the assurance that God will answer our prayers. How and when He answers our prayers is according to His will and purpose for us. For example, He may give us the ability to save money to buy what we want instead of making it happen right away. Or something good may come out of a bad situation that we are going through. Our responsibility is to pray. God will hear our prayers and answer them in the way He knows is best for us. Not only does God answer our prayers, the Psalmist goes on to tell us that God is with us in times of trouble and He will deliver us from it. Notice that we are going to have times of trouble. Becoming a Christian and following God does not exempt us from trouble. Satan loves to test our faith as he did with Job. But we have the assurance that God is with us and will deliver us from the trials we are facing. Jesus speaking in Matthew 28:20 assures us, 'and teaching them to observe everything I have commanded you. And surely I am with you always, to the very end of the age.' Take time to pray and seek God today. Tell Him your needs and then your wants. Trust Him to decide what is best for you at this time.

**Acknowledge** –Lord, You hear and answer our prayers.

**Confess** – Lord, forgive me when I ask selfishly for things I really don't need.

**Thanksgiving** – Lord, thank You for being with me in times of trouble.

**Prayer** – Lord, let my prayer life be more than a few minutes at night before I drift off to sleep.

# Day 223

> Psalm 92:1-2 It is good to praise the Lord and make music to Your name, O Most High, proclaiming Your love in the morning and Your faithfulness at night.

THE PSALMIST TELLS US THAT 'IT IS GOOD TO PRAISE THE LORD AND make music to Your name.' Let's explore several reasons why he makes that claim. First, God commands it. We will read later in Psalm 150:6, 'Let everything that has breath, praise the Lord.' In Luke 19:40, Jesus talking to His disciples during His triumphal entry into Jerusalem said, 'I tell you, if they keep quiet, the stones will cry out.' God loves and desires the praises of His people. He is the one who is worthy of our praise. Secondly, praise paves the way into His presence. Psalm 100:4 tells us, 'Enter His gates with thanksgiving and into His courts with Praise.' Our praise moves us from outside the gates of His presence, into His inner court. Next, God dwells in our praise. Psalm 22:3 says, 'Yet You are enthroned as the Holy One; You are the praise of Israel.' His presence is more real and more personal in our praise to Him. Lastly, praise changes our perspective on things. It takes our minds off our problems and focuses our total being on Him. Next, the Psalmist gives us instructions on when we should praise Him. He says our day should begin with praise. When God sent manna to the Israelites who were in the desert, the manna had to be gathered in the early morning before the heat of the day dried it up. Similarly, we should praise God early in the day before the heat and turmoil of the day dry up the freshness of our praise. God has given us another day. We should praise Him for it. Lastly, we should praise God at the end of the day. Praise Him for His faithfulness to you. He brought you through another day. If you don't already, spend time praising God in your prayers. Set aside time each morning and night to praise the God who loves you and enter into His presence. What a great way to start and end the day.

**Acknowledge** –Lord, You are worthy of our praise.

**Confess** – Lord, forgive me when I fail to praise You as I should.

**Thanksgiving** – Lord, thank You for allowing us to enter Your presence through our praises.

**Prayer** – Lord, remind me to offer up praise and worship to You each morning and night.

# Day 224

Psalm 92:5 How great are Your works, Lord, how profound Your thoughts!

THE PSALMIST IS PRAISING GOD BECAUSE OF HIS MIGHTY WORKS and the vastness of His thoughts. While we may not fully grasp the magnitude and complexity of God's works, it should be a part of our praise to Him. David said in 1 Chronicles 16:9, 'Sing to Him, Sing praise to Him; tell of His wonderful acts.' David offered up praise to God for His great works. We find other places in scripture where God is praised for His great works. Revelation 15:2-3 tells us, 'And I saw what looked like a sea of glass mixed with fire and, standing beside the sea, those who had been victorious over the beast and his image and over the number of his name. They held harps given them by God and sang the song of Moses the servant of God and the song of the Lamb: "Great and marvelous are Your deeds, Lord God Almighty. Just and true are Your ways, King of the ages."' During the tribulation, we see that people will be singing about God's great and marvelous deeds. These people were martyrs, killed because of their faith in God and their refusal to worship the beast or Anti-Christ. Why would they be singing about the greatness of God's deeds when they have been put to death? Could it be that because of their faithfulness, God revealed His plan of returning to conquer Satan? Or perhaps, it was because they witnessed first-hand God's faithfulness and love to them. Paul summed it up in Romans 5:8, 'But God demonstrates His own love for us in this: While we were still sinners, Christ died for us.' He loved you and me enough to send His one and only Son, to die a painful death on the cross to save us from the penalty of our sins and to restore our relationship with Him. That alone should give you reason to praise Him. Because of God's marvelous work on the cross and His perfect plan of salvation, we can spend eternity with Him in heaven. Praise Him for His mighty work on the cross.

**Acknowledge** –Lord, Your works are great and Your thoughts are profound.

**Confess** – Lord, forgive me for forgetting to praise You for saving my soul.

**Thanksgiving** – Lord, thank You for Your marvelous plan of salvation.

**Prayer** – Lord, I want to join with the multitudes in singing, 'great and marvelous are Your deeds. Just and true are Your ways.'

# Day 225

**Psalm 92:14** They will still bear fruit in old age, they will stay fresh and green.

Is the Psalmist talking about plants or is he using a metaphor to describe someone in the latter years of life? A few verses earlier, he writes, 'The righteous will flourish like a palm tree, they will grow like a cedar of Lebanon.' In others words, as the righteous grow older they will continue to bear fruit and stay fresh and green. Getting older is a fact of life. I have watched my parents grow older and witnessed the toll disease can take on an elderly person. I have also witnessed how even in old age they can still bear fruit. Around the age of 80, my mother was diagnosed with a form of Parkinson's disease which affects her memory and balance. She is now 87 years old. Over the last seven years we witnessed her declining health and loss of memory. Yet, she lights up when the great-grandchildren come over to see her. My father, on the other hand, is 87 years old but acts as if he is 67. He and I rebuilt a twenty-five-foot bridge that spans a narrow stream in my back yard and a massive playhouse and swing set combination for the grandchildren. Not only is he physically active, he is mentally active. After retiring, he went into full-time ministry. Papa has served five different churches and held the position of Director of Missions for the Wilmington Baptist Association. During COVID, he taught Sunday school by using Zoom. He has continued to bear fruit and learn and grow even in his old age. No one knows what the future holds. Our bodies may wear out, our minds may get foggy. However, no matter our circumstances we can still bear fruit. We can bear the fruit of patience, faith, and goodness. We can have the confidence that even in our latter years God still loves us and cares for us. We can proclaim as the Psalmist did in the very next verse, 'The Lord is upright; He is my Rock, and there is no wickedness in Him.' Trust Him today to lead you into old age.

**Acknowledge** –Lord, even in old age we can still bear the fruit of Your Spirit.

**Confess** – Lord, forgive me when I worry about the future.

**Thanksgiving** – Lord, thank You for being our Rock, our Salvation.

**Prayer** – Lord, I want to bear fruit and live for You into my last days of life.

# Day 226

Psalm 93:1 The Lord reigns, He is robed in majesty; the Lord is robed in majesty and armed with strength. Indeed, the world is established, firm and secure.

Psalm 93 speaks about the eternal sovereignty of God. In verse one, we learn that 'the Lord is robed in majesty and armed with strength. We also read that 'the world is established, firm and secure.' In verse two he says, 'Your throne was established long ago; You are from all eternity.' Later in verse five he tells us, 'Your statutes stand firm; holiness adorns Your House for endless days, O Lord.' The Psalmist leaves no doubt that God is in control, from the very beginning of time and throughout His endless days. We find ourselves somewhere in between the two, and still God is in control. Even during years like 2020 that are extremely challenging, where calamity and sickness hit every household, it is good to be reminded that God is in control. The Psalmist also tells us the Lord reigns. No matter what may be taking place on the earth, He reigns from above. Despite what we feel, whether it may be worry, uncertainty about the future, anxiety about our family, or just plain fear, remember that God is in control. Allow Him to be your peace and comfort. Isaiah 55:8-9 tells us, 'For My thoughts are not your thoughts, neither are your ways My ways, declares the Lord. As the heavens are higher than the earth, so are My ways higher than your ways and My thoughts than your thoughts.' God knows what He is doing and while it may look like chaos and Satan are winning, God is in control. Solomon writing in Ecclesiastes 3:11 tells us, 'He has made everything beautiful in its time. He has also set eternity in the human heart; yet no one can fathom what God has done from beginning to end.' We can trust that God has a purpose for all things that happen, whether good or bad. We may never understand God's purpose for some of the things that happen until we meet Him in heaven. Our role is to remain faithful and trust in God's sovereignty.

**Acknowledge** –Lord, You reign from the beginning of time to eternity.

**Confess** – Lord, forgive me when I lose faith and doubt You are in control.

**Thanksgiving** – Lord, thank You for being robed in majesty and armed with strength.

**Prayer** – Lord, when I begin to doubt, remind me that You are in control.

# Day 227

Psalm 94:1 The Lord is a God who avenges. O God who avenges, shine forth.

THE PSALMIST APPEALS TO GOD AS THE GREAT JUDGE OF THE EARTH to take vengeance on those who oppress the weak, the poor, widows, and orphans. I have heard the phrase, 'Vengeance is Mine, says the Lord.' It is found in Deuteronomy 32:35 which says, 'Vengeance is Mine, and recompense, at the time when their foot shall slide: For the day of their calamity is at hand.' This verse is actually part of a song recited by Moses to the Israelites just before his death. Moses tells us that vengeance is the Lord's and that He will repay. However, we also need to see what the New Testament has to say about vengeance. Paul writing in Romans 12:17-21 tells us, 'Repay no one evil for evil, but give thought to do what is honorable in the sight of all. If possible, so far as it depends on you, live peaceably with all. Beloved, never avenge yourselves, but leave it to the wrath of God, for it is written, "Vengeance is mine, I will repay, says the Lord." To the contrary, "if your enemy is hungry, feed him; if he is thirsty, give him something to drink; for by doing so you will heap burning coals on his head." Do not be overcome by evil, but overcome evil with good.' Paul is quoting two different scriptures, the verse from Deuteronomy 35, and also Proverbs 25:21-22. He also sounds very much like Jesus who said in Matthew 5:43-44, 'You have heard that it was said, "Love your neighbor and hate your enemy." But I tell you: Love your enemies and pray for those who persecute you.' I think the Bible is clear that vengeance belongs to the Lord. I am thankful that He is a loving, forgiving God that doesn't punish me as I deserve. I certainly don't have any right to judge or ask God to punish someone else. Jesus tells us to love our enemies. He tells us to pray for them. Are you praying for those you don't like? If not, add them to your prayer list. Ask God to help you change your attitude and thoughts towards them.

**Acknowledge** –Lord, vengeance is Yours.

**Confess** – Lord, forgive me for not loving and praying for my enemies as You have commanded.

**Thanksgiving** – Lord, thank You for not punishing me as I deserve.

**Prayer** – Lord, help me to love my enemies and pray for those who persecute me.

# Day 228

**Psalm 94:12** Blessed is the one You discipline, Lord, the one You teach from Your law.

THE PSALMIST TELLS US THAT THE ONE WHO GOD DISCIPLINES IS blessed. He is our Heavenly Father, and because of His love for us, He corrects us as an earthly father would do. Hebrews 12:5-6 tells us, 'And have you forgotten that word of encouragement that addresses you as sons: "My son, do not make light of the Lord's discipline and do not lose heart when He rebukes you, because the Lord disciplines those He loves and He punishes everyone He accepts as a son."' God's discipline is not punishment for doing wrong, but is designed to help us grow closer to Him. I have shared a couple of instances when I was punished for my wrongdoing as a child. I wasn't a bad child, but had my share of spankings. There was a time early in my childhood when my sister and I decided to dance on top of our father's car. Needless to say, that didn't go well for us. However, that was the last time we danced on top of a car. The writer of Hebrews goes on to say in 12:11, 'No discipline seems pleasant at the time, but painful. Later on, however, it produces a harvest of righteousness and peace for those who have been trained by it.' Notice he ends the verse by saying 'those who have been trained by it.' The designed effect of God's discipline is to help train us. We must learn from our suffering and pain, rather than just endure it until the next time. God can use all types of circumstances as his tools for our discipline. It could be a lost job, sickness, an accident, or even COVID-19. Yet, each is designed for our benefit. What are you going through today? Are you being trained and corrected by the situations you are facing or are you just trying to make it through? Dig deeper into His word and allow Him to point out things in your life that need correcting. Receive His blessing of discipline with an open heart.

**Acknowledge** –Lord, You discipline Your children.

**Confess** – Lord, forgive me for not learning from Your discipline.

**Thanksgiving** – Lord, thank You for loving me and wanting what is best for me.

**Prayer** – Lord, help me to recognize Your discipline and grow closer to You from it.

# Day 229

Psalm 94:22 But the Lord has become my Fortress, and my God the Rock in whom I take refuge.

Earlier in this Psalm, the writer tells us that the wicked are arrogant and boastful. They have banded together with those in charge to carry out their wickedness. But in today's verse, he declares there is one who can save him from the wicked. It is the Lord who has become his fortress and rock of refuge. In Him and Him alone is his safety. The world can rage around him, but he will keep his hope in God. How firm is your relationship with the God in whom you take refuge? The day is rapidly approaching when our faith and trust in God will be put to the test. If things are difficult now, they will only get more trying as the end of time draws closer. Jesus speaking about the end of the age in Matthew 24:12-13 said, 'Because of the increase of wickedness, the love of most will grow cold, but he who stands firm to the end will be saved.' Paul writing to Timothy in 2 Timothy 3:1 said, 'But mark this: There will be terrible times in the last days.' Are you prepared to live in this type of world? Wickedness and lawlessness will become even more rampant. In 2020, we witnessed lawlessness in the streets of many of our major cities. Businesses were looted and burned. Police officers were attacked with bricks, lasers, and molotov cocktails. Despite the violence, the news media and others called the riots, peaceful protests and even went as far as calling the looting, reparations. Sadly, as our world turns away from God, this type of behavior will become even more prevalent. If your relationship with God is not where it needs to be, go to Him in prayer. Ask Him to lead you to a deeper understanding and faith in Him. Then when difficult days arrive, you like the Psalmist will be able to declare that God is my Fortress and the Rock in whom I take refuge.

**Acknowledge** –Lord, You are my Fortress, the Rock in whom I take refuge.

**Confess** – Lord, forgive me for not trusting in You when times get difficult.

**Thanksgiving** – Lord, thank You for being my Fortress, one I can run to in time of need.

**Prayer** – Lord, difficult days are soon ahead. Help me to be prepared.

# Day 230

**Psalm 95:1 Come, let us sing for joy to the Lord; let us shout aloud to the Rock of our salvation.**

Today's Psalm was written as a call to worship for the Israelites as they assembled to enter the temple. Their call to worship included singing and shouting to the Lord. Music has also become an important part of worship today. No matter the type of music, we must be careful that our worship in song is done as worship to the Lord and not for the benefit of others. Psalm 100 tells us to, 'Make a joyful noise unto the Lord.' Today's verse provides us with several tips about our worship to God. First, singing is a vital part of worship. There are many other ways we can express our worship to God; such as, giving, helping someone in the name of Jesus, giving God your best in all you do, lifting someone up in prayer, and giving God thanks for all things are all forms of worship. However, singing praises to God is by far the primary form of worship. It engages everyone in worship. Secondly, the Psalmist tells us, 'let us sing for joy.' Without a doubt, our worship should be joyful. Psalm 33:1 says it this way, 'Sing joyfully to the Lord, you righteous; it is fitting for the upright to praise Him.' From experience, I know that it is almost impossible to leave your problems at the door of the sanctuary. They follow you wherever you go. However, as we focus our attention on the 'Rock of our Salvation' as the Psalmist does in the last part of today's verse, our troubles will not seem so important for the hour or two we are in the presence of our Savior. I like the way the chorus of 'In the Presence of Jehovah' says it; 'Troubles vanish hearts are mended in the presence of the King.' Have you experienced the presence of God, the 'Rock of your Salvation?' If not, try singing joyfully to the Lord. Enter into His presence through praise and worship. If those around you give you a funny look, sing even louder. God loves to hear your praise.

**Acknowledge** – Lord, You are the Rock of my Salvation. I love to sing praises to You.

**Confess** – Lord, forgive me for allowing my problems to overtake my worship for You.

**Thanksgiving** – Lord, thank You for accepting our praise.

**Prayer** – Lord, help me to praise You from my heart. Let my praise be genuine.

# Day 231

Psalm 95:7b-8 Today, if you hear His voice, do not harden your hearts as you did at Meribah, as you did that day at Massah in the desert.

HAVE WE HARDENED OUR HEARTS TOWARDS GOD AND NOT TRUSTED Him like the Israelites? Let's look in Exodus 17:1-7 and see what happened at Meribah and Massah. The Israelites had come to a place called Rephidim and set up camp. The Bible tells us, there was no water for them to drink, and it didn't take long for the people to get upset with Moses. Verse two says, 'So they quarreled with Moses and said, "Give us water to drink."' Moses replied, 'Why do you quarrel with me? Why do you put the Lord to the test?' But the people continued to grumble and complain about the lack of water. In frustration, Moses cried out to the Lord and said, 'What am I to do with these people? They are almost ready to stone me.' God told Moses to walk ahead taking the staff he had struck the Nile River with, and several of the elders. They came to a large rock at a place called Horeb. God told Moses to strike the rock, and water will come out of it for the people to drink. Moses obeyed and struck the rock, which produced enough water to satisfy the people and their livestock. Moses named the place, 'Massah' (Testing) and 'Meribah' (Quarreling) because the Israelites had not trusted the Lord. Jesus speaking about the Pharisees in Matthew 13:15 said, 'For this people's heart has become calloused; they hardly hear with their ears, and they have closed their eyes. Otherwise they might see with their eyes, hear with their ears, understand with their hearts and turn, and I would heal them.' The Pharisees were too caught up in following the law, rather than seeking a relationship with God. Therefore, their hearts were calloused, their eyes and ears closed. Have you closed your eyes and ears to the word of God? Now is the time to get your life right with Him. Open your eyes to His word, and your ears to His voice. Allow Him to soften your hardened heart and restore your relationship with Him.

**Acknowledge** –Lord, You desire to have a relationship with me.

**Confess** – Lord, forgive me for hardening my heart towards You.

**Thanksgiving** – Lord, thank You for restoring my relationship with You.

**Prayer** – Lord, I ask that You open my eyes to Your word and my ears to Your voice.

# Day 232

**Psalm 96:9** Worship the Lord in the splendor of His holiness, tremble before Him all the earth.

Psalm 96 is a call for all nations to worship the Lord. Verse one tells us to, 'Sing to the Lord a new song; sing to the Lord, all the earth,' encouraging us to add new songs to our worship. Today's verse tells us to worship the Lord in the splendor of His holiness and tremble before Him. Some translations use, 'beauty of His holiness' rather than 'splendor.' To get to this place of worship means that we recognize and bow before the majestic glory of God's Holiness in humbleness. We realize that our lives are far from being holy without the work of Jesus who paid the penalty for our sins and the Holy Spirit living within us. Compared to God's holiness, our holiness can be described like the Prophet Isaiah wrote in Isaiah 64:6, 'All of us have become like one who is unclean, and all our righteous acts are like filthy rags; we are shriveled up like a leaf, and like the wind our sins sweep us away.' The Apostle John had an experience on the Isle of Patmos where he found himself in the presence of God. Revelation 1:17-18 tells us how he reacted when he found himself face to face with a Holy God, 'When I saw Him, I fell at His feet as though dead. Then He placed His right hand on me and said: "Do not be afraid. I am the First and the Last. I am the Living One; I was dead, and behold I am alive for ever and ever! And I hold the keys of death and Hades.' John fainted when He beheld the awesomeness of God. The image he describes is one of beauty, purity, holiness, and righteousness. How do you approach worship? Is there excitement, anticipation, and joy when you enter into worship? Or has worship become mundane, sloppy, and superficial? Take time to evaluate your time of worship. Perhaps the words of the Phillips, Craig, and Dean Song, 'I'm coming back to a heart of worship' might help. Worship the God who loves you and saved you in the beauty of His Holiness.

**Acknowledge** –Lord, You are Holy.

**Confess** – Lord, forgive me when my worship has become mundane, sloppy, sinful, and superficial.

**Thanksgiving** – Lord, thank You for making me right with You.

**Prayer** – Lord, I pray that I will worship You in spirit and in truth, with excitement and a joyful heart.

# Day 233

> Psalm 96:13 Let all creation rejoice before the Lord, for He comes, He comes to judge the earth. He will judge the world in righteousness and the peoples in His faithfulness.

THE PSALMIST TELLS US TO REJOICE BECAUSE THE LORD IS COMING. In Matthew 24, the disciples ask Jesus about His return and the end of the age. Matthew 24:3 tells us, 'As Jesus was sitting on the Mount of Olives, the disciples came to Him privately. "Tell us," they said, "when will this happen and, and what will be the sign of your coming and of the end of the age."' Jesus answers them by providing a series of events that must take place before He returns. He also tells them in Matthew 24:36-39, 'No one knows about the day or hour, not even the angels in heaven, nor the Son, but only the Father. As it was in the days of Noah, so it will be at the coming of the Son of Man. For in the days before the flood, people were eating drinking, marrying and giving in marriage up to the day Noah entered the Ark; and they knew nothing about what would happen until the flood came and took them all away.' We can speculate on His return, but as Jesus told us, no one knows the day or hour. Jesus does tell us that people will be eating, drinking, getting married, and living life as normal. For some, His return will be a total surprise. Jesus told the disciples in Matthew 24:42-44, 'Therefore keep watch, because you do not know on what day your Lord will come. But understand this: If the owner of the house had known at what time of night the thief was coming, he would have kept watch and would not have let his house be broken into. So you must also be ready, because the Son of Man will come at an hour when you do not expect Him.' Are you prepared for His return? If not, repent and seek His forgiveness. Restore your relationship with Him so that you will rejoice at His return.

**Acknowledge** –Lord, one day soon You will return.

**Confess** – Lord, forgive me for allowing my life to drift away from You and Your Word.

**Thanksgiving** – Lord, thank You for reminding us to be alert and ready for Your return.

**Prayer** – Lord, no one knows the day or hour of Your return. Help me to be alert and watchful.

# Day 234

Psalm 97:9 For You, Lord, are most high over all the earth; You are exalted far above all gods.

Today's verse declares God is supreme. God speaking in Exodus 20:3-6 said, 'You shall have no other gods before me. You shall not make for yourself an idol in the form of anything in heaven above or the earth beneath or in the waters below. You shall not bow down to them or worship them; for I am a jealous God, punishing the children for the sin of the fathers to the third generation of those who hate Me, but showing love to a thousand generations of those who love Me and keep My commandments.' However, in Exodus 32:1 we already find the people disobeying God's command. 'When the people saw that Moses was so long in coming down from the mountain, they gathered around Aaron and said, "Come, make us gods who will go before us. As for this fellow Moses who brought us up out of Egypt, we don't know what has happened to him."' Exodus 32:4 states, 'He (Aaron) took what they handed him and made it into an idol cast in the shape of a calf, fashioning it with a tool. Then they said, "These are your gods, O Israel, who brought you up out of Egypt."' Moses confronted the people and Aaron about the idol they were worshiping. The real Aaron stepped up when he told Moses in Exodus 32:24, 'So I told them, "Whoever has any gold jewelry, take it off." Then they gave me the gold, and I threw it into the fire, and out came this calf.' Isn't that our favorite excuse when we are trying to get out of trouble, 'I don't know?' Yet God forgave Aaron and later appointed him as priest. Have we tried to substitute other things in place of God that don't have any lasting value or purpose? Our idols may not be a golden calf, but they are just as sinful. Ask God to show you what changes need to be made to put Him first in your life, then allow Him to restore your relationship with Him.

**Acknowledge** –Lord, You are exalted above all things.

**Confess** – Lord, forgive me for allowing other things to take Your place in my life.

**Thanksgiving** – Lord, thank You that You can use us, even if we make mistakes.

**Prayer** – Lord, help me to be careful not to let other things crowd out Your place in my life.

# Day 235

Psalm 97:12 Rejoice in the Lord, you who are righteous, and praise His Holy name.

Who are the righteous? Paul explains it to us in Romans 3:20,22, 'Therefore no one will be declared righteous in His sight by observing the law; rather, through the law we become conscious of sin. This righteousness from God comes through faith in Jesus Christ to all who believe.' The righteous are commanded to 'rejoice in the Lord.' However, to rejoice in the Lord, our relationship with Christ must go further than just acknowledging who He is. Our head knowledge of Christ and His love for us overflows to our hearts. It is from our hearts that we burst into joy and praise for what He has done. According to Paul, there is no excuse that prevents us from rejoicing and praising the Lord. Writing to the Philippians in 4:3 he said, 'Rejoice in the Lord always. I will say it again: Rejoice!' Acts 16:16-40 tells the story of Paul and Silas in Philippi, where they cast a spirit out of a young slave-girl that had been bothering them. This upset her owners because she had made them a lot of money by fortune-telling. They dragged Paul and Silas to the magistrate where they were accused of stirring up the entire city. They were stripped, beaten with whips, and locked up in jail. Acts 16:25 tells us, 'About midnight Paul and Silas were praying and singing hymns to God, and the other prisoners were listening to them.' They were beaten and bleeding, their feet locked up in stocks, yet they were praising God. Thankfully we find there are other places we can praise the Lord. Psalm 122:1 says, 'I was glad when they said unto me; let us go into the house of the Lord.' Every time we enter the sanctuary, we should enter rejoicing, with praise and thanksgiving. As Paul tells us, we should rejoice always. This means we are to rejoice anywhere and at any time. Take time today to rejoice in the Lord and praise His Holy name.

**Acknowledge** – Lord, You are worthy of our praise and worship.

**Confess** – Lord, forgive me for not opening my heart in praise to You.

**Thanksgiving** – Lord, thank You for all you have done for me. You are worthy of all praise.

**Prayer** – Lord, Your word tells us to rejoice in You always.

# Day 236

**Psalm 98:1** Sing to the Lord a new song, for He has done marvelous things; His Right Hand and His Holy arm have worked salvation for Him.

Psalm 98 foreshadows the coming of Jesus Christ. It is a proclamation that He has come to save the world. In verse one, the Psalmist tells us to sing a new song to the Lord, because of His marvelous work of salvation that God's Right Hand has done. Today we are going to look at several scripture references to God's Right Hand and its significance. Isaiah 41:10 tells us, 'Fear not, for I am with you; be not dismayed, for I am your God; I will strengthen you, I will help you, I will uphold you with My righteous Right Hand.' And Exodus 15:6 says, 'Your Right Hand, O Lord, glorious in power, Your Right Hand, O Lord, shatters the enemy.' In these verses, we find that God's Right Hand represents strength and power. His Right Hand has the strength to carry us and the power to defeat our enemies. We also find that God's Right Hand is a place of prominence and power. Acts 2:33 says, 'Being therefore exalted at the Right Hand of God, and having received from the Father the promise of the Holy Spirit, He has poured out this that you yourselves are seeing and hearing.' Also Acts 5:31, 'God exalted Him at His Right Hand as Leader and Savior, to give repentance to Israel and forgiveness of sins.' In these verses, the Apostle Peter is speaking about Jesus who was exalted to the Right Hand of God. Having completed His mission on earth, Jesus returned to heaven and took His rightful place at the Right Hand of God. What is Jesus now doing at the Right Hand of God? Romans 8:34 tells us, 'Who is He that condemns? Christ Jesus who died – more than that, who was raised to life – is at the Right Hand of God and is also interceding for us.' Jesus is at the Right Hand of the Father interceding for you and for me day and night. Aren't you glad He is there working on your behalf? Give Him praise today for all He has done for you.

**Acknowledge** – Lord, You have done marvelous things.

**Confess** – Lord, forgive me for doubting Your strength and power.

**Thanksgiving** – Lord, thank You for being at the Right Hand of the Father interceding for me.

**Prayer** – Lord, put a new song in my heart for the marvelous things You have done.

# Day 237

**Psalm 98:9** Let them sing before the Lord, for He comes to judge the earth. He will judge the world in righteousness and the people with equity.

The Psalmist tells us the Lord is coming to judge the earth with righteousness. Every Christmas, Christians around the world celebrate the first coming of Jesus. Many families read the story of Christ's birth from the Gospel of Luke. Luke 2:9-14 tells us, 'An angel of the Lord appeared to them, and the glory of the Lord shone around them, and they were terrified. But the angel said to them, "Do not be afraid. I bring you good news of great joy that will be for all the people. Today in the Town of David, a Savior has been born to you; He is Christ the Lord. This will be a sign to you: You will find a baby lying in a manger." Suddenly a great company of the heavenly host appeared with the angel, praising God and saying, "Glory to God in the highest, and on earth peace to men on whom His favor rests."' Can you imagine how terrified the shepherds may have felt? Right before their eyes, the night sky was illuminated by a multitude of 'heavenly hosts' praising God. Now fast forward several thousand years to the day Christ returns again. What does the Bible say about His second coming? 1 Thessalonians 4:16-17 tells us, 'For the Lord Himself will come down from heaven, with a loud command, with the voice of the archangel and with the trumpet call of God, and the dead in Christ will rise first. After that, we who are still alive and are left will be caught up together with them in the clouds to meet the Lord in the air. And so we will be there with the Lord forever.' We may not have witnessed the first coming of Christ, but we may very well hear the trumpet sound His second coming. Don't be caught off guard and surprised as the shepherds were. As Paul writes a few verses later, 'be alert and self-controlled. Be ready to meet Him in the air, singing praises to Him.

**Acknowledge** –Lord, You are coming again to judge and rule the earth.

**Confess** – Lord, forgive me for being like the shepherds, who were not expecting You.

**Thanksgiving** – Lord, thank You for providing the details of Your birth over 2000 years ago.

**Prayer** – Lord, help me to be alert and self-controlled, living as if You are returning today.

# Day 238

**Psalm 99:1** The Lord reigns, let the nations tremble, He sits enthroned between the cherubim, let the earth shake.

THE PSALMIST PROVIDES A GLIMPSE OF THE THRONE OF GOD AND His power. He tells us that God 'sits enthroned between the cherubim.' We find a description of that in Exodus 25 where God tells Moses to make a chest, called the Ark, and overlay it with gold. He also made a cover for the Ark, called the Mercy Seat. At each end of the Mercy Seat, cherubim were to face each other with their wings spread over the Mercy Seat. Inside the Ark, Moses put the tablets containing the 10 Commandments, a jar of manna, and Aaron's rod. The Mercy Seat became the place where God's presence would dwell. Exodus 25:22 says, 'There, above the cover between the two cherubim that are over the ark of the Testimony, I will meet with you and give you all My commands for the Israelites.' The Mercy Seat was God's throne on earth. The Ark was placed in the Holy of Holies in the tabernacle. The Holy of Holies was separated from the rest of the tabernacle by a thick veil. Only the High Priest was allowed to enter there once a year on the Day of Atonement, to sprinkle the blood of the sacrifice for the sins of the people on the Mercy Seat. This system of sacrifice and atonement for sins lasted thousands of years. 'Man' was unable to approach God and seek forgiveness by any other means. But Jesus' birth that we read about yesterday changed everything. His blood and His sacrifice on the cross, once and for all paid the penalty for our sin. No longer would animal sacrifices be required. No longer would the High Priest be required to enter the Holy of Holies to offer a sacrifice for our sins. Matthew 27:51 tells us, 'At that moment the curtain of the temple was torn in two from top to bottom. The earth shook and the rocks split.' Aren't you glad the earth shook on that day and the veil was torn? Have you approached the God who reigns and confessed your sins? Now is the perfect time to do so.

**Acknowledge** –Lord, You sit enthroned between the cherubim.

**Confess** – Lord, forgive me of my sins that separate me from Your presence.

**Thanksgiving** – Lord, thank You for tearing the veil that separated us from Your presence.

**Prayer** – Lord, I confess my sins to You. I ask that You forgive me.

# Day 239

Psalm 99:9 Exalt the Lord our God and worship at His Holy mountain, for the Lord our God is holy.

Today the Psalmist closes Psalm 99 by exalting the Lord and worshiping Him on His holy mountain. Did you know that God has a holy mountain? In Genesis 22, we read the story of God testing Abraham's faith by asking him to sacrifice his son Isaac. Genesis 22:2 says, 'Then God said, "Take your son, your only son, Isaac whom you love, and go to the region of Moriah. Sacrifice him there as a burnt offering on one of the mountains I will tell you about.' Abraham and Isaac travel three days into the wilderness and reach the mountain that God points out. They build the altar and Abraham is preparing to sacrifice his son as God commanded him. However, God intervenes and sends a ram to be sacrificed whose horns had been caught in a bush. You may be wondering what the significance of this story is. Fast forward a few thousand years and we read in 2 Chronicles 3:1 where Mount Moriah is mentioned again, 'Then Solomon began to build the temple of the Lord in Jerusalem on Mount Moriah, where the Lord had appeared to his father David. It was on the threshing floor of Araunah the Jebusite, the place provided by David.' Solomon built the temple on the very spot that God had led Abraham many years before to test his faith. Obviously, that spot in Jerusalem is a very special place for the Jews. However, one day in the future, it will have significance to those who have trusted Christ as their Savior. Revelation 21:10 tells us, 'And He carried me away in the Spirit to a mountain great and high, and showed me the Holy City, Jerusalem, coming down out of heaven from God.' One day we will worship Him on His holy mountain. However, the good news is that today we do not have to travel to a certain place to worship God. We can worship Him no matter where we are. Take time to worship Him today.

**Acknowledge** –Lord, You are Holy.

**Confess** – Lord, forgive me for not exalting You as I should.

**Thanksgiving** – Lord, thank You for the opportunity to worship You.

**Prayer** – Lord, I don't understand how Your plan will unfold, but I want to be ready to worship You on Your Holy Mountain.

# Day 240

**Psalm 100:3 Know that the Lord is God. It is He who made us, and we are His; we are His people, the sheep of His pasture.**

Psalm 100 is a call to praise the Lord. Today we read verse three that begins, 'Know that the Lord is God.' How well do you know God? I accepted Jesus as my Savior around the age of nine. Over the years my knowledge of God has grown through attending church, reading and studying the Bible, personal experiences, reading Christian books, and prayer. However, the older I get the more I realize how much more I have to learn about God. I may not understand His ways, but I know that He loved us enough to send His only Son to pay the penalty for our sin. Because I have trusted Him as my Lord and Savior, I owe Him my obedience, my trust, my submission, and my love. Next, the Psalmist tells us, 'It is He who made us and we are His…' God speaking to Jeremiah in chapter 1:5 said, 'Before I formed you in the womb I knew you, before you were born I set you apart; I appointed you as a prophet to the nations.' He knew you before you were born. Later in Jeremiah 29:11, God told Jeremiah, 'For I know the plans I have for you declares the Lord, plans to prosper you and not to harm you, plans to give you hope and a future.' God has a plan for your life as well. I have heard people use the term, 'he/she is a self-made person' about someone who has risen from nothing to greatness. Their stories are inspirational. However, their story is part of God's plan. It was God who created them, had a plan for them, and opened the doors of success for them. However, this doesn't mean they didn't have to work hard, stay focused on their goal, and persevere through trials to achieve success. Lastly, we are told, 'We are His people, the sheep of His pasture.' God made us, He has a plan for us, and He looks after us like a shepherd. What more can we want from our God? How well do you know Him?

**Acknowledge** –Lord, You alone are God.

**Confess** – Lord, forgive me for not knowing You as I should.

**Thanksgiving** – Lord, thank You for creating me and having a perfect plan for my life.

**Prayer** – Lord, You are the good shepherd who cares deeply for His sheep.

# Day 241

Psalm 101:1 I will sing of Your love and justice; to You, Lord, I will sing praise.

DAVID SINGS OF GOD'S LOVE AND JUSTICE AND PLEDGES TO APPLY these qualities as he rules over the people. These are also qualities we should strive for in our lives. What better example to follow than that of Jesus? We can observe His love and mercy in the way He forgives our sins. Yet we also witness His justice or discipline when we sin against Him. Thankfully, His justice is tempered with love and mercy. Are your feelings towards others tempered with love and mercy or just simply justice? Paul writing to the Colossians in 3:13 tells us, 'Bearing with one another and, if one has a complaint against another, forgiving each other; as the Lord has forgiven you, so you must forgive.' In verse two, David said 'I will be careful to live a blameless life' and asks for God's help. Our goal should be to live more like Christ each day. What are some of the qualities of living a blameless, Christ-like life: integrity, honesty, encouragement, helping others, and having pure thoughts? Like David, we should ask for God's help to live a blameless life each day. People will notice the difference when you make these qualities a priority in your life. In verse three, David vows not to look at anything that is worthless. Ask yourself; is what I spend most of my time watching bringing value, meaning, and purpose to my life? Just know that whatever captures your attention has long-term consequences. Paul writing to the Philippians in 4:8 said, 'Finally, brothers, whatever is true, whatever is noble, whatever is right, whatever is pure, whatever is lovely, whatever is admirable – if anything is excellent and praiseworthy – think about such things.' You will be amazed how much more time you have in a day to think, reflect, and talk to God rather than mindlessly scrolling on your phone. Put your phone down and talk to God, you will not regret it. Make a pledge today to pursue the qualities David sought for his life.

**Acknowledge** –Lord, I will sing of Your love and justice.

**Confess** – Lord, forgive me for allowing unhealthy things into my life.

**Thanksgiving** – Lord, thank You for David's example we can use to follow You.

**Prayer** – Lord, help me to live a blameless life, where I guard what I watch, and how I treat others.

# Day 242

Psalm 102:1 Hear my prayer, Lord; let my cry for help come to You.

Psalm 102 reads like a prayer of someone who is overwhelmed by their problems, troubled by their enemies, and depressed because of their physical condition. The Psalmist reaches a point of desperation and his only hope rests with God. He begins by crying out, 'Hear my prayer, Lord; let my cry for help come to You.' In the next several verses, the Psalmist tells God what he is going through. I love the colorful way in which he describes his situation. Verse three says, 'My days vanish like smoke; my bones burn like glowing embers.' Depression has snuffed out the fire that used to burn brightly in my life, now I am barely a glowing ember. Verse four, 'My heart is blighted and withered like grass; I forget to eat my food.' Anguish has taken away his energy. Grief has taken away his appetite. I have known several couples who have gone through divorce. Emotions of fear, anger, and grief overwhelm them taking away their appetite. Verse five, 'Because of my loud groaning I am reduced to skin and bones.' Verses 6-7, 'I am like a desert owl, like an owl among the ruins. I lie awake; I have become like a bird alone on a roof.' I am all alone among the ruins of my life. People have deserted me. Because of my sorrow, I prefer to be alone. Even worse, I can't sleep at night. I am up, alone with my thoughts that now haunt me day and night. What an awful place to be in. Sadly, many of us have been there or are headed in that direction right now. What can we do? We can do as the Psalmist does today. Cry out to the Lord. Cry out to the one who loves you and hears your every prayer. 1 Peter 5:7 says, 'Cast all your anxiety on Him because He cares for you.' Start casting your cares one by one on Him today.

**Acknowledge** –Lord, You hear my cry for help.

**Confess** – Lord, forgive me for waiting for things to blow up in my life before I reach out to You.

**Thanksgiving** – Lord, thank You for caring for me.

**Prayer** – Lord, life has its ups and downs, so I cast my sorrow on You. I cast my depression on You. I cast my fear on You. I cast my anger on You.

# Day 243

*Psalm 102:12 But You Lord, sit enthroned forever; Your renown endures through all generations.*

Today we turn our attention away from our problems and focus on the true source of our help. No matter the circumstances I may be facing, God is in control, I will not be afraid. We don't know if the Psalmist carried his problems to the Lord earlier, or if he waited until things had gotten to the point, he couldn't take it anymore. However, he is confident of God's sovereignty and faithfulness. How is your prayer life? Do you tend to hold on until things get bad before you bring them up to God in prayer? The year 2020 was a tough year for many. In early March when Covid-19 began to spread like wildfire in New York City where my son and his family live, it became a priority on my prayer list. As it continued to spread, it remained a priority in my daily prayers. However, it wasn't until someone I loved and cared for was in danger that I began to sincerely pray about this issue. For example, as parents we may sense something's not right in our children's lives. Because we love them, we start lifting them up in prayer as soon as we get that feeling. Or we sense something's not right with our marriage. Our spouse is acting differently. We begin to see our relationship breaking apart. As soon as these feelings begin to take place, we don't wait for things to get worse, we immediately pray about it. Yet, we may find ourselves in the same condition the Psalmist was yesterday. We have prayed for weeks or months, but things continue to get worse. Tensions are high. Nothing is going like it should. It is at those times we throw our hands up in surrender and say, Lord you are on the throne. Take control of my life. Help me to remember that You are faithful. You rule over all that is going on in my life today. Choose to trust Him and believe that He is in control. God can and does restore broken marriages. God can and does save our wayward children. He is enthroned forever.

**Acknowledge** –Lord, You sit enthroned forever.

**Confess** – Lord, forgive me when I doubt You are in control of my life.

**Thanksgiving** – Lord, thank You for being the same yesterday, today, and tomorrow.

**Prayer** – Lord, I ask for the foresight to pray for things that have yet to surface in my life.

# Day 244

**Psalm 102:19** The Lord looked down from His sanctuary on high, from heaven He viewed the earth.

TODAY WE GET A GLIMPSE OF THE POSTURE OF GOD AS HE SITS UPON His heavenly throne, looking downward toward earth. In verse 20, we find that God is looking down, 'to hear the groans of the prisoners and release those condemned to death.' God even cares for those condemned to death. Where were you before you accepted Christ as your Lord and Savior? Wasn't the penalty for your sin death? Paul writing in Romans 6:23 tells us, 'For the wages of sin is death, but the gift of God is eternal life in Christ Jesus our Lord.' You were facing the death penalty with no chance of parole. However, Romans 5:8 changed everything, 'But God demonstrates His own love for us in this: While we were still sinners, Christ died for us.' God loved you enough to send His Son to die in your place. Maybe you have not given your life to Christ and accepted Him as your Savior. God is still looking and watching over you. He wants you to repent of your sins and follow Him. 2 Peter 3:9 tells us, 'The Lord is not slow in keeping His promise, as some understand slowness. He is patient with you, not wanting anyone to perish, but everyone to come to repentance.' God is patiently waiting for you to turn to Him for salvation. He will not force you to accept Him as Lord of your life. Take time right now to ask Him to forgive you of your sins and to come into your life. What happens when you do? First, you will feel a release from the struggle of sin that has gripped your life. You will experience an inner joy and peace as the Holy Spirit comes into your heart. You will want to praise Him and tell others what He has done for you. What is God doing? Luke 15:10 tells us, 'In the same way, I tell you, there is rejoicing in the presence of the angels of God over one sinner who repents.' God tells the angels to 'crank up the band,' (fill in your name) has repented and come home.

**Acknowledge** –Lord, You look down from your sanctuary.

**Confess** – Lord, forgive me when I doubt Your love for me.

**Thanksgiving** – Lord, thank You for patiently waiting for me to turn to You.

**Prayer** – Lord, I pray that many will repent and come to know You today.

# Day 245

Psalm 102:25 In the beginning You laid the foundations of the earth, and the heavens are the work of Your hands.

GOD IS ETERNAL. HE WAS THERE TO LAY THE FOUNDATIONS OF THE earth and will be here long after they wear out. In verse 27 the Psalmist says of God, '...and Your years will never end.' This God who we cry out to for help, that we look up to, who sits on His throne, who looks down on us in love, laid the foundations of the earth and created the heavens. Genesis 1:1 says, 'In the beginning God created the heavens and the earth.' The Apostle John writing in John 1:1-2 gives us more details about the creation, 'In the beginning was the Word, and the Word was with God, and the Word was God. He was with God in the beginning.' Jesus is the 'Word' John is referring to. Jesus was with God at creation, yet He is God. What can we learn from what the Psalmist is telling us today? First, God had no problems creating the heavens and the earth. All He had to do was speak and the earth was created. In Genesis chapter one, we find the phrase 'And God said' nine times. Each time He spoke something new was created: the stars, the moon, the sun, the sky, the earth, vegetation, and all living creatures. This God who created all things, the one we look to for help, the one looking down on us in love, shouldn't have any trouble restoring our lives no matter how bad things have gotten. Most importantly, God can restore your relationship with Him. Have other things taken the place of God in your life? If so, call on the One who can restore your relationship with Him. Let Him fill your life with hope and peace. Paul writing in Romans 5:13 tells us, 'May the God of hope fill you with all joy and peace as you trust in Him, so that you may overflow with hope by the power of the Holy Spirit.' The hope and peace Paul speak about is there for you to have. All you have to do is ask Him.

**Acknowledge** –Lord, You are eternal.

**Confess** – Lord, forgive me when I doubt Your sovereignty.

**Thanksgiving** – Lord, thank You for Your power that can restore my walk with You.

**Prayer** – Lord, fill my life with joy and peace as I faithfully put my trust in You.

# Day 246

Psalm 103:2 Praise the Lord, my soul, and forget not His benefits.

David has not forgotten what God has done for Him. Over the next several verses, David begins to list some of the blessings from God. In verse three he says, 'Who forgives your sins and heals all your diseases.' Verse four, 'Who redeems your life from the pit and crowns you with love and compassion.' Verse five, 'Who satisfies your desires with good things so that your youth is renewed like the eagles.' Verse six, 'The Lord works righteousness and justice for all the oppressed.' Verse seven, 'He made known His ways to Moses, His deeds to the people of Israel.' Verse eight, 'The Lord is compassionate and gracious, slow to anger, abounding in love.' Verse nine, 'He will not always accuse, nor will He harbor His anger forever.' Verse 10, 'He does not treat us as our sins deserve or repay us according to our iniquities.' Perhaps the most important blessing to us, is that of God's grace and mercy. Until our sins are forgiven, the other blessings don't have as much meaning to us. Think back to the day your sins were forgiven and Christ came into your life. Can you remember the joy, peace, and happiness you felt because the burden of your sins had been taken away? In the 1980's, the Perry's sang a song written by Mary Spence about that experience, entitled, "I Remember the Day." The lyrics go, 'I was burdened down with sin, No happiness was found within, I never knew the meaning of joy down in my soul, When at last I finally knelt contentment filled my soul like I'd never felt, Heaven came down there was glory all around, When He saved my soul. I remember the day when the Lord saved me, All of heaven came down and I was happy and free, Glory filled my soul, For I knew the Lord had made me whole, I shall never forget, the day when the Lord saved me.' Do you remember the day you were saved? Think back to the day your sins were forgiven, and like David, praise the Lord today for His blessing of salvation.

**Acknowledge** –Lord, You are compassionate and gracious, slow to anger and abounding in love.

**Confess** – Lord, forgive me when I fail to offer my heartfelt praise for Your blessings in my life.

**Thanksgiving** – Lord, thank You for Your blessings of forgiveness and salvation.

**Prayer** – Lord, help me to never forget the day You saved me.

# Day 247

Psalm 103:11 For as high as the heavens are above the earth, so great is His love for those who fear Him.

DAVID TRIES TO DESCRIBE THE VASTNESS OF GOD'S LOVE. HE SAID IT was 'as high as the heavens above the earth.' To put it in perspective, the sun is approximately 93,000,000 miles from the earth. (www.solarsystem.nasa.gov) Traveling at 100 mph, 24 hours per day without stopping, it would take over 106 years to reach the sun. The very next verse, David writes, 'As far as the east is from the west, so far has He removed our transgressions.' Again, David provides us with another distance that can't be measured. Each step eastward takes you one step further from the west. Our God loves us immeasurably. He has forgiven our sins and removed the memory of them. If He doesn't remember them, neither should we. Have you found yourself digging up past sins and shame? Satan wants you to live in the shame and fear that God hasn't forgotten them as well. The next time you start to think I am not worthy of God's love, I don't deserve to be free from the guilt of my past, tell Satan that your past has been forgiven and that your sins have been removed as far as the east is from the west. Satan, I belong to the One who has forgiven me of my sins. Give God praise for His great love and forgiveness. However, David goes on to say in today's verse, '...so great is His love for those who fear Him.' We have learned earlier that the fear of God means a humble, heartfelt reverence of God and His authority. Godly fear is one of the first steps to receiving forgiveness. We come to the realization, that we are sinners, separated from God. Romans 3:23 says, 'All have sinned and come short of the glory of God.' Our only hope is Jesus Christ who paid the penalty for our sins. 1 John 1:9 tells us, 'If we confess our sins, He is faithful and just and will forgive us our sins.' We must humble ourselves before God, confess our sins and receive His forgiveness. God will do the rest.

**Acknowledge** –Lord, Your love for me is as high as the heavens.

**Confess** – Lord, forgive me for trying to bring up old sins You have forgiven and forgotten.

**Thanksgiving** – Lord, thank You for Your great love for me.

**Prayer** – Lord, never let me forget Your love for me.

# Day 248

Psalm 103:17 But from everlasting to everlasting the Lord's love is with those who fear Him, and His righteousness with their children's children.

God's love and blessings extend from generation to generation. Does that mean our faith in God automatically passes down to our children? David answers that question in verse 18 by saying, 'With those who keep His covenant and remember to obey His precepts.' This verse adds the condition that both the parents and their children should 'fear God' and obey His commands. I don't receive salvation based on the merits of my parents. My salvation is based solely on the decision I make to follow Him. Without God's love being personal to me, I would be less prone to obey Him and would be taking advantage of the grace extended to me from my parents. But what does David mean by God's love extending to the children's children of those who fear him? My grandparents grew up and lived in an era when things didn't come easy. They lived through the Great Depression and two world wars. My grandfather on my mother's side was killed in a land dispute and was buried the day my mother was born. My grandmother, in spite of her circumstances, served God and raised her daughter in a Christian home. My father's parents ran a small country store. They also trusted and served God. My grandparents were blessed and provided a great example for their children to follow. When my father and mother were married, they made a commitment to serve God and trust Him. God has tremendously blessed them. When Vivian and I were married, we also made a commitment to serve and trust God. Vivian's family history is one of faithfulness to God as well. I can say God has truly blessed our lives. We now have five beautiful grandchildren. Our prayer is that we will pass down to our children and their children our example of faithfully serving God. God will keep His promise of everlasting love to our family as long as we humble ourselves and give our lives to Him. What does your family history look like? You can start a legacy of everlasting love and grace upon yours.

**Acknowledge** – Lord, Your love is from everlasting to everlasting.

**Confess** – Lord, forgive me for not faithfully following You.

**Thanksgiving** – Lord, thank You for Your love that passes down from generation to generation.

**Prayer** – Lord, help me to start a legacy of everlasting love and grace upon my family.

# Day 249

Psalm 103:22 Praise the Lord, all His works everywhere in His dominion. Praise the Lord, my soul.

DAVID CALLS ON EVERYONE NEAR AND FAR TO PRAISE THE LORD. Perhaps he had a glimpse of heaven as John did when he wrote Revelation 5:11-12, 'Then I looked and heard the voice of many angels, numbering thousands upon thousands, and ten thousand times ten thousand. They encircled the throne and the living creatures and the elders. In a loud voice they sang: "Worthy is the Lamb, who was slain, to receive power and wealth and wisdom and strength and honor and glory and praise."' After witnessing the praise of the angels around the throne, John hears more praise rising up from every direction. Revelation 5:13 tells us, 'Then I heard every creature in heaven and on earth and under the earth and on the sea, and all that is in them singing: "To Him who sits on the throne and to the Lamb be praise and honor and glory and power, forever and ever!"' Like David, I don't want to be content with watching others praise God without taking part. Sadly, there are some days we can hardly get a 'thank You Lord' to roll off our lips. Life can be hard. We face disappointment, discouragement, trials, and temptation all the time. We tend to allow these things to take our attention away from the God who loves us, created us, watches over us, died for us, and is coming back to take us home with Him. No matter our circumstances, we can find something to praise the Lord about. As we lift our praise to Him, our problems begin to seem smaller. Not only that, it is God's will for our lives. 1 Thessalonians 5:16-18 tells us, 'Be joyful always; pray continually; give thanks in all circumstances, for this is God's will for you in Christ Jesus.' Start your day with praise to God. Give Him thanks for all He has done. Ask Him to fill your life today with peace and joy. Don't let the daily grind of life steal your praise.

**Acknowledge** –Lord, let everything that has breath, praise Your name.

**Confess** – Lord, forgive me when I allow the daily grind of life to take away my praise for You.

**Thanksgiving** – Lord, to You who sits on the throne and to the Lamb be praise and honor and glory and power, forever and ever!

**Prayer** – Lord, in everything I give thanks to You, for it is Your will in my life.

# Day 250

Psalm 104:1 Praise the Lord, O my soul. O Lord my God, You are very great; You are clothed with splendor and majesty.

After praising the Lord, the Psalmist acknowledges that God is great. At an early age, I was taught to say the blessing at mealtime, 'God is great, God is good, let us thank Him for our food. By His hands we all are fed. Give us Lord our daily bread, Amen.' This is a simple, yet powerful prayer that teaches us about the greatness of God. King Nebuchadnezzar, who was humbled by God, gives us a glimpse of the greatness of God in Daniel 4:34-35, 'At the end of that time, I, Nebuchadnezzar, raised my eyes toward heaven, and my sanity was restored. Then I praised the Most-High; I honored and glorified Him who lives forever. His dominion is an eternal dominion; His kingdom endures from generation to generation. All the peoples of the earth are regarded as nothing. He does as He pleases with the powers of heaven and the peoples of the earth. No one can hold back His hand or say to Him: "What have You done?"' The most powerful man on the earth at that time praises God's greatness. However, not only is God Great, He is also good. Jesus speaking to the Rich Young Ruler in Mark 10:18 said, 'Why do you call Me good? No one is good – except God alone.' His very nature is goodness, mercy, tenderness, patience, and kindness. If not, you and I would be on our way to eternal punishment. Lastly, the Psalmist tells us that God is clothed in splendor and majesty. While garments both conceal and reveal a person, they define who God is. Kids can get ridiculed for not wearing the right kind of clothes. However, God is not defined by what He wears. His garments are His creation, His plan of salvation, His miracle of life, His miracle of healing, and His preparation of a heavenly home for those who trust in Him. It is those things that give us a glimpse of who He is. He is a great God, clothed in splendor and majesty. Praise Him today for His greatness.

**Acknowledge** – Lord, You are great and greatly to be praised.

**Confess** – Lord, forgive me when I fail to see Your greatness at work all around me.

**Thanksgiving** – Lord, thank You for Your goodness and mercy shown to me.

**Prayer** – Lord, help me to acknowledge Your greatness and Your goodness.

# Day 251

> Psalm 104:2 The Lord wraps himself in light as with a garment; He stretches out the heavens like a tent.

Psalm 104 is a hymn to God the creator. Today we celebrate God's first two creations, light and the heavens. Genesis 1:2 says, 'And God said, "Let there be light," and there was light.' Moses had an encounter with the brightness of God's glory and presence. In Exodus 33, Moses asked God to show him His glory. In verse 19 the Lord said, 'I will cause all My goodness to pass in front of you, and I will proclaim My name, the Lord, in your presence…But you cannot see My face, for no one may see Me and live.' Then the Lord sent Moses to a place in the rocks where he could stand as the Lord passed by. God speaking in verse 22 said 'When My glory passes by, I will put you in a cleft in the rock and cover you with My hand until I have passed by. Then I will remove My hand and you will see My back; but My face must not be seen.' Moses was only capable of experiencing a portion of God's presence. After that, the Bible says that his face was so radiant, that Aaron and the rest of the Israelites were afraid to come near him. Next the Psalmist said, 'He stretches out the heavens like a tent.' Day Two of creation is found in Genesis 1:6-8, 'And God said, "Let there be an expanse between the waters to separate water from water." So God made the expanse and separated the water under the expanse from the water above it. And it was so. God called the expanse "sky." And there was evening, and there was morning – the second day.' How great is our God? He is a light so bright, that it cannot be seen by the naked eye. He is brighter than the sun. His brightness describes a God who is completely Holy and Pure. He created the universe, the stars, the moons, the sky, and the planets out of nothing as if it were nothing. Join with the Psalmist and sing, 'Praise the Lord O my soul.'

**Acknowledge** –Lord, You are Light.

**Confess** – Lord, forgive me when I try to compare Your likeness to something impure.

**Thanksgiving** – Lord, thank You for allowing me to have a tiny glimpse of Your presence when I worship You.

**Prayer** – Lord, if nothing else, Your creation points to Your greatness, so I should worship You.

# Day 252

**Psalm 104:5** He set the earth on its foundations; it cannot be moved.

WE SEE ANOTHER WORK OF GOD THAT MAKES HIM A GREAT GOD. 'God set the earth on its foundations.' The people of David's day knew very little about the heavens and how everything fits together. However, David wrote in Psalms 8:4-5, 'When I consider Your heavens, the work of Your fingers, the moon, the stars, which You have set in place, what is man that You are mindful of him, the son of man that You care for him?' David knew who created the heavens and put everything in place. He acknowledged and worshiped the Creator not the creation. It now seems as man continues to gain more knowledge and understanding of the heavens, the less they seem to acknowledge the Creator. We now have the Big-Bang Model to explain the creations of the heavens and the earth. According to Britannica.com, 'Its essential feature is the emergence of the universe from a state of extremely high temperature and density – the so-called big bang that occurred 13.8 billion years ago.' What is so surprising to me, are the assumptions that have to be accepted as fact for the Big-Bang Model to have any validity, yet it is the theory of choice over God's word about creation. I guess the smarter we seem to get, the less we need God. Maybe we should ask who else but God could put the earth in an elliptical orbit around the sun? Who else but God could place the moon, approximately 250,000 miles away, to orbit the earth every 27 days and while it is orbiting the earth, it is also rotating on its own axis at a pace of once every 27 days? (www.space.com) Who else but God could make the earth rotate on its tilted axis at just the right angle and speed to make one revolution every 24 hours? I could go on and on about the preciseness of God's handiwork in the heavens and earth. Don't get caught up in theory and assumptions about God's creation. Read His word, He will tell you how He put it all together.

**Acknowledge** –Lord, You set the earth on its foundations.

**Confess** – Lord, forgive me when I am tempted to believe man's explanation for Your creation.

**Thanksgiving** – Lord, thank You for creating the heavens and the earth.

**Prayer** – Lord, help me to understand and trust Your word.

# Day 253

*Psalm 104:24 How many are Your works, Lord! In wisdom You made them all; the earth is full of Your creatures.*

Our attention now moves from the heavens, to God's creation on the earth. In Genesis chapter one, we find that God spent a couple of days filling the earth with His creations. On the third day, He created the plants and trees. Genesis 1:11, 'Then God said, "Let the land produce vegetation: seed-bearing plants and trees on the land that bear fruit with seed in it, according to their various kinds." And it was so.' On day four, God set up the rotation of the earth around the sun as we learned about yesterday, to mark the seasons, days, and years. (Genesis 1:14-19) On day five, God was busy creating all the creatures that lived in water and all types of birds. Genesis 1:20, 'And God said, "Let the water teem with living creatures, and let birds fly above the earth across the expanse of the sky."' Day six was a very busy day for God. Genesis 1:24 tells us, 'And God said, "Let the land produce living creatures according to their kinds: livestock, creatures that move along the ground, and wild animals, each according to its kind." And it was so.' But God had not finished, for verse 26 tells us, 'Then God said, "Let Us make man in Our image, in Our likeness, and let them rule over the fish of the sea and the birds of the air, over the livestock, over all the earth, and over all the creatures that move along the ground."' It is amazing all the different types of birds, sea creatures, and land animals God created for you and me to enjoy and have control over. Yet, the Psalmist tells us, each one was wisely made. Each one fits in its place and has its own purpose. He even said the earth is full of God's creation. No matter where you are, God's riches abound. Praise Him today for all His creation, great or small. Thank Him for making His creation available for our use.

**Acknowledge** –Lord, the earth is full of Your creation.

**Confess** – Lord, forgive me when I begin to think Your creation just evolved from nothing.

**Thanksgiving** – Lord, thank You for Your creations on the land and in the water.

**Prayer** – Lord, Your works are many. Help me to appreciate and respect Your creation.

# Day 254

**Psalm 104:27** All creatures look to You to give them their food at the proper time.

GOD PREPARES FOOD FOR ALL HIS CREATION AND DISTRIBUTES IT at just the right time. That seems like an impossible task. It is hard enough for me to remember to feed my grandchildren's fish if they happen to be out of town. In Matthew 6:19-13, we find Jesus speaking at what is known as the Sermon on the Mount, where He teaches them how to pray, 'This, then, is how you should pray: Our Father in heaven, hallowed be Your name, Your kingdom come, Your will be done on earth as it is in heaven. Give us today our daily bread. Forgive us our debts, as we also have forgiven our debtors. And lead us not into temptation, but deliver us from the evil one.' Notice Jesus includes 'give us our daily bread' in His model prayer. He didn't say give us our weekly supply of bread, but specifically said, 'our daily bread.' This prayer works okay and our faith isn't tested as long as the grocery store shelves are full, or we can find an open restaurant. However, let a pandemic strike or a major hurricane rip through and our faith begins to waver. During the COVID-19 pandemic, I was surprised at the hoarding of all types of things, from food to toilet paper. Many of the grocery store shelves remained empty for weeks. Supplies were slow in coming in and people were loading their grocery carts as fast as the items could be restocked. Many stocked up months' worth of food and supplies just in case things continue to worsen. Because of the threat of hurricanes in our area, Vivian and I do try to keep enough supplies to last a week to weather the storm. That has always worked for us, and God has been faithful to provide. Have you taken Him at His word to provide your daily bread or are you hoarding up food and supplies that may never be used? Ask God for wisdom to know what and how much you should keep on hand. Then trust His answer. He will not fail to provide.

**Acknowledge** –Lord, all creatures including me, look to You to provide food at the right time.

**Confess** – Lord, forgive me when I doubt Your ability to provide for me.

**Thanksgiving** – Lord, thank You for Your faithfulness to me.

**Prayer** – Lord, I ask that You show me how to live by faith, not by sight.

# Day 255

Psalm 105:4 Look to the Lord and His strength; seek His face always.

DAVID GIVES US THREE REMINDERS TO KEEP OUR FOCUS ON GOD. He said we are to look to the Lord, look to His strength, and seek His face. First, we are to 'look to the Lord.' Jeremiah 29:13 tells us, 'You will seek Me and find Me when you seek Me with all your heart.' We have to seek God with our whole heart. After Adam and Eve sinned, did they seek God as they normally did each day? No, in fact they were hiding from Him. They were embarrassed by their nakedness which had been revealed as a result of their disobedience. Their unconfessed sin caused them to hide. Unconfessed sin in our lives can cause us to hide from God as well. However, 1 John 1:9 tells us, 'If we confess our sins, He is faithful and just and will forgive us our sins and purify us from all unrighteousness.' Confession and repentance restore our relationship with Him. Next, David said to look to His strength. We get tired. The pressures and stress of life can cause burnout and fatigue. God said to look to His strength. Isaiah 40:29 tells us, 'He gives strength to the weary and increases the power of the weak.' In verse 31 he said, 'But those who hope in the Lord will renew their strength. They will soar on wings like eagles; they will run and not grow weary, they will walk and not be faint.' Let Him renew you and give you strength to power you through the day. Lastly, we are to seek God's face or His presence. Although God is with us, there are times when we neglect God. We put him towards the rear of our priorities and thoughts. It is in those times we drift away from God and lose sight of Him. That is why David is reminding us to seek His face, to set our minds toward God in all circumstances. Have you lost sight of God? Draw close to Him and enjoy the peace and joy of His presence.

**Acknowledge** –Lord, You are our reward, worthy of the effort to seek You.

**Confess** – Lord, forgive me when I allow sin and disobedience to separate me from Your presence.

**Thanksgiving** – Lord, thank You for the comfort, peace, and strength that comes from being in Your presence.

**Prayer** – Lord, You are my Strength, my Shield, and my Stronghold. I seek You each day.

# Day 256

Psalm 105:8 He remembers His covenant forever; the promise He made, for a thousand generations.

God's word contains a number of promises. He promised to be with us. Isaiah 41:10 says, 'So do not fear, for I am with you; do not be dismayed, for I am your God. I will strengthen you and help you; I will uphold you with My righteous right hand.' Also, John 14:15-16 tells us, If you love Me, you will obey what I command. And I will ask the Father and He will give you another Counselor to be with you forever.' You are not alone. No matter the struggles you may be going through, God is with you. Secondly, God promises us He is in control. Your world may be a mess right now. Take heart, God knows what you are going through and He is in control. Jesus speaking in John 16:33 tells us, 'I have told you these things, so that in Me you may have peace. In this world you will have trouble. But take heart! I have overcome the world.' Paul writing in Romans 8:28 said, 'And we know that in all things God works for the good of those who love Him, who have been called according to His purpose.' Third, God loves you. He loves you even when you are at your lowest point. You may have done things that you think God could never forgive you for. Yet, He loves you in spite of anything you may have done. John 3:16 says, 'For God so loved (insert your name) that He gave His one and only Son, that whoever believes in Him shall not perish but have eternal life.' God loved you and me enough to send His one and only Son to die for our sins. Ephesians 3:18-19 urges us that we, 'may have power together with all the Lord's holy people, to grasp how wide and long and high and deep is the love of Christ, and to know this love that surpasses knowledge-that you may be filled to the measure of all the fullness of God.' That is a lot of love. Thank God for His promises today.

**Acknowledge** –Lord, You keep Your promises to a thousand generations.

**Confess** – Lord, forgive me when I doubt Your love and presence in my life.

**Thanksgiving** – Lord, I thank You for being in control of my life and all that goes on around me.

**Prayer** – Lord, help me to lean on the promises found in Your word.

# Day 257

Psalm 105:14 He allowed no one to oppress them; for their sake He rebuked kings.

DAVID IS REFERRING TO THE STORY OF ABRAHAM AND SARAH FOUND in Genesis 12. God prevented harm from coming to Abraham and Sarah at the hand of two different kings. God had told Abraham to leave and go to a land that He would show him. Abraham obeyed and left with his wife Sarah and nephew, Lot. Because of a famine, Abraham headed to Egypt. Uncertain how they would be treated in Egypt, Abraham devised a plan to tell everyone that Sarah was his sister, not his wife. Pharaoh took Sarah to be one of his wives, but God struck Pharaoh and his household with a serious disease because of it. Pharaoh, realizing something was wrong, discovered that Sarah was Abraham's wife, not his sister. He sent Abraham, Sarah, and their household out of Egypt unharmed. A few chapters later in Genesis 20, we find Abraham doing the same thing with King Abimelech. However, God appeared to him in a dream and said to him, 'You are as good as dead because of the woman you have taken; she is a married woman.' This dream scared Abimelech and he sent Abraham, Sarah and their household out of the land. King Abimelech also gave Abraham sheep and cattle, and to Sarah a thousand pieces of silver to cover any offense. Even in their dishonesty, Abraham and Sarah were protected by God fulfilling His covenant with them. We learned yesterday that God was with us, He loves us, and He is in control. Does that mean God will keep us from harm as well? Not really, we know that God does allow things to happen in our lives that can cause us pain and suffering. However, no matter what has happened or may happen to us, we can trust that God is in control and will equip us and protect us to complete His plan for us. Philippians 1:6 tells us, 'I am sure of this, that He who began a good work in you will bring it to completion at the day of Jesus Christ.'

**Acknowledge** –Lord, You have Your hand of protection on me.

**Confess** – Lord, forgive me when I allow the trials of life to doubt Your love for me.

**Thanksgiving** – Lord, I thank You for Your hand of protection.

**Prayer** – Lord, I pray that Your plan will be accomplished in my life, no matter the path it leads.

# Day 258

Psalm 105:17 And He sent a man before them – Joseph, sold as a slave.

NOTICE WHAT DAVID SAYS ABOUT JOSEPH'S JOURNEY, GOD SENT HIM. Later in his life, Joseph acknowledged God's purpose in Genesis 45:7, 'But God sent me ahead of you to preserve for you a remnant on earth and to save your lives by a great deliverance.' So how did Joseph get the call to go to Egypt? Did God say, 'Joseph, in about 15 – 20 years, there is going to be a great famine in the land, so I need you to take the next caravan to Egypt to get ready for it? Oh, by the way, you will have to convince Pharaoh there is going to be a terrible famine and that you are the perfect person to oversee the land to ensure no one starves to death. While this may seem like an impossible task, it isn't nearly as complicated as the way God made it happen. You can read the full story of Joseph in Genesis, chapter 37. Joseph was sold into slavery to the household of Potiphar, who was one of Pharaoh's officials. When Potiphar's wife tried to lure him into her bedroom, Joseph ran from her, but was accused of attacking her. He was put into prison and remained there several years until Pharaoh had a terrible dream that he wanted interpreted. None of Pharaoh's counselors could interpret it. However, one of Pharaoh's officials who had been in prison with Joseph remembered that Joseph had interpreted his and another official's dream while they were imprisoned. Joseph interpreted Pharaoh's dream which foretold of seven years of famine. Joseph was promoted and put in charge of managing the crops ahead of and during the famine. Throughout Joseph's life, God was working out a plan that was many years ahead. His journey prepared him for the work God had for him to do. What about your life? Is God preparing you for a task He has for you? Or, do you think your life is just a series of mistakes, bad luck, and misfortune? Can you say like Joseph in Genesis 50:20, 'You meant evil against me, but God intended it for good?'

**Acknowledge** –Lord, You have a plan for my life.

**Confess** – Lord, forgive me for not being patient in waiting for Your plan to unfold.

**Thanksgiving** – Lord, I thank You for the life of Joseph.

**Prayer** – Lord, help me to learn from Joseph's life and faith in You.

# Day 259

**Psalm 105:24** The Lord made His people very fruitful; He made them too numerous for His foes.

Today we learn that God can make you fruitful no matter where you are. It might seem as if your days are just routine and boring, or full of challenges. In either case, God is working in you and through you to accomplish His plan. God gave Noah an assignment to build an ark, large enough to hold pairs of all the animals in the world. It was a sunny day when Noah obeyed and started work on the ark. Years later, Noah's day consisted of the same thing he had done every day for the last several years. From sun up to sun down, he worked on the ark. By now the people were making fun of him. Noah continued to be faithful, and finished the ark approximately 120 years after he first started. He didn't give up and say, 'God this isn't worth it.' Or, 'God are you sure the earth is going to flood?' He remained true to the task God had given him and he was saved from the destruction of the earth. The Apostle Paul's life however was filled with challenges. After his conversion on the Road to Damascus, Paul's life was occupied with many missionary travels. His travels led him into trouble most everywhere he went. In 2 Corinthians 11:23-27 Paul describes the troubles he faced from beatings, stoning, being shipwrecked, in danger from bandits, going without sleep and food, and put in prison multiple times. Yet, it was in prison where Paul found the time to write several of the 13 letters which have become the backbone of the Christian faith and the New Testament. Paul was faithful and prospered where he was. He used the time in prison to write some of the most encouraging words for us today. What about you? Are your days like Noah's, faithfully 'building the ark' day in and day out? Or perhaps your days are like Paul's where no two days are the same. Take heart, God is working His plan in your life. Trust God to make you fruitful in whatever situation you find yourself in.

**Acknowledge** –Lord, You make us fruitful where we are.

**Confess** – Lord, forgive me for doubting You have a plan for my life.

**Thanksgiving** – Lord, I thank You for the examples of Noah and Paul.

**Prayer** – Lord, no matter my circumstances, You can make me fruitful and prosperous. Help me to trust You in all things.

# Day 260

Psalm 105:26 He sent Moses His servant, and Aaron, whom He had chosen.

How was Moses chosen by God to deliver His people from the bondage of Egypt? Did Moses rise up and tell Pharaoh what he was doing was wrong and to go easy on the Hebrews? Did he try to implement social justice reform and educate the Egyptians on the good qualities of the Hebrews? No, thinking no one had seen him, Moses killed an Egyptian who was beating a Hebrew slave. However, word spread to Pharaoh about the incident, and Moses fled for his life to a place called Midian where he remained for forty years. Moses got married, and found a job in Midian, tending the flocks of his father-in-law, Jethro. However, God had a plan for him. It was in the desert, at Mount Horeb, where God appeared to Moses in the burning bush. God speaking to Moses in Exodus 3:10-11 said, 'So now, go. I am sending you to Pharaoh to bring my people the Israelites out of Egypt. But Moses said to God, "Who am I, that I should go to Pharaoh and bring the Israelites out of Egypt?"' Notice that God said, "I am sending you." Just like Joseph, Moses was being sent by God to Egypt to fulfill his plan. Moses' response is much like ours when we hear God calling us to do something, "who am I?" God why are you calling me to lead this Sunday School Class? I am not good at speaking in front of crowds. God, why are you calling me to lead this group of people on a mission trip? I have never had any experience in leading a team. Wouldn't someone else do a better job? What did God tell Moses in verse 12? 'And God said, "I will be with you. And this will be the sign to you that it is I who have sent you: When you have brought the people out of Egypt, you will worship God on this mountain."' God will not call you to do something that you cannot do. You can trust Him to equip you and be with you all the way.

**Acknowledge** –Lord, You send ordinary people like me to accomplish Your plan.

**Confess** – Lord, forgive me for doubting my abilities to do what You want me to do.

**Thanksgiving** – Lord, thank You for sending me.

**Prayer** – Lord, help me to trust your plan for my life.

# Day 261

Psalm 105:42 For He remembered His holy promises given to His servant Abraham.

TODAY WE LEARN THAT GOD HAS A VERY GOOD MEMORY. MY MOTHER has a form of Parkinson's disease that affects her memory and balance. Her condition has progressed to the point she can't remember what she had for lunch an hour later. Some days, she doesn't recognize she is in her own home. Otherwise, her overall health is excellent for an 87-year-old. It is sad to watch your mother who was once bright and engaging, regressed to sitting around the house. However, today's verse is encouraging because it tells us that God remembers His promises. God doesn't forget even one small detail. Yesterday we read that Moses and Aaron were sent by God to lead the children of Israel out of Egypt to the Promised Land, keeping God's promise to Abraham. Exodus 12:40-41 tells us, 'Now the length of time the Israelite people lived in Egypt was 430 years. At the end of the 430 years, to the very day, all the Lord's divisions left Egypt.' What started out as a short-term plan to flee a famine, resulted in the Israelites becoming slaves in Egypt for 430 years. Yet, this was all part of God's plan and He hadn't forgotten His promise to Abraham. Although God delivered the Israelites from the hand of Pharaoh, the journey to the Promised Land, wasn't a short stroll in the park. They spent 40 years moving from place to place in the desert until they could enter the Promised Land. Several days ago, we read about three promises of God. We learned that God promised to be with us, that He is in control, and that He loves us. I want to add another promise of God. Philippians 4:19 tells us, 'And my God will meet all your needs, according to His glorious riches in Christ Jesus.' All along their journey, God provided food and water for the Israelites. He met their needs by miraculously sending manna and water out of a rock. If God can meet their needs, He can meet yours as well. He remembered a thousand-year-old promise to Abraham. He won't forget to provide for you.

**Acknowledge** –Lord, You remember Your promises, even if they are a thousand years old.

**Confess** – Lord, forgive me when I doubt Your promise to meet my needs.

**Thanksgiving** – Lord, thank You for Your great memory.

**Prayer** – Lord, even when things don't seem to be going like they should, You are still in control.

# Day 262

Psalm 105:45 That they might keep His precepts and observe His laws. Praise the Lord.

DAVID CLOSES BY STATING THE REASON WHY GOD FULFILLED HIS covenant with Abraham many years ago. God did it so they might keep His precepts and obey His laws. What started with Abraham being obedient to God, led to his descendants inheriting a land that God had promised years before, so they could live in obedience there. In Genesis 26:4-5, God told Isaac, 'Stay in this land for a while, and I will be with you and will bless you. For to you and your descendants I will give all these lands and will confirm the oath I swore to your father Abraham. I will make your descendants as numerous as the stars in the sky and will give them all these lands, and through your offspring all nations on earth will be blessed, because Abraham obeyed Me and kept My requirements, My commands, My decrees and My laws.' Because of one person's faithfulness and obedience to God, blessings flowed to his descendants. The Bible has much to say about obedience. God prefers our obedience over any sacrifice we offer Him. 1 Samuel 15:22 says, 'But Samuel replied: "Does the Lord delight in burnt offerings and sacrifices as much as in obeying the voice of the Lord? To obey is better than sacrifice, and to heed is better than the fat of rams."' Animal sacrifices are no longer made, so how does this apply to us? Perhaps you promised God that you would read your Bible for 30 minutes each day, give up certain habits, or stay off social media for 24 hours. These are examples of sacrifices, not obedience unless God has specifically told you to do so. Jesus speaking in John 14:15 said, 'If you love Me, you will obey what I command.' Obeying God demonstrates our love for Him. 1 John 5:2-3 says, 'This is how we know that we love the children of God: by loving God and carrying out His commands. This is love for God: to obey His commands. And His commands are not burdensome.' Lastly, God blesses and rewards obedience. Luke 11:28 tells us, 'Blessed rather are those who hear the word of God and obey it.' Enjoy God's blessings, be obedient to Him.

**Acknowledge** –Lord, You prefer obedience over sacrifice.

**Confess** – Lord, forgive me when I disobey You.

**Thanksgiving** – Lord, thank You for blessing those who hear and obey Your word.

**Prayer** – Lord, help me to be obedient to You.

# Day 263

Psalm 106:1 Praise the Lord; give thanks to the Lord, for He is good; His love endures forever.

This Psalm begins by giving praise to God and acknowledging His goodness and love. It is hard to understand the unending love and patience of God. His love extends to everyone, and endures forever. Without God's goodness and love for us, we would be destined to spend eternity apart from Him and our sins unforgiven. However, it is important for us to know that our forgiveness requires repentance. God does not forgive and forget our iniquities without repentance on our part. He does it because we are truly sorry for our sins and ask Him to forgive us. King Saul was appointed by God to be King of Israel. God's favor was upon him. However, Saul repeatedly disobeyed the commands of God and did not repent. 1 Samuel 15:24-25 tells us, 'Then Saul said to Samuel, "I have sinned. I violated the Lord's command and your instructions. I was afraid of the people and so I gave in to them. Now I beg you, forgive my sin and come back with me, so that I may worship the Lord."' Notice Saul acknowledged that he had sinned. He even asked Samuel to forgive him for what he had done. However, Saul does not seek God's forgiveness. Because of Saul's continued and reckless disobedience, God could no longer let his behavior go unpunished. 1 Samuel 15:26 tells us, 'But Samuel said to him, "I will not go back with you. You have rejected the word of the Lord, and the Lord has rejected you as king over Israel."' Our unconfessed sin has consequences. For Saul, it was his removal from office. It also led to a tormenting spirit that made him want to kill David. 1 Samuel 16:14 tells us, 'Now the Spirit of the Lord had departed from Saul, and an evil spirit from the Lord tormented him.' Are you carrying a load of unconfessed sin? Have you made excuses that God knows your weakness and because of it condones what you are doing? Sin is still sin in God's eyes and unconfessed sin has consequences. Whatever it may be, take it to God and confess your sins to Him.

**Acknowledge** – Lord, You are good, Your love endures forever.

**Confess** – Lord, forgive me for carrying around unconfessed sin in my life.

**Thanksgiving** – Lord, thank You for Your goodness.

**Prayer** – Lord, help me to recognize the sin in my life and confess it before You.

# Day 264

**Psalm 106:6** We have all sinned, even our ancestors did; we have done wrong and acted wickedly.

Several years ago, Franklin Graham led a nationwide campaign called 'Decision America,' going to each state capital holding a prayer vigil for our nation and challenging Christians to live according to God's word. I attended his stop at Raleigh, NC, where he used the story of Nehemiah as a model for calling our nation to repentance. Nehemiah was a Jew in exile, serving as a cupbearer for King Artaxerxes. Word had come to him about the poor condition of his home town, Jerusalem. Nehemiah 1:5-11 records his prayer that we prayed on that day. 'Then I said: "O Lord, God of heaven, the great and awesome God, who keeps His covenant of love with those who love Him and obey His commands, let Your ear be attentive and Your eyes open to hear the prayer Your servant is praying before You day and night for Your servants, the people of Israel. I confess the sins we Israelites, including myself and my father's house, have committed against You. We have acted very wickedly toward You. We have not obeyed the commands decrees, and laws You gave Your servant Moses. Remember the instruction You gave Your servant Moses, saying, "If you are unfaithful, I will scatter you among the nations, but if you return to Me and obey My commands, then even if Your exiled people are at the farthest horizon, I will gather them from there and bring them to the place I have chosen as a dwelling for My Name. They are Your servants and Your people, whom You redeemed by Your great strength and Your mighty hand. O lord, let Your ear be attentive to the prayer of this Your servant and to the prayer of Your servants who delight in revering Your Name. Give Your servant success today by granting him favor in the presence of this man."' Note that Nehemiah confessed the sins of his nation, his father and himself. Use Nehemiah's prayer as a guide today to confess the sins of our nation, the previous generation, and your own sins. God is faithful to forgive.

**Acknowledge** –Lord, You forgive us when we confess our sins to You.

**Confess** – Lord, forgive the sins of my nation, my parents, and most of all, my sins.

**Thanksgiving** – Lord, thank You for the gift of eternal life through Jesus Christ.

**Prayer** – Lord, I lift up men like Franklin Graham who are calling our nation to repentance.

# Day 265

Psalm 106:21 They forgot the God who saved them, who had done great things in Egypt.

WHAT A SAD COMMENTARY ON THE PEOPLE OF ISRAEL. THEY FORGOT about God. They were eating manna God provided, and drinking water out of a rock. However, no sooner had they left Egypt and crossed the Red Sea, they asked Aaron to make an idol for them to worship in the form of a golden calf. A few hundred years later after Gideon had defeated the Midianite army with only 300 men, we find the Israelites doing the same thing. Judges 8:33-34 tells us, 'No sooner had Gideon died than the Israelites again prostituted themselves to the Baals. They set up Baal-Berith as their god and did not remember the Lord their God, who had rescued them from the hands of all enemies on every side.' Before we rush to judgment, we might need to look at ourselves. When things get comfortable for us, what place does God take in our heart? Do we become ungrateful, forgetting to thank God for everything we have? Do we begin to overlook our time with God? Paul writing in 1 Corinthians 4:7 said, 'For who makes you different from anyone else? What do you have that you did not receive? And if you did not receive it, why do you boast as though you did not?' We owe our gratitude to God each day. Why do we forget God and lean towards ingratitude toward Him? The answer is simple, we were born with the desire to be in control of our lives. Paul said it this way in Romans 7:19, 'For what I do is not the good I want to do; no, the evil I do not want to do – this I keep on doing.' Our flesh or sinful nature puts us at odds with our spirit. It is a constant struggle to keep our hearts and minds focused on seeking God; yet, we need God's presence in our lives each day. Don't let success or a comfortable life cause you to drift away from Him. Also, don't base your relationship with God on your feelings. God is still working even if you don't see it or feel it. Seek His presence daily.

**Acknowledge** –Lord, You desire our daily companionship with You.

**Confess** – Lord, forgive me when I take any success I may have for granted.

**Thanksgiving** – Lord, thank You that You desire a relationship with me.

**Prayer** – Lord, help me to win the war against my fleshly nature.

# Day 266

**Psalm 106:30 But Phinehas stood up and intervened, and the plague was checked.**

THE STORY OF PHINEHAS IS FOUND IN THE BOOK OF NUMBERS. The people of Israel were camped in the desert across the Jordan River from Jericho. While there, the men began to indulge in sexual immorality with the local Moabite women. The Moabite women also invited the Israelite men to worship their gods. Numbers 25:3 tells us, 'So Israel joined in worshipping the Baal of Peor. And the Lord's anger burned against them.' God told Moses that those who were involved in worshipping Baal should be put to death. While Moses and the leaders of Israel were planning how God's orders should be carried out, an Israelite man paraded a Midianite woman in front of them to his tent. Numbers 25:7-9 tells what happens next, 'When Phinehas son of Eleazar, the son of Aaron, the priest, saw this, he left the assembly, took a spear in his hand and followed the Israelite into the tent. He drove the spear through both of them – through the Israelite and into the woman's body. Then the plague against the Israelites was stopped; but those who died in the plague numbered 24,000.' Because of Phinehas' action, God stopped a plague. He also recognized Phinehas for his faithfulness. Numbers 25:12-13 tells us, 'Therefore tell him (Phinehas) I am making my covenant of peace with him. He and his descendants will have a covenant of lasting priesthood, because he was zealous for the honor of his God and made atonement for the Israelites.' What can we learn from the story of Phinehas? First, God does not tolerate idolatry. Secondly, God honors those who faithfully follow Him. Thirdly, sin does not go unpunished. How does this apply to us today? Obviously, no one is going to take a spear and kill anyone living in sin. However, is anyone today standing up and calling sin, sin? Are we too intimidated to stand up and say what is right and wrong? You can be a Phinehas. Stand for what is right. Be a person of integrity. Let your friends know where you stand on important issues. Don't follow the crowd. Follow Jesus.

**Acknowledge** – Lord, You do not tolerate idolatry.

**Confess** – Lord, forgive me when I fail to take a stand for what is right.

**Thanksgiving** – Lord, thank You for examples like Phinehas who stand up for what is right.

**Prayer** – Lord, help me to be strong and courageous in calling sin, sin.

# Day 267

Psalm 106:32 By the waters of Meribah they angered the Lord, and trouble came to Moses because of them.

APPROXIMATELY 40 YEARS AFTER GOD HAD PROVIDED WATER FROM a rock, we find the people's faith had not changed. They were again camped in the desert, where there was no water supply. The people gathered against Moses and Aaron and quarreled with them about it. Moses and Aaron prayed to God for directions on how to provide water to the people. Numbers 20:7-8 gives us God's reply, 'The Lord said to Moses, "Take the staff, and you and your brother Aaron gather the assembly together. Speak to that rock before their eyes and it will pour out its water. You will bring water out of the rock for the community so they and their livestock can drink."' What did Moses do? Numbers 20:11 tells us, 'Then Moses raised his arm and struck the rock twice with his staff. Water gushed out, and the community and their livestock drank.' Wait, didn't God tell Moses just to speak the rock? Why did Moses strike the rock? I believe 40 years of frustration bubbled up within Moses and he let his temper get the best of him. In a moment of anger, He had disobeyed God's command. As we have learned, sin has consequences. Moses's disobedience had consequences as well. Numbers 20:12 tells us, 'But the Lord said to Moses and Aaron, "Because you did not trust in Me enough to honor Me as Holy in the sight of the Israelites, you will not bring this community into the land I give them."' Moses and Aaron would not be allowed to enter the Promised Land. However, Moses was allowed to see it from the top of a mountain. There are a couple of things we can learn from this story. First, sin has consequences. God will forgive, but we still face the consequences. Secondly, count to ten before you react out of anger. Don't allow someone to 'bait' you into a reaction that you will regret later. Lastly, ask God to give you wisdom each day with the interactions you have with others. Proverbs 15:1 says, 'A gentle answer turns away wrath, but a harsh word stirs up anger.' Always be ready with a gentle answer.

**Acknowledge** – Lord, our sin has consequences.

**Confess** – Lord, forgive me when I allow someone to bait me into overreacting.

**Thanksgiving** – Lord, thank You for second chances.

**Prayer** – Lord, I ask for Your wisdom to guide me through my daily interactions with others.

# Day 268

**Psalm 106:48** Praise be to the Lord, the God of Israel, from everlasting to everlasting, let the people say, 'Amen!' Praise the Lord.

David wrote Psalm 106 as a confession of Israel's long history of rebellion and a prayer for God to save His people. He used it as a part of the celebration during the return of the Ark to Jerusalem. The Ark which represented God's presence had been left at Obed-Edom's house. 1 Chronicles 15:3 tells us, 'David assembled all Israel in Jerusalem to bring up the Ark of the Lord to the place he had prepared for it.' With all of Israel there to celebrate and witness the Ark's return, naturally there was much joy and happiness among the people. Verse 28 tells us, 'So all Israel brought up the Ark of the Covenant of the Lord with shouts, with the sounding of rams' horns and trumpets, and of cymbals, and the playing of lyres and harps.' David got so caught up in the celebration that he was dancing as the Ark returned. 2 Samuel 6:18-19 provides us more detail about the celebration, 'After he (David) had finished sacrificing the burnt offerings and fellowship offerings, he blessed the people in the name of the Lord Almighty. Then he gave a loaf of bread, a cake of dates and a cake of raisins to each person in the whole crowd of Israelites, both men and women. And all the people went to their homes.' They left shouting 'Amen, Praise the Lord.' What a great celebration. The Ark, representing the presence of the Lord, was brought to the tabernacle. Everyone left happy, shouting 'Amen.' As I was growing up, I didn't give much thought to the word 'amen.' For many years I had the impression it meant 'the end,' or I am through with my prayer. However, it means much more than that. The literal meaning of 'Amen' is 'So be it.' It puts our dependence and faith completely in our Heavenly Father. I translate it as, Lord there is nothing else I can do, it is in Your hands to do as You will. Today as you close your prayer time, let your 'amen' ring out, 'so be it Lord.'

**Acknowledge** –Lord, I am totally dependent upon You.

**Confess** – Lord, forgive me when I take for granted Your Hand working in my life.

**Thanksgiving** – Lord, let my praises ring out to You, amen and amen.

**Prayer** – Lord, I let my amen be as earnest as my prayer to You.

# Day 269

Psalm 107:1,9 Give thanks to the Lord, for He is good, His love endures forever. For He satisfies the thirsty and fills the hungry with good things.

These verses remind me of Thanksgiving Day at my parent's house. My siblings and their families all gather at Dot's and Papa's house for a huge meal. There is so much delicious food that you can't get it all on your plate. Today's verse tells us that God 'fills the hungry with good things.' He prepares a better meal than we do on Thanksgiving. While we are here on earth, God feeds us with His word and satisfies us with His presence. God's Word brings peace and comfort. It also instructs us how to live for Him. His words are like honey, sweet and satisfying. The Prophet Ezekiel was given a scroll with God's words written on it and told to eat it. Ezekiel 3:3 tells us, 'Then He said to me, "Son of man, eat this scroll I am giving you and fill your stomach with it." So I ate it, and it tasted as sweet as honey in my mouth.' Are you feasting on God's word? Not only will God's word satisfy our hunger now, the Bible tells us that one day, everyone who has trusted Jesus as their Savior will gather for a huge banquet. Revelation 19:9 tells us, 'Then the angel said to me, "Write: Blessed are those who are invited to the wedding supper of the Lamb!" And he added, "These are the true words of God."' In Luke 14:15-23 we find Jesus telling a parable about 'The Great Banquet.' Jesus was eating at a Pharisee's house when someone at the table said, 'Blessed is the man who will eat at the feast in the kingdom of God.' Jesus replied with the parable. In the story, many who had been invited to the great banquet began to make excuses as to why they could not make it. So, the master of the house invited the poor, the crippled, the blind, and the lame to come to the banquet. What about you? Are you making excuses why you can't follow Christ? My prayer is that you don't miss out on the Lord's banquet.

**Acknowledge** – Lord, Your word is sweet as honey and satisfies my soul.

**Confess** – Lord, forgive me for making excuses not to follow You.

**Thanksgiving** – Lord, thank You for filling me with good things.

**Prayer** – Lord, I pray that I will be at the wedding supper of the Lamb.

# Day 270

Psalm 107:15 Let them give thanks to the Lord for His unfailing love and His wonderful deeds for mankind.

It is no surprise that the attributes of God's unfailing love and wonderful deeds show up over and over in the Psalms. Verses 13-14 give us an idea of what God did for them, 'Then they cried to the Lord in their trouble, and He saved them from their distress. He brought them out of darkness and the deepest gloom and broke away their chains.' God rescued them and restored them to their homeland even though they had been disobedient. God's love for us is not only unfailing, it is filled with forgiveness. Hopefully, we will never need God to rescue and restore us. However, all around us are the transformed lives of those who had become trapped by the bad choices they made. They were living in utter darkness with no hope of ever getting out. Yet God loved them, rescued them, and restored them. No matter how far they had drifted from God, or their rebellious lifestyle, God loved them and rescued them. God still works miracles in people's lives today. I want to share a story of someone Vivian and I know who God dramatically changed their life. He was headed in a downward spiral that had no way out. Somewhere in his journey, he recognized that he needed help and started attending Alcoholics Anonymous. Someone at AA planted seeds about Jesus and His saving power. Through the power of the Holy Spirit and the support of AA, his life changed dramatically. No longer was he a slave to drugs and alcohol. God had set him free. God had also given him a great voice. He began singing in the church choir and before long he was singing solos. His favorite song was 'Worth' by Anthony Brown. The lyrics go, 'You thought I was worth saving, So You came and changed my life, You thought I was worth keeping, So You cleaned me up inside. You thought I was to die for, So You sacrificed Your life. So, I could be free, So I could be whole, So I could tell everyone I know.' Thank God, because you and I were worth dying for too.

**Acknowledge** –Lord, Your love is unfailing.

**Confess** – Lord, forgive me for doubting Your transformational power.

**Thanksgiving** – Lord, thank You for thinking I was worth dying for.

**Prayer** – Lord, help me to share Your love with those who really need a Savior.

# Day 271

Psalm 107:21,32 Let them give thanks to the Lord for His unfailing love and His wonderful deeds for mankind. Let them exalt Him in the assembly of the people and praise Him in the council of the elders.

Before we start the celebration, I would like to add you and me to the names God has rescued. No matter how good we tried to live, we were still lost and destined to spend eternity apart from God. Our lives were controlled by the sinful nature we were born with. Paul said in Galatians 5:19-21, 'The acts of the sinful nature are obvious: sexual immorality, impurity, and debauchery; idolatry and witchcraft; hatred, discord, jealousy, fits of rage, selfish ambition, dissensions, factions and envy; drunkenness, orgies, and the like. I warn you, as I did before, that those who live like this will not inherit the kingdom of God.' We could try to live the best life possible, being a good person, but we were still lost, without hope. Ephesians 2:4-5 give us reason to celebrate and worship God, 'But because of His great love for us, God, who is rich in mercy, made us alive with Christ even when we were dead in our transgressions – it is by grace you have been saved.' It is God's grace that makes salvation worth celebrating. Paul went on to say in verses 8-9 in Ephesians 2: 'For it is by grace you have been saved, through faith – and this not from yourselves, it is the gift of God – not of works, so that no one can boast.' Salvation is a gift of God, there is nothing we can do to earn it. All we had to do was accept this free gift from God by believing in His Son, Jesus Christ. No matter our background, God's free gift of salvation is available to all. Isn't that worth lifting our praise to God with other believers who have received this free gift as well? The Message Bible translates today's verse as, 'Lift high your praises when the people assemble, shout Hallelujah when the elders meet!' Don't miss out on your opportunity to praise God. Lift high your praise in the sanctuary. God inhabits the praises of His people.

**Acknowledge** – Lord, it is by grace we are saved.

**Confess** – Lord, forgive me when I don't feel like praising You.

**Thanksgiving** – Lord, thank You for the opportunity to praise You in the assembly.

**Prayer** – Lord, I give You praise in the sanctuary, in the assembly of Your people.

# Day 272

Psalm 107:43 Let the one who is wise heed these things and ponder the loving deeds of the Lord.

THE WISE WILL NOT FORGET WHAT GOD HAS DONE. THIS REMINDS me of the parable Jesus told about the wise and foolish builders found in Matthew 7:24-27, 'Therefore everyone who hears these words of Mine and puts them into practice is like a wise man who built his house on the rock. The rain came down and the streams rose, and the winds blew and beat against that house; yet it did not fall, because it had its foundation on the rock. But everyone who hears these words of Mine and does not put them into practice is like a foolish man who built his house on sand. The rain came down, the streams rose, and the winds blew and beat against that house, and it fell with a great crash.' According to Jesus, what does it take to have a solid foundation of faith in Him? First, He said that we must hear His words. There are many ways to hear God's word. We hear it by going to church, attending a Bible Study Group, and reading the Bible, just to name a few. To get deeper into God's word, start a daily reading plan to read through the Bible in a year. Jesus' second requirement for having a firm foundation was to 'put them into practice.' James 1:22-24 tells us, 'Do not merely listen to the word, and so deceive yourselves. Do what it says. Anyone who listens to the word but does not do what it says is like a man who looks at his face in a mirror and, after looking at himself, goes away and immediately forgets what he looks like.' If you don't use God's word by putting it into practice, you will not benefit from it. James tells us in James 2:14, 'What good is it, my brothers, if a man claims to have faith but has no deeds? Can such faith save him?' If we truly love God, His word will move us to action. We will live out His word. Find true wisdom in His Word.

**Acknowledge** –Lord, we are called to be doers of Your word, not hearers only.

**Confess** – Lord, forgive me when I spend more time on Facebook than in Your word.

**Thanksgiving** – Lord, thank You for the many opportunities we have to hear Your word.

**Prayer** – Lord, help me to be a doer of Your word, not a hearer only.

# Day 273

Psalm 108:4 For great is Your love, higher than the heavens; Your faithfulness reaches to the skies.

DAVID DECLARES THE GREATNESS OF GOD'S LOVE AND FAITHFULness to us. We may never fully understand the greatness of God's love until we meet Him in heaven. However, many have tried to capture it in song. I am reminded of a hymn written by Frederick Lehman entitled "The Love of God is Greater Far." My favorite verse is verse three, 'Could we with ink the ocean fill, And were the skies of parchment made; Were every stalk on earth a quill, And every man a scribe by trade; To write the love of God above, Would drain the ocean dry; Nor could the scroll contain the whole, Though stretched from sky to sky.' The hymn concludes with the chorus, 'O love of God, how rich and pure! How measureless and strong! It shall forevermore endure – the saints' and angels' song.' The last verse really paints a beautiful picture of the vastness of God's love. If the oceans were filled with ink and every person had a pen to write about the love of God, there would not be enough ink to finish the job. Moreover, if the sky was a notebook, it wouldn't have enough pages to contain the writings about the love of God. 1 John 3:1 tells us, 'How great is the love the Father has lavished on us, that we should be called the children of God! And that is what we are! The reason the world does not know us is that it did not know Him.' As imperfect as we are, God loved us enough to die for us, not only that, He has adopted us into His family and calls us His children. There is nothing we can do that would stop God from loving us. John 3:17 tells us, 'For God did not send His Son into the world to condemn the world, but to save the world through Him.' I thank God that He did not condemn me, but loved me enough to send His Son to save me and call me His child. Have you experienced God's love and faithfulness?

**Acknowledge** – Lord, Your love reaches to the heavens and Your faithfulness to the skies.

**Confess** – Lord, forgive me when I begin to doubt Your love for me.

**Thanksgiving** – Lord, thank You for sending Your Son to save the world, not condemn it.

**Prayer** – Lord, help me to tell others about Your great love.

# Day 274

Psalm 108:5 Be exalted, O God, above the heavens; let Your glory be over all the earth.

Today David directs our attention to the greatness of God's glory. First, he exalts God and puts Him above the heavens, then in the next breath tells us that God's glory is over all the earth. Isaiah 6:3 tells us about God's glory filling the earth in a vision Isaiah saw of God and seraphs who were calling out, 'Holy, Holy, Holy, is the Lord of Hosts, the whole earth is full of His glory. God's glory is His unseen, but felt presence. It can also be described as the beauty of His Spirit that comes from His perfect being. Because of God's perfection and glory, we may try to hide our sins from Him. Jeremiah 23:24 tells us, 'Can anyone hide in secret places so that I cannot see him, declares the Lord? Do I not fill heaven and earth, declares the Lord?' Ezekiel 8:7-12 is a good illustration of God's all-knowing presence. God instructs Ezekiel to dig a hole in a wall and enter into a secret court. Once inside, He tells Ezekiel to see the wicked things 70 elders of the House of Israel were doing. They were worshiping pictures of idols that were drawn on a wall. Verse 12 states, 'He said to me, "Son of man, have you seen what the elders of the House of Israel are doing in the darkness, each at the shrine of his own idol?" They say, "The Lord does not see us; the Lord has forsaken the land."' The elders were hiding in a dark, inner room worshiping idols thinking God did not see them. Yet God knew where they were and the detestable sins they were committing. What can we learn from this scripture? There are no secret sins to God. He knows what goes on behind closed doors. He knows the websites you visit, and the thoughts you have, whether good or bad. You are not hiding anything from Him. If there are things you are trying to hide from God, confess them to Him today. He is willing and able to forgive you.

**Acknowledge** – Lord, there is nothing hidden from You.

**Confess** – Lord, forgive me for the sins I have tried to hide from You.

**Thanksgiving** – Lord, may You be exalted above the heavens.

**Prayer** – Lord, You know all and see all. Let Your glory fill the earth.

# Day 275

Psalm 108:13 With God we will gain the victory, and He will trample down our enemies.

David closes Psalm 108 with a verse he used in Psalm 60, which we read on Day 151. There we read about David using five stones to face Goliath and the victory God gave him. However, not all battles are won with five stones. Some are won by prayer and fasting, others by a shout to the Lord, and still others by obedience and patience. Take Esther for example. King Xerxes had issued a decree that all Jews in the land of Persia would be killed on a certain date. Unknown to King Xerxes, Esther, his wife, was also a Jew. Esther's uncle, Mordecai, appealed to her to save her people by asking the King to change the decree. Esther didn't go straight to the King and beg for the lives of her people. She went straight to God. Esther 4:16 tells us Esther's plan, 'Go, gather together all the Jews in Susa, and fast for me. Do not eat or drink for three days, night or day. I and my maids will fast as you do. When this is done, I will go to the King even though it is against the law. And if I perish, I perish.' God blessed Esther and gave her success. Battles are also won by shouting to the Lord. Joshua and the Israelites marched around the City of Jericho for six days without saying a word. On the seventh day, they marched around the city seven times. As they completed their seventh lap, Joshua commanded the people to shout, for God had given them the victory. While they were shouting, the walls collapsed and they took the city. Lastly, battles are won through obedience and patience. In 2 Samuel 5:22-25, David and his men were fighting the Philistines. David asked God for guidance and victory over the enemy. God instructed him to sneak behind the enemy and wait until he heard the sound of marching in the tops of trees. David waited for the sound of marching and attacked as the Lord had commanded. God gave him complete victory. What battle strategy has God given you? Trust Him for the victory.

**Acknowledge** –Lord, You give us the victory.

**Confess** – Lord, forgive me for not using Your battle plan.

**Thanksgiving** – Lord, thank You for the victories in my life.

**Prayer** – Lord, help me to seek Your plan before I try to battle the giants in my life.

# Day 276

Psalm 109:1 My God, whom I praise, do not remain silent.

DAVID IS ASKING GOD TO SPEAK UP AND SAY SOMETHING ON HIS behalf. Why? Because in verse two he tells us, 'For wicked and deceitful men have opened their mouths against me; they have spoken against me with lying tongues.' Unfortunately, we live in a wicked world where wicked people will say wicked things about us. They will say things that are not true, with no regrets of the suffering they produce because of their lies. Sadly, you don't have to look too far to find these types of attacks on someone's character. The negative political ads being aired today are vicious. The opposing candidate is portrayed as a self-serving, selfish, mean-spirited, and heartless person who doesn't care for anyone but themselves. Unfortunately, those are the nicer things that are said about them. If you believed all that was said about the person, you would never like them, much less vote for them. It is common to see a negative ad about one candidate, followed by a negative ad from their opponent. The response to the negative ads is, 'it's just politics.' But how do we handle the lies that hit closer to home? How do we deal with people who slander and try to defame our character? First, let the truth of your life speak for itself. Jesus, speaking in Matthew 10:26, tells us, 'So do not be afraid of them. There is nothing concealed that will not be disclosed, or hidden that will not be made known.' God doesn't want us to worry because the truth will eventually come out for all to see. Secondly, trust God and His promise to see you through any situation. 1 Corinthians 4:5 tells us, 'Therefore judge nothing before the appointed time; wait till the Lord comes. He will bring to light what is hidden in darkness and will expose the motives of men's hearts. At that time each will receive his praise from God.' Trust God's timing to bring to light the wrongs that have been said about you. Don't try to take matters into your own hands by seeking revenge. God will not remain silent.

**Acknowledge** –Lord, You will bring to light what is hidden.

**Confess** – Lord, forgive me for lashing out at those who tell untruths about me.

**Thanksgiving** – Lord, thank You for Your promise to see me through any situation.

**Prayer** – Lord, help me to live a righteous life, one that speaks for itself.

# Day 277

Psalm 109:6 Appoint someone evil to oppose my enemy; let an accuser stand at his right hand.

DAVID IS ON A ROLL TODAY. WHAT BETTER WAY TO PUNISH YOUR enemy than to have someone who is just like themselves to govern over them? How could someone complain if they are governed by a leader just like themselves? Today's leadership is a mixture of good, honest people of character and of those who are selfish, self-serving, and dishonest. Unfortunately, we elect these people, not based on their character but because of the political views they support. However, the day is soon coming when everyone in leadership will be corrupt and deceitful. It is during that time the 'lawless one' or the Antichrist will take charge and rule the entire earth for 3 ½ years. 2 Thessalonians 2:9-10 states, 'The coming of the lawless one will be in accordance with the work of Satan displayed in all kinds of counterfeit miracles, signs and wonders, and in every sort of evil that deceives those who are perishing. They perish because they refused to love the truth and so be saved.' Also, during that time, everyone will be forced to worship the Antichrist or be killed. Everyone will be required to display the number of the lawless one, '666' in order to hold a job and buy and sell. Revelation 13:16-17 tells us, 'He also forced everyone, small and great, rich and poor, free and slave to receive a mark on his right hand or on his forehead, so that no one could buy or sell unless he had the mark, which is the name of the beast or number of his name.' The good news for Christians is that Christ will come and take us to be with Him in heaven before all this takes place. 1 Thessalonians 4:17 tells us, 'After that, we who are still alive and are left will be caught up together with them in the clouds to meet the Lord in the air. And so we will be with the Lord forever.' Thank God that we don't have to live under the Antichrist's rule.

**Acknowledge** –Lord, You have told us what to expect during the end times.

**Confess** – Lord, forgive me when I fail to vote for people of character.

**Thanksgiving** – Lord, thank You for honest leaders.

**Prayer** – Lord, help me to share the good news of Your return.

# Day 278

Psalm 109:21 But You, Sovereign Lord, deal well with me for Your name's sake; out of the goodness of Your love, deliver me.

DAVID PUTS HIMSELF INTO THE HANDS OF THE LORD TO DEAL WITH him as He deems best. However, this is not the first time David has put himself at the mercy of God. In 1 Chronicles 21 we read that David had sinned by commanding a census be taken of the entire nation of Israel. Why was taking a census a sin? In verse one, we read that 'Satan rose up against Israel and incited David to take a census of Israel.' David sinned by yielding to Satan's temptation. We also find in Exodus 30:12 instructions God had given Moses, that when a census was taken, each person must pay a ransom for his life at the time he is counted so no plague will come upon them. David didn't follow these instructions either. In verse eight, David acknowledges his sin to God and says, '...I have sinned greatly by doing this. Now, I beg You, take away the guilt of your servant. I have done a very foolish thing.' Because of the great sin David committed, God gave Him a choice of three different punishments: three years of famine, three months of fleeing before his enemies, or three days of plague. The Bible doesn't tell us why God chose to punish the people. It may have been a lesson that everyone suffers when our leaders make mistakes. In any event, David chooses the third option because the first two would have depended on the mercy of man, while the plague was a direct punishment from God and they could look to Him for mercy. David even asked God to only punish him and his family because he was the one who had sinned. Verse 14 tells us that 75,000 men had already died of the plague and an angel was on the way to destroy Jerusalem when God had mercy and stopped the angel. God is merciful. He doesn't deal with us as we deserve. When you have fallen away from God, ask Him to deal with you out of the goodness of His love.

**Acknowledge** –Lord, You are Sovereign, Your love is endless.

**Confess** – Lord, forgive me for being disobedient to Your Word.

**Thanksgiving** – Lord, thank You for dealing with us out of the goodness of Your love.

**Prayer** – Lord, like David, help me to choose Your mercy.

# Day 279

Psalm 109:30 With my mouth I will greatly extol the Lord; in the great throng of worshipers I will praise Him.

DAVID LOVED TO PRAISE GOD. HE NEVER MISSED AN OPPORTUNITY to lift his voice in praise. Today he tells us that he has gathered with 'the great throng of worshipers' who are praising God. In David's day, worship took place at the temple in Jerusalem and today we typically worship at church or some other venue. In John 4:1-26, we find the story of Jesus talking to the Samaritan woman. As they were talking, she makes the comment that the Jews and the Samaritans each claim that they have the right place to worship God. Jesus answers her in verses 21-24 saying, 'Believe me, woman, a time is coming when you will worship the Father neither on this mountain nor in Jerusalem. You Samaritans worship what you do not know, we worship what we do know, for salvation is from the Jews. Yet a time is coming and has now come when the true worshipers will worship the Father in spirit and truth, for they are the kind of worshipers the Father seeks. God is spirit, and His worshipers must worship in spirit and truth.' What is Jesus teaching us in this encounter? First, where we worship is not important. We are not required to make a pilgrimage to a holy place to worship God. The important thing is that our worship is from the heart, motivated by our love for Him. Also, worship should not be a ritualistic ceremony, unless it has heartfelt meaning and purpose. Secondly, allow the Holy Spirit to work inside you, leading you to a deeper relationship with God. As that relationship grows, He will stir us to celebrate and give thanks to Him. But not only should we worship in spirit, we must also worship in truth. Our worship should be rooted in the truth of God's word. We need to know the one we worship. Worship without truth leads to more of an emotional experience rather than God-honoring worship. On the other hand, worship without spirit can lead to a dry legalistic form of worship. True worship incorporates both spirit and truth. Worship Him today in spirit and truth.

**Acknowledge** –Lord, You desire our worship.

**Confess** – Lord, forgive me when I fail to worship You in spirit and in truth.

**Thanksgiving** – Lord, thank You for times of worship.

**Prayer** – Lord, I love to join the 'great throng of worshipers' praising You.

# Day 280

**Psalm 110:5 The Lord is at your right hand; He will crush kings on the day of His wrath.**

PSALM 110, WRITTEN BY DAVID, DESCRIBES THE KINGSHIP OF CHRIST when He comes to rule the earth. He illustrates the type of king the people were looking for when the Messiah was to come. They were looking for an earthly king that would rule justly, judge the nations, and crush the enemies of the Jews. Sadly, many missed the Messiah while He was on earth because they were looking for an earthly king. Even the disciples didn't quite understand Jesus' mission. Mark 10:35-45 tells us that two of the disciples, James and John, who were brothers, asked Jesus to allow them to sit at His side when He set up His kingdom. They thought Jesus was going to set up an earthly kingdom and wanted the honor of sitting beside Him. When the other disciples heard their request, they were angry at them because they wanted those positions for themselves. It wasn't until after Jesus' death and resurrection that they all realized who Jesus was and His purpose for coming to earth. However, in Revelation 19:11-16 John gives us a description of Jesus' return to earth that sounds very much like David's. 'I saw heaven standing open and there before me was a white horse, whose rider is called Faithful and True. With justice He judges and makes war. His eyes are like blazing fire, and on His head are many crowns. He has a name written on Him that no one knows but He Himself. He is dressed in a robe dipped in blood, and His name is the Word of God. The armies of heaven were following Him, riding on white horses and dressed in fine linen, white and clean. Out of His mouth comes a sharp sword with which to strike down the nations. He will rule them with an iron scepter. He treads the winepress of the fury of the wrath of God Almighty. On His robe and on His thigh He has His name written: King of Kings and Lord of Lords.' One day soon, Jesus is coming to rule the earth. Are you looking for His return?

**Acknowledge** – Lord, You are our soon coming King.

**Confess** – Lord, forgive me when I take my eyes off You.

**Thanksgiving** – Lord, thank You for being patient with us.

**Prayer** – Lord, one day soon you will return to rule the earth. Help me to be prepared.

# Day 281

Psalm 111:10 The fear of the Lord is the beginning of wisdom; all who follow His precepts have good understanding. To Him belongs eternal praise.

THERE ARE NOT TOO MANY DAYS THAT GO BY THAT I DON'T ASK GOD for wisdom. I want to make good decisions and keep myself from making foolish mistakes. I also pray several verses related to wisdom to be specific and purposeful in my prayers. One of my favorites is Proverbs 16:3 that says, 'The prudent see danger and take refuge, but the simple keep going and suffer for it.' I add to it, Lord give me foresight to see what lies ahead, give me insight to see what is taking place, and give me hindsight to learn from the past. I also pray Psalm 32:8 which says, 'I will instruct you and teach you in the way you should go; I will counsel you and watch over you.' I wish I could say I always listened to God's instruction and followed His counsel. If so, I would not have made some of the decisions I have come to regret. The Psalmist tells us that all who follow God's precepts have good understanding. A precept is a general rule intended to regulate behavior or thought. (www.oxfordlearnersdictionay.com) He also tells us the fear or reverence and respect of the Lord is the beginning or entrance to wisdom. Solomon reiterates this thought in Proverbs 9:10, 'The fear of the Lord is the beginning of wisdom, and knowledge of the Holy One is understanding.' So, having reverence and respect for the Lord is the doorway to wisdom. It is not an automatic door that opens when you walk up. We have to take hold of the handle and open it. Seeking wisdom takes effort on our part. James 1:5 tells us, 'If any of you lacks wisdom, he should ask God, who gives generously to all without finding fault, and it will be given to him.' Are you asking God for His wisdom each day? If not, today is a great day to start. Ask Him to give you His Godly wisdom, foresight, insight, and hindsight to guide your path each day. As James tells us, 'He gives generously to all.'

**Acknowledge** –Lord, all who follow Your precepts have good understanding.

**Confess** – Lord, forgive me when I fail to use the Godly wisdom You give me.

**Thanksgiving** – Lord, thank You for giving me wisdom and understanding.

**Prayer** – Lord, help me to be a prudent person who foresees danger and takes precaution.

# Day 282

Psalm 112:1 Praise the Lord. Blessed are those who fear the Lord, who find great delight in His commandments.

YESTERDAY WE LEARNED THAT THE FEAR OF THE LORD IS THE BEGINNING of wisdom. Today the Psalmist tells us that those who fear the Lord are blessed. What are God's blessings? Do we equate them to material things such as financial success, a successful career, a beautiful family, and good health? All of these things are temporary and can disappear in the blink of an eye. The story of Job reminds us of that. Perhaps God's greatest blessing is the peace and assurance He gives us as we draw closer to Him in spite of life's circumstances. There are a number of verses in the Bible that identify God's blessings. Let's take a look at a few of them. Jesus speaking in Luke 11:28 said, 'Blessed rather are those who hear the word of God and keep it.' Our verse today said it this way, blessed are those who find great delight in God's commands. This tells me that blessings come with obedience. James 1:12 tells us, 'Blessed is the man who perseveres under trial, because when he has stood the test, he will receive the crown of life that God has promised to those who love Him.' What is James saying here? Did he say that a blessed person will undergo trials? Not only that, we will have to persevere through them. But the good news is that there is crown of life on the other side that has been promised to us. Every year, Vivian and I select a word for the year to steer the way we live that year. One year, my word was perseverance and my verse to support it was Hebrews 12:1, 'Therefore, since we are surrounded by a great cloud of witnesses, let us throw off everything that hinders and the sin that so easily entangles. And let us run with perseverance the race marked out for us.' Everyone's race is different. However, we are all called to be obedient to the race God has for us and to persevere to the end where He has a crown of life waiting for us.

**Acknowledge** –Lord, blessed are those who find great delight in Your commands.

**Confess** – Lord, forgive me for seeking material blessings over Your presence.

**Thanksgiving** – Lord, thank You for the race You have prepared for me.

**Prayer** – Lord, help me to run with perseverance the race You have marked out for me.

# Day 283

Psalm 112:5 Good will come to him who is generous and lends freely, who conducts his affairs with justice.

TODAY THE PSALMIST HITS US WHERE IT HURTS THE WORST, OUR wallet. However, he does it in a positive way showing the benefits of being generous. Solomon, writing in the Book of Proverbs, has a lot to say about generosity. Proverbs 11:24-25 says, 'One gives freely, yet grows richer; another withholds what he should give, and only suffers want. Whoever brings blessing will be enriched, and one who waters will himself be watered.' Proverbs 19:17 says, 'Whoever is generous to the poor lends to the Lord, and He will repay him for his deed.' Lastly, Proverbs 22:9, 'Whoever has a bountiful eye will be blessed, for he shares his bread with the poor.' Do you see the theme here? Generous people are blessed. The more they give, the more they seem to receive so they can continue to give more. This principle seems counter to today's philosophy of making sure 'I get mine.' However, this principle is not only found in Proverbs. It is found in the New Testament as well. 2 Corinthians 9:6 tells us, 'Remember this: Whoever sows sparingly will also reap sparingly, and whoever sows generously will also reap generously.' Perhaps the most generous person I ever met was Vivian's uncle, Deacon Jones. He was the son of a Church of God minister, who started out with nothing. Deacon started buying and selling cars, which grew into a large car dealership in Smithfield, NC. Deacon was always doing nice things for people. He supported local charities. He supported education on many levels. He set up an annual college scholarship at the local high school he graduated from. He donated the funds to build a student cafeteria for Lee University in Cleveland, Tennessee. At Christmas, he would go to NYC and buy out China Town, bring the items back and give them away. The more he gave, the larger his business grew. You could see God's promises fulfilled in the way he lived. How about you? Are you hoarding up what God has blessed you with or are you helping others? Be a blessing to someone today. Trust God's word.

**Acknowledge** –Lord, good will come to those who are generous.

**Confess** – Lord, forgive me for hoarding up and not sharing with others.

**Thanksgiving** – Lord, thank You for Your principle of giving and receiving.

**Prayer** – Lord, help me to be one who sows generously.

# Day 284

Psalm 113:5 Who is like the Lord our God, the One who sits enthroned on high?

THIS SEEMS LIKE A PRETTY SIMPLE QUESTION WITH A SIMPLE ANSWER, no one. However, it is not the only time it has been asked. Moses, speaking in Exodus 15:11, asks, 'Who among the gods is like you, O Lord? Who is like You – Majestic in holiness, awesome in glory, working wonders?' And in Micah 7:18 we read, 'Who is a God like You, who pardons our sin and forgives the transgression of the remnant of His inheritance? You do not stay angry forever but delight to show mercy.' Lastly, Isaiah writes in Isaiah 44:7, 'Who is like Me? Let him proclaim it. Let him declare and lay out before Me what has happened since I established my ancient people, and what is yet to come – yes, let him foretell what will come.' When Moses asked the question, he tries to describe God as majestic, awesome, and one who works wonders. Micah describes God as one who forgives our sins and shows mercy. And in Isaiah, God is asking the question 'who is like Me?' He asks 'who can tell what has taken place from the beginning of time, and turn around and foretell the future.' In these descriptions we get a glimpse of who God is. First, we see that God is omnipotent and sovereign. He created the heavens and the earth. He is majestic in His holiness, all-powerful, and works wonders. He is in total control. Yet, He loves us and pardons our sins. Secondly, we see that He is omnipresent. He is everywhere. He has been and will always be. Lastly, we see that God is omniscient or all-knowing. He asks the question 'who other than Himself can tell what has taken place or foretell what is going to happen?' He also knows our sins and still offers forgiveness. Give God glory today for being your God. There is no one like Him. I pray that you will get to know Him better each day. Lincoln Brewster along with Taylor Gall and Corbin Phillips wrote a song entitled 'There is No One Like Our God.' Take time to listen to it today.

**Acknowledge** – Lord, there is no one like You.

**Confess** – Lord, forgive me for not knowing You as I should.

**Thanksgiving** – Lord, thank You for Your Omnipotence, Your Omnipresence, and Your Omniscience.

**Prayer** – Lord, help me to tell others about Your greatness and love for them.

# Day 285

Psalm 115:1 Not to us, Lord, not to us but to Your name be the glory, because of Your love and faithfulness.

WHAT IS IN A NAME? TRY TO COME UP WITH A NAME FOR YOUR CHILD, then you will have a good idea of the time, thought, consideration, and options that it requires to settle on one. When our son, Bren, was born we wanted to incorporate some family member names from both sides of the family. We didn't know whether the baby was going to be a boy or a girl so we had to come up with names for both. Some names were easy to eliminate because they just didn't seem to fit. The name Zeke kept coming up for a boy, but finally got dropped because it was an uncle, not an immediate family member. We decided on Charles Bren which included the names of our grandfathers. He would go by his middle name since my name was Charles too. However, there was a slight problem. Vivian's grandfather spelled his name Leonard Breen Woodall. I didn't want the extra 'e' in Bren because I felt it would cause pronunciation issues. Everything appeared to be going well. Bren was a healthy, nine-pound baby boy. While we were still at the hospital, Vivian's grandfather came by to visit. He happened to see the baby's name tag and said there was a mistake. The middle name should have been 'Breen' instead of 'Bren.' We had to explain why we wanted the name spelled that way and would not be changing the birth certificate. Thankfully, he understood and had no hard feelings about the spelling. What about God's name? In Exodus 3:14 we find God telling Moses His name, "God said to Moses, 'I Am Who I Am. This is what you are to say to the Israelites: I Am has sent me to you.'" There are many different names for God, such as: El Shaddai, My Supplier, Adonai, My Master, and Jehovah Jireh, My Provider. However, for today let's just say His Name is Wonderful. Take a moment today to listen to the song by that name and give Him the glory.

**Acknowledge** – Lord, to Your name be the glory.

**Confess** – Lord, forgive me for using Your name in vain.

**Thanksgiving** – Lord, thank You for the power that is in Your name.

**Prayer** – Lord, Your name is the name above all others. Help me to glorify Your name.

# Day 286

Psalm 115:14 May the Lord cause you to flourish, both you and your children.

God's first blessing on mankind is found in Genesis 1:28, "God blessed them and said to them, 'Be fruitful and increase in number; fill the earth and subdue it. Rule over the fish of the sea and the birds of the air and over every living creature that moves on the ground.'" Again in Deuteronomy 1:11 we find this same blessing of increase, 'May the Lord, the God of your fathers, increase you a thousand times and bless you as He has promised.' I have a lot of respect for families who want to have lots of children. Raising the two Vivian and I had was no easy task. I can only imagine what two or three more adds to the equation. In the verses above, God is speaking about a physical increase in families. However, there is a spiritual side to God's command to increase. He wants us to grow His kingdom. 2 Corinthians 9:10 tells us, 'Now He who supplies seed to the sower and bread for food will also supply and increase your store of seed and will enlarge the harvest of your righteousness.' God promises to supply the seed and the soil in which to plant it. As we are faithful to plant, God is faithful to provide the harvest. A few verses earlier, Paul writes, 'Remember this: Whoever sows sparingly will also reap sparingly, and whoever sows generously will also reap generously.' Essentially Paul is saying, we reap what we sow. Paul also gives us an example of how God's harvest takes place. 1 Corinthians 3:6 says, 'I planted the seed, Apollos watered it, but God made it grow.' It is God who takes the seeds of His word that have been planted in someone's heart and causes them to grow and increase. You may plant the seed and it just sits there for some time. Someone else comes along and begins to water the seed you planted, causing it to take root. God provides the sunshine and nourishment that causes the tiny seed to grow for harvest. Are you planting seeds of God's word? If not, start your harvest today.

**Acknowledge** –Lord, You cause us to flourish.

**Confess** – Lord, forgive me for sowing sparingly.

**Thanksgiving** – Lord, thank You for the principle of increase.

**Prayer** – Lord, help me to generously sow the seeds of Your word.

# Day 287

> Psalm 116:5 The Lord is gracious and righteous; our God is full of compassion.

Today we learn that God is a God full of compassion. In John 4, we find the story of Jesus and the Samaritan woman. In Jesus' day, there was bitter hostility between the Samaritans and the Jews. Most Jews would cross the Jordan River and take a longer route just to avoid Samaria. However, we find Jesus traveling through the heart of Samaria. Jesus, tired from His journey, sat down at a well where a Samaritan woman was headed to draw water. The disciples had left to go into town for food. Jesus asks her for a drink of water. The Samaritan woman, knowing Jesus was Jewish, asks Him why He would want to drink water she had touched. Jesus begins to tell her about the living water He offers. He also tells her about her current marital situation which caught her off guard and causes her to try to change the subject. However, Jesus turns the conversation to the worship of God and that all who worship will worship in spirit and truth. The disciples returned and were surprised to find Jesus talking to the Samaritan woman who is leaving to go back into town to tell the people of her encounter with Jesus. The disciples try to get Jesus to eat, but He wasn't interested in eating. John 4:32 says, "But He said to them, 'I have food to eat that you know nothing about.'" He continued in verse 34-35, "My food, said Jesus, is to do the will of Him who sent Me and to finish His work. Do you not say, "Four months more and then the harvest?" I tell you, open your eyes and look at the fields! They are ripe for harvest." Verse 39 tells us, 'Many of the Samaritans from that town believed in Him because of the woman's testimony, "He told me everything I did."' From this story we see the compassion Jesus has for the lost, even the outcasts of society. He doesn't care about your past, where you came from, or where you are now. He is compassionate and full of mercy for all. Receive His love and mercy today.

**Acknowledge** – Lord, You are compassionate and full of mercy.

**Confess** – Lord, forgive me for my prejudice.

**Thanksgiving** – Lord, thank You for being gracious and full of compassion.

**Prayer** – Lord, where would I be if You had not had compassion on me?

# Day 288

Psalm 116:15 Precious in the sight of the lord is the death of His faithful servants.

BENJAMIN FRANKLIN WRITING TO JEAN-BAPTISTE LEROY IN 1789 about the Constitution said, '...But in this world nothing can be said to be certain except death and taxes.' (www.adamsmith.org) The writer of Hebrews said it this way in 9:27, 'Just as man is destined to die once, and after that to face judgement.' Each of us have an appointment with death. But the Psalmist gives us hope by telling us the death of a faithful servant of the Lord is special to Him. I have attended the funerals of people I knew who trusted God. There is something peaceful, comforting, and encouraging about those services. The presence of God is there. John 11:1-44 tells us the story of the death of Jesus' good friend Lazarus. The Bible tells us that Jesus was moved by the death of His friend. John 11:35 simply says, 'Jesus wept.' Later in verse 38 it tells us, 'Jesus, once more deeply moved, came to the tomb. It was a cave with a stone laid across the entrance.' You know the rest of the story. Jesus calls out to Lazarus to come out of the grave. Lazarus is raised back to life after being dead for four days. Jesus raises him back to life because of His love for His friend, and for the people to believe He was sent by God. Lazarus would die again; however, both times his death was precious in the sight of the Lord. Sadly, I have attended funerals of those who never accepted Christ as their Savior. These funerals seemed to be cold and hopeless. What makes the difference between a comforting and encouraging funeral versus a cold and hopeless one? The presence of the Lord. Take heart at the death of a loved one who knows Jesus. He is there to resurrect and take them to their new home in heaven. Their death is precious in His sight. If you know of family members who are not ready to face death, tell them about the love and mercy of Jesus. He loves them and wants them to be with Him in heaven.

**Acknowledge** –Lord, the death of Your faithful servants are precious in Your sight.

**Confess** – Lord, forgive me for not sharing Your grace and mercy with my loved ones.

**Thanksgiving** – Lord, thank You for preparing a place for those who love and trust You.

**Prayer** – Lord, I pray my funeral will be a time of rejoicing and celebration.

# Day 289

Psalm 117:2 For great is His love toward us, and the faithfulness of the Lord endures forever. Praise the Lord.

WITH ONLY TWO VERSES, PSALM 117 IS NOT ONLY THE SHORTEST Psalm, but it is also the shortest chapter in the Bible. Yet, it is packed with meaning and promise. Verse one says, 'Praise the Lord, all you nations; extol Him, all you peoples.' What is the importance of these verses? The Jewish people felt that God's love and faithfulness was for them alone. Yet, the Psalmist is telling everyone from every nation to praise the Lord for His great love. In Jesus' day, the first believers were Jewish. However, the gospel was spread to non-Jewish people as well. In Acts 10 we find the story of Cornelius, a Roman Centurion, who is believed to be the first non-Jewish person to be converted. The Bible tells us that he and his family were devout and God-fearing, who prayed regularly. However, they had not heard the story of Jesus and the plan of salvation. One day as he was praying, an angel appeared to Cornelius in a vision. The angel told Cornelius to send for Peter, who was staying with Simon the tanner in Joppa. The very next day, Peter had a strange vision about some 'unclean animals' that God told him to eat. While Peter was trying to understand the vision, Cornelius' men arrived looking for Peter. Taking this as a sign, Peter went with the men to Cornelius' house and preached to the people who had gathered there. Cornelius' entire household believed and were baptized. Peter speaking in Acts 10:34-35 said, "...I now realize how true it is that God does not show favoritism but accepts men from every nation who fear Him and do what is right." This message applies to us as well. God is moving and saving souls in many other parts of the world today, not just in the United States. For many years the U.S. led the world in sending overseas missionaries, but now many of the countries we once sent missionaries to are now sending missionaries to the U.S. As the Psalmist tells us, His great love is for everyone.

**Acknowledge** –Lord, Your faithfulness endures forever.

**Confess** – Lord, forgive me for being nearsighted with Your plan of salvation.

**Thanksgiving** – Lord, thank You for accepting people from every walk of life.

**Prayer** – Lord, help me to take the gospel to those who aren't like me.

# Day 290

**Psalm 118:7** The Lord is with me; He is my helper. I look in triumph on my enemies.

WHAT A GREAT PROMISE WE FIND IN TODAY'S VERSE; THE LORD IS with you. He is your helper. Isn't it great to know that God is always with us and there to help us? However, we find that His help may be much different than what we think it ought to be. Our thought may be that God's help would quickly get us out of a difficult situation we find ourselves in. Or it may be that God would immediately take away the pain and hurt we feel from a broken relationship. Or perhaps we pray for healing that doesn't immediately happen. In those times do you begin to doubt God's promise that He is with you? Do you feel like He is a million miles away or He doesn't care about your problems? On the other hand, you may be thinking God is using these situations to help you grow stronger in your faith and trust in Him and to help others who are going through similar situations. Paul writing in 2 Corinthians 1:3-4 says, 'Praise be to the God and Father of our Lord Jesus Christ, the Father of compassion and the God of all comfort, who comforts us in all our trouble, so we can comfort those in any trouble with the comfort we ourselves have received from God.' Paul knew what trouble was. He was not afraid or tried to avoid it. He was beaten, put in prison, stoned, shipwrecked, and bitten by a poisonous snake all for following God. Yet, he writes in Romans 8:31, 'What, then, shall we say in response to this? If God is for us, who can be against us?' No matter what happened, he knew that God was with him. He experienced the comfort God had given him in all the difficulties he faced and could share it with others. The writer of Hebrews said it this way in Hebrews 13:6, 'So we say with confidence, "The Lord is my helper; I will not be afraid. What can man do to me?"' Take heart, the Lord is your helper. God is bigger than our problems and He is in control. Do not be afraid.

**Acknowledge** –Lord, You are ever with us.

**Confess** – Lord, forgive me for doubting Your love for me.

**Thanksgiving** – Lord, thank You for helping me through difficult times.

**Prayer** – Lord, You are my helper, I will not be afraid.

# Day 291

Psalm 118:14 The Lord is my strength and my defense; He has become my salvation.

As a warrior, David recognized God through the lens of war. God was his strength and his defense. He had come to David's aid many times in battle, saving him from death and giving him many victories. But David also declares that God is his salvation. He owed his deliverance entirely on the Lord. However, there are many of us who have not had the same experiences as David and may not be able to relate to what he is saying. Perhaps we can relate to someone who was not a warrior like David. Let's look at the life of the person who said the following: 'But I, with a song of thanksgiving, will sacrifice to you. What I have vowed I will make good. Salvation comes from the Lord.' This was spoken by Jonah while he was floating around in the stomach of a large fish, not knowing if he was going to live or die. If you recall, Jonah had run from the Lord and the job God had given to him to go to Nineveh to preach repentance. While sailing in the opposite direction, there was a great storm. Jonah, realizing he was the cause of the storm, asked to be thrown into the sea to help calm the storm. No sooner than he landed in the water, a great fish came and swallowed him. Jonah remained in the fish for three days where he prayed to God and recognized and declared that salvation comes from the Lord. What is salvation? It is the deliverance from sin and its consequences of a life without hope. Our sin separates us eternally from God. How do we receive salvation? It is a free gift of God, through faith and trust in Jesus Christ. If you have trusted in God, declare Him as your salvation today. Like Jonah, sing a song of thanksgiving for what He has done for you. If you have yet to give your life to Christ, today you can receive salvation. Acknowledge your sins to God, ask Him to forgive you, and to come into your life and never leave you or forget you. He loves you and wants you to invite Him into your life.

**Acknowledge** –Lord, You are my salvation.

**Confess** – Lord, forgive my sin and come into my life.

**Thanksgiving** – Lord, I sing a song of thanksgiving for what You have done for me.

**Prayer** – Lord, You are my strength and my defense. You are my salvation.

# Day 292

Psalm 118:28 You are my God, and I will give You praise; You are my God, and I will exalt You.

Do you think David had a personal and intimate relationship with God? If there was any doubt, today's verse answers that question. Twice he proclaims, 'You are my God.' After declaring his relationship with God, he moves to offering praise which quickly grows into exaltation to Him. We have learned that praise is an expression of love and gratitude as an act of worship, while exaltation raises our praise to a much higher level. The Prophet Isaiah, writing in Isaiah 25:1, tells us why he praises and exalts the Lord. 'O Lord, you are my God; I will exalt You and praise Your name, for in perfect faithfulness you have done marvelous things, things planned long ago.' Note first, that Isaiah claims that the Lord is his God. Then he offers his praise and exaltation to the Lord, following the same pattern as David. Lastly, he tells us that God has done marvelous things, which were planned long ago. What type of relationship do you have with God? Do you know Him well enough to call Him, 'My God?' Do you talk to God each day in prayer? Or perhaps your only time with God is once a week at church or on special holidays such as Easter and Christmas. The more time you spend with God in prayer and in His word, the better you will know Him. You will also begin to see the things that God is doing in your life. Things that you may have thought were just good luck or happenstance were God's handiwork in your life. Spending time with Him will also open your eyes to His plan for you. Jeremiah 29:11 tells us, 'For I know the plans I have for you, declares the Lord, plans to prosper you and not harm you, plans to give you hope and a future.' Take the time to get to know God as David and Isaiah did. Learn to recognize His faithfulness in your life. Let Him open your eyes to the plans He has for you. It is worth the time.

**Acknowledge** –Lord, You are my God.

**Confess** – Lord, forgive me for not spending time with You.

**Thanksgiving** – Lord, I will exalt and praise Your name.

**Prayer** – Lord, You want to have the same relationship with me as You did with David and Isaiah. Help me to seek You more each day.

# Day 293

Psalm 119:2 Blessed are they who keep His statutes and seek Him with all their hearts.

Today we begin a three-week adventure into Psalms 119, which is the longest book in the Bible. It contains practical instruction for obtaining Godly wisdom. In both verses one and two, David declares that those who are obedient to God's laws and seek after Him are blessed. This is a very simple, but powerful promise of God. When we choose to obey the Lord blessings will follow. However, His blessings may likely not be in the form of a new car or some other material thing. God's blessings come wrapped in things such as peace, joy, and fulfillment. Take for example the promise of God's blessing in Ephesians 6:1-3, 'Children, obey your parents in the Lord, for this is right. Honor your father and mother – which is the first commandment with a promise – that it may go well with you and that you may enjoy long life on the earth.' Very simple, right? Obey your parents and you will enjoy a long life on the earth. However, it may not be as simple as it sounds. When I was growing up, my parents had rules. Some were easy to follow, others not so easy. One weekend, my friends wanted to go see a new movie that had just come out. My parents had told me that movie was not one I should be going to. The pull of my friends was stronger than the warning from my parents. This was in the day when you stood in line outside the movie theater to get tickets. Unfortunately for me, my parents happened to ride by the movie theater while my friends and I were in line. Needless to say, things didn't go well for me. That incident may have taken a year off my life. (Just kidding) The point is, obedience is not easy. It takes commitment and determination. The devil tells us, 'Rules are made to be broken.' That sounds good and maybe we can get away with breaking a few. But breaking God's commands has lasting consequences. Try following God and walk according to His law. Receive the blessings He has for your obedience.

**Acknowledge** –Lord, blessed are those who keep Your statutes.

**Confess** – Lord, forgive me for my disobedience.

**Thanksgiving** – Lord, thank You for the blessing You have given me.

**Prayer** – Lord, You desire our obedience over all else. Give me the determination to follow You.

# Day 294

**Psalm 119:11** I have hidden Your word in my heart that I might not sin against You.

WHAT TAKES UP THE MOST STORAGE SPACE IN YOUR HEART AND mind? Is it God's word? Is it the lyrics to some not so godly songs? Or perhaps it is images you have seen on TV or the web? What other things are there? How about anger, greed, lust, bitterness, and envy? Are thoughts filled with these ideas taking over your mind? Paul, writing in Philippians 4:8, tells us, 'Finally, brothers, whatever is true, whatever is noble, whatever is right, whatever is pure, whatever is lovely, whatever is admirable – if anything is excellent or praiseworthy – think about such things.' So how do I keep my mind on things that are true, noble, right, pure, lovely and admirable? For starters, we need a steady diet of God's word in our lives. Not only that, David tells us to hide God's word in our hearts. In other words, we need to memorize God's word. I wish there was some other way. Memorization is not one of my strengths. However, knowing God's word is powerful. It keeps us from sin and its consequences. I mentioned that Vivian and I are teaching the grandchildren Bible verses when we say the blessing over a meal. This exercise is not only teaching them God's word, but it is helping us to learn it as well. Knowing God's word is crucial because there will come a time when we need it. Ephesians 6:17 tells us, 'Take the helmet of salvation and the sword of the Spirit, which is the word of God.' The sword of the Spirit is the only offensive weapon God has provided us to stand against evil. A sword is meant to be used, not left in its sheath. Before Jesus began His ministry, Satan tempted Him three times. Each time Jesus combated the temptation by saying, 'It is written.' Jesus used the word of God to withstand the temptation. However, Satan knows God's word as well and will twist and manipulate it to confuse and trap us. That is why we need to have a solid foundation in God's word. Start today. Select a verse and memorize it. Make it a family project.

**Acknowledge** – Lord, Your word exposes sin.

**Confess** – Lord, forgive me for allowing things other than Your word fill my mind.

**Thanksgiving** – Lord, thank You for Your written word.

**Prayer** – Lord, give me the determination to hide Your word in my heart.

## Day 295

Psalm 119:18 Open my eyes that I may see wonderful things in Your law.

THIS IS A VERY DIFFERENT TYPE OF REQUEST BY DAVID. OBVIOUSLY, what he has seen in God's word has left him longing for more. It is as if David is asking God to remove any filters that may have dimmed his spiritual vision. He is not asking God for more blessings, but the ability to see more clearly what is in His word. What filters are you looking through when you read God's word? Have your problems clouded your vision of the promises in God's word? Has your faith been tested to the point you are unsure of God's love for you? In 2 Kings we find the story of Elisha, his servant, and an attacking army from Aram. The King of Aram was at war with Israel. Each time the King would set up for battle to attack the Israelites, God would tell Elisha their every move. This frustrated the King to the point, that he sent his army to capture Elisha. Elisha's servant woke up one morning to see the city surrounded by the Arameans and he panicked. 2 Kings 6:15-17 tells us what happened next, 'When the servant of the man of God got up and went out early the next morning, an army with horses and chariots had surrounded the city. "Oh, my lord, what shall we do?' the servant asked. "Don't be afraid," the prophet answered. "Those who are with us are more than those who are with them." And Elisha prayed, "O Lord, open his eyes so he may see." Then the Lord opened the servant's eyes, and he looked and saw the hills full of horses and chariots of fire all around Elisha.' Elisha's servant was looking at the problem at hand through the filter of his limited ability. His vision was clouded by a lack of faith. How much are we like Elisha's servant? Do we think of the worst possible outcome to our problems even before they happen? Or do we turn to God's word to find comfort and peace? If our eyes are open, we can find wonderful things in His word to comfort and see us through our problems.

**Acknowledge** –Lord, there are wonderful things in Your word.

**Confess** – Lord, forgive me for filtering Your word through the lens of lack of faith.

**Thanksgiving** – Lord, thank You for opening my eyes to Your word.

**Prayer** – Lord, remove any filters that cloud my vision of Your word.

# Day 296

Psalm 119:27 Cause me to understand the way of Your precepts that I may meditate on Your wonderful deeds.

It is one thing to casually know God's word and blindly obey it, as compared to having a deep insight into the practical meaning of it. All too often, we want to box Christianity into a list of do's and don'ts. Marking off a checklist is much easier than knowing the meaning behind God's word and having an ongoing relationship with the Father. It takes time and effort to get into God's word and to understand its meaning for our lives. How much do we rely on a pastor or small group leader to teach us what we need to know about God's word rather than studying it ourselves? Those resources are great to have, but they shouldn't be our only source for Bible study. In Jesus' day, the Pharisees were experts in the law and great at enforcing them all. They put heavy burdens on the people and did most things for show rather than out of obedience to God. Jesus told them in Luke 11:52, "Woe to you experts in the law, because you have taken away the key to knowledge. You yourselves have not entered, and you have hindered those who were entering." Jesus was telling them, the very ones who could have helped the people understand the law, made it complicated and confusing to the people. Not only did they misguide the people, the ones with the most knowledge of God's word in that day missed the Messiah. In fact, their passion for following the law and the status it provided them caused them to hate Jesus and put Him on the cross. Like David, we should want to have a deeper understanding of God's word. The more we learn about God, the more we are grateful for His love for us. Isaiah 48:17 tells us, 'This is what the Lord says – your Redeemer, the Holy One of Israel: "I am the Lord your God, who teaches you what is best for you, who directs you in the way you should go."' Get into God's word. Allow Him to teach you. Allow Him to direct you. Get to know God and His love for you.

**Acknowledge** –Lord, You are our teacher.

**Confess** – Lord, forgive me for relying on someone else to teach me Your word.

**Thanksgiving** – Lord, thank You for directing my steps.

**Prayer** – Lord, help me to dig deeper into Your word to get to know You.

# Day 297

Psalm 119:37 Turn my eyes away from worthless things; preserve my life according to Your word.

OUR EYES ARE THE PORTAL TO OUR HEART. ADVERTISERS LEARNED this a long time ago. Car commercials are the most tempting to me. The producer creates a scene of a nice shiny car zooming down the road or on some off-road adventure. They attempt to create a memory that you would like to experience yourself so that the next car you buy is the one you saw in their commercial. Aside from car commercials, our eyes take in a number of things each day. David is asking God for help by turning his eyes away from the worthless things he sees. Notice he didn't ask God to close his eyes, but to direct them to what is good. In Genesis, we find that it was through the eyes of Eve, sin first entered mankind. Genesis 3:6 tells us, 'When woman saw that the fruit of the tree was good for food and pleasing to the eye, and also desirable for gaining wisdom, she took some and ate it.' Isn't that the way sin sneaks into our hearts as well? Something that may not be good for us looks pleasing and desirable. David learned a hard lesson about looking at something he shouldn't have. In 2 Samuel 11:2, we pick up the story of David and Bathsheba. It states, 'One evening David got up from his bed and walked around on the roof of the palace. From the roof he saw a woman bathing. The woman was very beautiful.' From that one look, David's life was caught up in an affair with Bathsheba, the murder of her husband Uriah, and the death of a child they conceived. What are you looking at? Are you looking at things that you should not be? Perhaps you can even justify what you are looking at by saying it isn't hurting anyone. However, you may never fully know what kind of seeds are being planted by the things you are watching until it is too late. Ask God to turn your eyes away from the worthless things you are watching. Don't let your eyes lead you into sin.

**Acknowledge** –Lord, my eyes are the portal to my heart.

**Confess** – Lord, forgive me when I desire to look at the worthless things of life.

**Thanksgiving** – Lord, thank You for providing good and healthy things to look at.

**Prayer** – Lord, I need Your help in keeping my eyes on what is good and pure.

# Day 298

Psalm 119:41 May Your unfailing love come to me, Lord, Your salvation, according to Your promise.

WHAT IS GOD'S PROMISE OF SALVATION? IT IS THE DELIVERANCE from the penalty of sin and an eternity destined for hell. What do I do to earn salvation? Nothing, salvation is free for all. It costs us nothing, but it did cost God His only Son. Ephesians 2:8-9 tells us, 'For by grace you have been saved through faith, and that not of yourselves; it is the gift of God, not of works, lest anyone should boast.' Why has God given us this promise of salvation? Romans 5:8 tells us, 'But God demonstrates His own love toward us, in that while we were yet sinners, Christ died for us.' Paul tells us that it is only by God's unfailing love or His grace, that Christ died for us. What do I need to do to receive God's promise of salvation? John 3:16 tells us, 'For God so loved the world that He gave His one and only Son, that whoever believes in Him shall not perish but have eternal life.' Is receiving the promise of salvation that easy? The answer is yes and no. The first step to receiving God's promise of salvation is to believe in our hearts that Jesus was the Son of God and He came to pay the penalty for our sin. However, it would be very easy to claim Jesus as our Lord and Savior and continue to live the same lifestyle we did before we made that decision. Sadly, many people who claim to know Christ have stopped at this point and live no differently than before they accepted Jesus. God's word also tells us that we should also repent and turn from our sins. That means a change in our lifestyle is an important part of salvation. Paul, writing in Romans 6:1-2, said it this way, 'What shall we say, then? Shall we go on sinning so that grace may increase? By no means! We died to sin; how can we live in it any longer?' When we come to know Christ, we become a new person in Him. We should be living like it.

**Acknowledge** –Lord, You promise salvation to all who believe.

**Confess** – Lord, forgive me when I slip back into my old lifestyle.

**Thanksgiving** – Lord, thank You for sending Your Son for our salvation.

**Prayer** – Lord, help me share Your great plan of salvation with someone today.

# Day 299

Psalm 119:49 Remember Your word to Your servant, for You have given me hope.

David tells us that God's word offers hope. Yesterday we read about the promise of salvation that is available to all who receive it. It is this very same salvation that offers hope to a lost and dying world. However, after we receive Christ as our Savior, we still have problems. They do not mysteriously disappear when we start living for Christ. Where do you turn when you are confronted by those looming problems that will not go away? What do you do when your faith is put to the test? Do you diligently read and search God's word to find hope or do you sit around and worry about tomorrow? Not only does God's word offer hope, our God is a God of hope. Romans 15:13 tells us, 'May the God of hope fill you with all joy and peace as you trust in Him, so that you may overflow with hope by the power of the Holy Spirit.' This verse really changes our perspective on hope. Hope is not just something we try to convince ourselves that everything is going to be okay based on unfounded optimism. For a Christian, it is the assurance that our future is based on God's love for us. He loved us enough to send His only Son to die for our sins, how much more will He look after His children? However, hope requires action on our part. We must trust Him, even when times are difficult and life gets hard. But there is more. It is the Holy Spirit who plants and develops the seeds of hope in our hearts. He confirms our faith, strengthens our hope, and causes it to overflow. Not only does the Holy Spirit work in our lives to build hope, we can also find hope in God's word. Romans 8:31 says, 'What, then, shall we say in response to this? If God is for us, who can be against us?' This verse does not mean that everything will go our way, but that our eternal destiny is secure in the love of God. No matter how bad things may seem, God loves us and has a plan for us.

**Acknowledge** – Lord, in You there is hope.

**Confess** – Lord, forgive me for not trusting You.

**Thanksgiving** – Lord, thank You for the Holy Spirit who strengthens our hope.

**Prayer** – Lord, help me to put my hope and trust in You even when life is difficult.

# Day 300

Psalm 119:58 I have sought Your face with all my heart; be gracious to me according to Your promise.

WE HAVE LEARNED THAT SEEKING GOD'S FACE IS THE DESIRE TO BE in His presence. It implies a deeper relationship with Him. Notice in today's verse that David has already sought God's face with his whole heart. He has entered into the presence of God. Now that he is there, what is the first thing that David asks of God? He is asking for the promise of God's mercy that has been revealed in His word. David, a man after God's own heart, the anointed King of Israel, the warrior, the giant slayer, is asking for God's mercy. Why? Because he knew more than anything else, he was a sinner. He also knew that God would fill in the rest, if his heart was in tune with the Father. Do we have a relationship with God where we trust Him to fill in the details of our lives or are our priorities out of order? Speaking for myself, I probably give too much attention to the details of life. I like to be comfortable. I like to know when and where the next meal is coming from. I like to go to the closet and have plenty of options to wear. I like the security of a savings account. Jesus, speaking in Matthew 6:31-33, tells us, "So do not worry, 'saying what shall we eat?' or 'What shall we drink?' or 'What shall we wear?' For the pagans run after all these things, and your heavenly Father knows that you need them. But seek first His kingdom and His righteousness, and all these things will be given to you as well." That works well until the circumstances of our lives take a bad turn and the bottom falls out. Do we panic and worry about our circumstances? Or do we seek God and His presence? Do we realize, like David, that God's mercy becomes much more important to us than earthly possessions? One thing I have learned over the years is that no one is immune from problems. They are going to happen. I am thankful that I serve a God who is bigger than life's problems, one who allows me to come humbly into His presence.

**Acknowledge** –Lord, in Your presence is mercy.

**Confess** – Lord, forgive me for putting my priorities into earthly things.

**Thanksgiving** – Lord, thank You for the promises in Your word.

**Prayer** – Lord, help me to seek first Your kingdom and righteousness.

# Day 301

Psalm 119:64 The earth is filled with Your love, O Lord; teach me Your decrees.

David tells us that the earth is filled with God's love. If anyone should know, he should. While David was not a world traveler, he spent quite a bit of time in some very remote places hiding from Saul and his son, Absalom, who were trying to kill him. Even in those places David felt God's love and protection. David also trusted God to guide and direct his steps. In 1 Samuel 30, we find that David's camp had been raided by the Amalekites while he and his men were away. The Amalekites took everything. When David and his men returned to find their possessions and their families taken and the camp burned to the ground, they wept until they could weep no more. Then they became bitter at David and talked about stoning him. David was in deep trouble. He had lost everything and was being blamed by everyone else for their situation. 1 Samuel 30:6-8 tells us what David did, 'David was greatly distressed because the men were talking of stoning him; each one was bitter in spirit because of his sons and daughters. But David found strength in the Lord his God. Then David said to Abiathar the priest, the son of Ahimelech, "Bring me the ephod." Abiathar brought it to him, and David inquired of the Lord, "Shall I pursue this raiding party? Will I overtake them?" "Pursue them," he answered. "You will certainly overtake them and succeed in the rescue."' First, David found strength in the Lord. He was confident of God's love for him and didn't allow his circumstances to cause him to doubt God. Secondly, he asked God what he should do. He didn't rush into doing something that didn't have God's blessing and approval. What lessons can we learn from David's experience? No matter our circumstances, no matter where we are, we are never away from God's love. His love fills the earth. Also, God will teach us and direct us when we ask him. Too often we act first and then ask God to bless our actions. Before reacting to your problems, go to God first. Ask Him to guide and direct you. He will not let you down.

**Acknowledge** –Lord, Your love fills the earth.

**Confess** – Lord, forgive me when I act first and pray last.

**Thanksgiving** – Lord, thank You for teaching me Your ways.

**Prayer** – Lord, help me to find strength in Your love.

# Day 302

Psalm 119:66 Teach me knowledge and good judgement, for I trust in Your commands.

DAVID IS ASKING GOD TO TEACH HIM WISDOM AND KNOWLEDGE which comes from God's commands. Knowledge is typically obtained through reading and teaching. It is something we work at to acquire over time. While wisdom is having discernment and the ability to determine which facts are important in making a decision or choosing a solution to a problem. James 1:5 tells us, 'If any of you lacks wisdom, he should ask of God, who gives generously to all without finding fault, and it will be given to him.' According to James, it is our choice whether or not we have wisdom. It is available to all who ask God for it. We also know that Proverbs speaks a lot about wisdom and knowledge. In the first six verses of Proverbs, Solomon tells us why he wrote the book. In verses 2-3 he said, it was 'for attaining wisdom and discipline; for understanding words of insight; for acquiring a disciplined and prudent life, doing what is right and just and fair.' He sums it up in verse seven by saying, 'The fear of the Lord is the beginning of knowledge, but fools despise wisdom and discipline.' In other words, reverence and awe of God are the beginning of knowledge. A wise person is one whose foundation is in God and His word, while the fool has no foundation to build on. The fool makes decisions based on his limited understanding. Proverbs 14:15 says it this way, 'A simple man believes anything, but a prudent man gives thought to his steps.' A fool will believe what he or she is told, while the wise will weigh it against God's word. Proverbs 19:2 says, 'It is not good to have zeal without knowledge, nor to be hasty and miss the way.' Or translated it means enthusiasm without knowledge is not good. The person who seeks wisdom and knowledge will not make hasty uninformed decisions. They will pray and seek God over the decisions they are faced with. Are you searching God's word for knowledge and good judgement? Trust His word to guide you and instruct you in the way you should go.

**Acknowledge** – Lord, Your word is a lamp to my feet and a light to my path.

**Confess** – Lord, forgive me when I make hasty decisions without seeking Your wisdom.

**Thanksgiving** – Lord, thank You for teaching me knowledge and good judgement.

**Prayer** – Lord, help me to be a prudent person who gives thought to my steps.

# Day 303

Psalm 119:76 May Your unfailing love be my comfort, according to Your promise to Your servant.

DAVID CALLS GOD'S LOVE UNFAILING, HIS COMFORT, AND GOD'S promise to him. Despite his troubles, David knew God loved him. God's love had sustained him and kept him going through the most difficult days of his life. David, writing in Psalm 86:13, said, 'For great is Your love toward me; You have delivered me from the depths of the grave.' Would it surprise you to learn that God loves you and me just as much as He did David? However, if you are like me there are times when I don't always feel God's love. It is in those times God seems to be a million miles away. What do we do when those feelings take over our thoughts? As simple as it may sound, we need to turn to God's word during those times. You can open your Bible to most any place and read about God's love. Isaiah 49:15-16 tells us, 'Can a mother forget the baby at her breast and have no compassion on the child she has borne? Though she may forget, I will not forget you! See, I have engraved you on the palms of My hands; your walls are ever before me.' Isaiah is essentially saying, even if our own mother doesn't love us, God does. He has us in the palm of His hands. Jesus, speaking in Matthew 10:29-31, said, "Are not two sparrows sold for a penny? Yet not one of them will fall to the ground apart from the will of your Father. And even the very hairs of your head are all numbered. So don't be afraid; you are worth more than many sparrows." God knows the number of hairs on your head. That is amazing in light of the fact that every time I comb my hair, several fall out. He knows every detail about us and cares for us. Lastly, we can talk to God any time day or night. Hebrews 4:16 says, 'Let us then approach the throne of grace with confidence, so that we may receive mercy and find grace to help us in our time of need.' Let God's unfailing love be your comfort.

**Acknowledge** – Lord, Your love is unfailing.

**Confess** – Lord, forgive me when I doubt Your love for me.

**Thanksgiving** – Lord, thank You for loving me.

**Prayer** – Lord, help me to approach Your throne of grace with confidence.

# Day 304

Psalm 119:88 In Your unfailing love preserve my life, that I may obey the statutes of Your mouth.

Yesterday we read that God's unfailing love was David's comfort. Today, he makes the declaration that it is his life preserver. Our two-year-old granddaughter, Reese, is fearless when it comes to being around water. She loves to go swimming in the 'deep water' whether in a pool or the ocean. Needless to say, unless someone is holding her, she is wearing a life preserver. She is not ready to swim on her own and needs the security and protection of a life preserver. By next summer she will hopefully have grown and matured to where she could swim some on her own with an adult close by. In Matthew 14:22-33, we read about an incident the disciples had on the water. They had gotten into a boat to sail to the other side of the Sea of Galilee. Jesus had stayed behind to be alone and pray. The Apostle Peter, who was no stranger to water, was an experienced fisherman and had spent many hours at sea. In the early hours of morning, the disciples saw a figure walking on the water towards them. They were terrified and thought it was a ghost. Jesus told them, "Take courage! It is I. Don't be afraid." Peter said, "if it is really You Lord, tell me to come to You on the water." Jesus told Peter to come on, and so Peter did. Peter did well the first few steps, but then he became afraid and began to sink into the water. Peter cried out, "Lord, save me," and Jesus immediately reached out and caught him. Have you been where Peter was? Have you stepped out in faith only to have the winds and waves overtake you? Suddenly you find yourself sinking and the only thing you can do is cry out, 'Lord save me!' What does Jesus do? He reaches out His hand of love and mercy and gently pulls us out of the raging sea. What did Jesus ask Peter after He had saved him? Jesus asked, "why did you doubt?' Like David, give God thanks for His unfailing love for you. Never doubt His love.

**Acknowledge** –Lord, Your love preserves my life.

**Confess** – Lord, forgive me when I let the storms of life cause me to doubt You.

**Thanksgiving** – Lord, thank You for rescuing me.

**Prayer** – Lord, give me the confidence to step out into the water.

# Day 305

Psalm 119:90 Your faithfulness continues through all generations; You established the earth, and it endures.

To get a broader picture of the everlasting, faithful, and enduring word of God, we need to look at verses 89-91 which say, 'Your word, O Lord, is eternal; it stands firm in the heavens. Your faithfulness continues through all generations; You established the earth, and it endures. Your laws endure to this day, for all things serve you.' The God who created the heavens and the earth is the same God we serve today. A lot of things have changed since creation; however, God has not. He is a God who can make a promise like one found in Exodus 20:6 which says, 'but showing love to a thousand generations of those who love Me and keep My commandments.' Why? Because He doesn't change and He is faithful to remember His promises for thousands of years. We also know we can trust the promises in God's word because it doesn't change or become outdated. Jesus speaking in Matthew 24:35 says, "Heaven and earth will pass away, but My words will never pass away." Over the centuries, the Bible has survived and thrived even though some have tried to destroy it. Isaiah said it this way, 'The grass withers and the flowers fall, but the word of our God stands forever.' Even in places like China where it is illegal to have a Bible, God's word is finding its way to those who are hungry for it. God's word is not going away. Lastly, Jesus speaking in Matthew 5:17-18 said, "Do not think I have come to abolish the Law or the Prophets; I have not come to abolish them but to fulfill them. I tell you the truth, until heaven and earth disappear, not the smallest letter, not the least stroke of a pen, will by any means disappear from the Law until everything is accomplished." I hope you get the picture. God's word is eternal. It is not going to change. We can put our trust in the promises of His word. However, we must be careful not to think God's word is outdated and doesn't apply to us. It is just as real today as it was thousands of years ago.

**Acknowledge** –Lord, Your faithfulness continues to all generations.

**Confess** – Lord, forgive me for not trusting Your word.

**Thanksgiving** – Lord, thank You for never changing.

**Prayer** – Lord, because You never change, I can trust You completely.

# Day 306

**Psalm 119:103** How sweet are Your words to my taste, sweeter than honey to my mouth!

I CAN RELATE TO WHAT DAVID IS DESCRIBING IN THIS VERSE. SEVERAL years ago, my sister took up beekeeping as a hobby and at Christmas would give everyone a jar of honey. We would take the honey and drip it over a warm piece of buttered bread. Talk about a sweet treat. However, David in comparing the sweetness of God's word to honey claims hands down, God's word wins. What kind of taste does God's word leave in your mouth? Are His words sweeter than honey or are they bitter and hard to swallow? Do you find joy, peace, goodness, forgiveness, and love in God's word? Or maybe you are convicted of the sin God's word exposes in your life. Hebrews 4:12 tells us, 'For the word of God is living and active. Sharper than any double-edged sword, it penetrates even to dividing soul and spirit, joints and marrow; it judges the thoughts and attitudes of the heart.' It is a good thing that God's word is living and active, because we need it to survive. In Matthew 4:1-11 we read where Jesus was tempted by Satan in the wilderness. Satan preying on Jesus' hunger, tried to get Jesus to turn stones into bread. Jesus answered Satan saying, "It is written: 'Man does not live on bread alone, but on every word that comes from the mouth of God.'" Jesus was telling Satan that physical nourishment was not the only thing needed for a healthy life, we also need to be fed spiritually. Are you feeding on God's word each day? Are His words becoming sweeter as you get to know Him? Colossians 3:16 says, 'Let the word of Christ dwell in you richly, teaching and admonishing one another in all wisdom, singing psalms and hymns and spiritual songs, with thankfulness in your hearts to God.' The more of God's word we take in, the more our hearts will overflow with praise and thankfulness for what He has done for us. I agree with David on this one. God's word is sweet to the taste, like honey. Something that good, we shouldn't miss out on.

**Acknowledge** –Lord, Your words are sweeter than honey.

**Confess** – Lord, forgive me for not reading and studying Your word.

**Thanksgiving** – Lord, thank You for Your unchanging word.

**Prayer** – Lord, Your word is sweet like honey, but sharper than a two-edged sword. Help me to have a daily diet of it.

# Day 307

Psalm 119:105 Your word is a lamp for my feet, a light on my path.

IN TODAY'S TERMINOLOGY, DAVID COMPARES GOD'S WORD TO A GPS. It lights the path before him and keeps him on course. Our granddaughter, Tatum, has grown up in NYC. When she was almost three years old, Vivian and I kept her for several days while baby sister was being born. We would take Tatum to the park and other places to keep her entertained. However, her favorite thing to do was to get a bagel and smoothie. It was amazing how she knew exactly where the bagel shop was located. Her sense of direction even on the NYC streets that all looked the same to us, was spot on. She knew exactly where she was and where she was going. Proverbs 14:12 says, 'There is a way that seems right to a man, but in the end it leads to death.' What better way to say we need Godly direction in our lives? We may have a successful career, nice house, and a membership to a large country club. However, if God has not been included in our lives, these are just things that have no eternal value. Proverbs 3:5-6 says, 'Trust in the Lord with all your heart and lean not on your own understanding; in all your ways acknowledge Him, and He will make your paths straight.' Notice that Solomon didn't say God would make your path easy and take all the bumps out. In fact, straight in God's perspective doesn't mean our path will be easy, but that it is the only way to get us to the right destination. All too often when we encounter difficulties, we assume we have wandered off the path God had intended for us. When in fact, God may have placed us there for a purpose. That is why it is critical to have God's word light the path ahead of us. 2 Timothy 3:16 tells us, 'All scripture is God-breathed and is useful for teaching, rebuking, correcting and training in righteousness.' Dig deeper into God's word. Learn from it and allow it to light the path of your life.

**Acknowledge** – Lord, Your word is a lamp to my feet and a light to my path.

**Confess** – Lord, forgive me for leaning on my own understanding.

**Thanksgiving** – Lord, thank You for the usefulness of Your word.

**Prayer** – Lord, Your word teaches, rebukes, corrects, and trains. Help me to apply it to my life.

# Day 308

**Psalm 119:114** You are my refuge and my shield; I have put my hope in Your word.

DAVID DECLARES THAT HIS HOPE IS IN GOD'S WORD. HOPE AND faith go hand in hand with each other. Hebrews 11:1 defines faith and hope as, 'Now faith is being sure of what we hope for and certain of what we do not see.' The rest of Hebrews 11 provides the names of the 'Faith Hall of Fame.' Each verse starts out by saying, 'By faith...' and then describes what that person did. Faith requires trust and action on our part. When the Israelites crossed the Jordan River to enter the Promised Land, the water did not stop flowing until the priests carrying the Ark, stepped out into the water. They trusted God's promise and walked across a dry river bed. The stories in the Bible are nice to read, but what about faith in today's world? Is faith and hope still relevant today? Our faith examples may not make the 'Hall of Fame,' but they are just as important to God. For example, Vivian and I met someone not long ago who was given a vision by God to plant a church in a city about seven hours from where he was successfully serving as a youth pastor. Instead of questioning God, He stepped out in faith and left his comfortable job to move his family of six to a place he had never been before. Each step along the way, God has provided what they have needed. His hope is to fulfill the vision God has given him. By faith, he moved his family, was able to buy a house with no guarantee of a steady income, and meet the people who God has called to help launch the church. Like with the 'Old Testament Hall of Famers,' the task has not been easy or without obstacles. However, God has been faithful in seeing him through the challenges. God may not have called you to start a church, but perhaps He has planted a seed for you to do something else. Is God your refuge and your shield? Can you trust Him enough to step out in faith to do what He is leading you to?

**Acknowledge** –Lord, You are my refuge and my shield.

**Confess** – Lord, forgive me when my faith is weak.

**Thanksgiving** – Lord, thank You for the examples of faithful people in Your word.

**Prayer** – Lord, what are You calling me to do? Help me to be faithful.

# Day 309

> Psalm 119:125 I am Your servant; give me discernment that I may understand Your statutes.

First David declares that he is God's servant, not His equal. What an important reminder for us as well. I don't know about you, but at times the way I talk to God may sound more like I am right up there with Him, instead of His child. During those times, my prayers seem more demanding rather than asking in obedience to His word. That is why David's request for good judgment to better understand God's word is so appropriate. The better we understand God's word, the better we know God and what He desires. My goal each year is to read through the Bible. I have done so for a number of years. However, just reading God's word is not enough. Reading through it only gives us a glimpse of what is there. God's word also has direct application for our lives. We can miss the underlying meaning when we just gloss over it or only apply worldly intellect to understand it. 1 Corinthians 1:20-21 says, 'Where is the wise man? Where is the scholar? Where is the philosopher of this age? Has God not made foolish the wisdom of the world? For since in the wisdom of God the world through its wisdom did not know Him, God was pleased through the foolishness of what was preached to save those who believe.' God's plan of salvation is very simple. However, some of the smartest people have tripped over it and failed to understand it. Paul in Ephesians 3:9 refers to it as a mystery, 'And to make plain to everyone the administration of this mystery, which for ages past was kept hidden in God, who created all things.' This is all the more reason for asking God for discernment to understand His word. Thankfully there are a lot of resources available to help understand God's word. Even the Bible app with yearly reading plans include commentary on the scripture for the day. Take time to read and study God's word. Get to know God better through His word. Don't let it be a mystery to you.

**Acknowledge** –Lord, I need discernment to understand Your word.

**Confess** – Lord, forgive me when I act like I am entitled.

**Thanksgiving** – Lord, thank You for making Your plan simple so everyone can understand it.

**Prayer** – Lord, give me the desire to read and study Your word.

# Day 310

Psalm 119:130 The unfolding of Your words give light; it gives understanding to the simple.

THE MESSAGE BIBLE SAYS IT THIS WAY, 'BREAK OPEN YOUR WORDS, let the light shine out, let ordinary people see the meaning.' My translation is very simple, 'Lord when I dig into Your word, the light comes on in my soul, even someone as simple as me can understand it.' Have you had one of those moments when you read a verse that you have read many times before, but see something totally new this time? God is unfolding His words in your heart. He is revealing something that you need for that moment. God's word is full of those opportunities if we take the time to look for them. It also doesn't hurt to ask God to reveal things in His word to you. Paul writing in Ephesians 1:17 said, 'Keep asking the God of our Lord Jesus Christ, the glorious Father, may give you the Spirit of wisdom and revelation, so that you may know Him better.' How deep is your spirit of wisdom and revelation? Is it maturing or stuck in infancy? Are you asking God for spiritual wisdom and insight into His word? 1 Corinthians 3:1-3 says, 'Brothers, I could not address you as spiritual but as worldly – mere infants in Christ. I gave you milk, not solid food, for you were not yet ready for it. Indeed, you are still not ready. You are still worldly. For since there is jealousy and quarreling among you, are you not worldly? Are you not acting like mere men?' Paul tells us that not everyone is ready to dig deeper into God's word because some are acting like they did before they received Christ. If we haven't learned the basics, then we are certainly not ready to move forward into deeper spiritual truths. 1 Peter 3:18 tells us, 'But grow in the grace and knowledge of our Lord and Savior Jesus Christ. To Him be the glory both now and forever! Amen.' It is time to get off the milk of God's word and move towards spiritual maturity. Ask God to give you understanding and insight into His word. Let His word light up in your life, share it with others.

**Acknowledge** –Lord, Your words give light.

**Confess** – Lord, forgive me for still depending on spiritual milk instead of solid food.

**Thanksgiving** – Lord, thank You for revealing Your words to me.

**Prayer** – Lord, give me the spirit of wisdom and revelation as I study Your word.

# Day 311

Psalm 119:142 Your righteousness is everlasting and Your law is true.

DAVID DECLARES THAT GOD'S LAW TALKS ABOUT THE TRUTH. OR did he say, God's Law contains the truth? No, he tells us God's Law is truth. God's Law doesn't refer us to the truth, or imply what truth is. God's Law is truth. Most every time I hear the word truth, I am reminded of the famous line spoken by Jack Nicholson in the movie, 'A Few Good Men.' When asked for the truth, he replied, 'You can't handle the truth, you don't want the truth...' Unfortunately, that statement may be applicable to us and our relationship with Christ. God's Law exposes the sin in our lives that we may not want to face up to. Paul writing in Romans 7:22-23 said, 'For in my inner being I delight in God's law; but I see another law at work in the members of my body, waging war against the law of my mind and making me a prisoner of the law of sin at work within my members.' It is the Law that reveals God's standard for us, it tells us right from wrong. Without it, we would have no way to judge our sinfulness. Romans 7:7 says, 'What shall we say, then? Is the law sin? Certainly not! Indeed I would not have known what sin was except through the Law. For I would not have known what coveting really was if the Law had not said, "Do not covet."' Because of the convicting nature of God's Law, many have fallen into the trap of declaring there is no truth, except what I believe. That way, they can live as they prefer without fearing the judgment of God because they are convinced their way is right. I hope you are trusting and believing God's Law to be true. If you have slipped into making up your own rules for living, get back into God's word for direction because the Law doesn't stop at revealing our sin. It also reveals that God is still a gracious, faithful, and loving God who forgives sin. Ask Him to reveal the truth of His Law to you.

**Acknowledge** –Lord, Your Law is true.

**Confess** – Lord, forgive me when I make up my own rules instead of following Your Law.

**Thanksgiving** – Lord, thank You for exposing the sin in my life through Your Law.

**Prayer** – Lord, help me to be able to handle the truth of Your Law.

# Day 312

**Psalm 119:145** I call with all my heart; answer me, Lord, and I will obey Your decrees.

Have you ever cried out to God with your whole heart? Have you been at a place where trying to use the right words really didn't matter? That is where David is today. His whole soul pleaded with God. I have to admit there haven't been many times where I can honestly say I have been there. If asked to pray at a gathering of believers, my prayers tend to be short and safe. My prayers at home during devotion time are more conversational with God. Other times, I will pray scripture or the words of a song. 1 Peter 3:12 tells us, 'For the eyes of the Lord are on the righteous and His ears are attentive to their prayer, but the face of the Lord is against those who do evil.' It is comforting to know that God hears our prayers no matter how long, how short, how eloquent, how logical, or how sweet they are. But what about those times when we reach the point of desperation and all we can do is just cry out from the heart? It is those times words are hard to come by. I might be able to say, "Lord help me," or "Lord I can't keep going, do something," but that is about as far as I can go. My heart takes over and just cries out to God. Paul writing in Romans 8:26-27 said, 'In the same way, the Holy Spirit helps us in our weakness. We do not know what we ought to pray for, but the Spirit Himself intercedes for us with groans that words cannot express. And He who searches our hearts knows the mind of the Spirit, because the Spirit intercedes for the saints in accordance with God's will.' When we reach the point of desperation, the Holy Spirit intercedes for us. He knows what we are struggling with. He also knows God's will for our lives and directs our prayers in that direction. The Holy Spirit turns my cry of 'God do something' into 'God Your will be done in my life, give me patience and endurance to finish the race You have for me.'

**Acknowledge** –Lord, You hear our prayers.

**Confess** – Lord, forgive me when I don't think You hear my prayers.

**Thanksgiving** – Lord, thank You for the Holy Spirit that intercedes for us.

**Prayer** – Lord, help me to cry out with my whole heart more often.

# Day 313

Psalm 119:160 All Your words are true; all Your righteous laws are eternal.

On Day 311 David proclaimed God's law as truth. Today, he declares all God's words are true. As simple and logical as it may sound, this has created much debate and division even among believers. Everyone agrees that the Bible is God's Holy Word. Men were inspired to record God's plan and purpose for His creation. However, there are some who stop there and don't believe in the complete inerrancy of the Bible. That is the Bible, in its original manuscripts, is without error or fault. Paul writing in 2 Timothy 3:16-17 said, 'All scripture is God-breathed and is useful for teaching, rebuking, correcting and training in righteousness, so that the man of God may be thoroughly equipped for every good work.' Paul had no doubt about the accuracy and usefulness of God's word, calling it 'God-breathed' or from the mouth of God. Peter writing in 2 Peter 1:21 said, 'For prophecy never had its origin in the will of man, but men spoke from God as they were carried along by the Holy Spirit.' In other words, the Holy Spirit moved men to write the Bible. They used their own words and writing style, but were guided by the Holy Spirit to accurately record what God wanted them to say and how He wanted them to say it. 1 Corinthians 2:13 says, 'This is what we speak, not in words taught us by human wisdom but in words taught by the Spirit, expressing spiritual truths in spiritual words.' Paul also writes that his words didn't come from human teaching, but were inspired by the Holy Spirit. Where do you stand on the Word of God? Do you trust God's word to be the inspired, inerrant, authoritative record of God's plan and purpose? If not, I pray that you will dig deeper into God's word. Trust David, a man after God's heart, who said God's word is true. Trust Solomon, the wisest man ever to live who wrote Proverbs 30:5 which says, 'Every word of God proves true; He is a shield to those who take refuge in Him.'

**Acknowledge** –Lord, Your word is truth.

**Confess** – Lord, forgive me when I doubt the accuracy of Your word.

**Thanksgiving** – Lord, I thank You for Your words of truth that we can rely on.

**Prayer** – Lord, I pray for a deeper insight into Your, Holy, Inspired, Inerrant Word.

# Day 314

Psalm 119:169 May my cry come before You, Lord; give me understanding according to Your word.

HAVE YOU NOTICED THAT DAVID, A MAN AFTER GOD'S HEART, DOES a lot of crying out to God? Today he is crying to God for Godly understanding. David had a pretty good handle on understanding according to human judgment, but he wanted much more. He wanted understanding according to God's word. This is another example of how David trusted God's word and believed it to be true. Otherwise, he would not be asking for understanding from it. But why would David ask for understanding from God's word? God's word enlightens us to God and His righteousness. It draws us to Him and produces obedience in our lives. The Prophet Hosea wrote in Hosea 14:9, 'Whoever is wise, let him understand these things; whoever is discerning, let him know them. For the ways of the Lord are right, and the righteous will walk in them, but transgressors will stumble in them.' Just as the Prophet Hosea wrote, there are many intelligent people who are wise to the ways of the world, but stumble over the word of God. They don't understand how God sent His Son to die for their sins and offer them eternal life. Others choose to ignore it or discount that there is even a God. But God rewards those who trust and earnestly seek Him. Proverbs 3:13 says, 'Blessed is the one who finds wisdom, and the one who gets understanding.' We have learned that Godly understanding produces obedience and blessings in our lives; it also helps us distinguish between right and wrong choices. Not only that, it guides us to distinguish between better and best choices. 1 Corinthians 2:10 says, 'But God has revealed it to us by His Spirit. The Spirit searches all things, even the deep things of God.' What type of understanding are you searching for? Are you satisfied with worldly knowledge and understanding or are you like David, seeking the understanding that comes from God and His Word? As Matthew 6:33 tells us, 'But seek first His kingdom and His righteousness, and all these things will be given to you as well.'

**Acknowledge** –Lord, Your word enlightens us.

**Confess** – Lord, forgive me for seeking worldly wisdom over Godly wisdom.

**Thanksgiving** – Lord, thank You for rewarding me with Godly wisdom.

**Prayer** – Lord, give me understanding according to Your word.

# Day 315

Psalm 119:172 May my tongue sing Your word, for all Your commands are righteous.

THE KING JAMES VERSION OF THIS VERSE READS, 'MY TONGUE SHALL speak of thy word: for all thy commandments are righteousness.' Using either translation, it is clear that David doesn't have any trouble proclaiming God's righteousness. Outside of church how much do we speak about God and His word? For me, it is very easy to talk about grandchildren, a sporting event, or something posted on social media. At work, my conversations tend to be about business or something related to it. I may even be brave enough to talk about politics with a neighbor. But where do my conversations about God fit in? Why is it difficult to transition my conversation with someone to the love of God? Can you relate? God has strategically placed you around someone who needs to hear from Him. You have developed a relationship with that person, but seem to hit a brick wall when it comes to discussing spiritual topics. God's word has some help for us when that happens. Paul writing in Colossians 4:5-6 said, 'Be wise in the way you act toward outsiders; make the most of every opportunity. Let your conversation be always full of grace, seasoned with salt, so that you may know how to answer everyone.' Earlier in Colossians 4:2 he said, 'Devote yourselves to prayer, being watchful and thankful.' First, pray for the opportunities God gives you. Ask Him to make you alert to really hear what someone tells you. Begin by asking questions to help lead the conversation towards God. Paul said to 'season your conversation with salt.' Salt adds flavor and preserves our words. Use words that the person can relate to, not the King James Bible Version. Always be full of grace. In other words, we need to have the same compassion and love for that person as God does. If we truly love and care for them, we can offer the hope of Jesus Christ. Start today by carefully listening to what someone is telling you. Ask God to help you lead the conversation to where that person can see Him. Choose words that show you care. Let God do the rest.

**Acknowledge** –Lord, I need to speak Your word to others.

**Confess** – Lord, forgive me for the missed opportunities to share Your word.

**Thanksgiving** – Lord, thank You for leading me to people who need help.

**Prayer** – Lord, give me the confidence to share Your word with others.

# Day 316

Psalm 120:1 I call on the Lord in my distress, and He answers me.

WHAT IS THE ONLY ADVANTAGE OF HAVING TROUBLE IN OUR LIVES? It makes us, like David, call on God for help. What is even better than calling on God? He hears our prayers and answers them. Jonah, who we have talked about before, is a good example of someone who found himself in a big mess. It is one that he created for himself by disobeying God's call to go to Nineveh to preach repentance. Jonah 2:1-2 says, 'From inside the fish Jonah prayed to the Lord his God, He said: "In my distress I called to the Lord, and He answered me. From the depths of the grave I called for help and You listened to my cry."' While our problems may seem impossible to us, I think it would be hard to top being fish bait. Isn't it comforting to learn that God heard him in the midst of his trouble? Better yet, God didn't tell Jonah, "You got yourself into this mess, you can get yourself out." God delivered Jonah out of a seemingly impossible situation. If God can deliver Jonah out of the belly of a large fish, He should have no problem delivering you from any situation you are in. However, there is more to Jonah's story. God didn't deliver Jonah the first day he landed in the fish's belly. Jonah was inside it for three days. This should remind us that God's timing is completely different from ours. When I ask God for help, I want it right away. I want my circumstances to change immediately or at least start to get better. Although it is a difficult lesson to learn, God may be teaching us patience and how to carry on despite our circumstances. On the other hand, do we fail to call on God when there is trouble in our lives? Are we too ashamed to ask for His help because of the mess we have made of life? God loves you no matter how bad you have messed up. Call on Him in your distress and wait for Him to answer you. You will not be disappointed.

**Acknowledge** –Lord, You hear me when I call out to You.

**Confess** – Lord, forgive me for the mess I have made of my life.

**Thanksgiving** – Lord, thank You that I can call out to You.

**Prayer** – Lord, my life is in a mess, please help me.

# Day 317

**Psalm 120:2 Save me, Lord, from lying lips and from deceitful tongues.**

SADLY, NOT MUCH HAS CHANGED IN 3,000 YEARS. IN FACT, LYING AND slander seem to be the norm rather than the exception. Unfortunately, it will continue to get worse until Christ returns because of Satan and his attempts to deceive and turn us away from God. Jesus speaking to the Pharisees in John 4:44-45 said, "You belong to your father, the devil, and you want to carry out your father's desire. He was a murderer from the beginning, not holding the truth, for there is no truth in him. When he lies, he speaks his native language, for he is a liar and the father of lies. Yet because I tell the truth, you do not believe me!" Jesus called Satan the father of lies. There is no truth in him. From the very beginning of time, Satan has used lies and deception to cause man to fall away from God. In Genesis 3:4 we find the serpent talking to Eve, 'But the serpent said to the woman, "You will not surely die."' God had told Adam and Eve they could eat from any tree in the Garden of Eden except from the tree of the knowledge of good and evil. Genesis 4:17 says, 'But you must not eat from the tree of the knowledge of good and evil for when you eat of it you will surely die.' What type of lies is Satan using to turn your heart away from God? Is he telling you that you are not good enough to be a Christian? Or maybe he told you that it won't hurt to try something you know is wrong this one time. Then the next time, he says, 'that wasn't so bad was it? Nothing happened, you should try it again.' Or my favorite, 'no one will ever find out what you are doing, besides it isn't hurting anybody.' We have to be alert at all times. The devil knows our weak spots and will use them to turn us away from God. Paul writing in Ephesians 6:11 said, 'Put on the whole armor of God, that you may be able to stand against the schemes of the devil.'

**Acknowledge** –Lord, the devil is the father of all lies.

**Confess** – Lord, forgive me when I fall for the devil's lies.

**Thanksgiving** – Lord, thank You for providing armor so I can stand against the schemes of the devil.

**Prayer** – Lord, help me to be alert to the devil's lies.

# Day 318

Psalm 121:1-2 I lift up my eyes to the hills – where does my help come from? My help comes from the Lord, the Maker of heaven and earth.

The Book of Psalms has been the inspiration for a number of contemporary Christian songs. Today's verse is a great example of that. The Brooklyn Tabernacle Choir sings a song written by Esther David entitled, "My Help (Cometh From The Lord)" which was taken directly from Psalm 121. In verse one David asks a great question, "I lift up my eyes to the hills–where does my help come from?" It is a question that we should ask ourselves as well. Where do you look for help? David said he looked up to the hills. What was so special about looking at them? It may have been that the City of Jerusalem was built on a hill. The temple where the presence of God dwelt was on a hill in the city. Perhaps David was looking towards the area of the temple since he declared his help comes from the Lord. However, that hill has little or no meaning for you or me. Is there another hill we should look to? Outside the city gates of Jerusalem sits another hill. We find mention of it in John 19:17-18, 'Carrying His own cross, He went to the place of the Skull (which in Aramaic is called Golgotha). Here they crucified Him, and with Him two others – one on each side and Jesus in the middle.' You may recognize this place as Mount Calvary. When we look to this hill, we see the cross of Jesus Christ. It is on this hill Jesus suffered and died for our sins. This hill represents forgiveness and reconciliation. But most importantly, it represents hope. To a lost and dying world it offers the hope of salvation. To a Christian, it offers the hope of a risen Savior who has promised to never leave us or forsake us. What problems are you facing today? Do they seem insurmountable? If so, look to the hill of Mount Calvary where Jesus died for you. Thank Him for His love for you. Let His presence calm your troubled spirit.

**Acknowledge** –Lord, my help comes from You.

**Confess** – Lord, forgive me when I look to worldly solutions for my problems.

**Thanksgiving** – Lord, thank You for climbing the hill to Golgotha.

**Prayer** – Lord, help me to look towards the right hill for help.

# Day 319

Psalm 122:1 I rejoiced with those who said to me, 'Let us go to the house of the Lord.'

DAVID WAS EXCITED ABOUT GOING TO CHURCH. SINCE HE WAS rejoicing with others who said let's go, it doesn't appear that he was alone. I can imagine a packed church with people ready to worship and eager to hear the word of God. Sadly, that is not the case today. COVID-19 has impacted the way we worship and attend church. During the pandemic, most churches began offering worship services via live streaming or a video version on their website. Once churches began to reopen, most did by limiting their attendance to less than one half their seating capacity to meet social distancing guidelines. During this time, many people got out of the habit of going to church. They began to enjoy the convenience of watching a sermon from their house, and not having to get the family ready to go to church. However, meeting and worshiping together is still important. Hebrews 10:24-25 says, 'And let us consider how we may spur one another on toward love and good deeds. Let us not give up meeting together, as some are in the habit of doing, but let us encourage one another – and all the more as you see the Day approaching.' And Matthew 18:20 says, 'For where two or three come together in My name, there am I with them.' Besides the fact that God tells us we should worship together, there are benefits for gathering with other believers. Most importantly, it connects us with God. While we may have some spiritual moments at home, it is not all the time. However, walking into church puts us in a place where the primary focus is on God. It draws our attention to Him. Next, it connects us with other people who have the same type of struggles we have. But it also connects us with people who desire to worship and learn more about our Lord and Savior. Lastly, it provides the opportunity for us to give back to others with our time, talents, and money. Don't give up on church. It has a lot to offer you. Invite someone to go with you.

**Acknowledge** – Lord, I was glad when they said to me, let us go to the house of the Lord.

**Confess** – Lord, forgive me for not attending church.

**Thanksgiving** – Lord, thank You for Your church.

**Prayer** – Lord, I need to be in church. Help me to invite someone to go with me.

# Day 320

**Psalm 121:8** The Lord will watch over your coming and going both now and forevermore.

INVENTIONS SUCH AS THE TRAIN, AUTOMOBILE AND AIRPLANE HAVE improved our ability to travel much further and much quicker than ever before and people are taking advantage of them. The FAA reports that every day there are approximately 2.9 million airline passengers. (www.faa.gov) That is a lot of coming and going. Isn't it reassuring to know that God watches over our travels? However, there is another coming and going that God watches over. He watches over us from the cradle to the grave, and everywhere in between. We were no surprise to God when our mother gave birth to us. Nor is He surprised when we take our last breath here on earth. He watches over us and has a plan for our lives. Ephesians 2:10 tells us, 'For we are God's workmanship, created in Christ Jesus to do good works, which God prepared in advance for us to do.' So, what are you doing with the time you have between your coming and going? Are you trusting God and obeying Him? Or, are you on a rebellious path of wanting to do things your way? In Deuteronomy 28:1-2,6 we read that God promises His blessings for obedience, 'If you fully obey the Lord your God and carefully follow all His commands I give you today, the Lord your God will set you high above all the nations on earth. All these blessings will come upon you and accompany you if you obey the Lord your God: You will be blessed when you come in and blessed when you go out.' I heard someone say that each new day brings us one day closer to our last day. As you grow older, every new day becomes even more precious because you may not have many more. My advice to you is to not waste your days on things that do not have eternal value. Don't get to your last day only to look back wishing you had done things much differently. Start living like today is your last day. God promises to bless you and keep watch over you if you follow Him no matter how many days you have.

**Acknowledge** – Lord, You watch over our coming and our going.

**Confess** – Lord, forgive me for wasting my days on things that have no eternal value.

**Thanksgiving** – Lord, thank You for watching over me.

**Prayer** – Lord, I pray for Your blessings over my coming in and going out.

# Day 321

Psalm 123:1 I lift up my eyes to You, to You whose throne is in heaven.

On Day 318 David wrote, 'I lift up my eyes to the hills' and asked 'where does my help come from.' Today we find him fixing his eyes towards a higher place than the hills, to the very throne of God. Usually when Vivian and I go to the beach, she enjoys walking while I prefer to hunt for sharks' teeth along the edge of the water. As I am walking, my eyes are focused downward looking for anything black and shiny resembling a shark's tooth. There are shells and small stones that have the same color and shape, but are not sharks' teeth. I have bent down and picked up many shells that turned out not to be a shark's tooth. Also, my eyes get so focused downward that I sometimes fail to see someone sitting in the sand right ahead of me. Isn't that like life? We keep looking down, stuck in the routine of life. We search to find anything that can help solve our problems, continuing to pick up things that add no value to our lives. Our eyes get so focused on our problems and the next step in front of us that we fail to see what God has in store for us. With each new step, anxiety and helplessness begin to take over our thoughts. To what do you turn to when this starts to happen? Do you, as David, lift up your eyes to the God who loves you and cares for you? Or are your eyes focused on worldly solutions such as self-help books and advice from friends? Which do you trust more? Jesus speaking in Matthew 11:28 said, "Come unto Me, all you who are weary and burdened, and I will give you rest." Are you ready to find rest and peace from the burdens you are facing? Lift up your eyes to the Lord. Hand your problems to the One who can give you rest and keep your eyes focused on Him. Don't look down and try to take your problems back from Him. Let the peace of God guard your heart and mind.

**Acknowledge** –Lord, You promise rest to the weary.

**Confess** – Lord, forgive me for not looking to You for help.

**Thanksgiving** – Lord, thank You for guarding my heart and mind.

**Prayer** – Lord, I lift my eyes to You, help me find rest in Your presence.

# Day 322

**Psalm 124:8 Our help is in the name of the Lord, the Maker of heaven and earth.**

I THINK IT IS FAIR TO SAY THAT EVERYONE NEEDS HELP AT SOME TIME in their life. When it comes to the finer details about technology, I need help. I need someone who knows more about the subject to give me advice so I don't have to fumble through, trying to figure things out on my own. Without help, I invariably do something that creates a problem that has to be fixed. This has also been the case for several home repair projects I have taken on. Thank goodness for YouTube and the self-help videos that show you how to fix things. In today's verse, David tells us that the Maker of the heavens and the earth is our helper. His name is the Lord. As I mentioned, it helps to have someone who has the knowledge and experience we can trust to help when problems arise. That is why it was so important for Jesus to be born into the world and experience the same life issues we face. He knows what we are going through. He experienced disappointment, rejection, pain, persecution, and hatred. He dealt with the Pharisees who were pious and imposed unrealistic regulations on the people. He felt the pain of betrayal not only by Judas, but of Simon Peter as well. He fed people when they were physically and spiritually hungry. He wept over the death of his dear friend Lazarus and felt anger when the House of God was turned into a market. Suppose God had chosen another way for us to receive salvation without having to send Jesus to die on the cross. Would any of those ways have as much meaning to us? Hebrews 4:15-16 says, 'For we do not have a high priest who is unable to sympathize with our weaknesses, but we have one who has been tempted in every way, just as we are – yet was without sin. Let us then approach the throne of grace with confidence, so that we may receive mercy and find grace to help us in our time of need.' We have a God we can trust and has been where we are. Don't wait until you really mess things up, reach out to the Maker of heaven and earth for help.

**Acknowledge** –Lord, our help is in Your name.

**Confess** – Lord, forgive me when I forget Your sacrifice for me.

**Thanksgiving** – Lord, thank You for going before us.

**Prayer** – Lord, never let me forget that my help is in You.

# Day 323

> Psalm 125:1 Those who trust in the Lord are like Mount Zion, which cannot be shaken but endures forever.

David tells us that those who trust in the Lord are like Mount Zion. I really don't know much about Mount Zion and think it would be helpful to learn why he is making that comparison. In David's day, Mount Zion was the name of the hill that the City of Jerusalem was built upon. However, the name was also interchangeable with the City of Jerusalem and means the place where Yahweh dwells. Isaiah 8:18 says, 'Here am I, and the children the Lord has given me. We are signs and symbols in Israel from the Lord Almighty, who dwells on Mount Zion.' As Isaiah points out, God dwells on Mount Zion and David said we are like Mount Zion. What does this tell us? When we trust God as our Savior, God begins to dwell in us. 1 Corinthians 3:16 says, 'Do you not know that you are a temple of God and that the Spirit of God dwells in you?' Not only that, when God begins to dwell in us, He never leaves. Joshua 1:5 tells us, 'No one will be able to stand against you all the days of your life. As I was with Moses, so I will be with you; I will never leave you nor forsake you.' With God living in us, we should look to His strength when the storms of life come our way. 2 Timothy 1:7 says, 'For the Spirit God gave us does not make us timid, but gives us power, love and self-discipline.' We can live each day with the confidence of having the Holy Spirit working inside us. The prophet Jeremiah 17:7-8 said it this way, 'Blessed is the man who trusts in the Lord, whose trust is the Lord. He is like a tree planted by water, that sends out its roots by the stream, and does not fear when heat comes, for its leaves remain green, and is not anxious in the year of drought, for it does not cease to bear fruit.' Live with confidence each day knowing that God is with you every step of the way.

**Acknowledge** –Lord, those that trust in You are like Mount Zion.

**Confess** – Lord, forgive me for not trusting You through the storms of life.

**Thanksgiving** – Lord, thank You for dwelling in me.

**Prayer** – Lord, the more I trust You, the stronger I become. Help me to grow my trust.

# Day 324

Psalm 126:5 Those who sow with tears will reap with songs of joy.

DAVID USES A PICTURE OF FARMING TO DESCRIBE THE REALITIES OF life. This summer we laid off a small area in my daughter's back yard for a garden. My granddaughter, Brynlee, was so excited about the prospects of planting various vegetables and watching them grow. However, she also learned there was work involved in a garden. It had to be watered. Weeds had to be pulled. Even though she doesn't like them, she was so proud when the first tomato appeared. David tells us that our sowing may be with tears. In other words, life is hard. We go through difficult seasons in our life when we feel like giving up. During those times we would rather go home, close the door, and not come out until things are better. However, David said these are the times when we need to keep going, keep planting seeds because there will be joy at the end of the harvest. Paul writing in Galatians 6:7-9 talks about sowing and reaping, 'Do not be deceived: God cannot be mocked. A man reaps what he sows. The one who sows to please his sinful nature, from that nature will reap destruction; the one who sows to please the Spirit, from the Spirit will reap eternal life. Let us not become weary in doing good, for at the proper time we will reap a harvest if we do not give up.' What kind of seeds are you sowing? Are you sowing selfish seeds or are you sowing seeds of goodness? Paul also gives us one more piece of knowledge about sowing seeds in 2 Corinthians 9:6, 'Remember this: Whoever sows sparingly will also reap sparingly, and whoever sows generously will also reap generously.' No matter what type of seeds we sow, how we sow them makes a big difference in the reaping. Don't let the difficulties of day to day life hinder you from sowing seeds. Sow the seeds of love, joy, peace, kindness, goodness, faithfulness, gentleness and self-control and experience the unspeakable joy that comes with the harvest.

**Acknowledge** –Lord, we reap what we sow.

**Confess** – Lord, forgive me for letting the daily struggles of life hinder me from sowing seeds.

**Thanksgiving** – Lord, thank You for the joy that comes with the harvest.

**Prayer** – Lord, when life starts crashing in, help me to sow through the tears.

# Day 325

Psalm 127:1 Unless the Lord builds the house, the builders labor in vain.

WHEN OUR HOUSE WAS BEING BUILT, WE INVOLVED OUR ENTIRE family in writing their favorite Bible verses on the framing of the house. Underneath the sheetrock of every room is at least one Bible verse. Our desire was for God to be the builder of our home. We wanted the word of God to surround us and protect our home from the attacks of Satan. In Genesis 11:1-9 we find the story of the Tower of Babel. After the flood, Noah and his family began to multiply. The whole world had one language and settled together. Verse 4 says, 'Then they said, "Come, let us build ourselves a city, with a tower that reaches to the heavens, so that we may make a name for ourselves and not be scattered over the face of the earth."' Notice they didn't include God in their building plans. They used phrases such as; 'let us' and 'so that we.' Verse 8 tells us what happened to their great plans, 'So the Lord scattered them from there all over the earth, and they stopped building the city.' In today's verse, a house can represent more than just our home. First, it represents our relationship with God. Each one of us is a temple of the Holy Spirit. Is God the foundation of our faith? Have we allowed Him to build and grow our faith in Him? Next, God should be the head and builder of our home. Do we have family devotions? Is God's word taught in our homes? If not, what type of building are we constructing? Lastly, God should be the head and builder of our country. Sadly, we have pushed God out of our government to where His Word is hardly recognized. 1 Corinthians 3:12-13 says, 'If any man builds on this foundation using gold, silver, costly stones, wood, hay or straw, his work will be shown for what it is, because the day will bring it to light. It will be revealed with fire, and the fire will test the quality of each man's work.' What type of building materials are you using?

**Acknowledge** –Lord, unless You build our house, our work is in vain.

**Confess** – Lord, forgive me for not including You in my building plans.

**Thanksgiving** – Lord, thank You for Your firm foundation in my life.

**Prayer** – Lord, help me to build my house on Your firm foundation.

# Day 326

> Psalm 127:3,5 Children are a heritage from the Lord, offspring a reward from Him. Blessed is the man whose quiver is full of them. They will not be put to shame when they contend with their opponents in court.

Solomon tells us that children are a reward from God, a blessing to the man who has a house full. Vivian and I felt like our quiver was full with two, but thankfully our children have added five grandchildren to our family. However, it breaks my heart to hear about unborn children whose lives have been ended by abortion and will never get the chance to bless someone's family. God doesn't give children to be a burden to us. They are our inheritance. However, raising children is not easy nor should be taken lightly. Each have their own unique personalities that require different approaches for teaching them. I quickly learned that my children's interests were much different from the ones I had when I was growing up. The good news is that God has given us instructions on how to raise our families. The Book of Proverbs has several verses that teach us about raising children. Perhaps the most important is Proverbs 20:7, 'The righteous man leads a blameless life; blessed are his children after him.' Children watch and imitate their parents. If they see you putting God first, praying, reading your Bible, and making church a priority, the more likely they will model your behavior. However, you must be very careful because they see you every day. What do you teach them if they hear you say one thing and do just the opposite? Be a godly leader in your home by giving them someone to imitate. Another verse is Proverbs 22:6, 'Train a child in the way he should go, and when he is old he will not turn from it.' Children are naturally inclined to go their own way. If we are modeling and teaching them to walk in the path of righteousness, their inclination will be to respond and act in that way. That is not to say our children will not rebel and go down a path of disobedience, but God's word tells us they will turn back to Him.

**Acknowledge** – Lord, children are a blessing from You.

**Confess** – Lord, forgive me for not doing a better job of modeling You to my children.

**Thanksgiving** – Lord, thank You for my children and grandchildren.

**Prayer** – Lord, help me to train my children and grandchildren in the way they should go.

# Day 327

Psalm 128:1-2 Blessed are all who fear the Lord, who walk in obedience to Him. You will eat the fruit of your labor; blessings and prosperity will be yours.

BLESSINGS OR HAPPINESS FOLLOW THOSE WHO WALK IN OBEDIENCE to God's word. We have learned that obedience is not a list of do's and don'ts. It is all about our relationship with God and the desire to follow Him. Jesus speaking in Mark 12:30-31 clearly tells us what obedience looks like, "Love the Lord your God with all your heart and with all your soul and with all your mind and with all your strength. The second is this: Love your neighbor as yourself." Our obedience comes down to loving God and loving people. Jesus also said in Luke 11:28, "Blessed rather are those who hear the word of God and obey it." So, it is more than just hearing God's word, it is a matter of putting it into practice. We demonstrate the love of God by treating others with kindness and looking for opportunities to help someone. It could be as simple as giving an encouraging word to someone, or taking the time to listen to someone share their problems. It could be helping a neighbor with yardwork, or looking after their children for an hour. Paul writing in 1 Corinthians 15:58 said, 'Therefore, my dear brothers, stand firm. Let nothing move you. Always give yourselves fully to the work of the Lord, because you know that your labor in the Lord is not in vain.' Paul tells us that serving the Lord by helping others is not a waste of time. David testifies that blessings and prosperity will be ours. His blessings may not be dollars in our pockets, but something more lasting and fulfilling. Isaiah 1:19 says, 'If you are willing and obedient, you will eat the best from the land.' What does 'eat from the best of the land' mean to you? I interpret it as a generous portion of God's blessing of satisfaction, contentment, and peace. Have you tasted of God's blessings lately? What, could taste better or be better for you?

**Acknowledge** –Lord, blessed are those who walk in obedience to You.

**Confess** – Lord, forgive me when I fail to love others as You have commanded.

**Thanksgiving** – Lord, thank You for the opportunity to help others.

**Prayer** – Lord, help me to never stop looking for opportunities to share Your love with someone.

# Day 328

Psalm 129:4 But the Lord is righteous; He has cut me free from the cords of the wicked.

When I was in Middle School, there were a couple of kids in my class that I got to know and become friends with. However, it did not take long for me to learn that they were doing some things that I knew were wrong. Their acceptance and friendship were important, but I also knew that I didn't want to get involved with the things they were doing. They were very friendly and the pull to fit in with them was very strong. Because I knew what they were doing was wrong, I would make up excuses for not being able to hang out with them. Regrettably, I wasn't bold enough to tell them they needed God in their lives. I was stuck in the middle of trying to fit in with them and holding on to what I knew was right and wrong. For any teenager, the lure to fit in can be overwhelming and costly. Fortunately for me, our classes got changed and I was moved to a different class. After that, I didn't see those guys as much and began to hang out with some kids from our Youth Group. I often wonder where I would have wound up had I continued down the path I was headed. Would I have gone with the crowd or would I have tried to witness to them? Paul writing in 1 Corinthians 15:33 says, 'Do not be misled: Bad company corrupts good character.' How true that is. We need to be careful who we spend our time with. More often than not, their behavior influences us to be like them. Proverbs 22:24-25 says, 'Do not make friends with a hot-tempered man, do not associate with one easily angered, or you may learn his ways and get yourself ensnared.' I do believe that it was God's hand at work moving our classes around when I was in Middle School. He cut me free from the guys who were leading me down a wrong path. God can do the same for you. Ask Him to cut you free from the cords of those who are leading you down the wrong path.

**Acknowledge** –Lord, bad company corrupts good character.

**Confess** – Lord, forgive me for getting entangled with the wrong crowd.

**Thanksgiving** – Lord, thank You for rescuing me from the cords of the wicked.

**Prayer** – Lord, help me to get close enough to share Your forgiveness with others.

# Day 329

**Psalm 130:1-2** Out of the depths I cry to You, Lord; Lord, hear my voice. Let Your ears be attentive to my cry for mercy.

THIS IS NOT THE FIRST VERSE WE HAVE READ WHERE THE PSALMIST is crying out for God to hear his plea. We have already learned that God hears our cry and answers our prayer. However, it doesn't hurt to be reminded that God loves us and hears our cries. Today's verse reminded me of the story of Bartimaeus found in Mark 10:46-52. The thing that caught my attention is the part where the Psalmist asks the Lord to 'be attentive to my cry for mercy.' As a blind man, Bartimaeus' sense of hearing was likely enhanced to compensate for his loss of sight. He relied heavily on being able to hear people as they drew near so he could beg for money or food from them. On this day as he was sitting by the roadside, like he did every day of his life, he heard something different. Verse 47-48 says, 'When he heard that it was Jesus of Nazareth, he began to shout, "Jesus, Son of David, have mercy on me!" Many rebuked him and told him to be quiet, but he shouted all the more, "Son of David, have mercy on me!"' Can you picture Bartimaeus, unable to see what is going on, shouting for Jesus to have mercy on him? People around him are telling him to be quiet, he is just a blind, useless individual, not worth Jesus' time. Bartimaeus had two choices: believe the crowd, sit back down, be quiet and remain a blind beggar the rest of his life, or he could cry out even louder in hopes that Jesus would hear and heal him. Bartimaeus chose hope, he didn't want to live in blindness the rest of his life. What are you facing today that you need Jesus' help? Like Bartimaeus, you have two choices. You can be quiet and continue to suffer, or you can cry out even louder to Him. He will hear your cry for help and answer your prayer. Which one do you choose?

**Acknowledge** – Lord, You hear our cries for help.

**Confess** – Lord, forgive me for not trusting You.

**Thanksgiving** – Lord, thank You for hearing and healing Bartimaeus.

**Prayer** – Lord, help me to be bold like Bartimaeus and trust You to answer my cry for help.

# Day 330

Psalm 130:3 If You, Lord, kept a record of sins, Lord, who could stand?

BEFORE COMPUTERS, BUSINESS RECORDS WERE KEPT IN A LEDGER. Every transaction was recorded. At the end of the month, the books were tallied to provide a record for the month, and ensure the records were in balance. Before coming to know Jesus as my Lord and Savior, I envisioned God sitting on His throne, watching over the earth. Every time I did something wrong, I would get a 'tick' mark in His giant ledger book. I told a story, and bam, I get a 'tick' mark. I was mean to my sister, another 'tick' mark. I disobeyed my parents, another 'tick' mark. Pretty soon, I am overwhelmed by the number of 'tick' marks and realize there is no way I can balance the ledger book by offsetting the bad marks with good deeds. As much as I tried, I couldn't keep up. Then I read scriptures like 1 John 1:8 that says, 'If we say we have no sin, we deceive ourselves, and the truth is not in us.' Or Romans 3:23 that says, 'For all have sinned and fall short of the glory of God.' I thought I might as well give up, because there was no way I could impress God by trying to balance out my sins by being good. Then I read Ephesians 2:8-9 which turned my life around, 'For it is by grace you have been saved, through faith – and this not from yourselves, it is the gift of God – not by works, so that no one can boast.' What a relief. My relationship with God wasn't based on the good things I did. It was through His grace or unearned favor that I could be saved. Better yet, when we ask God to forgive our sins, He does and goes one step further. Isaiah 43:25 says, 'I, even I, am He who blots out your transgressions, for My own sake, and remembers your sins no more.' Aren't you glad God doesn't keep a giant ledger book on your shortcomings? Have you asked Him into your life and to forgive you of your sins? Trust Him today, He is faithful to forgive and remember our sins no more.

**Acknowledge** –Lord, You remember our sins no more.

**Confess** – Lord, forgive me for trying to impress You with good deeds to hide my sins.

**Thanksgiving** – Lord, thank You for forgiveness.

**Prayer** – Lord, I need Your forgiveness every day.

# Day 331

Psalm 131:1 My heart is not proud, Lord, my eyes are not haughty; I do not concern myself with great matters or things too wonderful for me.

A FAMILIAR CREDIT CARD COMMERCIAL ASKS THE QUESTION, 'What's in your wallet?' David takes aim at the heart today and declares that humility and contentment are in his. Before we rush to judgment about the condition of David's heart, let's learn more about the heart. Jeremiah 17:9 says, 'The heart is deceitful above all things and beyond cure. Who can understand it?' And Matthew 15:19 says, 'For out of the heart come evil thoughts, murder, adultery, sexual immorality, theft, false testimony, slander.' These things do not leave much room in our hearts for humility and contentment. However, Jesus speaking in Luke 6:45 said, 'The good man brings good things out of the good stored up in his heart, and the evil man brings evil things out of the evil stored up in his heart. For out of the overflow of his heart his mouth speaks.' Jesus tells us there are two types of hearts. One where good is stored up and one where evil is stored up. How do we obtain a good heart? 2 Corinthians 5:17 tells us, 'Therefore, if anyone is in Christ, he is a new creation; the old has gone, the new has come.' And Ezekiel 11:19 says, 'I will give them an undivided heart and put a new spirit in them; I will remove from them their heart of stone and give them a heart of flesh.' In other words, when we accept Christ as our Savior, He performs heart surgery on us. He takes away the arrogance and evil thoughts and replaces them with humility and contentment. His Holy Spirit moves into our hearts to teach and guide us. John 14:26 says, 'But the Counselor, the Holy Spirit, whom the Father will send in my name, will teach you all things and will remind you of everything I have said to you.' Are you struggling with the things that are going on in your heart? Is there a battle between good and evil? Ask God to fill your heart with His Holy Spirit. Allow Him to guide you and enjoy the peace and contentment He gives.

**Acknowledge** –Lord, You give us an undivided heart.

**Confess** – Lord, forgive me for allowing Satan to control my thoughts.

**Thanksgiving** – Lord, thank You for Your Holy Spirit who lives in us.

**Prayer** – Lord, come into my life today. Fill me with Your Holy Spirit.

# Day 332

> Psalm 132:13 For the Lord has chosen Zion, He has desired it for His dwelling.

ON DAY 323 WE READ THAT THOSE WHO TRUST IN THE LORD ARE like Mount Zion. As believers, His Holy Spirit dwells in us and will never leave us. However, there is another dimension to Zion that we will look at today. 1 Peter 2:4-6 says, 'As you come to Him, the Living Stone – rejected by men but chosen by God and precious to Him – you also, like living stones, are being built into a spiritual house to be a holy priesthood, offering spiritual sacrifices acceptable to God through Jesus Christ. For in the Scripture it says: "See, I lay a stone in Zion, a chosen and precious cornerstone, and the one who trusts in Him will never be put to shame."' Peter identifies Jesus Christ as a living stone. Stones have no life, so how can Peter make the comparison to Jesus as a stone? Jesus died and was buried, but rose from the grave on the third day. Jesus, rejected by people, was chosen by God to be the cornerstone, the most valuable stone, on which to build His kingdom. Because He is the resurrected, living stone, we can have a personal relationship with Him. Peter calls those who trust in God, building blocks in His kingdom. As building blocks, we are being used to build a spiritual house. In other words, we are God's temple and a part of His family. We find that our lives have purpose and meaning if our foundation is Jesus Christ, the cornerstone of God's church. However, if our faith is in anything else, the cornerstone meant to be our foundation will become a stumbling block. 1 Peter 2:7-8 says, 'Now to you who believe, this stone is precious. But to those who do not believe, "The stone the builders rejected has become the capstone", and, "A stone that causes men to stumble and a rock that makes them fall." They stumble because they disobey the message – which is also what they were destined for.' Is Jesus Christ the foundation or stumbling block of your life? Trust Him today to develop you into His spiritual house.

**Acknowledge** – Lord, Your Son, Jesus Christ is the cornerstone on which Your kingdom is built.

**Confess** – Lord, forgive me for not having a deeper relationship with You.

**Thanksgiving** – Lord, thank You for the purpose and meaning You add to my life.

**Prayer** – Lord, help me to be a spiritual building block for Your kingdom.

# Day 333

Psalm 133:1 How good and pleasant it is when God's people live together in unity!

DAVID TELLS US THAT LIVING IN UNITY IS BOTH GOOD AND PLEASANT. However, it is easier said than done even within a group of believers. Throughout the years I have witnessed churches that have split over the most insignificant things; such as, changing the color of the carpet. Our opinion, pride, and personal interests can sometimes take over and affect our relationship with others. Add to our selfish desires, the daily pressures of life and stress which can put a strain on relationships causing simple disagreements to turn into ugly arguments. Ugly arguments open the door to hurt feelings and broken relationships. We end up hurting each other and ruining any unity we may have had. 1 Peter 5:8 says, 'Be self-controlled and alert. Your enemy the devil prowls around like a roaring lion looking for someone to devour.' The devil wants no more than to cause division among us. However, God has called His people to live in unity. Paul writing in 1 Corinthians 1:10 said, 'I appeal to you, brothers, in the name of our Lord Jesus Christ, that all of you agree with one another so that there may be no divisions among you and that you may be perfectly united in mind and thought.' Paul tells us that we should agree with one another and be united in mind and thought and not fight over the color of the carpet. With so many opinions and ideas, how do we come to an agreement with each other? Philippians 2:3 says, 'Do nothing out of selfish ambition or vain conceit, but in humility consider others better than yourselves.' Unity requires humility. We must put others ahead of ourselves. Ephesians 4:2-3 says, 'Be completely humble and gentle; be patient, bearing with one another in love. Make every effort to keep the unity of the Spirit through the bond of peace.' We see that word 'humility' again in Ephesians. Paul goes on to say it takes work to keep unity. However, it is worth the effort if we trust David's words today. Seek unity and find out how good and pleasant it is.

**Acknowledge** –Lord, it is good and pleasant when Your people live in unity.

**Confess** – Lord, forgive me for not humbling myself for the sake of unity.

**Thanksgiving** – Lord, thank You for teaching me how-to live-in unity with others.

**Prayer** – Lord, help me to do nothing out of selfish ambition.

## Day 334

**Psalm 134:2** Lift up your hands in the sanctuary and praise the Lord.

DAVID DOESN'T HOLD BACK HIS WORSHIP OF THE LORD. WE HAVE seen him dancing for 'joy before the Lord,' bowing before the Lord, playing songs, shouting praise, and lifting his hands in the sanctuary. This doesn't sound like your traditional Baptist Church service. However, as we have learned God honors all types of worship as long as it is genuine and directed to Him. Worship means to honor or praise God. He desires our worship. 1 Chronicles 16:29 says, 'Ascribe to the Lord the glory due His name. Bring an offering and come before Him; worship the Lord in the splendor of His holiness.' Worship is more than just singing praise and worship songs. It is one of the reasons we were created. Isaiah 43:21 tells us, 'The people I formed for myself that they may proclaim my praise.' Why is lifting hands an important part of worship to David? First, worship involves more than just our hearts and minds. It also involves our physical body and the posture we take. Kneeling, standing, hands outstretched towards heaven, clapping our hands, lying prostrate before Him, head bowed, eyes closed, or eyes open and lifted towards heaven are just some of the ways our body participates in worship. The lifting of hands can take on several meanings. When we raise both hands towards heaven, we are lifting our lives in surrender to Him. We drop whatever we are holding and surrender our lives to Jesus. Another aspect of lifting hands is that it brings us closer to the Father. Our outstretched hands are reaching to heaven with the praise of our lips following right behind them. Lastly, it helps us focus on the one we are praising. Our hands are not busy doing something else. Whether or not you raise your hands in worship is between you and God. No one should force you to raise your hands. 1 Timothy 2:8 says, 'I want men everywhere to lift up holy hands in prayer, without anger or disputing.' I don't think Paul is saying that it is contrary to God's will for us to pray without lifting our hands, but when we pray with our hands raised, they should be holy.

**Acknowledge** –Lord, You created us to worship You.

**Confess** – Lord, forgive me when my worship is simply going through the motions.

**Thanksgiving** – Lord, thank You for accepting my worship.

**Prayer** – Lord, I lift up holy hands in total praise to You.

# Day 335

Psalm 135:3 Praise the Lord, for the Lord is good; sing praise to His name, for that is pleasant.

How well do you know God? Do you know Him well enough to say, God is good all the time, and all the time God is good? Our God is a good God. But how do we know He is good? First, God's word tells us He is good. Psalm 107:1 says, 'Oh give thanks to the Lord, for He is good, for His steadfast love endures forever.' And Nahum 1:7 says, 'The Lord is good, a stronghold in the day of trouble; He knows those who take refuge in Him.' And Jesus speaking in Mark 10:18 said, "Why do you call me good? No one is good – except God alone." God's word is pretty clear about His goodness. His goodness is a foundation on which we can build our faith and trust. We also experience His goodness every day. Each new day is a gift from God. The air we breathe, the food we eat, the clothes we wear, the place we live are the result of the goodness of God. But what about the times when things start to fall apart in our lives? You lose your job. You get bad news from the doctor. Your child is having problems in school. The list goes on and on. As our problems continue to mount, the goodness of God can seem like a distant memory. Complaining about our circumstances doesn't change anything, it only keeps us chained to them. Holding pity parties with our friends doesn't help. It is in those times we have to look past our circumstances and remember the promises in God's word. Promises like Psalm 23:6 which say, 'Surely goodness and mercy will follow me all the days of my life; and I will dwell in the house of the Lord forever.' Do you remember this promise we studied several months ago? No matter our circumstances, God's goodness and His mercy are with us every day of our life. He is with you in the good times and the bad. Like David, begin to sing praises to Him for His goodness. Allow Him to fill your heart with His promises of goodness.

**Acknowledge** –Lord, You are good all the time.

**Confess** – Lord, forgive me for allowing my circumstances to doubt Your goodness to me.

**Thanksgiving** – Lord, thank You that Your goodness and mercy are following me.

**Prayer** – Lord, help me to rely on the promises of Your word.

# Day 336

Psalm 135:13 Your name, Lord, endures forever, Your renown, Lord, through all generations.

My first car was a 1973 Toyota Corolla which held up long enough to get me through college. By now the metal in it has probably been recycled several times. Since then, I could not tell you how many cars I have owned over the years. They are not made to last forever. In fact, there are only a handful of things that last forever. Today, the Psalmist tells us that God's name will last forever. Closely related to God's name is His word that will also last forever. Isaiah 40:8 says, 'The grass withers and the flowers fall, but the word of our God stands forever.' What God's word said thousands of years ago is just as true and relevant today as when it was written. It will continue to be just as true a thousand years from now. Even in the midst of changes in our world, God's word remains. We can trust it. However, there is another thing that will last forever. It is you and me. While our time on earth is short, our souls will continue to live on. No matter what some scientist may tell you, your soul will live on into eternity. The question is where in eternity will your soul live? Jesus speaking in Matthew 25:36 said, "Then the King will say to those on His right, 'Come, you who are blessed by My Father; take your inheritance, the kingdom prepared for you since the creation of the world.'" Later in verse 41 He said, "Then He will say to those on His left, 'Depart from Me, you who are cursed, into the eternal fire prepared for the devil and his angels.'" The great thing about accepting Christ as your Savior is that eternal life doesn't begin when your physical body dies, it starts the moment He comes into your life. You begin an eternal relationship with God. Have you taken that step into eternity with Him? If not, ask Him to come into your heart today.

**Acknowledge** –Lord, Your name will last forever.

**Confess** – Lord, forgive me when I put my trust into earthly things that don't last.

**Thanksgiving** – Lord, thank You for Your Word that lasts forever.

**Prayer** – Lord, I want to start eternity with You today, come into my heart today.

# Day 337

Psalm 136:1-3 Give thanks to the Lord, for He is good. His love endures forever. Give thanks to the God of gods. His love endures forever. Give thanks to the Lord of lords: His love endures forever.

YESTERDAY WE LEARNED THAT GOD'S NAME, HIS WORD, AND OUR lives will last forever. Today we discover that His love also lasts forever. However, this is not the first time we have read about the enduring love of God in the Psalms. Sometimes though, it helps being reminded that we serve a God whose love never ends. It did not stop when Jesus was nailed to the cross for our sins. Nor did it end when Jesus rose from the grave on the third day. It didn't end when He ascended to heaven in plain view of the disciples some 40 days after His resurrection. His love does not end when you and I disobey Him. His love doesn't end when we try to run and hide from Him. His love doesn't end when life's problems come crashing in on us. His love doesn't end when we are terminally ill. Nor does His love end when we take our final breath. Can you give thanks to the Lord, for His never-ending love? Paul tells us in Romans 8:37-39 that nothing can separate us from the never-ending love of God, 'No, in all things we are more than conquerors through Him who loved us. For I am convinced that neither death nor life, neither angels nor demons, neither the present nor the future, nor any powers, neither height nor depth, nor anything else in all creation, will be able to separate us from the love of God that is in Christ Jesus our Lord.' We did nothing to earn God's love, nor do we deserve it. Just like the shepherd in the parable of the one lost sheep found in Luke 15:1-7, God cares for each of us. If one of us is lost or goes astray, He searches for us until He finds us and brings us back to the fold. As Corey Ashbury's song, "Reckless Love" tells us, God's love is overwhelming, never-ending, and reckless. Thank Him for loving you.

**Acknowledge** –Lord, Your love endures forever.

**Confess** – Lord, forgive me for thinking You don't love me.

**Thanksgiving** – Lord, thank You for searching for the one lost sheep.

**Prayer** – Lord, help me to experience Your never-ending, overwhelming love.

# Day 338

Psalm 136:25 He gives food to every creature. His love endures forever.

According to the Psalmist, God operates the largest feeding program in the world. He provides food to every creature. We have read about God providing manna to the Israelites for 40 years while they were headed to the Promised Land. He also sent enough quail to feed over 2 million people. In Matthew 14:13-21, we find that Jesus fed five thousand men along with women and children with five loaves and two fishes. Not only that, there were 12 basketfuls of broken pieces left over. Later in Matthew 15:29-39, Jesus feeds another four thousand men along with women and children with seven loaves of bread. Afterwards, the disciples collected seven basketfuls of food. In both cases, everyone ate until they were satisfied. Jesus teaching the disciples how to pray in Matthew 6:9-13, included 'Give us today our daily bread.' We can trust God to provide us with food to eat. However, God doesn't stop there with supplying our physical needs with food. He provides us with spiritual food each day. Jesus speaking in John 6:35 said, "I am the bread of life. He who comes to Me will never go hungry, and he who believes in Me will never be thirsty." Are you taking in your daily consumption of God's word? Using devotionals such as this one helps, but it is crumbs compared to reading and consuming God's word straight from the Bible. In John 6:37, Jesus said, "Do not work for food that spoils, but for food that endures to eternal life, which the Son of Man will give you. On Him God the Father has placed His seal of approval." In other words, the spiritual food he provides offers eternal life. On top of that, God has placed His seal of approval on it. God's seal has much more authority and importance than the USDA's seal of approval. Begin today by reading one chapter a day in the Bible. As you read it, make notes on anything that really speaks to you. Put a question mark by something you may not understand. Purchase a study Bible that can help answer your questions. Before you know it, you will be feasting on God's word.

**Acknowledge** –Lord, You give food to every creature.

**Confess** – Lord, forgive me for not taking in Your word on a daily basis.

**Thanksgiving** – Lord, thank You for providing my daily bread.

**Prayer** – Lord, I want to taste of the spiritual food You have to offer.

# Day 339

**Psalm 137:1** By the rivers of Babylon we sat and wept when we remembered Zion.

The Israelites that had not died of starvation or who had not been killed by the Babylonian army were led away into captivity to Babylon. This was a 1,600-mile trip, made on foot and carrying what belongings they could take with them. There they would live under the Babylonian rule for 70 years. They were treated harshly and made to worship the Babylonian gods. The Book of Daniel provides some insight into their captivity there. It was during their captivity when King Nebuchadnezzar made an image of gold that he required everyone to bow and worship. Three of the Jewish captives, Shadrach, Meshach, and Abednego refused to worship the statue and were thrown into a fiery furnace. God delivered them from the fiery furnace because of their faithfulness to Him. However, the captives had to learn to live and adapt to the ways of the Babylonians. Today's verse lets us know they missed their homeland and were homesick for Jerusalem. They had taken a lot of things for granted before they were captured by the Babylonians. They were living in prosperity and had fallen away from their worship of God. They had begun to worship idols and consult mediums and spiritists. (2 Kings 23:24) Because of their disobedience, they now find themselves sitting by the banks of the rivers of Babylon weeping and longing for home. Have we found ourselves in the same place as the Israelites right before they went into captivity? As a Christian, this world is not our home. Heaven is our home. However, like the Israelites, we have drifted into a place of contentment and prosperity. For many, worshiping God has taken a lower priority. We have replaced our worship of God with the worship of ourselves, money, and social status. How long will it be before God takes away the things we are now worshiping instead of Him? What will it take for us to repent and come back to worshiping Him? My prayer is that we don't wait until we find ourselves held captive by our sin, crying on the banks of a river, longing for the presence of God.

**Acknowledge** –Lord, You desire our worship.

**Confess** – Lord, forgive me for allowing other things to take Your place in my life.

**Thanksgiving** – Lord, thank You for drawing us back to You.

**Prayer** – Lord, help me to learn from the mistakes of the Israelites who were put into captivity.

# Day 340

**Psalm 138:2** I will bow down toward Your holy temple and will praise Your name for Your unfailing love and Your faithfulness, for You have so exalted Your solemn decree that surpasses Your fame.

DAVID MAKES THE DECLARATION THAT HE WILL BOW DOWN towards God's holy temple, the place where the presence of God dwelt. He will offer his praise to God's name because of His love and faithfulness and because God's name is above all things. First, let's get an understanding of what bowing down means. When we bow before something or someone, we are humbling ourselves before them recognizing their authority and submitting to it. Growing up in church or at the dinner table, the phrase 'Let's bow our heads in prayer,' was heard all the time. It was a call for everyone to humble themselves before God in preparation for prayer. However, now it seems as if bowing down in worship has become more uncommon. The emphasis tends to be more towards lifting our heads and our hands in worship. There is a place for both, but we should be careful not to neglect humbling ourselves before God. Philippians 2:10-11 tells us, 'That at the name of Jesus every knee should bow, in heaven and on earth and under the earth, and every tongue confess that Jesus Christ is Lord, to the glory of God the Father.' This verse is not talking about a far-off event. Matthew 2:10-11 speaking about the Magi writes, 'When they saw the star, they were overjoyed. On coming to the house, they saw the child with His mother Mary, and they bowed down and worshiped Him. Then they opened their treasures and presented Him with gifts of gold and of incense and of myrrh.' Also, in Mark 5:6 we read about a demon-possessed man who bowed before Jesus, 'When he saw Jesus from a distance, he ran and fell on his knees in front of Him.' As Paul tells us in Philippians, there is coming a day when we will all bow before Jesus. Have you submitted your life to Christ and bowed before Him? Give Him the reverence and honor He deserves for saving your soul.

**Acknowledge** – Lord, Your Name is the Name above all names.

**Confess** – Lord, forgive me for not humbling myself before You.

**Thanksgiving** – Lord, thank You for Your unfailing love and faithfulness.

**Prayer** – Lord, I bow my head in worship and praise Your mighty name.

## Day 341

Psalm 138:7 Though I walk in the midst of trouble, You preserve my life. You stretch out Your hand against the anger of my foes; with Your right hand You save me.

The year 2020 will be remembered by many because of the troubles caused by the Corona Virus and the prolonged presidential election. A saying came out of 2020 for the many problems countless people faced which said, 'I have been 2020'd.' If David were writing this Psalm today, he could have easily said, 'I have been 2020'd,' instead of saying, 'I walk in the midst of trouble.' Troubles come in all shapes and sizes. However, we quickly learn that one size fits all and no one is immune from them. As in the case of Jacob and his brother Esau found in Genesis 27, we can create problems for ourselves. Jacob, the younger brother, deceived his father Isaac by pretending to be Esau, to steal the blessing of the first born from him. Genesis 27:41 says, 'Esau held a grudge against his brother Jacob because of the blessing his father had given him. He said to himself, "The days of mourning for my father are near; then I will kill my brother Jacob."' Jacob fearing for his life, had to leave and go far away to the home of Laban, his mother's brother. However, in the midst of his trouble, God had a plan and purpose for Jacob to go there. It was there he married Leah and Rachel and had twelve sons, who later became the twelve tribes of Israel. Just as we have no idea what lies ahead of us, Jacob had no idea what would become of him when he ran away. We have to trust God and His word that He will take care of us. Zephaniah 3:17 says, 'The Lord your God is with you, He is mighty to save. He will take great delight in you, He will quiet you with His love, He will rejoice over you with singing.' Our God is with us through the troubles and He is mighty to save. Allow Him to bring peace and quietness to your soul. Trust Him to carry you through your 2020.

**Acknowledge** –Lord, we will face trouble in this world.

**Confess** – Lord, forgive me when I fail to trust Your love for me.

**Thanksgiving** – Lord, thank You for bringing peace and quiet to my soul.

**Prayer** – Lord, You are mighty to save, please save me.

# Day 342

Psalm 139:1-2 You have searched me, Lord, and You know me. You know when I sit and when I rise; You perceive my thoughts from afar.

In today's verse we get a glimpse of the all-knowing presence of God. We learn there are no secrets with God. We may think we are hiding things from our friends, family, and even God, but more often than not, the truth comes out. When my brother was in high school, he and my father restored an old Ford Falcon. They invested a lot of time and work in that car to get it running. However, from time to time it would break down and leave my brother stranded. On one such occasion, his frustration got the best of him and he took a tire iron and started beating the car. Nothing was said or mentioned about the incident. A few days later, someone came into the dentist office where my sister worked and said she saw someone that looked like our brother beating his car. Naturally, my sister had to say something to him about it. Since then, the incident has become a favorite family story at Thanksgiving. Something that he thought would never be known has now become a family story. I am glad that God doesn't operate that way and expose my failures to everyone. However, as David tells us, God searches our hearts to know what is there. Jeremiah 17:10 also tells us that God searches our hearts, 'I the Lord search the heart and examine the mind, to reward a man according to his conduct, according to what his deeds deserve.' God knows our every thought and movement. He knows the good, the bad, and the ugly. He even knows the motives that drive the words that come out of our mouth. The world is full of temptation. For that reason, it is important that we guard our hearts. What is the Lord finding when He searches your heart? Is He finding you aligned with His Holy Spirit, making God-honoring choices and having pure thoughts? Or, is He finding you being led by your sinful nature, doing whatever pleases you?

**Acknowledge** –Lord, You search my heart and know me.

**Confess** – Lord, forgive me when I allow my sinful nature to lead my heart.

**Thanksgiving** – Lord, I thank You that You know the real me.

**Prayer** – Lord, I want my heart aligned with Your Holy Spirit, come in and clean me up.

# Day 343

Psalm 139:7 Where can I go from Your Spirit? Where can I flee from Your presence?

OUR GRANDCHILDREN LOVE TO PLAY HIDE AND SEEK. ONE OF THEIR favorite hiding places is a chair in our dining room that has a cloth covering which surrounds the legs and hangs down to the floor. They crawl underneath the covering and hide. However, their feet hang out beyond the bottom of the covering and are visible when we walk into the dining room to look for them. Their first question after we find them is, 'how did you find me?' We always say it was a lucky guess and never tell them we could see their feet sticking out from under the chair. Just like our grandchildren playing hide and seek, we can't run and hide from God. No matter where we are or where we go, God's presence is there with us. Hebrews 4:13 tells us, 'Nothing in all creation is hidden from God's sight. Everything is uncovered and laid bare before the eyes of Him to whom we must give account.' There have been times when I wanted to hide from God because I was ashamed of what I had done, or because I didn't want God to see what I was doing. The good news is that He was right there, but never stopped loving me. However, there have been other times when my problems have overwhelmed me and I wanted God's presence and help. During those times I have felt that God had abandoned me and left me to suffer all alone. But the same God who is with us when we have wandered away from Him is the same God who is with us when troubles take over our lives. Paul writing in Romans 8:38-39 gives us the assurance that God is with us no matter our circumstances, 'For I am convinced that neither death nor life, neither angels nor demons, neither the present nor the future, nor any powers, neither height nor depth, nor anything else in all creation, will be able to separate us from the love of God that is in Christ Jesus our Lord.' By the way, the answer to David's questions in today's verse is nowhere.

**Acknowledge** –Lord, nothing is hidden from Your sight.

**Confess** – Lord, forgive me when I try to hide from You.

**Thanksgiving** – Lord, thank You that nothing can separate me from Your love.

**Prayer** – Lord, Help me to seek Your presence each day.

# Day 344

Psalm 139:10 Even there Your hand will guide me, Your right hand will hold me fast.

To understand what David is talking about, we need to look back a couple of verses. In verse seven, David asked was there any place he could go and be away from God. In verses eight and nine he begins to answer his own question, 'If I go up to the heavens, You are there; if I make my bed in the depths, You are there. If I rise on the wings of the dawn, if I settle on the far side of the sea.' David said even in those places, God's hand would guide him and hold him fast. David was confident of God's presence and guidance. Isaiah 58:11 says, 'The Lord will guide you always; He will satisfy your needs in a sun-scorched land and will strengthen your frame. You will be like a well-watered garden, like a spring whose waters never fail.' God has called many people to the mission field. They have left their home to go to a foreign land where they have no family or friends in order to follow God. Many spend their entire lives pouring into the communities they serve. They have trusted God to guide them and hold them in His hand. They followed the words of Jesus in Matthew 28:18-20 which says, 'Then Jesus came to them and said, "All authority in heaven and on earth has been given to Me. Therefore go and make disciples of all nations, baptizing them in the name of the Father and of the Son and of the Holy Spirit, and teaching them to obey everything I have commanded you. And surely I am with you always, to the very end of the age."' God promises to be with us, no matter where we go. Has God placed a burden on your heart to go to another country to serve Him? Or perhaps, He is calling you into the ministry as a pastor or youth pastor. No matter the call, God's hand will be with you. Answer the call and trust God to do the rest.

**Acknowledge** –Lord, Your right hand holds me.

**Confess** – Lord, forgive me for not answering Your call to serve.

**Thanksgiving** – Lord, thank You missionaries and pastors who have answered Your call.

**Prayer** – Lord, what are You calling me to do? Help me to step out in faith to follow You.

# Day 345

Psalm 139:13-14 For You created my inmost being; You knit me together in my mother's womb. I praise You because I am fearfully and wonderfully made; Your works are wonderful, I know that full well.

According to data from the United Nations, the current world population is 7.8 billion people, with approximately 385,000 babies being born each day. (theworldcounts.com). Begin counting from the first child born to Adam and Eve until today and the number of babies that have been born reaches numbers that are mind-boggling. Yet David tells us that each one was created and knit together by God. He said that we are fearfully and wonderfully made. This means that God intimately knows every detail about us. He also created us in His own image. Genesis 1:27 tells us, 'So God created man in His own image, in the image of God He created him; male and female He created them.' Today's technology allows us to watch a baby develop from an embryo to a child, ready to enter the world. We can watch the miracle of God's Hand at work, knitting together billions of cells to create a new person, complete with their own unique personality and identity. According to Whattoexpect.com, at six weeks a baby will measure $1/6^{th}$ of an inch from head to rump. By the end of the pregnancy, the baby will measure anywhere from 18 to 21 inches and weigh around six to eight pounds. During that time, God takes great care in creating human life. Because we are fearfully and wonderfully made, all life is sacred and each person is valuable to Him. God doesn't create any junk. Not only did He take the time to create us, He has a plan for our lives. Sadly, many unborn children have had their lives ended before they were even born. It grieves the Father to see His creation treated that way. It should grieve us as well. All life is precious in His sight. Jesus speaking in Luke 12:6-7 said, "Are not five sparrows sold for two pennies? Yet not one of them is forgotten by God. Indeed, the very hairs on your head are all numbered. Don't be afraid; you are worth more than many sparrows." Thank God today for fearfully and wonderfully creating you.

**Acknowledge** – Lord, You created my inmost being.

**Confess** – Lord, forgive me for not valuing all life.

**Thanksgiving** – Lord, thank You for creating me.

**Prayer** – Lord, help me to value and protect the unborn.

# Day 346

Psalm 139:16 Your eyes saw my unformed body. All the days ordained for me were written in Your book before one of them came to be.

USING AN ANALOGY FROM ONE COMMENTARY, WHILE OUR UNFORMED bodies were on the potter's wheel, God saw us as complete.[3] He knew who we were and what we would look like, while an embryo in our mother's womb. Our newest grandson, Luke, is only seven weeks old. It is amazing to witness the change in his looks since he was born. He has grown and his facial features look completely different now. He is also beginning to look around and focus his eyes on things. In a few short months, he will be up and crawling around. Even as simple as his days are right now with just eating and sleeping, each one was ordained by God. God also knows the very details of our lives. Those details include a unique plan for each one of us. Ephesians 2:10 tells us, 'For we are His workmanship, created in Christ Jesus for good works, which God prepared beforehand, that we should walk in them.' Also, Jeremiah 1:4-5 tells us, 'The Word of the Lord came to me, saying, "Before I formed you in the womb I knew you, before you were born I set you apart; I appointed you as a prophet to the nations."' I don't think God's plan for us involves a detailed, day to day blueprint telling us what to do and when to do it. However, God does call people like He did Jeremiah for a specific purpose. Pastors, missionaries, and others in full-time ministry are called by God to serve Him. God's plan for your life might involve being a Christian husband, wife, father, or mother raising your children to follow Him. His plan could be for you to have a career in the medical, business, education, or construction field where your actions and behaviors reflect Him. Paul said in Colossians 3:17, 'And whatever you do, whether in word or deed, do it all in the name of the Lord Jesus, giving thanks to God the Father through Him.' What is God's plan for you? Start by living for Him where you are. Then let Him open doors for you.

**Acknowledge** –Lord, You saw me before I was created.

**Confess** – Lord, forgive me for not following Your plan for my life.

**Thanksgiving** – Lord, thank You for Your plan for me.

**Prayer** – Lord, help me live my life according to Your plan for me.

# Day 347

Psalm 139:23-24 Search me, God, and know my heart; test me and know my thoughts. See if there is any offensive way in me, and lead me in the way everlasting.

Psalm 139:1 says, 'O Lord, You have searched me and You know me.' If God already knows his heart, why is David inviting God to search His heart and test His thoughts again? Maybe David wanted to make sure that he was not harboring anything in his heart that was offensive to God, or there were things he didn't consider to be offensive, but could have been to God. Asking God to search our hearts takes courage, because we need to be ready to repent and deal with the things He reveals. How does God reveal what is wrong in our hearts? First, God reveals things through His word. You may read a particular verse that speaks to your heart and convicts you of something there. God also reveals things through a sermon. Have you ever listened to a sermon and thought, that was meant just for me? It may have been. Next, God can reveal things to us through a family member or friend. As a child, our parents know us very well. They can sense when something is not right in our lives or we are heading down the wrong path. We may not like or want their correction, but it could save us from making some very bad choices. Lastly, God reveals things through His 'Still, Small, Voice' that speaks to us. Why is it important for God to search our hearts and reveal what is there? Jesus speaking in Mark 7:21-23 said, "What comes out of a man is what makes him unclean. For from within, out of men's hearts, come murder, adultery, greed, malice, deceit, lewdness, envy, slander, arrogance and folly. All these evils come from inside and make a man unclean." Jesus does not paint a pretty picture of what thoughts can lurk inside us. We need His presence in our lives each day to keep our hearts and minds clean. David said in Psalm 51:10, 'Create in me a pure heart, O God, and renew a steadfast spirit in me.' Ask God to search your heart and renew your spirit today.

**Acknowledge** –Lord, You know my heart.

**Confess** – Lord, forgive me for harboring unconfessed sin in my heart.

**Thanksgiving** – Lord, thank You for revealing sin in my life.

**Prayer** – Lord, search me, know my heart, and test my thoughts.

# Day 348

Psalm 140:1-2 Rescue me, Lord, from evildoers; protect me from the violent, who devise evil plans in their hearts and stir up war every day.

THROUGHOUT DAVID'S LIFETIME, A NUMBER OF PEOPLE WERE OUT to harm him. In those times, he sought refuge and protection from God. He knew that God could save him from his enemies, sustain him when he was under attack, and give him victory over them. Like David, we may not be able to avoid evildoers who intend harm for us. Do we seek God and His deliverance, or do we try to take matters into our own hands when those times arise? In the Book of Esther, we read that Haman had a decree issued for all the Jews in the kingdom of King Xerxes be killed because of his hatred for one person, Mordecai. Esther 5:9 says, 'Haman went out that day happy and in high spirits. But when he saw Mordecai at the king's gate and observed that he neither rose nor showed fear in his presence, he was filled with rage against Mordecai.' Esther 4:1 tells us, 'When Mordecai learned of all that had been done, he tore his clothes, put on sackcloth and ashes, and went out into the city, wailing loudly and bitterly.' In his day, this was a sign of mourning and humbling himself before God. Because of Haman's position, Mordecai had no other option but to appeal to God. Where are the attacks on your life and the lives of your family coming from? Are they coming from an unseen enemy or someone we think is in higher authority? If so, we may be in the same situation as Mordecai and have no other option but to appeal to God for help. Jesus speaking in Luke 10:19 said, I have given you authority to trample on snakes, and scorpions and to overcome all the power of the enemy; nothing will harm you.' He also concluded his model prayer in Matthew 6:9-13 with, "And lead us not into temptation, but deliver from the evil one.' Are the attacks on your life and the lives of your family coming from the evil one? Seek His protection and deliverance today. Ask God to 'deliver you and your family from the evil one.'

**Acknowledge** –Lord, You protect us from the evil one.

**Confess** – Lord, forgive me for trying to rely on my own strength.

**Thanksgiving** – Lord, thank You for your model prayer.

**Prayer** – Lord, lead me not into temptation, but deliver me from the evil one.

# Day 349

Psalm 141:3 Set a guard over my mouth, Lord; keep watch over the door of my lips.

SAYING THE WRONG THING AT THE WRONG TIME CAN CAUSE YEARS of pain and sorrow. How many marriages, friendships, and even families have been ruined because of the words spoken to each other. Having God keep watch over the door of our lips and guard what comes out of our mouths is priceless. I have the tendency to blurt out something sarcastic in an effort to be funny. However, some of my comments aren't received as they were intended and hurt someone's feelings. I have asked God to put a guard over my sarcasm to only say things that build instead of cut down. However, that doesn't mean those thoughts do not enter my mind and race to my lips. Thankfully, God is there to intercept them and prevent them from coming out; although, one may still sneak out from time to time. Proverbs 13:3 says, 'Whoever guards his mouth preserves his life; he who opens wide his lips comes to ruin.' James 3:2-6 talks about taming the tongue, 'We all stumble in many ways. If anyone is never at fault in what he says, he is a perfect man, able to keep his whole body in check. When we put bits into the mouths of horses to make them obey us, we can turn the whole animal. Or take ships as an example. Although they are so large and driven by strong winds, they are steered by a very small rudder wherever the pilot wants to go. Likewise, the tongue is a small part of the body, but it makes great boasts. Consider when a great forest is set on fire by one small spark. The tongue also is a fire, a world of evil among the parts of the body. It corrupts the whole person, and is itself set on fire by hell.' James has little good to say about the tongue. In verse 10 he says, 'Out of the same mouth come praise and cursing. My brothers, this should not be.' That is why we need a guard at our lips. We need the Holy Spirit checking our words and controlling our conversations. Ask God to set a guard over your mouth and take control of your conversations.

**Acknowledge** –Lord, from our mouth comes both praise and cursing.

**Confess** – Lord, forgive me for saying things that hurt and divide.

**Thanksgiving** – Lord, thank You for guarding my mouth.

**Prayer** – Lord, help me to be careful with the words I use.

# Day 350

Psalm 142:6 Listen to my cry, for I am in desperate need; rescue me from those who pursue me, for they are too strong for me.

When I was a young boy, I loved to arm wrestle with my father. Occasionally, he would let me win, boosting confidence in my strength. Having the strength to beat my dad in arm wrestling, I would pretend to be Superman. However, it did not take long to find out that there was always someone, bigger, stronger, and faster than me. David found himself in the same situation and cried out to God to rescue him. Jesus speaking in Luke 11:21-22 tells us, "When a strong man, fully armed, guards his own house, his possessions are safe. But when someone stronger attacks and overpowers him, he takes away the armor in which the man trusted and divides up the spoils." Jesus told this story to those who accused him of casting out demons by the power of Satan. Jesus pointed out that the power He had to cast out demons didn't come from Satan, for if it did, Satan would be supporting an attack on himself. Jesus' power came from God. Jesus established the fact there is no one, including Satan who is stronger than He. Jesus speaking in Revelation 1:18 said, "I am the Living One; I was dead, and behold I am alive for ever and ever! And I hold the keys of death and Hades." Jesus went to the cross and died for our sins, rose on the third day, and is alive forever. He conquered sin and the grave and has power over them. Not only does He have power over them, He has power over Satan as well. Hebrews 2:14 says, 'Since the children have flesh and blood, He too shared in their humanity so that by His death He might destroy him who hold the power of death – that is, the devil.' Just like I discovered, we are going to face situations in our lives that are bigger, stronger, and faster than we are. Where are you going to look for help? Call out to the One who conquered sin and the grave and has power over all. There is nothing too hard for Him.

**Acknowledge** –Lord, there is nothing too hard for God.

**Confess** – Lord, forgive me for trying to rely on my own strength.

**Thanksgiving** – Lord, thank You for coming to conquer sin and death.

**Prayer** – Lord, I cry out to You, the only One who can save me.

# Day 351

Psalm 143:5 I remember the days of long ago; I meditate on all Your works and consider what Your hands have done.

Have you ever said the phrase, "those were the good old days?" Usually, we start looking back and reflecting on the past when things are not going so well for at the moment. We long for the times when life seemed simpler and with less problems. The fallacy with our memory is that we tend to leave out the difficult days that are mixed in with the good. That is exactly what David is doing today. He is reflecting back on the times he witnessed God's hand at work in his life. For David, that was pretty much most of his life. He may have recalled the day as a young teenage boy, being called from the fields and anointed king by Samuel. He may have thought back to the day he stood in front of Goliath with a slingshot and took him down. Perhaps he thought about the times he dodged a spear thrown at him by Saul, or the times God saved him from Saul and his men who were chasing him. He may have thought about the day he and his men rescued their families from the Amalekites who had taken them captive or the number of victories God gave him over the Philistines. He may have even thought about the goodness of God's forgiveness he experienced for his sin with Bathsheba and Uriah. When you think about the "good old days" are you simply taking a trip down memory lane and longing for what seemed to be a simpler time in your life? Or, are you reflecting back on the times you witnessed God's hand working in your life? Isaiah 64:8 tells us, 'Yet, O Lord, You are our Father. We are the clay, You are the Potter; we are all the work of Your Hands.' As you look back, do so with the perspective of God's Hand at work, leading and guiding you through the difficult seasons. Reflect back on His forgiveness, His restoration, His provision, and His love for you. Then thank God for all He has done for you.

**Acknowledge** –Lord, You are the Potter, I am Your clay.

**Confess** – Lord, forgive me when I forget Your Hand is at work in my life.

**Thanksgiving** – Lord, thank You for the times You have led me through.

**Prayer** – Lord, help me to think about the "good old days" in the right perspective.

# Day 352

Psalm 143:8 Let the morning bring me word of Your unfailing love, for I have put my trust in You. Show me the way I should go, for to You I lift up my soul.

SOME OF THE LONGEST NIGHTS ARE WHEN YOUR CHILDREN ARE SICK and running a fever. For some reason when our children were sick, their fever was low and manageable during the day. However, it always seemed to spike and be at its worst late at night after the doctor's office had closed. On several occasions, Vivian had the children in the tub trying to cool them down and lower their fever. It was a long night, with hopes that morning would soon come. Daylight offered hope that they might have turned the corner and begun to feel better. Or if no better, get them to the doctor. Mornings are special. They offer hope. They signal the dawning of something fresh and encouraging for us. David writing in Psalm 30:5 said, 'For His anger lasts only a moment, but His favor lasts a lifetime; weeping may remain for a night, but rejoicing comes in the morning.' The verses leading up to today, indicate David was being pursued by his enemies. Yesterday, he reflected on how God had delivered him before. Today, David wants the morning to bring him a fresh anointing of God's love. He knew that God loved him and had delivered him in the past, but he needs the reassurance of God's love in his life. Aren't we the same? It is great to have the memories of what God has done for us, but we need more than memories. We need to experience and see God's love working in our lives right now. Our problem is that we want God to move and act on our time schedule. However, God didn't say that our morning would come tomorrow. Like David, we have to put our trust in God and His timeline. We need to ask God to lead us through the long night we are going through and wait for morning to come. God is faithful to see us through the long nights. Lift up your soul and worship the God who loves you.

**Acknowledge** –Lord, You promised joy comes in the morning.

**Confess** – Lord, forgive me when I fail to trust You.

**Thanksgiving** – Lord, thank You for new mornings.

**Prayer** – Lord, help me to be patient as I wait on Your timing.

# Day 353

Psalm 144:3 Lord, what are human beings that You care for them, mere mortals that You think of them?

David asks a great question, why does God love us? Who are we, what have we done, what is it that causes God to love us? It certainly isn't because we are lovable people or have done anything to deserve it. We are not adorable, loveable, or good. In fact, we are sinful, disobedient, and rebellious towards God. Paul writing in Romans 3:11-18 said, 'There is no one who understands, no one who seeks God. All have turned away, they have together become worthless; there is no one who does good, not even one. Their throats are open graves; their tongues practice deceit. The poison of vipers is on their lips. Their mouths are full of cursing and bitterness. Their feet are swift to shed blood; ruin and misery mark their ways, and the way of peace they do not know. There is no fear of God before their eyes.' Paul's description is one that would make it hard for our own mother to love us. Yet, God loves us. In fact, God is love. 1 John 4:16 says, 'And so we know and rely on the love of God has for us. God is love. Whoever lives in love lives in God, and God in him.' God demonstrated His love by sending His Son to die on the cross for our sins. Romans 5:8 says, 'But God demonstrates His own love for us in this: While we were still sinners, Christ died for us.' I would offer to die in the place of someone I really loved, like my wife, children, or grandchildren, but would be hard-pressed to die for someone else. Have you rejected God's love by turning away from Him and living as Paul described? Or, have you accepted God's love and asked Him to live in your heart? When we accept Christ, God cleans all the wickedness and sinfulness from our hearts and sends His Holy Spirit to live within us. Jesus speaking in John 14:26 said, "But the Counselor, the Holy Spirit, whom the Father will send in My name, will teach you all things and will remind you of everything I have said to you.' As the old saying goes, smile, God loves you.

**Acknowledge** –Lord, You are love.

**Confess** – Lord, forgive me when I doubt Your love for me.

**Thanksgiving** – Lord, thank You for loving me.

**Prayer** – Lord, help me to share Your love with others.

# Day 354

> Psalm 144:9 I will sing a new song to You, my God; on the ten-stringed lyre I will make music to You.

My grandparents grew up in the Primitive Baptist Church where no musical instruments are used to accompany the singing. They believe that the use of musical instruments is not authorized in the New Testament. Singing a cappella can be a worshipful experience. Occasionally, when singing praise songs, our praise leader will have the instruments stop playing while the congregation still sings. The harmony and sound of our voices rising in praise to God moving. However, I am like David, get out the ten-stringed lyre and play along. The music helps drown out my sour notes and poor rhythm. I have mentioned that I grew up in the Baptist Church singing from the Broadman Hymnal. Although the hymnal was over 400 pages, it seemed as if we went through a rotation of the same songs. We sang them enough, that I still remember the words to many of the songs. Some churches still use the Broadman Hymnal and love to sing from it. As long as it comes from our lips as worship to God, He honors our worship. Paul writing in Ephesians 5:19 said, 'Speak to one another with psalms, hymns, and spiritual songs. Sing and make music in your heart to the Lord.' In this verse, Paul covers all types of music. However, God should be the subject of our singing, not the beneficiary. We are the ones being drawn into His Presence through our worship. Paul said in Colossians 3: 16, 'Let the word of Christ dwell in you richly as you teach and admonish one another with all wisdom, and as you sing psalms, hymns and spiritual songs.' David did not have the benefit of knowing Christ as his Savior, yet he was diligent in his worship of God. David's love for God manifested itself in using the talents God had given him. He wrote many new songs which we are learning from today. Has God given you the talent to write music or play an instrument? If so, use that talent to serve Him. If that is not your talent, you can still sing along and worship the God who saved you.

**Acknowledge** –Lord, You love our worship.

**Confess** – Lord, forgive me when I fail to worship You in song.

**Thanksgiving** – Lord, thank You for those who use the talents You have given them.

**Prayer** – Lord, I want to sing a new song to You.

# Day 355

**Psalm 145:8** The Lord is gracious and compassionate, slow to anger and rich in love.

According to David, God is gracious, compassionate, slow to anger and rich in love. We read in Exodus 34:5-6 where God spoke to Moses from a cloud when he went to receive the second set of Ten Commandments, 'Then the Lord came down in the cloud and stood there with him and proclaimed His name, The Lord. And He passed in front of Moses, proclaiming, "The Lord, The Lord, the compassionate and gracious God, slow to anger, abounding in love and faithfulness."' David may have read this, but more importantly he could speak from first-hand experience about the character of God. Nehemiah 9:17 also speaks about God's compassion, 'They refused to listen, and did not remember Your wonderous deeds which You had performed among them; so they became stubborn and appointed a leader to return to their slavery in Egypt. But You are a God of forgiveness, gracious, and compassionate, slow to anger and abounding in lovingkindness; and You did not forsake them.' What does this mean for us? First, God is gracious to us. He offers us the gift of eternal life through the death and resurrection of His Son, Jesus Christ. We cannot earn our salvation. It is a free gift, graciously given to us. Next, God is compassionate. Looking down from heaven, he saw our need. He had compassion on us and did for us what we could not do for ourselves. God is also slow to anger. This is a blessing. How many times have we disobeyed God? How many wrong choices have we made that grieve His Heart? Yet, He does not treat us as our sins deserve. He is patient with us. Lastly, God is rich in love. Most of us would rather be rich in material things. However, God is rich in love. Jesus speaking in John 3:16 said, "For God so loved the world that He gave His one and only Son, that whoever believes in Him shall not perish but have eternal life." Can you, like David, speak from your heart about the gracious, compassionate God who is slow to anger and rich in love? If not, get to know Him today.

**Acknowledge** –Lord, You are gracious, compassionate, slow to anger, and rich in love.

**Confess** – Lord, forgive me when I shut You out of my life.

**Thanksgiving** – Lord, thank You for Your grace.

**Prayer** – Lord, I open the door to my heart to You.

# Day 356

**Psalm 145:17** The Lord is righteous in all His ways and faithful in all He does.

HAVE YOU EVER HEARD SOMEONE ASK, WHY WOULD A LOVING GOD allow this to happen? On the surface it sounds like a good question, but it doesn't consider the character of God. David tells us that the Lord is righteous in all His ways. Everything that God does is right. He does no wrong. However, we tend to blame God for the bad decisions and wickedness done by man. Moses speaking in Deuteronomy 32:4 said, "He is the Rock, His works are perfect, and all His ways are just. A faithful God who does no wrong, upright and just is He." Moses points out that God is also upright and just. Therefore, He loves things that are good and hates things that are evil. Today, our concept of good and evil has been turned upside down. What used to be good is now evil, and what was evil is now good. God has not changed His opinion and still judges by His standards. Thankfully, a righteous God doesn't punish us as we deserve. No matter how hard we try to live a good and righteous life, we fall miserably short of God's standard. Romans 3:23 says, 'For all have sinned and fall short of the glory of God.' What is our just punishment for not living up to God's righteousness? Romans 6:23 says, 'For the wages of sin is death, but the gift of God is eternal life in Christ Jesus our Lord.' We deserve the death penalty for the wickedness that is in our hearts. Paul tells us in Romans 2:2 that God's judgment on us is based on His truth not our concept of it, 'Now we know that God's judgment against those who do such things is based on truth.' How are we made righteous in God's sight and receive eternal life? Romans 10:9 tells us, 'That if you confess with your mouth, "Jesus is Lord," and believe in your heart that God raised Him from the dead, you will be saved.' It is simple, but also hard for many to grasp. Share His plan of salvation with someone today.

**Acknowledge** –Lord, You are righteous and faithful in all You do.

**Confess** – Lord, forgive me for my sins.

**Thanksgiving** – Lord, thank You for Your plan of salvation.

**Prayer** – Lord, help me to share your plan of salvation with someone today.

# Day 357

Psalm 146:2 I will praise the Lord all my life; I will sing praise to my God as long as I live.

David loves to worship God through music. David said in Psalm 144:9, 'I will sing a new song to You, O God…' Today, David vows to praise God as long as his life continues. Twice David commits to praising God by saying 'I will.' What about our commitment to praise God? It is easy to praise God as long as things are going well. How committed are we at praising God when we experience times of disappointment, sickness, pain, and suffering? David knew that praise wasn't about him or his feelings. Praise is about worshiping God for who He is. What are some reasons we should praise God? 1. God created you. We read in Psalm 139 that God created our innermost being, and knit us together in our mother's womb. Not only that, He has a plan for our lives. 2. God loved us enough to send His Son, Jesus, to die on the cross for our sins. He paid the penalty for our sins and made a way for us to have eternal life with Him. 3. God provides for us. Jesus speaking in Matthew 6:26 said, 'Look at the birds of the air; they do not sow or reap or store away in barns, and yet your heavenly Father feeds them. Are you not much more valuable than they?' 4. God desires our praise and even commands it. Psalm 150:6 says, 'Let everything that has breath praise the Lord.' 5. Praise ushers us into God's presence. Psalm 100:4 says, 'Enter His gates with thanksgiving and His courts with praise; give thanks to Him and praise His name.' 6. It is God's will for us to praise and give thanks. 1 Thessalonians 5:16-18 says, 'Be joyful always; pray continually; give thanks in all circumstances, for this is God's will for you in Christ Jesus.' 7. He has prepared a place for you and me in heaven. Jesus said in John 14:2, In My Father's House are many rooms; if it were not so, I would have told you. I am going there to prepare a place for you.' Isn't that reason enough to praise Him?

**Acknowledge** –Lord, You are worthy of my praise.

**Confess** – Lord, forgive me for not making praise a priority in my life.

**Thanksgiving** – Lord, thank You for the many reasons to praise You.

**Prayer** – Lord, I will praise You the rest of my days.

# Day 358

Psalm 146:5-6 Blessed is he whose help is the God of Jacob, whose hope is in the Lord his God, the Maker of heaven and earth, the sea, and everything in them – the Lord, who remains faithful forever.

THE PSALMIST TELLS US THAT THOSE WHOSE HELP COMES FROM THE God of Jacob are blessed. We will also learn that God blesses those who bless the lineage of Jacob. Why is Jacob so important? Who is Jacob and why are blessings associated with him? Jacob is the grandson of Abraham, the son of Isaac and Rebecca, and twin brother of Esau. In Genesis 25:23, God speaking to Rebecca about her unborn sons said, "Two nations are in your womb, and two peoples from within you will be separated; and one people will be stronger than the other, and the older will serve the younger." Although twins, Jacob and Esau were completely different boys. When it came time for Isaac to give his blessing on the older son, Jacob disguised himself as Esau and received the blessing of the firstborn. Genesis 28:29 records his blessing, "May God give you of heaven's dew and of earth's riches – an abundance of grain and new wine. May nations serve you and peoples bow down to you. Be lord over your brothers, and may the sons of your mother bow down to you. May those who curse you be cursed and those who bless you be blessed." Many years later, Jacob was headed back to his homeland with his family. One night while on the way, Jacob wrestled with an angel. Genesis 32:26-28 tells us, "Then the 'man' said, "Let me go, for it is daybreak." But Jacob replied, "I will not let you go unless you bless me." The 'man' asked him, "What is your name?" "Jacob" he answered. Then the man said, "Your name will no longer be Jacob, but Israel, because you have struggled with God and with men and have overcome." Jacob received two blessings that have set the course of history. He became the father of the 12 Tribes of Israel. And, Isaac's blessing on those who bless him and curse on those who curse him still applies to the Nation of Israel today. Praise God for His blessings and His faithfulness.

**Acknowledge** –Lord, You are faithful forever.

**Confess** – Lord, forgive me for not trusting in You.

**Thanksgiving** – Lord, thank You for Your blessings.

**Prayer** – Lord, I pray blessings and safety for the Nation of Israel.

# Day 359

Psalm 147:3 He heals the brokenhearted and binds up their wounds.

After Jesus was baptized and spent 40 days in the wilderness preparing for His ministry, He went to the synagogue in His hometown, Nazareth, and was handed a scroll. Luke 4:17-18 records what happened, 'The scroll of the prophet Isaiah was handed to Him. Unrolling it, He found the place where it is written: "The Spirit of the Lord is upon me, because He hath appointed Me to preach the gospel to the poor; He hath sent me to heal the brokenhearted, to preach deliverance to the captives, and recovering of sight to the blind, to set a liberty them that are bruised." What is broken in your life? Is it your marriage? Your finances? Relationships with children or family members? Are you like many who suffered from depression and isolation during the COVID-19 pandemic? Have you contemplated suicide to end the pain and suffering of your situation? Friends and family can help, they can comfort and listen to you, but they have no power to heal you. Take heart, Jesus came to heal all types of brokenness. He can take your situation and make it better than it was before. However, we have to trust in His Word, and ask Him to heal us. Jesus just didn't walk up and heal blind Bartimaeus. Bartimaeus had to tell Jesus what he wanted Him to do. Mark 10:51 says, '"What do you want Me to do for you?" Jesus asked him. The blind man said, "Rabbi, I want to see." Reach out to Jesus, and tell Him your pain. Ask Him to heal your brokenness and heartache. Ask Him to restore whatever has been taken away from you. Then give Him time to work. His healing may not take place overnight. In 2 Kings 5:1-19, we find the story of Naaman the leper. He was told by the Prophet Elisha to go dip seven times in the Jordan River to be healed. Naaman went away angry because of how and what he was told to do to be healed. Nevertheless, he went and did as Elisha said and was completely healed. Take your brokenness, your sickness, and your heartaches to Jesus. He heals the brokenhearted.

**Acknowledge** –Lord, You heal the brokenhearted.

**Confess** – Lord, forgive me for not seeking Your healing power.

**Thanksgiving** – Lord, thank You for healing me.

**Prayer** – Lord, restore what depression and heartache have taken away from me.

# Day 360

> Psalm 147:10 His pleasure is not in the strength of the horse, nor His delight in the legs of the warrior;

TODAY WE LEARN ABOUT THE AREAS WHERE GOD DOES NOT PLACE His delight and confidence. We also discover that God's perspective on the strength or wealth of a person or nation is completely opposite of ours. We tend to think that bigger is better, that more is security, that strength represents power, that might is right. This has not changed over the centuries. The nation with the bigger army, the more advanced weapons, and the most horses was thought to be the most powerful. God has a different perspective. In Deuteronomy 17:16 we find, 'The king, moreover, must not acquire great numbers of horses for himself or make the people return to Egypt to get more of them, for the Lord has told you, "You are not to go back that way again."' Also, in Deuteronomy 20:1 we find, 'When you go to war against your enemies and see horses and chariots and an army greater than yours, do not be afraid of them, because the Lord your God, who brought you up out of Egypt, will be with you.' God is warning the people that the accumulation of horses will tempt them to trust in their own military power rather than to trust in the power of God to save them. Later in 1 Kings 4:26, we find that Solomon didn't follow God's word about acquiring horses, 'And Solomon had forty thousand stalls of horses for his chariots, and twelve thousand horsemen.' In addition to horses, Solomon acquired a lot of everything else, including wives. It was his wives that turned his heart away from God and led him into idolatry and the eventual downfall of the nation of Israel. Solomon had established a pattern of disobedience to God, relying on his wealth, his ideas, and his military power instead of God. What do you trust in? Are you focused on acquiring more, like Solomon, for your security? Or, are you trusting God? 1 Corinthians 1:25 says, 'For the foolishness of God is wiser than man's wisdom, and weakness of God is stronger than man's strength.' Put your trust in God's strength and protection.

**Acknowledge** – Lord, You have no pleasure in the strength of man.

**Confess** – Lord, forgive me for trusting in my own power and strength.

**Thanksgiving** – Lord, thank You for Your wisdom and strength.

**Prayer** – Lord, help me to trust in Your strength, not my own.

# Day 361

Psalm 147:11 The Lord delights in those who fear Him, who put their hope in His unfailing love.

Isn't it odd that the Psalmist tells us that God delights in the person who fears the One in who we put our hope? How does that work? I have a healthy fear of roller coasters. Standing on the platform waiting to board, I always get a little nervous. However, watching others ride, I have a confident hope that all will go well when I get in. We have learned that the fear of God is a holy reverence of Him. Hope is a confident expectation of a desired outcome that stems from faith. A wish is hope without faith. It is something we desire that we have no confidence will happen. Hebrews 11:1 says, Now faith is the substance of things hoped for, the evidence of things not seen.' Faith and hope have substance, there is something tangible to hold on to. Where do we find hope? Psalm 62:5 tells us, 'Find rest, O my soul, in God alone; my hope comes from Him.' Our hope comes from God and His promises. Our salvation is based on the hope we have in God's Word and the promise of Jesus' work on the cross. We put our lives in His hands and depend on His love for salvation. And that is why God takes pleasure in those who hope in His unfailing love. His saving grace is glorified and He is magnified. Our weakness demonstrates His strength. When we recognize our weaknesses, our trust in God becomes that much stronger because we know that without God, we cannot accomplish anything. Paul writing in 2 Corinthians 12:9-10 said, 'But He said to me, "My grace is sufficient for you, for My power is made perfect in weakness." Therefore, I will boast all the more gladly about my weaknesses, so that Christ's power may rest on me. That is why, for Christ's sake, I delight in weaknesses, in insults, in hardships, in persecutions, in difficulties. For when I am weak, then I am strong.' Have you fully trusted God and given your weaknesses to Him? God delights in those who rely on Him.

**Acknowledge** –Lord, You delight in those who fear You.

**Confess** – Lord, forgive me when I doubt Your grace and power.

**Thanksgiving** – Lord, thank You for the hope we have in Your salvation.

**Prayer** – Lord, I put my trust in Your unfailing love.

# Day 362

Psalm 148:1 Praise the Lord. Praise the Lord from the heavens; praise Him in the heights above.

As we come to the end of our journey through the Psalms, we are going to concentrate on praising God. Notice the command 'to praise' is given three times in this short verse. The first call to praise the Lord is to whoever is reading this Psalm. He created you, loves you, provides for you, and desires your praise. No matter where you are, how you feel, or what you are doing, stop and praise the Lord. Next, he elevates his call to praise the Lord to the heavens. All who dwell in the heavens praise the Lord. The Book of Revelation gives us several glimpses of the praise and worship that takes place in the heavens. John tells us in Revelation 1:1 that his book is about, 'The revelation of Jesus Christ, which God gave him to show his servants what soon take place.' One of the primary activities taking place in heaven will be the worship and praise of our Lord and Savior, Jesus Christ and God the Father. Revelation 7:9-12 says, 'After this I looked and there before me was a great multitude that no one could count, from every nation, tribe, people and language, standing before the throne and in front of the Lamb. They were wearing white robes and were holding palm branches in their hands. And they cried out in a loud voice: "Salvation belongs to our God, who sits on the throne, and to the Lamb." All the angels were standing around the throne and around the elders and the four living creatures. They fell down on their faces before the throne and worshiped God saying: "Amen! Praise and glory and wisdom and thanks and honor and power and strength be to our God for ever and ever. Amen!"' Lastly, the Psalmist said we should not only praise God from the heavens, we should praise Him looking up to the heights above. What a great picture of praise to our heavenly Father. I look forward to the day we will be standing around the throne, joining with the uncountable numbers of people praising God.

**Acknowledge** –Lord, You desire our praise.

**Confess** – Lord, forgive me when I fail to praise You as I should.

**Thanksgiving** – Lord, thank You for the picture John paints of the multitudes praising You.

**Prayer** – Lord, I give you praise. I don't want to wait until I get to heaven to praise You.

# Day 363

Psalm 149:1 Praise the Lord. Sing to the Lord a new song, His praise in the assembly of His faithful people.

Obviously, God loves to hear new songs about Him and to Him since this is not the first time the Psalmist has directed us to sing a new song. He adds that we should offer our praise in the assembly of other believers. In 2020, due to COVID-19 the assembling together for worship was forever changed. Many aspects of worship that we took for granted are either more complicated or completely changed. No matter the format, there are certain things about our assembly, whether on-line or in person, that should never change. The first is singing. Ephesians 5:19-20 says, 'Speak to one another with psalms, hymns and spiritual songs. Sing and make music in your heart to the Lord, always giving thanks to God the Father for everything, in the name of our Lord Jesus Christ.' Lifting our praise and giving thanks to God unites us. Moreover, God inhabits the praises of His people. Next is corporate prayer. Jesus speaking in Matthew 18:19 said, "Again, I tell you that if two of you on earth agree about anything you ask for, it will be done for you by My Father in heaven." There is power in our prayers when we come together in agreement. Next is the preaching of God's word. Acts 2:14 tells us, 'Then Peter stood up with the Eleven, raised his voice and addressed the crowd: "Fellow Jews and all of you who live in Jerusalem, let me explain this to you; listen carefully to what I have to say."' On that day, about three thousand people received Peter's message of salvation and were baptized. There is saving power in the Word of God. Lastly is giving. Malachi 3:10 says, '"Bring the whole tithe into the storehouse, that there may be food in My House. Test Me in this," says the Lord Almighty, "and see if I will not throw open the floodgates of heaven and pour out so much blessing that there will not be room enough to store it."' God honors and rewards our giving. Don't miss out on the power of worshiping together.

**Acknowledge** –Lord, You desire to see us worship together.

**Confess** – Lord, forgive me when I fail to meet with others in worship.

**Thanksgiving** – Lord, thank You for the freedom we have to worship You.

**Prayer** – Lord, help me not to neglect the assembling together with other believers.

## Day 364

Psalm 149:4 For the Lord takes delight in His people; He crowns the humble with victory.

GOD CROWNS THE HUMBLE WITH VICTORY WHICH IS COMPLETELY opposite of what I have always been taught. I grew up hearing things like, 'only the strong survive.' But one thing I have learned from reading the Bible and observing others is that it takes real strength to be humble. It takes someone who is confident in God's love and mercy to always put other's needs ahead of their own. It takes a person who is obedient to God's word to be humble when those around them seem to be getting ahead at their expense. Perhaps the greatest example of someone living a life of humbleness is Jesus Christ. Paul writing about Jesus in Philippians 2:6-8 said, 'Who, being in very nature, God, did not consider equality with God something to be grasped, but made Himself nothing, taking the very nature of a servant, being made in human likeness. And being found in appearance as a man, He humbled Himself and became obedient to death – even death on a cross.' Jesus did not have to die a painful death on the cross. He chose to. Even as He hung on the cross and people were hurling insults at Him, taunting Him to come down, He chose to stay there for you and me. What did Paul say in the very next verse, 'Therefore God exalted Him to the highest place and gave Him the Name that is above every name.' If you are reading this devotion on December 30th and considering New Year's Resolutions, why not commit yourself to humbleness. Micah 6:8 provides a guide for getting started, 'He has showed you, O man, what is good. And what does the Lord require of you? To act justly, and to love mercy and to walk humbly with your God.' What better way to start the year than to live like Christ? 2 Timothy 4:8 says, 'Now there is in store for me the crown of righteousness, which the Lord, the Righteous Judge, will award me on that day – and not only to me, but also to all who have longed for His appearing.' With faithfulness comes victory.

**Acknowledge** –Lord, You crown the humble with victory.

**Confess** – Lord, forgive me when I am selfish and arrogant.

**Thanksgiving** – Lord, thank You for the example we have in Jesus Christ.

**Prayer** – Lord, help me to act justly, love mercy and walk humbly with You.

# Day 365

Psalm 150:6 Let everything that has breath praise the Lord. Praise the Lord.

Praise the Lord! You have finished your journey through the Psalms. My prayer is that you have learned something and found treasures along the way that have encouraged you and grown your faith in God. I would like to praise God for His goodness and faithfulness in making this book a reality. It was God who planted the idea in my heart to write this devotional for my children, grandchildren, and anyone who wanted to learn more about the Psalms. For someone who had no writing experience prior to beginning this book, God was faithful to provide the words and the time to write. It is amazing what God can do if we listen and obey Him. What about you? What is God calling you to do? Are you thinking God has made a mistake or maybe that it wasn't Him planting that seed in your heart? Trust God and take the first step. When I had finished writing the first 31 days of devotions, I thought, I only have 334 more to go. The task looked daunting and it was filled with stops, restarts, and rewrites along the way. However, some wise counsel from my wife who said, 'don't count how many you have left, but focus on how many have been written' kept me going. God will encourage you and send you help to accomplish His plan for you. When you are following His plan for your life, praising Him will be easy. It will start as a desire to praise Him, for He is worthy of our praise. Next, your praise will flow into a prayer of praise. A prayer of praise is praying the scriptures. You are in agreement with God's word and lifting it back to Him in praise. Praying verses like Jeremiah 32:17 that says, 'Ah, Sovereign Lord, You have made the heavens and the earth, by Your great power and out-stretched arm. Nothing is too hard for You.' Lastly, your praise will be a celebration of God's work in your life. I leave you with this blessing, "The Lord bless you and keep you; the Lord make His face to shine on you and be gracious to you; the Lord lift up His countenance upon you and give you peace."

**Acknowledge** –Lord, You desire our praise.

**Confess** – Lord, forgive me for not listening to Your call.

**Thanksgiving** – Lord, thank You for choosing me to serve You.

**Prayer** – Lord, I lift my praise to You O Lord.

# Song List

Day 18: "How Majestic is Your name" written by Michael W. Smith
Day 18: "Everything is Beautiful" written by Ray Stevens
Day 31: "I Sing Praises to Your Name" written by Terry Macalmon
Day 36: "Turn Your Eyes Upon Jesus" written by Helen Howarth Lemmel
Day 46: "Surrounded" written by Elyssa Smith
Day 47: "I Will Call Upon the Lord" written by Michael O'Shields
Day 48: "He's Everything to Me" written by Ralph Carmichael
Day 55: "Praise Him, All Ye Little Children" Music by Carrie Bonner
Day 61: "God is so Good" written by Paul Makai
Day 63: "King of Glory" written by Bradley Avery, David Carr, Johnny Mac Powell, Mark Lee, Samuel Anderson
Day 68: "Surely the Presence" written by Lanny Wolfe
Day 70: "In the Presence of Jehovah" written by Geron Davis
Day 79: "Trust in You" written by Lauren Daigle, Paul Marbury, Michael Farren
Day 85: "The B I B L E" author unknown
Day 85: "He's Been Faithful" written by Carol Cymbala
Day 93: "Goodness of God" written by Ed Cash, Ben Fielding, Jason Ingram, Brian Johnson, Jenn Johnson
Day 95: "Your Love O Lord" written by Bradley Avery, David Carr, Johnny Mac Powell, Mark Lee, Samuel Anderson
Day 105: "This Little Light of Mine" written by Harry Dixon Loes
Day 106: "Praise Him! Praise Him! Jesus our Blessed Redeemer written by Fanny J. Crosby
Day 111: "As the Deer" written by Martin Nystrom
Day 117: "There's Something About That Name" written by Bill and Gloria Gaither
Day 148: "I Could Sing of Your Love Forever" written by Martin Smith
Day 159: "Jesus Paid it All" written by Elvina M. Hall
Day 169: "Way Maker" written by Osinachi Okoro

Day 174: "Ain't no Rock!" written by La Marquis Jefferson
Day 178: "There is None Like You" written by Lenny Leblanc
Day 191: "Wonderful Peace" written by Don Moen
Day 214: "I Could Sing of Your Love Forever" written by Martin Smith
Day 230: "In the Presence of Jehovah" written by Geron Davis
Day 232: "The Heart of Worship" written by Matt Redman
Day 246: "I Remember the Day" written by May Spence
Day 270: "Worth" written by Anthony Brown
Day 273: "The Love of God is Greater Far" written by Frederick Lehman
Day 284: "There is No One Like Our God" written by Lincoln Brewster, Taylor Gall, and Corbin Phillips
Day 318: "My Help (Cometh From the Lord)" written by Esther David
Day 337: "Reckless Love" written by Corey Ashbury, Caleb Culver, and Ran Jackson

# ENDNOTES

1  Charles Haddon Spurgeon, updated by Roy H. Clarke, *The Treasures of David* (Nashville, Tennessee: Thomas Nelson, Inc., 1997), 25

2  Spurgeon, *The Treasures of David,* 658

3  Spurgeon, *The Treasures of David,* 1425

CPSIA information can be obtained
at www.ICGtesting.com
Printed in the USA
LVHW062208040822
725253LV00023B/469